# EXTREME
## DEVIANCE

# TITLES OF RELATED INTEREST FROM PINE FORGE PRESS

*Sociology: Exploring The Architecture of Everyday Life, Fifth Edition,* by David M. Newman

*Sociology: Exploring The Architecture of Everyday Life, Readings, Fifth Edition,* edited by David M. Newman and Jodi O'Brien

*Social Problems,* by Anna Leon-Guerrero

*McDonaldization of Society, Revised New Century Editon,* by George Ritzer

*Second Thoughts: Seeing Conventional Wisdom Through the Sociological Eye, Third Edition,* by Janet M. Ruane and Karen A. Cerulo

*Sociological Theory in the Contemporary Era: Text and Readings,* by Scott Appelrouth and Laura Desfor Edles

*Illuminating Social Life, Third Edition,* by Peter Kivisto

*Key Ideas in Sociology, Second Edition,* by Peter Kivisto

*Cultures and Societies in a Changing World, Second Edition,* by Wendy Griswold

*The Social Theory of W. E. B. Du Bois,* edited by Phil Zuckerman

*Explorations in Classical Sociological Theory,* by Ken Allan

*The Globalization of Nothing 2,* by George Ritzer

*Enchanting a Disenchanted World, Second Edition,* by George Ritzer

*McDonaldization: The Reader,* edited by George Ritzer

*Development and Social Change, Third Edition,* by Philip McMichael

*Investigating the Social World, Fourth Edition,* by Russell K. Schutt

*Race, Ethnicity, Gender, and Class: The Sociology of Group Conflict and Change, Third Edition,* by Joseph F. Healey

*Diversity and Society: Race, Ethnicity, and Gender,* by Joseph F. Healey

*Race, Ethnicity, and Gender: Selected Readings,* edited by Joseph F. Healey and Eileen O'Brien

# EXTREME
## DEVIANCE

EDITED BY

## ERICH GOODE
*State University of New York*
*at Stony Brook*

## D. ANGUS VAIL
*Willamette University*

PINE FORGE PRESS
An Imprint of Sage Publications, Inc.
Los Angeles • London • New Delhi • Singapore

*For information:*

Pine Forge Press
An Imprint of Sage Publications, Inc.
2455 Teller Road
Thousand Oaks, California 91320
E-mail: order@sagepub.com

Sage Publications Ltd.
1 Oliver's Yard
55 City Road
London EC1Y 1SP
United Kingdom

Sage Publications India Pvt. Ltd.
B 1/I 1 Mohan Cooperative Industrial Area
Mathura Road, New Delhi 110 044
India

Sage Publications Asia-Pacific Pte. Ltd.
33 Pekin Street #02-01
Far East Square
Singapore 048763

Printed in the United States of America

*Library of Congress Cataloging-in-Publication Data*

Extreme deviance / [edited by] Erich Goode, D. Angus Vail.
    p. cm.
Includes bibliographical references and index.
ISBN: 978-1-4129-3722-1 (pbk.)
    1. Deviant behavior. 2. Marginality, Social. I. Goode, Erich. II. Vail, D. Angus.

HM811.E97 2008
302.5′42—dc22                    2007014506

This book is printed on acid-free paper.

07  08  09  10  11   10  9  8  7  6  5  4  3  2  1

| | |
|---|---|
| *Acquisitions Editor:* | Benjamin Penner |
| *Editorial Assistant:* | Camille Herrera |
| *Production Editor:* | Catherine M. Chilton |
| *Copy Editor:* | Diana Breti |
| *Typesetter:* | C&M Digitals (P) Ltd. |
| *Proofreader:* | Liann Lech |
| *Indexer:* | Diggs Indexing Services, Inc. |
| *Cover Designer:* | Edgar Abarca |
| *Marketing Manager:* | Jennifer Reed |

# CONTENTS

## PART 6

# EARTH FIRST! GOING TO EXTREMES TO SAVE THE ENVIRONMENT 173

## PART 7

# ENGAGING IN S&M SEXUAL PRACTICES 201

# Introduction

## The Significance of Extreme Deviance

### *Erich Goode*

In Amherst, New York, a suburb of Buffalo, anti-abortion activist James Koop stood in the dark outside the house of Barnett Slepian, a physician who performed abortions. Spying Slepian in the kitchen, Koop fired one bullet from a high-powered rifle into the doctor's brain, killing him instantly. The killer was arrested two and a half years later, in France. At his trial, Koop, a devout Catholic, claimed that killing abortion doctors is "morally permissible and, under some circumstances, obligatory conduct" (Messenger, 2003).

Erik Sprague is "slowly transforming himself into a reptile." Not literally, of course, but in appearance. He has green, scale-like tattoos all over his body, from head to foot. He convinced surgeons to implant a bony ridge on his forehead and cut his tongue into a forked shape. His fingernails form long claws and several of his teeth are filed down to look like "crocodile-like chompers." Sprague says he discovers who his real friends are by their willingness to remain friends even after he has dramatically altered his appearance ("He's shedding his human skin," 2000; Goode, 2001, p. 317).

NAMBLA—the North American Man-Boy Love Association—is "strongly opposed to age of consent laws and all other restrictions which deny men and boys the full enjoyment of their bodies." The organization's goal "is to end the extreme oppression of men and boys in mutually consensual relationships." The criminal justice system, claims the association's Web site, "blindly condemns loving relationships between younger and older people." Youths and adults should have the right, NAMBLA asserts, "to choose the partners with whom they wish to share and enjoy their bodies."

Most sociologists define "deviance" as *behavior, beliefs, or physical characteristics that violate a social rule (or "norm") and are likely to elicit negative, condemnatory reactions*. We refer to the persons who evaluate behavior, beliefs, and characteristics and react to the people who enact, express, or possess them as audiences—and audiences could be almost anyone.

More than half a century ago, sociologist Edwin Lemert (1951) made a distinction between "primary" and "secondary" deviation (pp. 75–76). This distinction still has validity today. *Primary* deviation (or deviance) refers to simple non-normative behavior, anything that violates a rule and is likely to elicit censure, condemnation, or punishment from the members of a given group, social circle, or society. In other words, primary deviation is the simple violation itself—anything, really, that designated "audiences" or observers don't like. Primary deviation could be secret or public, trivial or serious, an action, belief, or physical characteristic that is punished or unpunished, but referring to it as deviance or deviation doesn't automatically assume that there are serious consequences for the violation or the reactions the violation elicits. In fact, *most* primary deviation is of transitory significance. Most rule violations, to begin with, are fairly trivial—shoplifting, lying, slacking off at work, cutting class, illegal parking, speeding. And most of the time, such violations aren't detected; even if they are, the condemnation they generate from audiences is usually trivial: a slap on the wrist, a harsh word, a small fine.

In contrast, *secondary* deviation takes the deviance process several steps further. When censure, condemnation, or punishment—deviance labeling—is so serious, so pervasive in violators' lives that audiences begin thinking of actors, believers, or possessors who violate the norms *as* deviants—as the sorts of people who are unacceptable—and when these people begin acquiring the *identity* of a deviant when they are scorned, isolated, and stigmatized—when they take on a deviant *role* defined by and consequent to this social reaction to them and their behavior, beliefs, and traits—their deviation is secondary (Lemert, 1951, p. 76).

The distinction between primary and secondary deviation is what made this book necessary. Here, we explore people whose lives are unambiguously immersed in the universe of secondary deviation.

## EXTREME DEVIANCE

Nearly all of us engage in behavior, express beliefs, or possess physical characteristics that some others, even persons in our own social circles, don't like and feel are objectionable. But the vast majority of deviance, as we said, is trivial, mild, and unserious: the little lie, the shoplifting episode, one drink too many, the stolen kiss. Sometimes we are caught; usually we aren't. If caught, the criticism or punishment we receive for these peccadilloes is usually minor—if anything, the proverbial slap on the wrist. The same applies to beliefs and physical characteristics: *slight* variations from the norm usually produce *mildly* negative reactions from others. This is society's everyday, garden-variety deviance: the mildly transgressive acts in which all of us engage that stimulate mildly negative reactions from an audience, that keep us comfortably within our social groups, still well within the bounds of respectability. The lives of very few of us revolve around one or another of those violations; most of us follow the norms most of the time. And the criticisms

that greet these violations *very rarely* exclude violators from mainstream society. Most of the time, when people don't like what we do, believe, or how we look, they still accept our right to circulate among them; to interact with them and their friends; to sit down and break bread with them; to be a normal, functioning member of the groups to which they belong. In other words, in spite of engaging in acts of occasional deviance, most of us do not acquire a deviant *identity* in the eyes of others.

But normative violations are a matter of degree: They range from *mild* to *serious*. And truly serious normative violations generate very strong negative reactions from others—much more than just a frown, a hostile remark, or a slap on the wrist. In other words, behaviors, beliefs, and physical traits can be arranged along a continuum from those that, when detected, are *highly* likely to generate outsiders to those that are *unlikely* to do so. Thus, it is true that smoking cigarettes is more deviant than it was a generation ago, but, aside from having to take their nasty habit out into the open air, in most circles, smokers are not social outcasts. No one gasps or shrinks in horror at the revelation that someone they just met has an almost indiscernible lisp (Ellis, 1998), is divorced (Gerstel, 1987), a redhead (Heckert & Best, 1997), or a white collar offender (Benson, 1985). But try telling someone you just met that you murder people for a living (Levi, 1981), suffer from AIDS (Siegel, Lune, & Meyer, 1998), plan to blow up the Empire State Building, or endorse sex between grown men and pre-adolescent boys (www.angelfire.com/tx/reachme/NAMBLA.html). Or try telling your parents that you plan to marry a 300-pound man or woman (see Part 3), or someone who is transforming himself or herself into a tiger ("Tiger Man Wants Fur Graft," 2005), or a person who must be spanked (see Part 7) or strangled (Lowery & Wetli, 1982) to achieve sexual arousal. Performing "mental experiments" such as these speculations provides evidence that deviance comes in degrees, and extreme deviance does not have the same consequences as mild deviance.

In short, some normative violations are so serious that they cast the violator outside mainstream society, beyond the pale, and exclude him or her from respectability. This book takes a look at normative violations that earn the violators a deviant identity in the eyes of the members of mainstream society. And violations so serious, likewise, that the lives of violators *do* revolve around the actions, the beliefs, or the characteristics, as well as the consequences of such violations, mainly with respect to the social reactions they generate in others. When others really don't like what you do, believe, or are, they usually let you know that in no uncertain terms, and that is likely to drastically alter your life. In other words, when we refer to "extreme" deviance, we are looking at the process and consequences of creating what Howard Becker (1963) refers to as *outsiders*.

As a general rule, the *less serious* the normative violation, the more *common* it is. Conversely, the more *extreme* the violation, the *rarer* it tends to be. Acts, beliefs, and physical characteristics that shock us, repel us, that cause us to expel their perpetrators, believers, and possessors from polite society are usually, in relation to the whole, relatively rare. Murder is thousands of times rarer than simple theft, and mass or serial murder is vastly rarer still. When we wander into the arena of extreme deviance, we are exploring a rarified atmosphere of statistically unusual phenomena.

Many sociologists feel uncomfortable with rare phenomena. We generally like to study the general, the common, the statistical norm. No, Virginia, we remind our students, "exceptions to the rule" do not disprove a generalization. Most discussions of deviance avoid exotic forms as atypical, relinquishing their study to the psychiatrist and the abnormal psychologist. When journalists write about extreme, unusual behavior—satanic ritual abuse, multiple school shootings, office workers "going postal," or the use of the latest exotic drug—as if it were "right around the corner from where you live," "sweeping the country," "invading every corner of every community in the nation," sociologists insist on the atypicality (or even, in a few cases, nonexistence) of these acts.

Almost by definition, sociologists of deviance study the atypical. Heterosexuality is more common than homosexuality; drinking alcohol in moderation is more common than alcoholism; what most of us regard as psychological normality is more common than schizophrenia. Still, the bulk of the curriculum of the deviance courses taught in the United States center on the "big five" subjects, the meat-and-potatoes, nuts-and-bolts of deviance: crime; alcoholism; illicit drug use; mental disorder; and sexual deviance, usually homosexuality. Unlike milder forms of deviance, such as stealing from the cookie jar, these five are "deviant" enough to qualify as instances of deviance, but they are common enough to satisfy the sociologist's insistence on what's fairly widespread.

Extreme deviance is behavior, beliefs, or physical traits that are so far outside the norm, so unacceptable to a wide range of different audiences, that they elicit *extremely* strongly negative reactions. For many of the people who know about these behaviors, beliefs, and traits, ordinary, routine interaction becomes almost impossible. Their reaction frequently borders on horror; they reject, stigmatize, and abhor the persons who have engaged in the behavior, hold the beliefs, or possess the traits. They regard such people as, in Erving Goffman's (1963) terms, "not quite human" (p. 5)—in every sense of the word, an abomination. The vast majority are excluded from conventional society.

Social exclusion can be as powerful as institutionalization or imprisonment. Picture a man who is tattooed over his entire body, including his face and his head, which is shaved bald. Try to imagine a respectable, conventional person—a minister, a priest, a rabbi, a high school principal, a Wall Street lawyer, an elected official—meeting and interacting with the man. How do such persons act toward or speak to this man? Conjure up a mental image, if you will, of this man showing up at the house of a middle-aged couple, announcing that he wants to marry their daughter. Can you imagine an extremely heavily tattooed person being elected senator or governor?

Visualize a college student telling her physics class she was abducted, sexually assaulted, and impregnated by aliens. Envision someone you know admitting that he plans to assassinate the president. Or burn down a housing development to save the environment. Or fly a plane into a large building to protest the treatment of Native Americans. Visualize a 400-pound woman showing up for a blind date. Or walking onto a beach, clad in a bikini. Or simply trundling a shopping cart down the aisle in a supermarket.

What's your reaction? What's the reaction of the people who see and hear such people, their behavior, or the expression of their beliefs? Do they condemn, make fun of, or punish such normative transgressors? Do the people who are very far from the norm have a place in society? What are the intersections at which such people make contact with and interact with the more conventional members of the society? What happens when such interaction takes place? Are such people allowed to interact with the rest of us on a more or less routine basis? Or is their relationship with us derailed, subverted, rendered tense, awkward, uncomfortable? Are these people accepted—or socially isolated and marginalized? Do they even want to interact with conventional others? Do they form their own, semi-secret mini-society of people similar to themselves? Do they even trust the rest of us?

Why extreme deviance? Many sociologists are likely to say that the cases we discuss in this book, and countless others like them, are too rare and exotic. But can we find the norm in the extreme? Can we learn about deviance in general from what we've referred to as extreme deviance? Do we see a

reflection of ourselves in offbeat, statistically unusual behavior, beliefs, and traits? Will the bearers of such deviance stray too far beyond the pale for us to identify with? Extreme deviance offers something of a test case for sociology's capacity to empathize with its subjects.

Goffman (1963) opens *Stigma* with a (fictional) case of a teenage girl born with no nose. Her anguish touches us, arouses our compassion. Who wouldn't raise her question, if afflicted with such a condition: "What did I do to deserve such a terrible bad fate?" In contrast, when we learn of deliberate exploitative behavior, acts that shock us to the core of our being, what one of us hasn't thought: "How could somebody do such a thing?" In other words, our outrage is mixed with curiosity. When horrendous cases of murder, let's say, or rape, or torture, are played out in court, relatives of the victims typically tell reporters, "I want to stare him in the eye and ask him one question: *Why*?" Why indeed? That "Why?" question challenges the defendant to translate his horrific act into terms that we, the representatives of civil, law-abiding society, can understand and empathize with.

*Why extreme deviance?* Three reasons.

One is implied, as we suggested above, by Edwin Lemert's (1951) distinction between primary and secondary deviation: Only by looking at the more *serious* deviations, that is, those that cause the group or society to stigmatize and isolate the normative violator, do we enter the realm of secondary deviance. Whereas primary deviation, by itself, is a *truncated version* of the sequence of violations and social reactions, extreme deviance typically allows us to explore the *full range* of the consequences of normative violations. The transitory significance of primary deviation is *typical,* but its sociological significance is mainly in individual variation. In contrast, the creation of the deviant role for the normative violator is atypical—but of *immense* sociological significance.

Consider, for a moment, some examples of mild or moderate deviance that sociologists have studied over the years: smoking marijuana; deer poaching; cohabitation; listening to rap, hip-hop, and heavy metal music; being a strip club patron; being a rodeo groupie; playing bingo; ticket scalping; shoplifting; underage drinking; gambling; cheating on exams in high school and college; watching and betting on dog fights. Now, being apprehended at some of these activities may have serious consequences. But not one of them entails violating society's most strongly held norms, and apprehension does not typically result in the transgressor being stigmatized or isolated from mainstream society. Studying any and all of them is a worthwhile research endeavor, revealing many important mechanisms of deviance and society's reaction to deviance. But all of them are engaged in by participants who are, in large measure, integrated into mainstream society. Again, an investigation of these activities entails lopping off the social control apparatus at a less extreme point than the phenomena we look at in this book. Very few, if any, of them result in the escalation from primary to secondary deviation.

The second reason we decided to put together a book on extreme deviance is that the concept encompasses *dramatic* examples of normative violations, those that are pedagogically effective, those that stick in the students' minds. When we read about students cheating on exams, teenagers smoking marijuana or drinking too much, doctors performing unnecessary surgery, or corporate executives committing white collar crimes, most of us shrug and ask, "What's the big deal?" There are segments of the population, including law enforcement, who may react more harshly, but society's majority is likely to react mildly, if at all. Not so with our examples of extreme deviance. They are difficult to forget.

And last, these examples of extreme deviance challenge our capacity to *empathize* with the norm violators. They are so far off the map that most of us are likely to ask, "Why would anyone *do* such a thing?" "How could someone *believe* something

like that?" "How could anyone *get* that way?" The reasons why less serious normative violations take place are easy to come by; the motives seem obvious and hence, need not be engaged. More serious normative violations lead to puzzlement, which demands an answer. Hence, these examples.

## RELATIVISM

The question sociologists always raise when the word "deviance" is bandied about is, *"Deviance to whom?"* What *you* consider wrong, a violation of *your* interpretation of the rules, may be different from what someone else considers wrong. We may decide that the "norm" that is violated should be the norms of the majority, but that begs the question of what constitute normative violations in different groups or social circles. Getting tattooed in a motorcycle gang is considered good and conforms to the rules—*of a motorcycle gang*. Getting tattooed among Orthodox Jews is considered bad, a violation of the rules—*among Orthodox Jews*. Different audiences, different definitions of what's acceptable or deviant.

It is something of a cliché that deviance is "relative" to time and place. "Everything is relative," we learn. Like more than a few clichés, this one is not completely true, but it does contain at least a grain of truth. Whether or not someone receives negative social reactions from audiences depends not merely on the nature of the act, the belief, or the trait, but on time and place. It is true that some things are very nearly universally condemned, so for them, time and place don't count for very much. For instance, every society has a rule against the unprovoked killing of a member of the group. Every society has rules against rape and robbery. But even these few universals have to be qualified.

It's important to note that the *nature* of these supposedly universal rules against harming others is not the same everywhere. As it turns out, throughout most of human history, rules have stated that it was acceptable to kill someone in a *different* group—you just can't do it in your own. Same thing with rape: During much of human existence, men were allowed to force *some* women to have sex, but not others. In other words, sure, there were rules everywhere against unauthorized killings, rape, and robbery. But a lot of the acts we *now* call murder, rape, and robbery were *not* condemned at other times and in other places (Curra, 2000). And in fact, in some societies, this is still true (Cowell, 1994; Greenberg, 1995, 1999). Consider the civil war in Iraq, violence in Israel and the West Bank, the actions of rebels and government forces in Sri Lanka and Congo, the obliteration of villages in Darfur, Sudan: Such acts are condemned by nearly everyone in the outside world, but not by everyone within those societies. Even today, some people in many places in the world believe that their norms command them to kill those whom they regard as their enemies.

The same applies to relativism over historical time. Norms change, and hence, the judgment of audiences concerning what's deviant also changes from one era to another. One observer claims that over time, deviance has been *defined down*: A lot of what was disapproved of years ago is now tolerated and accepted (Moynihan, 1993). Another writes that deviance has been defined *up*, that relatively harmful behavior that was once tolerated and accepted is now condemned, mainly because of vocal interest groups who demand that their vision of right and wrong be imposed on the rest of the society (Krauthammer, 1993). Both are true: Though some rules change and some remain the same, some things that got you in hot water years ago are shrugged off today, and what you could say years ago without consequence now touches off anger and denunciation. "Down" or "up"—the same principle applies: What is considered deviant or wrong is *relative* to the time period we're talking about.

Years ago, students could smoke in class and office workers could smoke on the job; today they can't. In the past, premarital intercourse was

considered a form of deviance; indeed, one deviance textbook written more than a generation ago even devoted a chapter to the subject (Bell, 1976, pp. 37–87). Today, sex before marriage is so common and acceptable that it is regarded as a type of deviance only by a minority of the society, mainly religious conservatives. (But notice: It is still deviant *to* the members of those minorities.) Throughout Europe during the fifteenth and sixteenth centuries, supposed heretics, blasphemers, witches, and persons who "consorted with the devil" were burned at the stake for their crimes (Ben-Yehuda, 1985, pp. 23–73). Today, the younger generation of most Europeans cares little about a person's religious belief or nonbelief. Before the 1960s, if a motion picture actress bore an out-of-wedlock child, the scandal was so great her career would be ruined. Today, on talk shows, actresses chat, endlessly it seems and without shame, about having children outside wedlock as a perfectly normal, routine event.

Deviance is also relative to *context*: Meaning changes according to its social surroundings. Embedded in every situation is a set of rules that says that certain acts, expressions of belief, or physical characteristics are appropriate or inappropriate—*in that situation*. Instructors are not allowed to consume alcoholic beverages in front of a class, but those same instructors can consume them at a New Year's Eve party. Having sex with one's spouse is perfectly acceptable—but not in a hotel lobby. Mentioning a relative's or friend's serious defects is fine—to an even closer relative or friend, in private. But doing the same thing in a eulogy at that friend's or relative's funeral, or in an obituary, is a definite no-no. Different social contexts transform the meaning of what's done and said from acceptable to unacceptable. What's regarded as conventional and normative in one social setting may be denounced as deviant in another.

Does historical, group, and situational relativism mean that "Everything is relative"? That an act that is approved at one time and in one place has a *random* chance of being condemned elsewhere, in another social group, during some other historical period—as some misinformed critics of relativism claim (Costello, 2007)? No, not really. Some things are simply more relative than others.

Societies are not made up of random jumbles of rules and norms, entirely different from one group and collectivity to another. For one thing, within the same society, deviance has a *hierarchical* quality. If the size and power of a given audience is enormous—for instance, the majority of the society, along with its ruling elite—someone who violates its norms is highly likely to get into trouble. If the audience is small and powerless, that likelihood tends to be a lot smaller. As a result, most of what sociologists refer to as deviance is condemned by a *lot* of people rather than a few, by people who have *more* influence in the lives of most of us rather than less. A club of "swingers" or "mate swappers" may define sexual exchange among married couples as acceptable—but it's still frowned upon in the society at large. At the same time, whether the audience is small or large, powerful or powerless, sociologically, what's regarded as deviant *is* relative to time, place, and social location. Thus, even something that violates the rules in a small, powerless group is nonetheless deviant—*to* the members of that group.

Consider the examples that opened this Introduction. A minuscule minority of opponents of abortion believe murdering doctors who terminate pregnancies is a righteous act. The vast majority of the society—even most opponents of abortion—disagrees, and condemns such killings. There's a small but vigorous community of advocates of extreme body modification whose members chop off digits, insert metal rings into their genitals, and tattoo major portions of their anatomy. Again, the majority in this society does not condone such actions, indeed, finds their practitioners bizarre, even repellent. And some pedophiles likewise believe that it is acceptable for adults to have sex with minors. To the majority, endorsing—and even worse, engaging in—such practices is anathema, heinous, seriously stigmatizing. But that *some* members of the society—albeit very few—endorse such beliefs and behavior is a fact, a reality that we, as students of deviance, cannot ignore. What makes these cases examples of deviance is that the persons who engage in or endorse the actions they describe are *very* likely to get into trouble from the rest of us, that is, the majority, mainstream society's "audiences."

Sociologists say that deviance is *socially constructed*. The norms, as well as all the social reactions, past, ongoing, and future, that greet the violators of rules are part of how an action is constructed by the society, or by sectors of the society. The *beliefs* we have about what's unacceptable behavior, and the *actions* we take when we discover normative violations, are what sociologists *mean* when they talk about the social construction of deviance. To say that a norm or rule or reaction is socially constructed is simply to say that it is a product of the social life of a group, a society, or any collectivity of people. It was created at a particular time and place, and it is sustained as part of who that group or society is. If important aspects of that collectivity change, its rules are likely to change as well, along with how it deals with transgressors.

The fact that deviance varies from one social category to another demonstrates its socially constructed nature. What may be praiseworthy in one sector may be condemned in another. What does being "socially constructed" mean? Every thought that everyone in a society has about violating the rules, every reaction they put forth to behavior, beliefs, and traits they consider unacceptable makes up, defines, or *constitutes* the social construction of deviance. All of this includes informal norms and interpersonal reactions, such as a social snub by a friend, or criminal laws, along with other formally prescribed norms, such as the rules that prevail in a corporation, a university, or a hospital. Sociologists of deviance are interested in *how* and *why* rules are created; why some people *violate* those rules; how people come to be *judged* as violators; whether and to what extent such judgments cast violators *out* of the groups that are making such judgments; and what the consequences of such reactions are for the rule violators (Pfuhl & Henry, 1993). Whenever a norm is created, broken, or reacted to, the interest of the sociologist of deviance is aroused.

Are we saying that social norms are completely arbitrary, that they have *nothing to do* with protecting its members from harm, danger, and catastrophe? What about rape, robbery, and murder? Aren't social rules devised to ensure society's survival? And if society's norms are not preordained and do not drop down from the skies, then why are so many of these norms similar from one society to another? Why do all societies have laws and norms protecting their members from actions that would, if permitted, tear the organized society apart at the seams?

Human collectivities could not long survive if some of their members were allowed to exploit, abuse, and corrupt others at will. But the concept of deviance is separate from and independent of physical and even social harm. Some forms of deviance are indeed harmful to society's constituent members and to the society as a whole. But some are not. And likewise, many conventional, law-abiding, traditional behaviors are socially harmful. Consider warfare, which has wiped innumerable societies off the face of the Earth. For the most part, wars have been endorsed by the majority of societies, their leaders included, since humans gathered together into social collectivities. Hence, most of the time, waging war—a harmful action—is conventional and normative. Whether and to what extent a given behavior, belief, or trait is harmful to the functioning of a society has very little to do with whether it is or is not deviant.

In fact, objectively speaking, phenomena designated as deviant have very little in common—period. Consider the people described in this book: the hugely obese; men who are sexually attracted to, and who have sex with, hugely obese women; ecological terrorists; the extremely heavily tattooed; persons who claim to have been abducted by aliens; men who have sex with minors or who endorse adults having sex with minors; people who engage in sado-masochistic sexual practices; people who advocate the racial superiority of Caucasians and the inherent inferiority of Jews and non-whites. What do they have in common?

Internally, substantively—in their core or essence—nothing whatsoever. Some manifest their deviance through their behavior. Others are considered deviant by virtue of their physical characteristics. Still others hold beliefs many people believe are deranged. Some are, by all common agreement, harmful; others harm no one. Some are criminal, most are not. The people who enact, profess, or possess these actions, beliefs, or traits are tied together by no intrinsic common thread at all. If we were to seek out a cause-and-effect explanation for how and why these people came to do, believe, or be what the society condemns, we would come up empty. Despite the claims of advocates of numerous sociological schools of thought that have attempted to explain the phenomenon of deviance, a single origin of what it is that violates a norm cannot be found. *Is* there a common thread among the forms of deviance in this book?

The *conventional* view of deviance is that it is behavior that deserves to be punished or beliefs or conditions that deserve to be corrected. It is bad, harmful, pathological—it does not deserve to exist. There's something wrong with it. It's society's job to eradicate this sort of behavior, by passing laws if necessary, or by snubbing, shunning, condemning, or informally punishing wrongdoers in our midst; to educate mistaken believers into a correct view; or to treat physical conditions to make the possessor of deviant traits whole, complete, or healthy. According to the conventional view, we must abandon relativism and tolerance for deviance and return to conventional morality, which recognizes a sin or sickness when faced with it. Good is good, bad is bad, and everyone knows exactly what each is (Costello, 2007; Hendershott, 2002).

In contrast, the *romantic* view of deviance is that persons condemned or punished by conventional society do not deserve the condemnation or punishment they receive, that the deviant is a victim, "more sinned against than sinning." According to this view, society punishes normative violators out of "mere prejudice" or an "irrational morality." It's "nobody's business" if some of us engage in harmless actions in private (McWilliams, 1993). We ought to accept diversity, celebrate unconventional beliefs, embrace the physically different, and refuse to punish the deviant.

The sociological view of deviance is *neither* conventional *nor* romantic. It is, instead, *naturalistic* (Matza, 1969, p. 8); it attempts to understand the role of non-normative acts, beliefs, and characteristics in the society. Many observers unacquainted with the sociologist's conceptualization of deviance assume something that is referred to by a specific term must have at least one important quality in common. The problem is, deviance is not a quality *inside* or *intrinsic to* something or someone. It is imposed from the outside, external to it—*extrinsic* rather than intrinsic. It is defined and constituted by the reactions of others. Hence, from the point of view of a common thread, it encompasses extremely miscellaneous phenomena. The people that are defined as deviant don't have to have anything in common. In fact, their common thread comes from beyond the phenomenon itself: what others think of them, how others treat them and interact with them. Deviance has nothing to do with "good" or "bad" in the abstract. It has everything to do with what some people

*consider* good or bad, acceptable or unacceptable, in need of remediation or not—and what they do about it. The fact is, the deviant status of behavior, beliefs, and physical conditions is *solely* a question of a social judgment by a particular audience, whether the majority of a society or a segment of the society. Whether any such judgments about good or bad are "right" in the cosmic sense is not a question a sociologist can answer.

Even scientific assertions for which evidence is overwhelming are matters of diverse judgments by different audiences. The *fact* of these different judgments—for instance, that the Earth is flat—is a reality that has to be acknowledged. The sociologist can weigh the evidence, just as anyone can, and conclude that the Earth is approximately round, but that conclusion does not deny the fact that some people *do* believe the Earth is flat; that belief plays a role in their lives, and it is the sociologist's obligation to understand what that role is. While some people may find this moral and scientific relativism distressing, it is exactly where our definition of deviance leads. As students and researchers of deviance, we must learn to live with its conclusion and use it to grapple with and understand the many paradoxes of this most paradoxical of subjects.

## STIGMA

Throughout this book, we'll be referring to the work of Erving Goffman, a sociologist whose book *Stigma* (1963) remains one of the two or three most important works on deviance. The parallels between stigma and deviance are obvious. To be stigmatized is to possess an attribute "that is deeply discrediting" (p. 3). All of us hold certain assumptions about what the person with whom we are interacting should be like; we have demands with respect to acceptable or appropriate behavior, beliefs, physical characteristics, even race and ethnicity. When that person fails to live up to our expectation of normalcy, he or she "is thus reduced in our minds from a whole and usual person to a tainted, discounted one." In our eyes, such a person possesses "a failing, a shortcoming, a handicap" (p. 3).

Goffman (1963) distinguishes three types or sources of stigma. First there are physical characteristics or traits ("abominations of the body"), of which there are two subtypes, aesthetic violations (such as obesity, extreme ugliness, disfigurement) and physical impairment (like blindness, using a wheelchair, deafness). Second, there are "blemishes of individual character," those attributes that are perceived as "weak will, domineering or unnatural passions, treacherous and rigid beliefs, and dishonesty," and include "mental disorder, imprisonment, addiction, alcoholism, homosexuality, unemployment, suicidal attempts, and radical political behavior." And third, "there are the tribal stigma of race, nation, and religion, these being stigma that can be transmitted through lineages and equally contaminate all members of a family" (p. 4). Sociologists of deviance usually focus on stigmatizing behavior, only occasionally physical characteristics, rarely beliefs, and almost never race or ethnicity.

Interacting parties are usually aware of the expectations of others, aware of what others might see as their shortcomings, and may conceal discrediting evidence of them. Goffman (1963) distinguishes persons who are *discredited* from those who are *discreditable*. The "discredited" are persons who have *already* been stigmatized, identified and labeled as deviants, discredited in the eyes of the "normal" majority. Even more interesting are the "discreditable," the persons who harbor deviant, stigmatizing attributes but have not been found out by those who consider themselves normative or, in Goffman's terminology, "normal." The discreditable possess a "guilty secret" and are able to navigate in a sea of *putative* condemnation, that is, they are aware that others would condemn them if they knew about these discrediting attributes. Most wisely keep such attributes from conventional others and exercise impression management or "information control" (Goffman, 1959). The person with strongly discrediting attributes has a great deal to lose if those attributes are revealed to disparaging others and, hence, uses a variety of strategies to conceal them. Their very concealment indicates their deviant, stigmatizing status.

Relevant to the discredited/discrediting distinction, Goffman (1963, pp. 48–51) also introduces the concepts of *evidentness* and *obtrusiveness* into the deviance equation. In all face-to-face encounters, being hugely obese is instantly evident, literally impossible to hide or minimize. In contrast, most circumstances do not smoke out or expose the drug addict, the child molester, the illiterate, who are more likely to be able to hide their stigmatizing conditions. Additionally, the inability of most people to "disattend" to a given stigmatizing quality distinguishes one type of deviance from another. Most participants at a business meeting can ignore the fact that one of the people present is sitting in a wheelchair; it is not a disruptively obtrusive characteristic. But a severe stutterer intrudes himself or herself on the interaction in a way that someone sitting in a wheelchair does not. Hence, the obtrusiveness of a particular type of deviance is, in some measure, context-specific. On top of the inherently intrusive character of certain traits, humans often *define* qualities as deviant in such a way that those qualities become obtrusive *to them*. Many fundamentalist Christians cannot interact with atheists without being continually reminded of the latter's corruption and one-way ticket to damnation. Many politically correct liberals find it difficult to socialize with right-wingers without feeling a sense of revulsion. The *mechanics* of social interaction (e.g., being unable to speak without stuttering) should not be confused with the creation of rules that make salience—and therefore obtrusiveness—an issue. In the latter case, the norms dictate repugnance, and the repugnance *forces* obtrusiveness on the interaction.

Many—probably most—deviant behaviors can be concealed from conventional others if they are enacted alone or exclusively in the company of coparticipants. Most deviance is enacted in secret (Becker, 1963, pp. 20–22). Even if these acts involve victimizing non-consenting others, the identity of the predator can be concealed. It is when the deviant actor is apprehended and identified that the mechanism of labeling and stigmatization is set into motion. For the sociologist of deviance, this is crucial because it generates a sociologically distinct social animal, one that is qualitatively different from the enactor of "secret deviance." Once identified, the actor faces a series of social consequences, including stereotyping, shunning, condemnation, ridicule, and the like. The importance of discovery and labeling does not mean that the person who enacts deviance in secret is identical to the conventional, law-abiding individual. After all, persons who possess discrediting attributes tend to be aware of that fact and act accordingly. Still, labeling unleashes a series of social consequences that need to be attended to. But secret deviance is a category unto itself, one with distinctive and unique characteristics, one that offers special rewards—and challenges—for the sociologist of deviance.

## PATHOLOGY VERSUS APPRECIATION

There is at least one yawning gulf between the way that the psychiatrist and the clinical psychologist address mental disorder and the way a sociologist studies deviance. Psychiatrists and psychologists describe their cases in terms appropriate for practitioners of medicine who take normality as a baseline: a loss of capacity, impairment, defect, excess, and so on—in short, *pathology* and *malfunction*. They make it clear that their patients live a life in which normal mental functioning has been derailed; they express a profound sense of loss for what their patients could have been had their minds functioned normally.

In contrast, for the most part, sociologists do not address the issue of normality or abnormality

at all. We do not regard deviance as a condition in need of treatment or correction. Years ago, even in sociology, the term "deviance" had a connotation of pathology, abnormality, a taint of sickness about it. Today, sociologists regard that meaning as archaic, obsolete, distinctly out of date. For the sociologist, no taint of pathology clings to the term. Nowadays, most sociologists mean by deviance one thing and one thing only: non-normative behavior that generates a negative reaction in others.

The sociologist of deviance enters the world of the deviant not only to empathize with that world but to *appreciate* it. We do not expect most of the people we study to make a recovery or get "better"—because we do not make judgments about what's "better" or "worse." We try to understand the *experience* of the person who engages in the deviant behavior, professes the deviant belief, possesses the deviant characteristic.

David Matza (1969) puts the matter this way: "Appreciation is especially difficult when the subject of inquiry consists of enterprises that violate cherished and widely shared standards of conduct and morality. Almost by definition, such phenomena are commonly *un*appreciated; indeed, they are condemned." The problem with trying to get rid of deviant phenomena—an approach Matza calls the *correctional* perspective—is that it "systematically interferes with the capacity to empathize and thus comprehend the subject of inquiry" (p. 15). Only through appreciation, he continues, "can the texture of social patterns and the nuances of human engagement with those patterns be understood and analyzed. Without appreciation and empathy . . . we will fail to understand . . . its meaning to the subjects involved and its place in the wider society" (pp. 15–16). No, we must not romanticize our subjects, deceive ourselves into imagining they are something they are not, grander, more noble, and better than they are. And no, appreciation does not mean endorsing any and all of the normative violations we study. But yes, trying to judge, treat, or "correct" them *interferes with understanding them*.

Appreciation, it must be stressed, is far from an easy exercise. Indeed, for many acts, beliefs, and traits, *especially* for our cases of "extreme" deviance, it is not only difficult but, for some of us, all but impossible. How do we empathize with a rapist? A terrorist who murders dozens—or thousands—of innocent victims? A chief executive officer who earns tens of millions of dollars, loots, guts, then destroys a corporation, throwing his employees on the unemployment line, sucking their pensions dry, and causing the company's stockholders to lose billions of dollars? What do we say to someone who insists the world is flat? Or that aliens have taken over the bodies of key power holders everywhere and are living among us as "pod people" in order to conquer the Earth? How do we "appreciate" what these people do, say, or believe? Outrage or disdain, not appreciation, is usually our initial response.

But surely there must be curiosity as well. The very outrage we feel when encountering some cases of extreme deviance leads us to wonder why some people would do or say such things. We rarely pause to wonder why people do or believe what we consider normal, routine, unproblematic; why even raise the question? It is those actions and beliefs we find troublesome and untoward that demand an explanation. And the more they depart from our expectations, the more curious we are about how they came to exist. Hence, the importance of appreciation.

## Accounts of Deviance

All social beings in the contemporary world navigate through social life aware of the fact that their way of life, their view of things, and who they are may be challenged or questioned by some other members of the same society. The more substantial the challenge, the more we are called upon to defend ourselves, our sense of self, our dignity and self-respect.

People whom the majority regard as "deviants" most especially need to justify themselves *to* themselves. In other words, all of us—but most notably persons who violate strongly held conventional norms—render accounts or statements for an "untoward" action, belief, or trait (Lyman & Scott, 1970, p. 112; Scott & Lyman, 1968). "Untoward" phenomena are those deemed by others as unacceptable, blameworthy, improper—in a word, deviant. When others find out we engaged in the behavior, hold the belief, or possess the trait regarded as unacceptable, chances are we will be called upon to provide an explanation, an account, a justification. Even in advance, even if it is simply to ourselves, anticipating that we might be challenged, we usually justify what we are doing, what we believe, who we are.

When we encounter the accounts of others that we find implausible, many of us regard them as "mere rationalizations," that is, blatantly untrue, in all likelihood, a product of self-delusion. But the fact is, they bubble up from inside all of us as a result of the need to maintain a positive self-image, to restore a sense of dignity and self-worth. And yes, rapists explain, justify, or account for their hurtful behavior in terms that attempt to construct themselves as honorable, dignified human beings (Scully & Marolla, 1984), as do terrorists (Martin, 2003, pp. 57–64; Sarraj & Sprinzak, 2004), hit men or people who kill for profit (Levi, 1981), and white collar and corporate criminals (Benson, 1985). As sociologists, we don't have to believe in the *validity* of these accounts, but the person who renders them often does, and understanding how someone comes to justify untoward behavior represents a major step in understanding deviance. Deviant accounts are the social *face* that those whom many members of the society wish to discredit present to themselves and to others. They are the "passport" of deviance, permitting persons to navigate in a world in which their sense of self-worth is under attack. As such, they are of immense value in getting a sense of where people who are, or are likely to be, stigmatized are "coming from." Reading them enables us to enter the world of deviance.

As we'll see, accounts that attempt to neutralize the stigma of deviance don't always work. Persons whom society discredits aren't necessarily able to wash away the human stain that taints them. As sensitive sociologists, we are forced to take note of the social contexts in which accounts are created and what their creators attempt to accomplish by rendering and using them. People render accounts because they *anticipate* that their actions, beliefs, and traits will elicit negative reactions from observers or audiences, and they seek to neutralize the implications of that negativity for their self-image. Accounts represent an attempt to restore dignity and self-respect to the person who engages in potentially deviant acts, holds potentially deviant beliefs, bears deviant characteristics. As such, they are products of society; they enable us to gaze not only upon the world of deviance but the world of conventionality as well. They reveal that even serious miscreants among us seek a place at the table, an honorable position among all humanity. We don't have to honor that quest, but as sociologists of deviance, we have to recognize its significance.

Is it possible for people who commit even the most tabooed behavior—murder for hire—to offer deviance-neutralizing accounts? Ken Levi's classic "Becoming a Hit Man" (1981) lays out the central argument we use in this book: More extreme forms of deviance introduce conceptual and theoretical issues not found in milder forms. Levi discusses deviance neutralization, as we saw, a process common among persons who engage in untoward behavior, hold unorthodox beliefs, or possess unacceptable characteristics. But his argument applies to all aspects of deviance as well: By examining extreme deviance, we discover aspects of the subject we won't find with marijuana use, being a poker player or an unwed father, or using shady techniques to sell shoes.

How do people who kill for a living explain and justify their horrendous actions? It would seem that murder for hire is beyond the pale, an act so despicable that no one who does it can successfully neutralize the stigma it inevitably produces. Levi (1981) interviewed a professional hit man, eliciting an explanation of how the killer managed to make himself feel better about the negative implications of his acts. To live with himself, Levi explains, the hit man "reframes" his acts—casts them into a context that makes them seem less horrendous, indeed, necessary and justified. After all, killers say to themselves, in warfare soldiers take human lives, but the "frame" they use to think about their homicidal actions is warfare, not murder. But the soldier's interpretation of his actions is backed up by the military enterprise—his commanding officers, his fellow soldiers, the general public. In contrast, the hit man has no such support groups and hence, must generate self-justifications on his own. As Levi explains, excuses for the more inexcusable forms of deviant behavior are less easy to come by, so the very serious offender will probably begin engaging in the behavior in question with few of the usual defenses.

The foundation of Levi's (1981) argument is *self-image*: People tend to protect a positive self-image. But if this is true, how does one engage in an action that attracts widespread and intense public scorn? Even if one overcomes this inhibition, how does one maintain a positive self-image if one is engaged in an action he or she knows attracts that self-same scorn? Techniques of deviance neutralization provide the answer to these questions. This argument suggests that persons who enact mildly condemned behavior do not find it as necessary to engage in similar techniques of neutralization. It is when we anticipate condemnation from others that we resort to justifications for behavior we know those others find reprehensible.

## THE READINGS

Why did we include the topics that appear in this book? Because they comprise a diverse range of deviances. All too often, deviance texts and collections of readings on the subject focus entirely on behavior. (Not to mention, they include many fairly trivial forms of deviance.) But people can be condemned, punished, and stigmatized for more than behavior alone. We've attempted to correct that deficiency. Two chapters—extreme tattooing and obesity—typify *physical* or *bodily deviance*; one (tattooing) is distinctly voluntary, while the other (obesity), many argue, is not. Two of our articles discuss a deviant *belief* that is expressed largely to disbelieving, judgmental others—the belief that one has been abducted by aliens and the belief that whites are superior, and should be separate from, the other races. Engaging in sado-masochistic sexual practices and having sex with minors are, of course, forms of behavior. (Even *advocating* sex with minors is a form of extreme deviance.) And belonging to Earth First!, a self-admitted "extreme" social movement activity, is both a form of behavior and a system of beliefs. The last of these is a bit different from the others in that it exemplifies a form of *collective* deviance. Members of less radical social movement organizations (or, in Rik Scarce's terminology, "interest groups") have attempted to discredit and stigmatize Earth First! To them, both the movement, taken as a whole, as well as its constituent members are extreme deviants. The general public may not denounce Earth First! members to the same degree that conservatives and moderate environmentalists do, but the process by which others have tried to stigmatize this decidedly radical movement is instructive for anyone wanting to know about how deviance works. Moreover, several of our chapters discuss forms of deviance that are directly political (white supremacy, being an active member of Earth First!), while most are only *indirectly* political, in that their definitions are an outcome of a struggle over what the behavior, belief, or condition

means. It is this range, this rich brew of non-conforming behavior, beliefs, and physical characteristics, we contend, that will enable us to understand the intriguing, multifaceted phenomenon sociologists refer to as deviance.

## REFERENCES

Becker, H. S. (1963). *Outsiders: Studies in the sociology of deviance.* New York: Free Press.

Bell, R. R. (1976). *Social deviance: A substantive analysis* (2nd ed.). Homewood, IL: Dorsey Press.

Benson, M. L. (1985, November). Denying the guilty mind: Accounting for an involvement in a white-collar crime. *Criminology, 23,* 589–599.

Ben-Yehuda, N. (1985). *Deviance and moral boundaries.* Chicago: University of Chicago Press.

Costello, B. J. (2007). Deviance is dead and cultural relativism killed it. *Sociological Spectrum, 27*(1).

Cowell, A. (1994, October 17). Israeli's death: Atrocity or act of war? *The New York Times,* p. A11.

Curra, J. (2000). *The relativity of deviance.* Thousand Oaks, CA: Sage.

Ellis, C. (1998). I hate my voice: Coming to terms with minor bodily stigmas. *Sociological Quarterly, 39,* 517–537.

Gerstel, N. (1987, April). Divorce and stigma. *Social Problems, 34,* 172–186.

Goffman, E. (1959). *The presentation of self in everyday life.* Garden City, NY: Doubleday-Anchor.

Goffman, E. (1963). *Stigma: Notes on the management of spoiled identity.* Englewood Cliffs, NJ: Prentice Hall/Spectrum.

Goode, E. (2001). *Deviant behavior* (6th ed.). Upper Saddle River, NJ: Prentice Hall.

Greenberg, J. (1995, February 17). Shared hate: Jews and Arabs mark mosque slayings. *The New York Times,* p. A3.

Greenberg, J. (1999, December 30). Israel destroys shrine to mosque gunman. *The New York Times,* p. A6.

Heckert, D. M., & Best, A. (1997). Ugly duckling to swan: Labeling theory and the stigmatization of the redhead. *Symbolic Interaction, 20*(4), 365–384.

Hendershott, A. (2002). *The politics of deviance.* San Francisco: Encounter Books.

He's shedding his human skin. (2000, January 28). *The Chronicle of Higher Education,* p. A12.

Krauthammer, C. (1993, November 22). Defining deviancy up. *The New Republic,* pp. 20–25.

Lemert, E. M. (1951). *Social pathology: A systematic approach to the theory of sociopathic behavior.* New York: McGraw-Hill.

Levi, K. (1981). Becoming a hit man: Neutralization in a very deviant career. *Urban Life, 10*(1), 47–63.

Lowery, S. A., & Wetli, C. V. (1982, January-March). Sexual asphyxia: A neglected area of study. *Deviant Behavior, 3,* 19–39.

Lyman, S. M., & Scott, M. B. (1970). *A sociology of the absurd.* New York: Appleton-Century-Crofts.

Martin, G. (2003). *Understanding terrorism: Challenges, perspectives, and issues.* Thousand Oaks, CA: Sage.

Matza, D. (1969). *Becoming deviant.* Englewood Cliffs, NJ: Prentice Hall.

McWilliams, P. (1993). *Ain't nobody's business if you do: The absurdity of consensual crimes in a free society.* Los Angeles: Prelude Press.

Messenger, T. (2003, March 18). Doctor's killer claims moral duty as defense. *Columbia Daily Tribune,* p. 1.

Moynihan, D. P. (1993, Winter). Defining deviance down. *The American Scholar, 64,* 25–33.

Pfuhl, E. H., & Henry, S. (1993). *The deviance process* (3rd ed.). New York: Aldine de Gruyter.

Sarraj, E., & Spinzak, E. (2004). What makes suicide bombers tick? In A. Thio & T. C. Calhoun (Eds.), *Readings in deviant behavior* (3rd ed., pp. 104–108). Boston: Allyn & Bacon.

Scott, M. B., & Lyman, S. M. (1968, February). Accounts. *American Sociological Review, 33,* 46–62.

Scully, D., & Marolla, J. (1984, June). Convicted rapists' vocabulary of motive: Excuses and justifications. *Social Problems, 31,* 530–544.

Siegel, K., Lune, H., & Meyer, I. H. (1998). Stigma management among gay/bisexual men with HIV/AIDS. *Qualitative Sociology, 21*(1), 3–24.

Tiger man wants fur graft. (2005, April 7). Retrieved from http://www.anova.com/news/story/sm_365440.html

## Discussion Questions

1. Why do the authors believe that a study of "extreme" deviance is more revealing than investigating less serious forms of deviance, such as shoplifting, marijuana smoking, and getting divorced?

2. Sociologists argue that involuntarily acquired physical characteristics such as ugliness, curvature of the spine, and obesity should be considered a form of deviance. Is this fair? Does it make moral sense to regard physical traits as deviance? Does it make theoretical sense?

3. Over time, society has defined deviance both "up" and "down." Give some examples of each. What does this movement of the deviance bar up and down tell us about how sociologists define the concept?

4. Some people have argued that social norms were designed to ensure society's survival and to protect its members from harm. Is this true? Is this why some form of behavior has been condemned everywhere? What's wrong with this explanation?

5. What are deviant "accounts" and why is understanding them an important tool in understanding deviance?

6. What does Ken Levi's "Becoming a Hit Man" tell us about the process of engaging in extreme deviance?

# PUBLISHER'S ACKNOWLEDGMENTS

Pine Forge Press gratefully acknowledges the contributions of the following reviewers:

Hank J. Brightman
*Saint Peter's College*

Philip Collin Campbell
*University of Maryland, European Division*

Jennifer Dabbs
*Lubbock Christian University*

Dan Dexheimer
*University of Florida, Gainesville*

Michael Garr
*Wilkes University*

Robert J. Homant
*University of Detroit Mercy*

Rick Jones
*Marquette University*

Claudia Kowalchyk
*Bloomfield College*

Marv Krohn
*University at Albany*

Karen E. B. McCue
*University of New Mexico*

Michael Messina-Yauchzy
*Keuka College*

Simon Singer
*Northeastern University*

Karen Sternheimer
*University of Southern California*

Jeffery Ulmer
*Pennsylvania State University*

# ABOUT THE EDITORS

**Erich Goode** received a PhD in sociology from Columbia and has taught at New York University, the University of North Carolina, The Hebrew University of Jerusalem, and the University of Maryland. He is the author of 10 books and the editor of six, mainly on deviance and drug use, and has published over 40 academic articles, as well as dozens of articles in newspapers, magazines, and literary journals. He recently completed a master's degree in nonfiction writing, focusing on memoir. Goode is currently Sociology Professor Emeritus at the State University of New York at Stony Brook, where he taught for more than 30 years.

**D. Angus Vail** is Associate Professor of Sociology at Willamette University in Salem, OR, where he teaches courses in Deviance, Theory, Qualitative Methods, Social Psychology, and Art and Culture. He has published articles on fine art tattoo collectors and artists and is coauthor, with Clinton R. Sanders, of the second edition of *Customizing the Body: The Art and Culture of Tattooing*. He is currently working on a book about the fine art tattoo world. He wears the work of 15 artists.

# PART 1

# EXTREME TATTOOING

# BOD MOD TO THE MAX!
## An Introduction to Body Modification as Deviance

As we saw in the Introduction, deviance is a matter of definition. People make sense of the behavior, beliefs, and physical characteristics of others in a variety of ways so that those behaviors, beliefs, and characteristics become social objects; in other words, they are socially constructed. Which kinds of social objects they become, and to whom, will depend to a large extent on social context: In what contexts do these behaviors take place, how are these beliefs expressed, and who possesses these traits or characteristics?

Along similar lines, other kinds of social objects—people's hairdos, their clothes, the makeup they choose to wear, the size of their feet—are all bodily objects, but they become what they are to us through the same process of social definition. Thus, people learn to see heavy eye liner, skinny neckties, beehive hairdos, and polyester leisure suits as appropriate, attractive, silly, fun—or grotesquely outdated—and/or vintage aspects of the ways people can present themselves. In fact, most of us spend a considerable amount of time in any given week changing the ways we look. We might wear a t-shirt or a sweatshirt bearing our favorite team's logo after a win but choose not to after a loss. We rarely wear the same outfit when we go to a job interview as we do when lounging around the living room, watching television. We might wear a baseball cap backwards when we're hanging out with friends but turn it around when we're actually playing baseball. Some professors who wear shoes while teaching will put on flip-flops while barbecuing in the back yard. In fact, most of the ways that people alter their appearances are relatively easy to correct or change if they make the "wrong" impression on others, and we make those changes frequently. Bad haircuts grow back, cold cream will remove makeup without much hassle, and even bright purple hair can be re-dyed to a more suitable color.

One has to invest considerable time, energy, and money to become heavily tattooed and/or pierced, which makes body modification a pretty clear example of a behavior that people choose. People can and do employ a variety of strategies to control information about themselves to make personal characteristics either visible or less visible. People dress to accentuate or hide their physiques; they use makeup (or the lack of it) to change the appearance of their faces; they use different kinds of physical props to look one way or another. Some of these choices make differences less apparent; others make them blatantly obvious. One major difference, however, is that body modification is seen as voluntary and, therefore, worthy of judgment. Not many people would say the same about a person who is missing a limb and uses a prosthetic leg. Hence, in the case of extreme tattooing, the question many people ask is *Why?* Why would someone do such a thing? Why become heavily tattooed? The articles in this chapter address these questions.

Both the Vail and the Atkinson and Young articles in this section work well together for a variety of reasons, and the Vail personal account illustrates some of the principles in both articles. Vail and Atkinson and Young are intimately familiar with body modification culture; both articles are based on rich qualitative data that give voice to the perspectives of those who live in and contribute to body modification culture, and both of them do a nice job of explaining body modification in terms that make it seem like the understandable choice that, in fact, it represents. While their similarities provide a strength to their inclusion in this collection, their differences are also important, and it is perhaps their differences that make them such a strong match for one another.

As sociologists, we are trained to look for social and collective explanations for behavior where other scholars might look exclusively within the individual. Yet, naturalistic inquiry necessarily lies at the intersection of the individual and the social, which is also where these two articles take divergent paths.

Atkinson and Young take us inside the experience of "neoprimitive" practitioners of body modification. As such, the authors show us why a person would want to become heavily tattooed, pierced, branded, burned, and/or scarred. They explain how these neoprimitives have come to label their bodies and the jewelry, pigment, and scar tissue that have changed their appearance in such a way that their "flesh journeys" represent the personal choices they have made, the aspects of their personal biographies that are important to them, the interpersonal and subcultural connections that they value, and their interpretations of how their modified bodies communicate this information to others, both within and outside their social worlds.

Thus, as you read Atkinson and Young's article, think about the ways that labeling or social definition works as people define and apply social meanings to themselves and their experiences in life. If you don't have tattoos or "radical" piercings, what methods do you use to communicate information about yourself to others? Do you wear jewelry? Do you dye your hair? Grow it in distinctive ways? Which parts of your attire communicate important information about you? Do you wear tie-dyed t-shirts? Trendy, color-coordinated outfits? Now, how about your props: Do you carry a water bottle to class? A travel mug? A full knapsack or a tiny pocketbook? What information about you do these choices communicate to other people? How do those other people react to your presentations of yourself? Are you effectively communicating what you want to communicate?

Now, switch gears for a moment. How did you learn to make those choices? How do you know whether you look like a jock or a prep? Who teaches you how to be trendy and whom would you never trust to teach you how to dress? As social actors, we make individual choices throughout the courses of our lives, but those choices do not come out of a vacuum; they follow from social contexts that affect the range of choices we are likely to make, and this is where Vail adds to our understanding of body modification.

Building on David Matza's (1969) model from *Becoming Deviant*, Vail takes us inside the process through which people learn to become collectors of tattoos. This process involves three separate analytical moments, each of which helps the collector make sense of the enterprise of building a tattoo collection, navigating others' reactions to that collection, and defining these reactions and meanings in such a way as to allow these collectors to see their lives as part of the collecting process and vice versa. In order to become a collector, people have to learn to see collecting tattoos as a potentially rewarding activity; they also need to learn properly how to respect their canvasses, thus making sense of their bodies as sites for artistic manipulation and modification. Finally, they also need to learn how to make sense of their identities as "collectors" of art, not just people who have tattoos. Each of these analytical moments involves a learning process. Thus, collecting tattoos and being a collector are individual experiences, but they are also part of a social process that involves making sense of the social connections and interconnections that define tattooing in a variety of positive and not-so-positive ways.

Thus, Vail draws our attention to the intersubjective processes through which people learn how to make the decisions that lead them down the road of collecting, and Atkinson and Young help us understand how those people make sense of those choices. Recall the choices you have made to present a particular version of yourself to others. How did you learn how low your low-rise jeans should be? Who showed you how to style your hair so that it doesn't look styled? Who helps you, even now, to refine your choices? Are all these influences from friends, or do some of them come from people you don't even like? What kinds of reactions to your presentation of self do you find satisfying, and how did you learn to like those reactions?

Neoprimitives and tattoo collectors likely have dramatic kinds of information control that will affect how they get through the day. They have to worry about the consequences that accompany showing body modifications, and you probably don't have those same concerns. But aside from the deviance of extreme body modification, are their methods of communicating who they are to others and themselves really so different from yours? Both say, "I have constructed a physical presentation, both to myself and to others, that symbolically announces: I am a certain kind of person." In this sense, we are all the same. Extreme body modification has both a universal quality (the use of physical symbols to communicate our identities) and a more unusual or specific quality (these physical symbols are deviant from the mainstream); hence, it is fascinating to deviance specialists, to sociologists, and to the general public as well.

# Tattoos Are Like Potato Chips . . . You Can't Have Just One
## The Process of Becoming and Being a Collector

### *Angus Vail*

People of all stripes and colors have long enjoyed modifying their bodies. In fact, a July, 2003 Harris Poll indicated that some 40 million Americans, around 16% of the population of the country, have tattoos (Coleman, 2005). In the following pages, I discuss how those who are largely responsible for tattooing's growth become collectors.

## INTRODUCTION

People learn how to become deviant. How each individual learns his or her particular brand of deviance depends on the kind of deviance in which he or she participates. Professional thieves learn their trade from other professional thieves (Sutherland, 1937), marijuana users learn how to smoke marijuana and how to interpret the drug's effects from other marijuana users (Becker, 1963), and tattoo collectors learn how to interpret tattoos from those who wear them.

That deviance is a learned process is well-documented (e.g., Becker, 1963; Burgess & Akers, 1966; Glaser, 1956; Matza, 1969; Sutherland, 1939; Sutherland & Cressey, 1974). Deviance theories have explained many expressions of deviance (both formal and informal) in many contexts (whether subcultural or individualistic phenomena). One form of deviance not yet examined in the sociological literature, however, is tattoo collecting. While Sanders' (1989) watershed work addresses tattooing, in the following pages, I will build on that work to discuss how tattoo collectors come to treat getting tattooed as an explicitly artistic endeavor, much in the same way that collectors of other kinds of art collect those media.

In discussing how one becomes a tattoo collector, I will discuss how collectors learn about aesthetics appropriate for their body suits, the motifs that appropriately and accurately convey their ideas, iconographies appropriate for those motifs, and choosing an artist(s) to complete their collections. I will frame this discussion in Matza's (1969) theory of affinity, affiliation, and signification and the phenomenology of Alfred Schutz (1962, 1967).

## METHODS

Data for this paper have been collected using a variety of qualitative methods. Most interview data were collected at a recent, four-day tattoo convention in the southeastern United States. I conducted in-depth, semi-structured interviews with tattoo collectors and artists at the convention site. I have also conducted formal interviews with artists and collectors in California and Connecticut.

Informal field conversations with tattoo artists and collectors (from Austria, Australia, France, Japan, Switzerland, California, Connecticut, Michigan, New Jersey, New Mexico, Ohio, Oregon, and Texas), participant observation at tattoo conventions, participation in the tattoo subculture for the past 12 years, and over 150 hours getting tattooed have all provided me with preliminary data on which to base my suppositions. The data taken from these less formal observational techniques have been recorded in ethnographic field notes over the past four years. I have collected further secondary interview data from videos focusing on prominent fine art tattoo artists from the San Francisco Bay area.

## SCHOLARLY RESEARCH ON TATTOOING

Tattooing and the people that practice it are burgeoning areas in several scholarly fields. Recent articles and books focusing on dermographic embellishment have been written by psychologists, sociologists, researchers of marketing practices and theory, and anthropologists. Within these fields, the focus runs the gamut from psychological determinism to postmodernism.

The empirical research in the psychological literature has tended to focus on tattooing as a sign of psychopathology (see Sanders, 1989 for a review), although recent research (Copes & Forsyth, 1993) has examined tattoos as a sign of extroversion. Since extroverts require more social and physical stimulation, according to Copes and Forsyth, they are more likely to engage in behaviors deemed socially unacceptable. As a result, they are often labeled pathological. Hence, tattoos are not indicative of psychopathology. Rather, those who wear them are merely boisterous and likely to be labeled troublemakers.

Those who study tattooing from a marketing perspective have focused primarily on what is attractive about the tattoos themselves. Some marketers, for example, have focused on the freedom and hedonism associated with bikers (a prototypical tattoo community). Hence, marketing researchers have, as have psychologists, tended to look for intrapersonal explanations for becoming tattooed. In both cases, researchers seem to have drawn the conclusion that tattooing provides a way for one to flaunt his or her individuality, sometimes to the level of assuming a criminal or pseudo-criminal image.

Interdisciplinary studies of popular culture have examined recent trends in fashion models wearing tattoos, current or passing cultural impressions of tattoos as symbolic of criminality, and analyses of the contexts in which we are exposed to tattoos in the mass media. These analyses have tended to be less judgmental than their psychological and marketing counterparts, but they have largely ignored collectors and trends in fine art tattooing.

The anthropological literature has touched on cross-cultural perspectives and analyses of tattooing in America and abroad, employing ethnographic, descriptive analyses and postmodernist "discourses." Of the anthropologists, DeMello is currently the most prolific. Her *Bodies of Inscription* (2000) examines current changes in the American tattoo community as it expands across class and gender lines, and her discussions of the history of tattooing in America and tattoo publications are informative and insightful.

The sociological literature has, until recently, consisted solely of Sanders' (1989) seminal work on tattooing. Sanders described the interaction strategies used by tattooers and tattooees as they navigated the process of becoming tattooed. Atkinson (2003) has added to Sanders' work by studying the tattoo culture in Canada. My own work has focused on the fine art tattoo world.

Taken en masse, the scholarly literature is rich with analyses of people who wear tattoos, the context in which they wear them, and how non-tattooed people view those tattoos and the people who wear them. Excepting my work to date, researchers in the social sciences have avoided looking at those for whom tattoos have become a master status (Becker, 1963; Schur, 1971). I have, elsewhere, looked at one way that collectors form and solidify their identities as tattooed people (i.e., by attending tattoo conventions). I turn now to the process of becoming and being a collector.

## BECOMING AND BEING A COLLECTOR

Becoming a tattoo collector is a transformative experience in more ways than one. This transformation is physical (i.e., one actually alters skin pigmentation), psychological, and subcultural. Becoming a collector involves not only changing the way that light reflects off one's skin but also the way that others view that skin and the person inside it. The images one chooses, and the ways she or he combines them say a lot, not only about the person who has chosen them, but also about who has influenced those choices. For example, Chris, an arborist, describes his collection as follows.

> For my arm-band, I went out in the woods and cut a piece of branch with bittersweet around it . . . because . . . I climb trees and work outdoors . . . a lot doing tree removals and pruning and shit like that. . . . And this one over here . . . is sort of like . . . a protector. That's my climber line with my protecting dragons on either end. And then the third one [is] my back. . . . That design [a graphic depiction of a bare tree] came from . . . my belt buckle. . . . [My tattoo artist] did both of these pieces [on the lower legs]. This one here, I said, "I want some leaves in it. I want the Polynesian design, [Celtic] design, a band around my calf, but I want leaves in it." What he did was put in unfolding springtime ferns.

In Japanese tattoo iconography, the floral motifs, deities, and mythological characters all carry specific meanings. For example, because of their association with the Japanese card game of *hana-fuda*, peonies tend to be the most masculine of flowers, and cherry blossoms symbolize impermanence. The placement of a design and those surrounding it have significance as well.

Unlike Japanese tattooing, however, American fine art tattooing is, in many respects, a melting pot of motifs and aesthetics. The current tattoo renaissance encompasses such diverse styles as photorealism, cybertech, traditional Japanese style, neotribalism, and any number of combinations of the above. Artists have also made profound technical advances.

In many respects, the work of fine art tattoo artists like Filip Leu, Bill Salmon, Paul Booth, and Guy Aitchison have brought respectability to tattooing. Fine artists' abilities to use different motifs have allowed tattoo collectors to create individually designed body suits that are truly postmodern in impact. Hence, we see Japanese aesthetics used to create body suits composed entirely of different depictions of Godzilla (Bannatyne, 1992, pp. 22–24) or traditional Polynesian aesthetics used in a tattoo of M. C. Escher's *Metamorphosis*.

Although the meaning of specific tattoos is inherently individual, people learn how to build their collections from other people. It takes a great deal of research for one to become intimately familiar with a particular motif and the iconography appropriate to use within it. It takes still more comparative research to figure out what styles and/or motifs one will employ in building his or her collection. Some do this research using tattoo magazines (DeMello, 2000) and some learn through symbolic interaction with other collectors and artists. In the end, however, collectors learn how to become collectors (Glaser, 1956; Matza, 1969; Sutherland, 1939).

### Learning to Become a Collector: Affinity

Matza (1969) discusses the process of becoming deviant. Although tattoos are less a statement of deviance than they once were, becoming heavily tattooed still stands outside social norms. Becoming a collector requires devotion to a lifestyle that is more marginal than that associated with fraternities or "tasteful" flowers. In short, one must want to become a collector. This desire is what Matza (1969) calls "Affinity." "[Affinity] may be regarded as a natural biographical tendency borne of personal and social circumstance that suggests but hardly compels a direction of movement" (p. 93). In essence, affinity refers to a person's desire to become deviant. Comments like Chris's were common among respondents both in formal interviews and in informal field conversations: "My wife's been collecting for about 20 years, off and on, small pieces. And I've always wanted one, I just, y'know, never came across the right idea or the right person to do it." Chris is not alone in "always wanting" tattoos. However, not everyone who gets one tattoo becomes a collector.

In order to make the jump from having tattoos to being a collector, one must first have an affinity for being a collector. Here, I mean not only wearing tattoos (often, but not necessarily, many of them), but conceiving of oneself as tattooed.

> Several of the people that I talked to discussed becoming collectors in terms of starting with just one tattoo and building their collections from that starting point. The experience of getting several small, bad tattoos as a start seems to be a common one. It is only after they start to conceive of themselves as collectors, however, that they begin to visualize their collections as conceptual and stylistic wholes. This becomes apparent by starting their collections by covering their old, small tattoos. This cover work tends to evolve in either geographic (i.e., specific areas of the body) or conceptual patterns. (Field Notes)

This excerpt from my field notes speaks to how people express themselves differently once they have conceived of themselves as "tattooed" as opposed to wearing tattoos. The tattoos with which they started are pictures in their skin. The collections that they have started to build represent a new self-image: that of the tattoo collector. Part of what allows the collector to fully realize this transition is what Matza (1969) calls "Affiliation."

## Learning to Become a Collector: Affiliation

"Affiliation describes the process by which the subject is *converted* to conduct novel for him but already established for others" (Matza, 1969, p. 101). This process has also been analyzed by Sutherland

(1937, 1939) as "Differential Association." According to both Sutherland and Matza, deviance is taught in symbolic interaction with successful deviants. "[Sutherland's] method of affiliation harbors an idea of conversion. . . . Unless one always was deviant, in which case little illumination is required, *becoming deviant* depends on being converted" (Matza, 1969, pp. 106–107). Thus, the collector learns how to feel good about becoming a collector, as well as learning where to place his or her tattoos. She or he learns how to become a collector from other collectors and tattooers.

As previously mentioned, in order for this conversion to be successful, one must want to be converted. Hence, affinity and affiliation work together in creating both deviance and deviants.

Respondents typically talked about tattooing as a desirable experience, the quality of which affected the perceived quality of the tattoo more than the crispness of lines or the boldness of the shading. In this way, collectors and artists alike see becoming collectors in terms of recruitment. Consider Luke's comments:

> What goes into a great tattoo is, I guess, is the experience, because it's like a personal album or something. . . . It's like a montage of your life. That's why the Japanese said I got tattooed for memories, and he got tattooed for a story. Some stupid fuckin' Japanese, Oriental story, he got tattooed for, y'know?

The pejorative "some stupid fuckin' Japanese, Oriental story" shows how Luke views the appropriate way to become tattooed. For Luke, collectors should get tattooed to hold on to their memories. For him, the Japanese notion of getting tattooed for a story is inappropriate.

Other collectors view tattoos as a means to express personal spirituality and thus, a moral enterprise. Sherrill illustrates this point nicely.

> For me to do a tattoo on somebody that runs against the grain of my philosophical life, it's impossible, it's just not going to happen. Y'know, if somebody

comes to me and says, "I want a tattoo of dismembered babies and whatever" I'm like, "Sorry." Y'know? Wrong guy. Go see [somebody else], y'know what I mean? Don't come to me with this stuff. It's not my life, it's not my style, it's not my belief system. I'm not going to violate that. And by doing that, I've always held close to my beliefs.

In this statement, Sherrill shows how he goes about recruiting select people into his philosophical approach to tattooing. Not only is he concerned with expressing himself artistically, but he is concerned with teaching people that tattoos should be a positive self-expression. By turning away work that he finds indicative of destructive tendencies, he is not only strengthening the resolve of those he tattoos; he is also telling those on whom he refuses to work that their notion of what is acceptable for tattooing is flawed. In essence, he is recruiting "the right kind of people" into the tattoo world.

Sherrill also recruits through means other than tattooing or showing his collection. The following exchange shows how his beliefs about the appropriate reasons for becoming tattooed run counter to common misconceptions about the exhibitionistic tendencies of tattoo collectors. In essence, becoming a collector involves learning how to act like one. Consider Sherrill's response to my asking whether he ever shows his collection publicly:

No. Because they're real personal, my tattoos. I always get asked to take my clothes off, but I never do. And the line that I always give . . . is that when you start taking your clothes off, nobody listens to what you have to say. You lose credibility real fast. This is a culture which does not . . . which has demonized the body. I'm not going to go on a big blabber about American culture's demonization of the body, but I'm writing a book on it, so it's consumed the last five years of my writing on tattooing.

Here, Sherrill shows how recruitment is not just a matter of preaching to the proverbial choir. By appearing in mass media outlets, Sherrill shows both those who are and those who are not tattooed

how to be tattooed and respectable at the same time. In essence, then, he recruits collectors into acting "the right way." He also recruits those who will never become tattooed into a culture that finds tattooing, if not acceptable, at least not reprehensible.

Both tattooers and collectors teach other collectors about appropriate "use of the canvas." Fine art tattoos take into account musculature, size, shape, and texture of a given area of the collector's body. Fine art back pieces, for example, incorporate the breadth of the collector's shoulders and narrowness of his or her waist in the design. Another example is Filip Leu's watershed color portrait of Jimi Hendrix (Bannatyne, 1992, p. 52), done on my right thigh in 1992. Since the thigh is roughly the same size as a face and follows similar outlines (roughly oval), the portrait used all of the canvas and used it appropriately.

Interviewees often spoke of beginning their collections with smaller tattoos that did not incorporate the structure of the body well. As their collections grew, however, they started to learn about appropriate designs for their specific canvases.

Colin [a collector and tattooer] just talked about the transition from large, bright color fantasy work [at the shoulders and chest] into a slightly narrower section of color fantasy and music as represented by the Muppet band [on his stomach], into the smaller black and grey photo-realistic depictions of [rock] musicians directly below. Each of those sections has a particular style appropriate for it, and the concept dictated the style and motif. (Field Notes)

Colin's collection began with smaller tattoos on the arms (now covered), but once he began thinking of himself as a tattoo collector, he began using his canvas to its full advantage. The front torso of Colin's collection is in a "V" shape. The fantasy-style tattoos on the chest caps are bold and striated (much like pectoral musculature); the Muppet band members are round and fuzzy (much like Colin's stomach); and the portraits at the bottom follow, both singularly and collectively, the contours of his hips and lower abdomen. In talking further about his collection, Colin discussed his back. He talked about how he loves all of his tattoos, but he got a sort of small piece early on, on his shoulder blade, which ruined taking up the entire back with one design. He now realizes, for instance, that the outside of the thigh is roughly half of a back.

We see, therefore, that Colin has learned how to conceptualize the human canvas in terms of what kinds of tattoos best fit where, and he learned this from working in his wife's tattoo shop and from discussing collections with other fine art collectors. Alfred Schutz (1967, pp. 75–78) helps us understand an important point here. While a great deal of this process may appear perfectly logical and in accordance with plans, collectors often assign meanings to their collections in "casting a reflective glance" on the work they already wear.

Another collector, Sadie, learned about appropriate use of the canvas from her husband (a tattoo collector and motorcycle mechanic). Her collection, still in its initial stages, is of gargoyles.

Currently, she has four gargoyles, all of similar size and style. They begin on her left shoulder and descend down the center of her back. Eventually, they will finish on her right hip, connected by vines. She was not ready to get a full back piece, but she had seen other women's backs, tattooed in the same basic shape, in tattoo magazines. As she described it to me, the contours of the string of gargoyles accent her figure. Also, the design leaves two fairly large open canvases. (Field Notes)

Hence, Sadie has learned about appropriate use of the canvas and has shown respect for its shape and possibilities. She learned about use and respect for the canvas from other collectors (her husband and collectors in tattoo-oriented publications) and from her artists.

These interviewees have been recruited, and continue to recruit others, by learning and sharing what makes a tattoo (and/or a tattooer) good.

Although every respondent talked about the artistic ability of his or her tattooer(s), 75% said that technique was less important than rapport. For example, when I asked Sherrill why he chose to visit a particular artist, he responded,

The professional quality of his studio is what struck me the most. The shop he had . . . on Sunset strip, was so clean, and the presentation was so beautiful, I was stunned when I saw it. You could have eaten off the floors in that place, it was so clean. Every bottle was labeled. This was a guy that was working with gloves and protecting himself long before anybody in the vicinity. And his work was way in advance of anybody I have ever seen. . . .

*Talk to me about how you learned what goes into a good tattoo.*

Well, it was just exposure. Most of us learn by experience. After a while, I began to see what was possible with tattooing and the level of quality that could be achieved. . . . For me, after a few bad experiences with personalities, I began to make decisions about getting tattooed from a whole different direction. It has more to do with the person. Even more to do with the person than with technique, actually.

Thus, the rapport between Sherrill and his artist is more important to him than artistic ability. In a sense, his collecting is based more on feeling a connection with an artist than acquiring "fine art." Now that he sees himself as a collector, he is going to make this self-applied label work for him. This is the final element of Matza's (1969) process of becoming deviant: signification.

## Learning to Become a Collector: Signification

After one learns the techniques of being deviant, he or she often reconceptualizes his or her life in terms of that deviance. In discussing "indication," Matza (1969) elaborates on this notion of identity-building among professional thieves:

Quite different from consequence, indication points the subject to a consideration of himself; to the question of the unity of meaning of the various things he does and the relation of those things to what he conceivably is. To consider the possibility that the theft was important in the sense of being indicative of him puts the subject well into actively collaborating in the growth of deviant identity by building its very meaning. (p. 165)

In essence, once deviants have internalized their deviant labels, they reconceptualize their actions in terms of being appropriate for people who are "like that." Tattoo collectors see collecting as appropriate for tattooed people. This can have profound effects on how they view their collections as well as appropriate ways to display them.

As I said in the section on affiliation, once collectors begin to think of themselves as collectors, they often begin to plan how each new tattoo will work within the canvas. An aspect of collecting that exhibits signification is working around public skin (i.e., easily visible skin like the neck, hands, and face). Cody illustrates this point nicely.

Cody is working on a full body suit, accompanied by facial piercings, and satyr horn implants on either side of his widow's peak at the hairline. The following excerpt from field notes shows how Cody has planned his suit, at various stages, to combine his tattooed identity with one that is acceptable to those outside the subculture.

> [Before] he became a full-time tattooer and piercer . . . his crew chief wouldn't let him work with any . . . tattoos showing. So, he had to get long-sleeved t-shirts to cover the tattoos that went to his elbow. He [has subsequently covered his arms] down to the wrists and is now going on to the tops of his hands. He said that he . . . is thinking about leaving the collar untattooed, and that way, he can take out the facial piercings and put on a hat and go out in public with a long-sleeved shirt and still look somewhat respectable.

**Photo 1.1**    Alistair's Tattoos. Body modification runs the spectrum from one or two small tattoos that can be concealed by clothes to more drastic physical alterations that are publicly observable. Tattoos that cover the neck can be observed, and commented on, by strangers in public, sometimes making the tattooed person an object of derision.

SOURCE: Angus Vail.

Thus, even though Cody is obviously devoted to body modification, he still is concerned with getting along in normative society. By leaving open canvas at the collar, he will be able to "pass" more easily. Other collectors are less concerned with passing than with planning their remaining space (see Photo 1.1).

Luke's collection has been complete for about 20 years, but in the following excerpt from our interview he recalls when he realized what he had to do to finish the collection.

Well, yeah. You look at yourself and you just, y'know, you see that there are these spaces that just need to be filled up. It's not that you're comparing yourself to someone else, or some kind or image, it's just that those spaces aren't complete. It's like you're on a course and you've gotta finish it. . . . most tattoo suits fit within standard barriers. Some people go above and beyond, but the prescribed cover job is like, a neck band, ankle bands, wrist bands, put a cargo net underneath your nuts and then just fill the rest of it up. So, when it's done, you can tell.

Thus, Luke completed his collection within "standard barriers." He filled his canvas from those barriers into the body of the suit. Other collectors work within a section at a time, while remaining cognizant of how to expand on what is already covered. The following excerpt from an interview with Chris shows how he has collaborated with an artist within the constraints of neotribalism.

And what I learned from [my tattoo artist] is that the pieces he's done on my legs . . . he's left 'em open to continue. 'Cause I . . . was always told when you put an arm band . . . around, that defines an end. But he says "Yeah, that's right, but I always leave an opening so I can move it in a different direction." That's what he did with this, too.

Thus, Chris has left room for expansion, should it be necessary. Yet, the tattoos can stand on their own. He conceived of his back piece, a sparse, solid black depiction of a bare tree, in a similar way.

This was interesting. That design came from [my belt buckle]. My wife gave me this 25 years ago, right after we first got married. I've always liked the design, and I brought it up to [my other artist], and all she did was add on the roots at the bottom, 'cause she said "Without the roots, it's gonna tip over."

*Do you think of yourself as a collector?*

Yeah. A beginning collector, but the pieces I've collected are a hell of a start. . . . The back piece

was . . . that was . . . I mean getting tattooed here was interesting. With the back piece, to me, that was like "I am really getting into this fucking tattoo shit."

*Talk to me about that.*

I mean, this is a tattoo [pointing at his arm]. This [his back], is a tattoo. I mean, it's just so much deeper into the cult, not, well, maybe the cult, but the . . . I keep going back to the industry. I mean, maybe that's not right, but I keep going back to the fact that it's hard core. . . . This was . . . it just crossed the line into the fact that I knew I was gonna get a whole lot more tattoos. We did the outline [of the tree] and I looked at it and I said, "Wow! That's my whole back." It just sunk in.

*Are you working toward a full body suit?*

No. I don't think so. . . . Mainly because a full body suit is too much for me. Too confusing. . . . It's confusing to follow it. . . .

*So, what will you leave out of the body suit?*

If I put . . . the chest piece that I have planned, if I put anything else here, it's gonna fuck it up. You know what I mean? The tree, everybody keeps saying, "Well, why don't you fill it in? Where the fuck are the leaves?" Y'know? I says, "No, that's it." I had originally thought of putting an eyeball in the middle, an owl behind it, y'know? It's just, fuck that. Just leave it simple.

This excerpt shows how Chris conceives of his collection in the future perfect tense (i.e., as a collection that will have been done; Schutz, 1962, 1967) in several ways. He does not want to ruin the impact of his back piece or his yet-to-be-applied chest piece. He also sees his collection as respectful of his canvas. Other collectors, while conscious of their open canvas, are less concerned with what specific designs will fill their remaining space. Rather, they are concerned with saving canvas for specific artists. The following excerpt from field notes describes such a collector:

I just spoke with a tattooer on the floor who said that she bases her choices on who to get work from on personality (although she has work from some wonderful artists, which shows that she is concerned with collecting fine art, too). I asked her what her plans are for future work and she said that she gets mostly small pieces, one or two a year, so that she won't run out of space when someone new that she really likes comes along. She has full sleeves and is working on her legs now.

Hence, collectors collect pieces (e.g., Chris's collection of arborist tattoos), artists (e.g., above excerpt from field notes), concepts (e.g., Colin's musical and fantasy themes), and/or styles (e.g., Luke's collection within "standard barriers"). Regardless of what they collect, however, collectors work toward a collection as it will be when it is done. They respect their canvases by collecting in "appropriate" ways.

## Conclusion

Collecting tattoos is both an individual and collective journey. Collectors must choose their own designs for their own reasons. Yet, they learn how to incorporate those designs into collections from others who have been successful in building collections. Some have attempted to explain what these collections mean. I believe this is a fruitless endeavor. However, studying the tattoo collection process sheds light on several broader sociological and phenomenological issues.

Tattoo collecting incorporates all three of Matza's (1969) stages of becoming deviant (i.e., affinity, affiliation, and signification). Because becoming a collector involves both considerable financial commitment and physical and stigmatic discomfort, it requires devotion to the process. In short, a collector's affinity must be strong.

Collectors must also learn how to become collectors. They must learn how to evaluate tattoos and tattooers. This involves learning how to evaluate technique and how to build rapport. Collectors must also learn how to best represent the tattoo subculture. This involves learning techniques of passing and consensus building. They learn these things through affiliation with other collectors.

Finally, collectors learn how to mitigate their new master statuses (Becker, 1963; Schur, 1971) as collectors, not as just people with tattoos. They begin to view their collections in the future perfect tense (Schutz, 1962, 1967), as collections that will have been completed. This process of navigating signification from both within and without the tattoo world involves respecting the canvas as it is and as it will be.

In becoming tattooed, the collector learns not only how well-established members of the tattoo world conceive of "proper" use of form and iconography in building a collection, but also how to see himself or herself as a tattooed person. Although some may consider the distinction between those who have tattoos and those who are tattooed a semantic one, semantics, in this case, are important.

In discussing those who have tattoos, the analyst (whether a sociologist, anthropologist, or psychologist) assumes a possessive relationship between the person and the dermographic embellishment that she or he has purchased. In essence, this person's tattoos are no different from the car she or he drives or the hair style she or he sports on any given day. Like these adornments, tattoos represent possessions that can be considered with or without the individual who wears them.

The collector, on the other hand, sees himself or herself *as tattooed*, not just the owner of the pigments residing in the first layer of his or her dermis. The images that adorn the collector's canvas are, as Luke so colorfully stated earlier in this article, his or her memories made physical. To the collector, tattoos are not something one owns. Rather, they are a part of him or her, no less important than the color of his or her hair or skin, no more easily removed from his or her identity than his or her deepest beliefs, most profound concerns, or his or her idiosyncratic sense of humor. In short, the collector does not see himself as John who *has tattoos* but as John who *is tattooed*.

Since, for the collector, tattoos represent a master status, all of his or her actions, beliefs, fears, and hopes can be seen in his or her collection. How those personal characteristics become part of the collection, only the collector knows. That they are there, however, is irrefutable. The fact that they are there affects not only the ways that collectors see themselves, but also the ways that others see them. In short, their tattoos have profound effects on their interactions with intimates and non-intimates alike.

The recent attention that the news media have paid to tattooing speaks volumes about the relevance of this topic. With tattoo shops being ranked among the six fastest-growing industries in the nation and the recent legalization of tattooing in New York City, we, as sociologists, have a unique opportunity to demystify the processes involved in enacting a cultural phenomenon that is rapidly losing its deviant status.

## REFERENCES

Atkinson, M. (2003). *Tattooed: The sociogenesis of a body art.* Toronto: University of Toronto Press.

Bannatyne, B. (Ed.). (1992). *Forever yes: Art of the new tattoo.* Honolulu, HI: Hardy Marks.

Becker, H. S. (1963). *Outsiders: Studies in the sociology of deviance.* New York: Free Press.

Burgess, R., & Akers, R. (1966). A differential association-reinforcement theory of criminal behavior. *Social Problems, 14,* 128–147.

Coleman, T. (2005, October). Pigments or poisons—Health risks from tattoo inks get bloody. *Skin and Ink, 10,* 11–13.

Copes, J. H., & Forsyth, C. J. (1993). The tattoo: A social psychological explanation. *International Review of Modern Sociology, 23,* 83–89.

DeMello, M. (2000). *Bodies of inscription: A cultural history of the modern tattoo community.* Durham, NC: Duke University Press.

Glaser, D. (1956). Criminality theories and behavioral images. *American Journal of Sociology, 61,* 433–444.

Matza, D. (1969). *Becoming deviant.* Englewood Cliffs, NJ: Prentice Hall.

Sanders, C. R. (1989). *Customizing the body: The art and culture of tattooing.* Philadelphia: Temple University Press.

Schur, E. M. (1971). *Labeling deviant behavior.* New York: Harper & Row.

Schutz, A. (1962). *Collected papers, vol. I: The problem of social reality* (M. Natanson, Ed.). Boston: Martinus Nijhoff.

Schutz, A. (1967). *The phenomenology of the social world* (G. Walsh & F. Lehnert, Trans., G. Walsh, Intro.). Evanston, IL: Northwestern University Press.

Sutherland, E. H. (1937). *The professional thief.* Chicago: University of Chicago Press.

Sutherland, E. H. (1939). *Principles of criminology* (3rd ed.). New York: Lippincott.

Sutherland, E. H., & Cressey, D. R. (1974). *Criminology* (9th ed.). Philadelphia: Lippincott.

# Flesh Journeys

## The Radical Body Modification of Neoprimitives

### *Michael Atkinson and Kevin Young*

Body decoration takes three forms: body painting, body ornamentation, and body modification. Our focus here is on the third of these forms, body modification, or permanent modes of body decoration. There are virtually endless ways to modify a body in what might be referred to as a "flesh journey," or the intentional reconstruction of the corporeal to symbolically represent one's identity, relationships, or thoughts. We would like to look at the more radical contemporary varieties of tattooing, piercing, branding, and scarification, or nonmainstream forms of body modification.

We estimate that roughly 10% to 20% of North Americans have engaged in tattooing or other lasting body modifications. Moreover, body modification cuts across the demographic categories of age, ethnicity, gender, and economic status. Once associated more or less exclusively with society's fringes—gangs, sailors, prisoners, outlaws, and bikers—a late-twentieth-century rebirth of body modification ushered in a new era of cultural expression and ideological representation. The long-standing argument that in Western society radical body modification and deviance and social stigma tend to go hand in hand maintains credibility, yet this formulation often limits the analysis of such practices as legitimate and viable forms of art and personal expression.

Here, we would like to look at the neoprimitives, an emerging strand within the Canadian body modification scene, who represent one of the more outspoken and radical groups of body modification enthusiasts. Neoprimitives challenge the deviant stereotypes associated with tattooed, pierced, branded, scarred bodies; they encourage a reexamination of the cultural meanings of radical body modification. Our discussion is broken down into four main parts. We begin with a review of the literature; then proceed to a discussion of the neoprimitive movement, leaning on terms and categories adopted by the participants themselves; and finally discuss six main rationales neoprimitives use to explain radical body modification and examine how these understandings are shared within the group.

## LOOKING AT THE CULTURALLY INSCRIBED BODY

How and why is culture inscribed upon the physical body? The physical body is like a text, rich in social, cultural, political, and religious significance. The body can emerge in the strictly biological sense, for instance, through illness. Or it can be socially constructed, in the sense that physical changes are voluntarily manufactured as a site for creating and affirming social and cultural meaning.

Chris Shilling (1993) refers to body modification as an intentionally designed "body project," arguing that such projects help symbolically construct a person's self and social identity. For Shilling, the body is always in a process of *becoming* because its size, shape, and appearance are subject to reconstruction on an ongoing basis, often in socially deviant ways. A full array of body projects or "flesh journeys" has been the topic of investigation for sociologists. These include the hyper-muscular body (Monaghan, 2001), the emaciated body (Lupton, 1996), the transgendered body (Segal, 1994), the cosmetically altered body (Davis, 2003), and the cybernetic body (Balsamo, 1996). As both radical and non-radical forms of "body work" (Gimlin, 2004) have blossomed as a means of self-expression, we see a proliferation of social research on how people modify their bodies to achieve social and personal ends.

While at first glance seemingly dissonant, what unifies these and other forms of cultural expression is the conscious attempt to alter the body's natural parameters in some way, to inscribe upon the body a set of symbols that distinguish it from the mainstream and connect it affiliatively or disaffiliatively with other marked-up bodies and groups. Definitions of deviance are socially constructed—and consciously resisted—by social groups and categories; as a result, we must consider how actors anticipate social reaction to their behaviors, expressions of belief, and physical characteristics. In presenting radical and confrontational styles such as non-mainstream body modification, individuals are often seeking to elicit a negative response from others. Deviance, then, may be instrumental for those interested in resisting social norms and conventions. The deliberate presentation of a profane or marked body is, as Hebdige (1979) writes, offered to be interpreted in a negative way.

Like sport, the body is contested terrain. Just as meanings of sport in our society are disputed, the experience of the body in sport is subject to context-specific definitions and interpretations. For example, pushing the body to its physical limits during a marathon might be lauded by other athletes, coaches, and spectators as emblematic of one's commitment to excellence, while engaging in the same degree of physical exertion during training runs might be viewed as risky, irrational, or counterproductive. Here, we argue that what

makes the radical body sociologically interesting is the cultural struggle over legitimate ways of using the body.

Until recently, sociologists have been somewhat inattentive to the study of non-mainstream body modification. Sanders' (1989) work on tattooing represents the most comprehensive analysis of radical body modification in Western society. His book, *Customizing the Body: The Art and Culture of Tattooing*, should be a starting point for anyone interested in this area. Sanders points to the changing meaning of tattooing in our culture, specifically a return to alternative body styles, a reinvigorated youth movement, and a boom in tattooing among females.

In contrast, the work of many psychologists has limited our understanding of radical body modification. Theorizing that tattoos are physical indicators of individual pathology, psychologists and sociologists of health have often attempted to correlate tattooing with risk taking, homosexuality, criminal tendencies, and low self-esteem (Ceniceros, 1998; Roberts & Ryan, 2002). Such perceptions have done much to produce an inaccurate picture of the cultural meanings associated with body modification. Further, they do not permit participants to speak for themselves using their own terms and categories.

In sum, while sociological investigations of radical body modification have introduced the subject and laid the groundwork, a full portrait of how the body, particularly the deviant body, is inscribed has just begun to be painted.

## NEOPRIMITIVES

We conducted semi-structured interviews with body modification artists (N = 20) and their clients (N = 35). We also observed work conducted at body modification studios and group body modification rituals and ceremonies and attended body modification ceremonies. All names used are pseudonyms. Our interviews and observations are drawn mainly from two cities in Canada (Toronto and Calgary), with occasional references to the American scene. Perhaps 5% to 8% of all persons in Canada who have been tattooed are affiliated with the neoprimitives.

While non-Western forms of body modification have never stopped being adopted as bridges to the past (New Zealand Maori tattooing is an obvious example), subcultural adoption of so-called primitive styles is a recent phenomenon. Neoprimitive body modification reflects an array of rituals of the flesh. As we indicated above, the four most prevalent forms of body modification are *tattooing*, characteristically done in black and red ink with large designs that resonate with tribal markings whose shapes follow the body's natural contours; *piercing*, most notably stainless steel, wood, or "bone" rings placed in the face, ears, and nipples; *branding* or *burning*, typically done in small patterns located on the limbs or upper back; and *scarification*, the least common form of body modification, involving a small but generally ornate cutting of the flesh.

The neoprimitive movement perhaps began with an interest in tribal lifestyles and artwork that developed in the late 1970s in Los Angeles, San Francisco, New York, and Toronto (Rosenblatt, 1997; Vale & Juno, 1989). The tribal tattoo styles of the New Zealand Maori, the Dyak of Borneo, and the Haida of the Pacific Northwest figured prominently at this stage, leading to non-Western body modification practices more generally and a growth in related print sources, such as the magazines *Body Play and Modern Primitives* and *Tattoo*

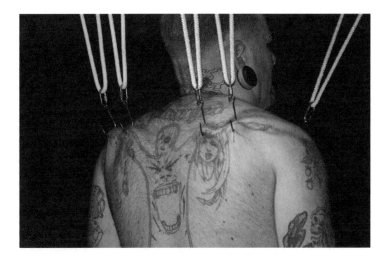

**Photo 1.2**   Another dimension of body modification is how much it violates cultural and normative standards of appearance and propriety. Some physical alterations provoke the question in observers: "Why would anyone want to *do* something like that to his body?"

SOURCE: Aaron D. Settipane.

*Savage,* to promote and support an expanding appetite for information about the movement.

An early statement of extreme body modification, Vale and Juno's *Modern Primitives* (1989), stressed the significance body art has played in human history and explored a number of directions such practices could lead, including body encumberments (neck encasements), body compression (bondage), body burning (branding), body suspension (through the use of hooks penetrating the flesh), and body penetrating (piercing, tattooing, and scarring). Vale and Juno argue that North American society is at a crossroads of body modification, in that there exists a desire here to return to the primitive meanings behind body modification (see Photo 1.2).

Part of the neoprimitive return to primitive sensibilities about radical body modification has included a re-conceptualization of how the modified body is displayed to others. Neoprimitive group members do not hide or "pass" their physical differences, but rather relish in the exhibition of their modified bodies. Tattoos are placed in normally exposed areas, such as hands, face, arms, neck, and legs. Piercings made from stainless steel, plastic, or bone (in the form of rings, barbells, screws, and plugs) are inserted into various parts of the body. Generally, these include body protrusions (such as ears, nose, nipples, or genitalia) or places where the skin can be stretched or manipulated to accommodate a piercing (such as eyebrows, lips, cheeks, or the neck). Branding involves burning a forged metal design into the skin, and scarification involves cutting a pattern or design into the skin with a sharp, normally metal, implement. As the practices can be quite painful, can heal with less than artistically pleasing results, and do not have long-standing traditions in North America, the use of branding and scarification by neoprimitives can present disruptive images of the body. This seems especially true where gender codes are concerned. In a culture still deeply stratified along gender lines, publicly displayed multiple tattoos and piercings represent a direct affront to traditional notions of femininity.

Another central characteristic of the neoprimitive group is the diversity of its members. Neoprimitives come from a cross-section of social backgrounds representing variations in age, ethnicity, occupation, and sexual orientation. Their commonality is a preference for urban life. According to our respondents, what defines an individual as a neoprimitive is both an identification with a set of focal concerns expressed by the group—including the alienation and isolation originating out of the experience of urban culture—and the active participation in alternative social activities, such as body modification, that arise distinctly in urban culture. As a social movement, then, neoprimitivism incorporates traditions of body modification from various tribal cultures, links these practices and their associated meanings to current social and political concerns, and does all this within the framework of a futuristic vision of popular cultural expression. In the words of Jane, one of our respondents, "We are not interested in the return *to* the primitive; we are interested in the return *of* the primitive."

## BODY MODIFICATION: INTERPRETATIONS AND MEANINGS

The rationales of neoprimitives for participating in what we call flesh journeys are grounded in diverse cultural philosophies and ideologies, but are linked in the sense that they attempt to align modern forms of body modification with historically meaningful practices. Neoprimitives would argue that while the technology used for performing body modification is markedly different from tools used in the past, the purposes behind doing it remain strikingly similar. For neoprimitives, the flesh is simultaneously an accessible canvas to be manipulated in a deeply personal, private way and a billboard to be displayed socially. Our interviews suggest that these experiences and intended outcomes may be classified into six main areas: subcultural membership and resistance, personal status passage, creativity and individuality, physical endurance and pain thresholds, beauty and art, and spirituality. We did not impose these categories on our respondents' accounts; rather, they arose from the insider vocabularies our respondents used.

### Subcultural Membership and Resistance

Many group members bond together in a manner perceived by the majority as deviant; that membership is regarded as an attempt to oppose, transform, or undermine the dominant order. Group members of some deviant collectivities seek to resist feelings of social disenfranchisement. In this sense, collectivized body modification celebrates tribal styles that help members cohere through a sense of problem sharing and solving.

During the interviews, neoprimitives frequently spoke of their personal dissatisfaction with contemporary urban life. Their physically marked bodies are literally designed to be socially disruptive markers of discontent. Adopting a voluntary social stigma by acquiring and displaying profane or defiling body marks, individuals establish bonds with others who are not only irreverent with respect to such social stigma, but even relish the aura of being socially distinct. In the words of Phil, one of our interviewees,

No matter how much disdain people show me for my tattoos and brandings, I find solace in the fact that I know so many others who share my experiences in life; we cling to one another in times [of] doubt and pain. There's a great sense of community that emanates out of this studio . . . something you don't experience if you go to Smoky Joe's tattoo shop and get "Number 23" [a standard design or "flash"] and never speak to anyone there again. There's a family of members here that know things about me, and I know personal details about them as well. That's what these [points to tattoos] stand for.

While body modification itself is not the only practice or value members collectively share, it serves the fundamental purpose of designating membership both to insiders and to nonmembers.

The concept of *bricolage* is central to understanding how neoprimitives create a common set of symbols that are meaningful to one another. Bricolage refers to the process of creating new and often socially deviant uses and meanings for cultural objects. Drawing heavily on the body modification imagery and styles of Polynesians, Melanesians, the Dyak of Borneo, North American Native cultures such as the Haida, the Aztec, and various African tribes, neoprimitive body modification obviously reflects eclectic influences and gives new meaning and rationale for wearing the designs. The use of primitive body modification styles and techniques attempts to recapture the collective sense of community and belonging the

neoprimitives believe was achieved through tribal uses of body modification. In the words of Renata, one of our respondents,

In other cultures, getting a tattoo means that you're "one of us." It's a mark of pride, a coming of age that no one can take away from you after it's over. I love that about my tattoos; I feel as if I'm a member of a tribe, one of the pack.

Many modern subcultural groups, such as the Goths, Skaters, Club Kids, Psychobillies, Ravers, Straightedgers, and Skinheads, also use radical body modification as an integral aspect of group membership and disaffiliation with other groups and with mainstream society generally. Clearly, body modification is not utilized universally or with the same rationale or intent across groups. Also key here is that group members experience and understand body modification in an *intersubjective* sense. Still, even though flesh journeys are deeply personalized and unique, group members explore the expressive capabilities of the modified body by sharing their experiences with others similarly committed to body modification. Thus, the meaning behind the modification of the body both reflects personal biographies and is ultimately crystallized and understood within a group context (see Photo 1.3).

**Personal Status Passage**

Neoprimitives use radical body modification for personal catharsis. As Shilling (1993) comments, North Americans' body projects are often highly individualized, reflecting an individual's private search for a new self, a new identity. Some members of the neoprimitive movement claim that for people who have endured emotional pain—such as illness and sexual or physical abuse—body modification rituals help to resolve such experiences and purge the associated trauma. For some female respondents, for example, this involved coming to terms with an experience of sexual assault. Jenny puts the matter in these words:

> I can't believe it, even now when I'm sitting here talking to you [about the assault]. I was out of my body for almost two years. I can't really find any other way of explaining this to you [other] than by saying I felt numb. I tried not to think about my body because I felt dirty, ashamed, and, like, you know, I wanted to crawl out of myself. . . . Then I met the people at [the neoprimitive studio]. I went in one day with a friend of mine who was getting a tattoo to commemorate the passing of her dad, and after speaking with a couple of the receptionists and one of the artists, I started thinking about getting a tattoo. I thought a tattoo might help me reclaim my body, bring it back to my control, you know. I lost my body when I was raped; I was a stranger in my own skin. . . . I cried the whole time I was being tattooed; all of the fear, and hate, and sorrow came to the surface, and every time the needles struck me I relived the pain of the rape. I don't think any amount of talk, with whoever, could have forced me to get back in touch with my body like that. . . . I consider that day my second birthday, the day I really started moving on with my life.

For some gay male respondents, radically modifying the flesh along tribal themes served as a marker of their coming out and as a part of the declaration of their gay identity. Buddy puts it this way:

> I finally mustered up the courage to come out to my family and friends about three years ago, after almost 15 years of hiding who I am. I'd just entered into a serious relationship with a man I met in the United States, and after several months of enduring a long-distance affair, he moved to Canada with me. I love Carl and want to be with him the rest of my life. . . . My tattoo [of a Gay Pride flag/banner] symbolizes the commitment I have made to Carl and to myself. This is me; this is who I am and I want people to know that I'm not living in shadows anymore.

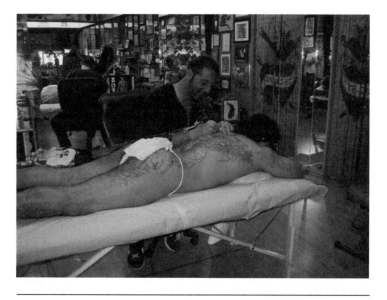

**Photo 1.3**   Tattoo by Shad at Diamond Club, San Francisco. In some traditional cultures, body modification is obligatory; the society demands that members undergo scarification, tattooing, or even the amputation of digits. In contemporary Western society, body modification is nearly always freely chosen, although usually emblematic of group membership.

SOURCE: Angus Vail. Tattoo by Shad, at Diamond Club, San Francisco.

In these ways, a vital part of the body modification process for many members of the neoprimitive movement is the ritual cleansing of a previously damaged body and self-identity.

In brief, neoprimitive flesh journeys represent personal status passages that involve the ritualistic purging of painful emotional experiences. Marking the skin becomes a text to chronicle the passage from one point in a person's life to another. A status passage can be kept private and hidden and be shared by only a few intimates, or it may be openly displayed as a means of encouraging others to explore the possibility of personal growth associated with the practices. In either situation, body modification is both an inward and outward symbol that the person has made a conscious life choice that binds himself or herself to a desire to move beyond a former identity or experience.

## Creativity and Individuality

For neoprimitive members, radically modifying the body often represents a political statement against limitations to personal expression and creativity. Feeling that they are prisoners of social conformity, members claim that many people feel limited in the potential range of personal or bodily expression available, given the mores of mainstream culture. As the sense of community is in decline in the modern urban metropolis and people are being dehumanized through technology, computers, e-mail, PINs, credit cards, and driver's licenses, neoprimitives claim they are searching for a method of injecting individuality into mainstream culture. Brian puts the matter this way:

See, all of this, this is about me and nobody else. This is like, like another way of introducing myself, another name I have. No one else will look like this, ever, because the designs I have done are custom; that's what we believe in. . . . [It's] like another signature or thumb print; it's all about me.

For this reason, the standard forms of body modification neoprimitives adopt are predominantly custom work. Tattoos, brandings, and piercings are typically designed for and sometimes by the individual, taking into consideration the idiosyncratic biography of the person, the contours and shape of his or her body, and artist-client negotiated ideas of the aesthetic appearance of the prospective work. As noted by Aaron, a 29-year-old artist,

Every person that walks through the door comes in because they're searching for something. My job is to lead them down the path of discovery. I have to

get to know them, to become friends so I can get into their heads and help them become who they want to be. So, I think an artist needs to be a shaman, a healer, and a soothsayer that guides a mystic journey. . . . The mark that remains in the skin is only the end of the process, man; it remains when the journey is over, or to mark that [the journey] has only begun. That's why I don't tattoo designs off the wall, and it's why we sit down together and draw out something for every soul who walks in here.

Normally, neoprimitives are well-acquainted with the artist performing their work, and it is not uncommon for modifications to take place after several consultations. Even though the markings are unique to the individual, the general pattern or structure of the neoprimitive style is generic enough that members of the group are able to recognize, read, and decode the symbols. This is partly achieved through a collective knowledge of primitive—that is, tribal—art and the personal relationships fostered between and among many neoprimitives.

## Physical Endurance and Pain Thresholds

One of the most obvious possibilities open to radical body modification practitioners is to allow participants to engage in group and individual pain rituals (Vale & Juno, 1989). Body modification experiences, especially the more radical forms, provide participants with contexts to learn how to understand pain as a sensory experience open to social construction and interpretation. As a marker of physical toughness and the ability to endure painful ordeals, radical body modification carries social messages about the wearer's ability to experience and relish practices for which many people exhibit and express a personal distaste. As Rosenblatt (1997) points out, North American neoprimitives share this orientation toward body pain as a cultural rite of passage with tribal cultures around the globe. In this way, rituals of the flesh can be used to challenge Western notions of the female body's ability to endure pain, separate from and independent of childbirth. And, these rituals accent the desire to experience and embrace physical pain as a means of personal growth. Neoprimitives see the experience of physical pain as a vehicle to conjure altered physical and mental states. They regard the experience as something not to be feared and avoided, but rather collectively respected as an austere illustration of personal integrity and growth. Sue, one of our interviewees, puts the matter in the following words: "We [members of Western society] revel in the discussion of emotional pain but treat the topic of physical pain like it's fucking deviant, right?" In contrast, she says, "I want everyone I talk to to understand that when you feel that steel slip through your skin, you have to embrace it and understand what you will be after it's over— changed for life."

The process of accepting and using the pain associated with body modification is another facet of the group affiliation process. Just as the tattooed image or piece of surgical stainless steel inserted under the skin can be read by audiences, so can the implicit experience of pain behind the marks. Members of the neoprimitive movement read, appreciate, and even hierarchize each others' experiences, understanding in an instant the kind and level of pain implied by particular markings. Again, these deconstructions are used as an integral part of forming a collectivity of individuals who coalesce around intersubjective understandings of the body.

Neoprimitive members seek to turn on its head the mainstream cultural understanding of pain and injury as entirely negative by participating in painful flesh journeys that are widely believed to help individuals actually expand the capability of their bodies and selves. Jay puts the matter in the following words:

> Every time I'm pierced there's a rush of adrenaline. I'm so jacked up because the feel of the cold needle is like a drug; it hurts but it's sweet. Some people get

on roller coasters and some jump out of airplanes to feel it, and that's cool, but you don't have anything more than a memory after you do it. My body is a living testimony to my desire to push the envelope. I've got 17 piercings and I've been tattooed 10 times. . . . I don't *think* I'm stronger and more confident as a person; I *know* it! You know, when I look down at myself and see what I have created, I like it.

Rather than passively accepting dominant social constructions about how bodily pain is to be avoided or hidden, neoprimitive rituals are intended to be brought to the forefront. They are discussed almost as a black eye or a lacerated face is to be displayed, as a badge of honor to some. The pain associated with a piercing or a tattoo is less an unfortunate consequence of the body modification process than one of the core reasons for participation. Mike, a neoprimitive, explains it this way:

> I have a t-shirt that simply says, "Yes, it does hurt." I don't mind if people ask if a tattoo hurts; in fact, I had to get used to it about five years ago when I first started [as a tattoo artist] 'cause it's the first [question] out of most people's mouths. My perspective is that it sets me apart from people who are afraid, and I suppose if it didn't hurt, everyone would have one, and a tattoo wouldn't mean as much.

Often shunned as repugnant self-mutilation, painful forms of radical body modification are not viewed by neoprimitives as acts that symbolically destroy the self, but rather a means of constructing physically stronger bodies and emotionally empowered social selves. Although other forms of body modification intended to empower the individual, such as plastic surgery, may also be physically painful, the outcome of that practice—the thinner thigh, the enlarged breast—tends to be the catalyst to increase esteem, not the pain process itself. In contrast, neoprimitives overturn this definition and deal with pain as a positive experience, actively seeking it out.

## Beauty and Art

Perhaps the most-cited rationale neoprimitive members provide for engaging in forms of body modification is their desire to provide alternative definitions of beauty and art. Says Peter,

> There's an elegance but [also] a raw, primal lure that invigorates every hormone racing through my body. I think [piercings are] more beautiful than anything you'll ever see in *Vogue*. It's exactly what the stale brand of beauty we revere desperately needs . . . a good shaking up.

Collectively rejecting mainstream notions of what is aesthetically pleasing as banal and uninspired, neoprimitives consider deviant forms of body expression and appearance to be appealing. Attempting to break free from what they see as repressive Western conceptualizations of beauty and art, neoprimitives stress the importance of taking personal control over the body in a culture that ultimately seeks to regulate, restrict, and prohibit the completely free pursuit of sensuality. Erin says,

> When I was a kid, I always used to draw on my jeans. All the kids did it. Remember that? I bet you did it. But my mom would tear a strip off me when I came home after school and she found pen [marks] all over me. She said it made me look like trash or something. . . . And when I got to be older and I started to wear a pound of makeup every day, and people had problems with that, calling me a tramp or a whore. . . . All my life I've wanted to color myself, design my body into art work, you know? But every time I tried people hassled me, saying it wasn't appropriate or it looked tacky. Like people have the right to make me toe the line with what *they* think is beautiful. So after I had my first tribal tattoo finished, I said to myself, "This is beautiful, this is me, and it ain't coming off no matter how much people complain." All of my life I've wanted this, to be a piece of art, and now I am.

According to Erin and her peers, the body modification of neoprimitives consciously symbolizes a form of resistance against the Puritan ethos of the body that members feel stifles human expression and individuality.

In this pursuit, neoprimitive members are adamant about how their practices of body modification challenge gender codes regarding appropriate femininities and masculinities. As the body is the main canvas upon which normative cultural expectations of gender are inscribed, neoprimitives utilize the radical modification of the flesh to undermine constraining codes of bodily idiom and conventional ways of being masculine and feminine. Women in the neoprimitive movement are the key in this social drama by adopting extravagant forms of body modification that explicitly subvert Western conceptualizations of the beautiful body. In the words of Renata,

> I'm so encouraged that more and more women are turning to body mod as a way of flexing their feminine muscles. There's a new understanding that [we] have about what a woman can be, and I hope that we [at the studio] are playing a role in educating women that "our bodies our selves" is more than a catchy feminist slogan. . . . I think women who are painted [tattooed] are beautiful because the tattoo just exudes confidence. So it's beautiful, but not in the traditional way that women were tattooed as biker molls [a person who has been roughly handled and is damaged] or circus freaks, and certainly not in any bubble-gum, Betty Boop, "I'm a helpless bitch" way.

Emphasizing tribal rituals behind neoprimitive body modification, replete with notions of femininity and female sexuality, female members are quick to underscore that cultural expressions of beauty and the female body are historically varied. For example, neoprimitives point out that women have participated equally with men in all forms of body modification around the world. In ancient Egypt, men were not allowed to be tattooed; only women engaged in the practice and used the tattoos as emblems of fertility and sexuality. In the Mayan culture, women were widespread users of tattooing, piercing, and scarification to aesthetically enhance the body. Women in Borneo tattoo designs on their body as indicators of their social lineage. Nubian women scar themselves to represent their fertility to males. And Tiv women endure painful scarification to proclaim individual qualities such as strength, courage, and fearlessness. In these ways, Pitts (1998) suggests that the contemporary renaissance in tattooing, piercing, and branding practices confront notions of docile femininity by appearing at least playfully theatrical or even provocatively grotesque when compared to traditional gender expectations.

Similarly, male neoprimitive members stress that body modification can be used as a means of exploring a variety of masculine styles and identities. Queer theory has repositioned the study of the male body by focusing on how dominant or hegemonic definitions of masculinity typically marginalize certain types of male bodies. Through the use of body modification, neoprimitives demonstrate that the male body is a cultural site, and codes of acceptable masculinity are as equally contested as codes of appropriate femininity. Thus, for neoprimitives, modifying the male body can also represent a deliberate attempt to overturn hegemonic notions of power, sexuality, and masculinity. According to Cole,

> People already think because I'm gay, I'm less of a man. They think I'm not classically macho because I've chosen a lifestyle that runs contra to what we consider to be manly. But I think I appreciate the male body and being masculine more than others because I truly love the male body in all its forms. That's why I admire male bodies that are marked [tattooed] in ways that question what we consider to be manly and point out that gay men possess qualities of strength and courage that straight men egotistically claim ownership over. . . . People need to know that gay men are strong but don't have to be overbearing and aggressive to prove it.

For neoprimitives, body modification becomes a conscious attempt to resist oppressive cultural ideology regarding what counts as beautiful and artistic.

## Spirituality

The neoprimitive quest for meaning is grounded in an attempt to collectively overcome difficulties associated with the fragmentation of life in the late modern urban setting while providing members with a set of practices that promotes personal growth. In an increasingly secular society, neoprimitive members give kudos to the rediscovery of a particular kind of spirituality. Numerous commentators argue that because of this fragmentation and secularization, many members of contemporary society find alternative forms of religious and spiritual expression appealing. In order to reclaim the spiritual purpose of our tribal ancestors, body modification is used by neoprimitives to mark the important individual and group events in their lives and symbolically tie the individual to something greater than the present-centered individual self. According to Joanna,

> We connect to each other and to the history of our planet through body marking. The spirits of our ancestors are swirling around us in the breeze, and if we ignore them we are ignoring ourselves. . . . So we do what they did, explore ourselves by exploring the past and how our ancestors fought to make something uniquely human out of life.

Neoprimitives draw on a diverse set of religious and philosophical doctrines to create a New Age spirituality that reflects contemporary concerns. Neoprimitive perspectives on the body, culture, and art are developed from a pastiche of historical influences that imply a postmodern spirituality. Neoprimitives question the criticisms that such borrowing disrespects the very cultural traditions members venerate. Says David,

> I've heard the complaint a million times, and I've run through an entire gamut of emotion about the accusations. I don't know if it's jealousy over the attention people in the community have given us, or

whether they just can't understand that we have so much respect for people all over the world. I have a degree in cultural anthropology, so I know that [tribal] designs and customs have evolved over centuries, and I defy anyone to find a culture that hasn't taken inspiration from others.... I've heard so much about raping and pillaging of cultures that neoprimitives do, but that makes me sick to think that people have such misconceptions of body art. It's particularly disconcerting and professionally deflating when it comes from other body artists.

In spite of such criticism, neoprimitives reshape iconography from other cultures in order to signify new spirituality in the West built on a respect for the past and for other cultures. As part of a collective search for identity in an increasingly mass-marketed, commodified, and fragmented world, neoprimitives articulate this respect by conducting voyages of spiritual, personal, and social discovery through their body markings.

## CONCLUSION

Like most sociological researchers on tattooing and other body modification, we have sought to situate neoprimitivism within the deviance literature. But of equal importance to us is looking at skin modification as a "body project" (Shilling, 1993) and a form of "identity work" (Pitts, 1998). In combining both approaches—viewing the body both as an evocative social text and a vehicle of social resistance—we have traced recent developments in meaning and form within the neoprimitive subculture.

As members of the larger body modification scene, neoprimitives have created a renaissance of innovative and flamboyant marking practices. Members stress the spiritual, emotional, and practical rewards of modification for persons entrenched within and ultimately oppressed by hegemonic boundaries of physical expression in the modern metropolis. Such boundaries relate especially to codes of beauty, gender, sexuality, and personal creativity. Radical and creative flesh

journeys tend to be met with disdain and distrust. Whether we reduce radical body modification practices to naïve individualism, the impetuousness and egocentrism of youth, or the passing fancies of hyper-commercialism, Western society seems clearly ambivalent about the meaning and implications of altering the surface of the skin. At the same time, body modification, including the more profane forms we've looked at, seems to be growing in appeal.

In experimenting with tribal expressions, the neoprimitives have expanded the potential uses of the body for persons interested in using the skin as a personal journey and a symbol of something larger. Body alteration practitioners develop and share understandings of their respective flesh journeys. The practices are carefully scripted joint activities replete with agreed-upon meanings and goals. Radical body modification is constructed to express an intersubjectively shared social commentary, signified by the specific styles prevalent in the scene. This commentary is grounded in the neoprimitive intent to explore the skin as a means of personal growth and as a political canvas upon which resistance to certain aspects of mainstream culture can be etched.

Neoprimitive behavior indicates that bodies are always involved in a process of becoming. Using the body as a site of identity work, neoprimitives mark significant events in their lives by developing the flesh. As the individual unfolds over the life course, the body is used to chronicle the maturing self and the varied triumphs and tragedies. In this sense, the self and the flesh that acts as its marker grow conjointly rather than being separated. The conjoining of social experience and the flesh has, of course, characterized a range of other categories, such as gang members, sailors, and prisoners. However, it may be that their flamboyant tribal use of body modification is not only more inclusive across a wider diversity of social groups, it is also at least as politically charged and subject to suspicious audience reading. Will the more widespread adoption of neoprimitive styles dilute and co-opt the movement's authenticity and more radical goals? If the neoprimitives are committed to changing cultural perceptions regarding uses of the flesh and what those uses imply about gender, sexuality, beauty, strength, and other issues, a mass turn to body modification and to a primitive style might be instrumental in realizing the group's goals.

## REFERENCES

Balsamo, A. (1996). *Technologies of the gendered body: Reading cyborg women.* Durham, NC: Duke University Press.

Ceniceros, S. (1998). Tattooing, body piercing and Russian roulette. *Journal of Nervous and Mental Disease, 186*(8), 199–204.

Davis, K. (2003). *Dubious equalities and embodied differences: Cultural studies and cosmetic surgery.* New York: Rowman & Littlefield.

Gimlin, D. L. (2004). *Body work: Beauty and self image in American culture.* Berkeley: University of California Press.

Hebdige, D. (1979). *Subculture: The meaning of style.* New York: Methuen.

Lupton, D. (1996). *Food, the body, and the self.* London: Sage.

Monaghan, L. (2001). *Bodybuilding, drugs and risk.* London: Routledge.

Pitts, V. (1998). Reclaiming the female body: Embodied identity work, resistance, and the grotesque. *Body and Society, 4*(3), 67–84.

Roberts, T., & Ryan, S. (2002, December). Tattooing and high-risk behavior in adolescents. *Pediatrics, 110*(6), 1058–1063.

Rosenblatt, D. (1997). The antisocial skin: Structure, resistance, and "modern primitive" adornment in the United States. *Cultural Anthropology, 12*(3), 287–334.

Sanders, C. (1989). *Customizing the body: The art and culture of tattooing.* Philadelphia: Temple University Press.

Segal, L. (1994). *Straight sex: The politics of pleasure.* London: Virago.

Shilling, C. (1993). *The body and social theory.* London: Sage.

Vale, V., & Juno, A. (1989). *Modern primitives: An investigation of contemporary adornment and ritual.* San Francisco: Re/search.

# Personal Account of a Tattoo Collector

## *Angus Vail*

Retail establishments, like nursing homes and hospitals, have code words that the employees use to call security's attention to potential trouble. At my father's nursing home, an announcement that "Mr. Green" was in a particular hall indicated that a resident with dementia was wandering there. At the Safeway near my apartment in Portland, it was "Johnny." I know this because I heard many a call for "Johnny" to come to my aisle as I was shopping during the summer, and every time it was followed by a security guard standing, very conspicuously, at the end of the aisle, watching me. During the school year, Johnny became unnecessary. Why the seasonal change? During the school year, I used to stop into Safeway on my way home from teaching, usually wearing jeans with a shirt and tie. During the summer, though, I walked to Safeway from my apartment, usually wearing shorts and a tank top. Shorts and tank tops don't do an especially effective job at covering close to 100 hours' worth of tattoos. Without visible tattoos, I was innocuous, no "trouble" at all; when my tattoos showed, I was dangerous—a "trouble" maker.

Like most people who go on to become fairly extensively covered in tattoos, I have found them fascinating for almost as long as I can remember— sometimes beautiful, sometimes scary, sometimes pathetic, but very rarely unworthy of attention.

Perhaps unlike many of my colleagues in the rainbow tribe, however, I have a very firm recollection of the first time tattoos made a serious impact on me. Where I grew up, in Bedford, NY, if there were any tattooed people—and there must have been—they weren't out of the proverbial closet, so my exposure to tattooing when I was young was severely limited, but I had bad allergies that required shots every two weeks or so for a period of years. My allergies brought me into New York City with my mother, where I ran into all manner of interesting people whom one was not likely to encounter in Bedford. On one allergy shot trip, my mother and I were walking down the sidewalk, hand in hand, when I noticed a biker and his "old lady" walking toward us. He was a tall and burly man, dressed in jeans and a leather vest with no shirt on underneath. What really caught my eye, though, was the dramatic effect of his set of full sleeves and the extensive work on his chest. Because he was a biker, and this was in the early 1970s, the work was all black and gray, and with the beard, the leather, and the denim, he cut an imposing figure. I tugged on my mother's arm and said, "Wow, Mom, look!" She responded, "Wow, Angus, don't" and moved me over to her other side. It was all over from that point on—I had discovered something that would elicit that kind of reaction in my parents. While I wasn't inclined toward rebellion quite yet, that thought remained with me.

I came from fairly affluent roots. Kids at my grade school didn't even really contemplate going to the public high school. Instead, the only real questions were which boarding school you would attend and whether you were going to go beginning in 9th grade or 10th. I opted for 9th and went to Brooks School in North Andover, MA. Before they accepted girls, Brooks was the place you went if you got kicked out of Andover, a top of the line prep school, but now that it was accepting girls, its star was rising. It was a small school—300 students—that provided all manner of academic advantages, like one-on-one writing courses and courses in Latin and Ancient Greek. There are

disadvantages to being in a setting like that, though, primary among which, as far as I was concerned, was that it was very difficult not to get caught when breaking rules. To make matters worse, I never really favored wearing khakis and pastel Izod shirts or Topsiders, and especially not without socks. I was more the Black-Sabbath-tour-shirt-with-torn-jeans-and-long-hair type. We were few and far enough between that we were exceptionally visible, and when we smelled like we had been smoking grass, we didn't get away with it.

I learned many a painful lesson about the power of labels in my first two years at Brooks, especially when my advisor voted to have me kicked out of school in my third disciplinary committee meeting. Fortunately for me, the head of the music department came to my defense and I was given one more chance. Soon after returning from my week-long unscheduled vacation, I met a beautiful girl and we fell in love. She didn't tolerate my chewing tobacco or smoking; she didn't want me to get kicked out of school, so she kept me from drinking and smoking grass on campus. She never quite got me away from t-shirts, but I moved more in the direction of tie-dye and away from Black Sabbath. Thanks largely to her influence, I earned a new-found respectability and was actually elected a school prefect in my senior year, which meant I had to serve on and vote in disciplinary committee meetings.

Of course, once we got off campus, the rules lifted and I went back to being young and experimental. On one train trip home for vacation, as we always did, the Brooks students took over the last car on the train and christened it "The Roach Coach." We came on with our cases of beer, bottles of booze, and other recreational substances and, of course, boom boxes and guitars. On this trip, I was introduced to two albums that would change my life in profound ways: Jorma Kaukonen's *Quah* and Hot Tuna's self-titled live acoustic album. This was guitar as I had never heard it played before—subtle, complex, rhythmically astounding, and precise. As I tend to do with most things that grab my attention this way, I collected everything I could that had Jorma playing on it, and I started looking for opportunities to see him play live.

Around this time, he was experimenting with solo electric work along with his standard acoustic repertoire, and I attended every show I could, taping a few of them for posterity. When I saw him in Boston, the crowd was a bit preppy for my taste, but his almost-shaved head, combined with the gold tooth and the tattoos covering his upper arms, made him look like a Nordic marauder, and that made things more interesting. When I saw him for the first time at the Lone Star Café in New York, however, everything changed. I don't think I'm exaggerating when I say that fully half the people in the bar for any of his sets were fairly heavily, and quite visibly, tattooed, and these were not your standard tattoos like panthers and Warner Brothers cartoon characters. These were incredibly intricate designs in what I would later realize was the Japanese style. Each image in the design merged into another, and all of them were connected with waves crashing behind them, wind sweeping through them, and fire enveloping them. This was a whole realm of artistic expression that I had never even considered possible. And, just to make it all that much more appealing, I thought it would terrify my parents.

I toyed around with the idea of getting tattooed for a couple years, but I didn't really have any way to get into the tattoo world, other than attending Jorma shows and Hot Tuna concerts. Then, in my freshman year at Denison University, my girlfriend at the time was given an assignment for her acting class; she was to do something she had never done before with someone she knew well. With a devilish look on her face, she popped in the door of the room we shared and suggested that we go get me my first tattoo. I broke out the Yellow Pages and we selected Marty Holcomb's shop in Columbus, Ohio. His advertisement had a cooler dragon than Jan's (i.e., the other tattoo shop in Columbus), so we picked up a six-pack of beer, thinking that you were supposed to get drunk to deal with the pain

of the tattooing process, and headed into Columbus. Much to our chagrin, his shop was not open on Mondays, but we resolved to go back on another day, and we stuck to our word.

When I showed up with my beer, Marty told me that he wouldn't tattoo me if I drank even one, and thus began my education. He asked why we had come to him as he was drawing up a sketch of the black rose that I wanted put on my hip. I responded that his ad was cooler than Jan's and he told me that, unlike Jan, he was not a "stencil man." Every tattoo that Marty did was freehand and unique. When he showed me the sketch I agreed, we settled on a price, and I sat down in the barber's chair. About 35 minutes later, I realized that tattoos really don't hurt that much after all and left with a grin on my face and instructions for proper healing of a new tattoo.

Over the course of the next year or so, I must have dropped my trousers at least once a week, on average, to show off my tattoo. One such time was at a Jorma show in Columbus at a nightclub called Stache's. Jorma played his two sets and then I waited for him to come out and get his equipment. When he came back out, I went up to the stage and introduced myself. I told him that I had gotten a tattoo and, before he could protest, I peeled my pants down and my boxers up to show him my black rose. He looked at it for a moment, actually paying it more attention than I thought he would, and said, "That's nice. Don't worry, you'll get more." At first I didn't believe him, but as time passed the temptation to get another one increased. Then, one vacation, I saw an advertisement for Jorma Kaukonen playing with his brother Peter at the Lone Star Café. I was not going to miss this opportunity because I loved Peter's album *Black Kangaroo* and had never had the chance to see him before. Those shows were a lot of fun because both brothers played well alone and together, and I started thinking that it would be a lot of fun to get one or both of them to play at Denison. I knew from reading an interview with Peter in *Relix* magazine that he lived in Des

Moines, so I called Information and asked for his number. The long shot paid off, and I contacted him and set up the first of three concerts of his that I would produce and promote at Denison.

Peter, it turned out, was also heavily tattooed, wearing work by some of the genuine mavericks and forerunners in the artistic explosion that began in the 1970s that fine art tattoo collectors call "the tattoo renaissance." When Peter came to Denison, we talked tattoos and he educated me about what makes a good tattoo good and what makes a bad one bad. He had one of the first portrait tattoos—Jimi Hendrix on his bicep—and a variety of other beautiful black and gray work, much of it done by the late Greg Irons. When I asked him to whom I should go, he recommended either Henry Goldfield or Bill Salmon in San Francisco. Since Greg worked for Henry with Bill, I started off with Henry, who put a Gypsy on my leg. About two years had elapsed between tattoos.

During those two years, I had met another woman and we had fallen in love with one another and the music of Joni Mitchell at the same time, and now I started thinking about getting a portrait of Joni. I checked a few references and set up an appointment with Shotsie Gorman in New Jersey. He had a policy of refusing to do "Traditional Americana" designs like panthers, which indicated his serious commitment to tattooing as an art form. It also turned out that he was a big Joni Mitchell fan, so I paid him a visit and, while listening to *Court and Spark*, I got my first portrait. This time, only a year had passed between tattoos, and I was starting to realize what people meant when they said that "tattoos are like potato chips; you can't have just one."

More designs followed and they came more frequently with each piece. They also got bigger and eventually they started getting more visible. As my commitment to artistic tattooing increased, I started to think of myself as a collector. I developed close relationships with a number of world-class tattoo artists, most of whom worked on me at one time or another, and I began to conceive of tattoos in a different light. No longer were these fun

ways to scare parents or strangers on the street; they had become bookmarks in my life. I began remembering things in relation to which work I was getting at the time, and I began planning the rest of my body. What would be the back piece and when would I get it? What would go on my ribs? Would I "finish" my sleeves, or would I stay with short sleeves ending above the elbows? My artist friends helped me work these questions out. They helped me plan and they helped me design.

I guess the height of my activity as a collector was probably in 1992 or thereabouts. This was right around the time that, at Bill Salmon's suggestion, the Swiss wunderkind, Filip Leu, tattooed a life-size portrait of Jimi Hendrix's face on the back of my right thigh. Photos of that portrait, both in its unfinished black and gray and full-color incarnations, made their way onto the pages of newly-launched tattoo magazines *Skin Art* and *Tattoo Review*.

This portrait was the first of its size and it was the first color portrait, which makes it a really very important tattoo in the tattoo world. As word about it spread, one of my artists approached me about being in a book of custom tattoos. The photos that would ultimately be in the book would also be in an art gallery exhibit called *Forever Yes*. I posed for the photos and looked forward to seeing the book, even if it was unlikely that I'd be able to make the opening. I remember thinking that this was all very exciting, but also very normal, somehow. Tattooing and my involvement in it had become a standard, taken-for-granted part of my life.

Not long after that, Filip returned to San Francisco from Lausanne and put a blue portrait of John Coltrane next to Jimi. A couple days after finishing the 'Trane portrait—it still hadn't healed completely—I drove a group of tattoo artists down to Hollywood for the first annual Inkslinger's Ball. While there, I served as a gofer for the artists working in our booth. I answered questions for the people waiting in line to get work, I went out for coffee, and I hung around and tried not to get in the way. I also entered two competitions for most realistic tattoo and best portrait, both of which I won.

Now, I found myself featured in a variety of magazines for a fair amount of time, and I also became fairly active on the convention circuit.

As my commitment to tattooing grew, my commitment to my "day job" at Tower Records slid, and I was eventually fired for closing the store five minutes early and playing unapproved music in the store. Not really wanting to do much else at this point, I approached a friend of mine who had done a considerable amount of work on me about the possibility of his apprenticing me to become a tattoo artist. We toyed around with the idea for a while and I eventually gave it a try. The apprenticeship didn't last long because it was interfering with our friendship, so I began a half-hearted search for employment, which really amounted to my hanging out at the shop, getting work done, and just passing time.

This period lasted close to a year, and somewhere along the line I had a memorable, if brief, conversation with my mother. Since I was spending all my time in tattoo shops, I broached the topic with my parents every now and then, but we had never really discussed my involvement in tattooing. Eventually, my mother asked me whether I had a tattoo. I toyed around with the idea of saying something like, "Well, it all depends on how you count," but I wasn't quite in the mood for picking a fight or freaking my parents out. The fact is that I had been trying to figure out a way to introduce them to the art form, figuring that if they saw it as legitimate art, maybe it wouldn't bother them. As all this was rolling around in my mind, I opted for a potentially dangerous answer. "I'll answer that question, and any other question you ever have about tattooing, if you understand that the answer that I will give will be complete and honest." Return of serve, successful! The ball was back in her court. She thanked me for my candor and dropped the topic. I guess, much to my chagrin, tattooing really hadn't become more acceptable, even though my right thigh was famous in the United States and Europe.

My parents were, by all accounts, relieved when, following a year of unemployment and hanging out in tattoo shops, I asked whether I might return to live with them while I learned some marketable skills. We established rules of the house and I started learning typing and basic computer literacy. While I was living with my parents, a friend of mine got married in Bedford and had the reception at her mother's house. They had a great band that played a combination of swing, blues, and rock and was immensely successful at getting everyone in attendance dancing. When they were taking one of their breaks, I approached their singer and asked, while pulling up the leg of my shorts, whether they knew any John Coltrane. He gasped and said, "No way! You're the guy who wears that tattoo? This is the last place I would have expected to see that!" We talked tattoos for a while, and I began thinking that maybe tattooing had become more acceptable.

The next year, I headed up to Storrs, Connecticut for graduate school and to study with Clint Sanders, who had written *the* book on tattooing: *Customizing the Body: The Art and Culture of Tattooing.* A couple years into graduate school, I met a woman at a friend's Halloween party. Inhibitions relaxed by a few beers, I was convinced to show a group of people my tattoo collection, and she was intrigued. One thing led to another, and we began seeing quite a bit of each other. One day at the mall, however, she would not allow me to get close to her. If I approached whatever she was browsing, she would move on to something else, and her responses to my attempts at conversation were curt and dismissive. I tried not to be put off by her antisocial behavior and occupied myself with browsing and people watching, which can often be quite amusing when you're heavily tattooed and it's hot outside. After our shopping was done, I asked her what was wrong, and she told me she was horrified that I would go out in public wearing cut-off shorts and a tank top with all my tattoos showing. I tried to talk it out with her, but she did not change her perspective; she had been humiliated by being seen with a heavily tattooed man, even if, as far as I could tell, we hadn't made much of a spectacle at all.

About a month later, we had tickets to see Deborah Voigt sing a Wagner program with the New York Philharmonic, including the famous *Liebestod* (or "love/death") from *Tristan und Isolde*. I called the day before the show to settle our plans for the following day and was hit with an unexpected "dear John" tone of voice. "You're not going to like to hear this, but I can't go and I don't think we should see each other any more. I just can't stop thinking about what our neighbors would say seeing you mowing the lawn with all your tattoos showing." It's hard to argue with that logic. Clearly, despite my best intentions and attempts at educating her, tattoos may have been fine with the lights out and in private, but they were not okay in public. I moved on with my life and continued writing my dissertation; I presented papers and wrote articles about the ways that people become elitists in art worlds by looking at tattoo collectors and artists, and I figured that next time I encountered that kind of labeling I would not allow it to hurt me.

The next time, the labeling was a little different and, while it didn't really hurt, it didn't feel especially good either. I was presenting a paper on tattoo collecting at a small conference. When it came time for questions, my first question was from a person who wanted me to take my clothes off. When I told her that people stop listening to what you have to say when you get naked, everyone laughed and we moved on. As the conference continued, though, I was asked repeatedly to show my tattoos. When I finally gave in at a post-conference party, a large semi-circle formed around me as people gasped, pointed, and offered compliments. Along with the compliments came the standard barrage of questions that make collectors shudder. "Didn't that hurt?" "What are you going to do when you get older?" "What did your mom say?" "Do you regret any of them?" And, the worst of them all, "How much did that cost?" Well-meaning curiosity reminds me from time to time that I'm really glad that I can keep my tattoos covered.

It's been a while since I've written anything new about tattooing—I've moved on to other topics for the time being—but I still encounter these issues once a year. In my deviance class, we have a segment on body modification and my students usually ask to see my tattoos. I bring in books of tattoos and tell them that they're welcome to figure out which ones are me. Sometimes they succeed, sometimes they don't, but I doubt they're likely to stop asking. In the meantime, it's nice to maintain a little mystery, and again, I thank goodness that I've kept away from tattooing public skin. As the preceding pages show, judgments and labels come from the most unexpected places and at the most unexpected times; it sure is nice to have some modicum of control over the topic.

## Discussion Questions

1. Tattoo collectors and modern primitives share some practices and differ in others. If you were explaining the world of "extreme tattooing" to someone who knows nothing about it, how would you explain the differences between two different segments of what seems like a unified world? Your answer should include a discussion of labeling the self and identity work.

2. Choose a clearly conformist social world or segment of the population. How is becoming heavily tattooed similar to it? What kinds of social activities and issues of definition of the situation and the self make these two worlds sociologically the same?

3.  Some in the tattoo world think that tattoos should "just be tattoos." How are modern primitives likely to respond to such a claim? How about tattoo collectors? Is one side more easily justified than the other? What does such a debate tell us about the processes through which we justify any realm of social activity?

4.  Sociologically speaking, what makes a good tattoo good? Your answer should include a discussion of negotiated definitions of the situation and the social construction of beauty.

5.  A modern primitive, a tattoo collector, and Edwin Lemert have decided that they are going to do a sociological analysis of your class. How would they do it? What features of your school make it similar to the world of "extreme tattooing"? What kind of definitions of legitimacy do you face in your class, and how do you negotiate those definitions? How do they affect your identities as a student, an individual, and/or a member of a family?

# PART 2

# BELIEVING THAT ONE HAS BEEN KIDNAPPED BY EXTRATERRESTRIALS

# BEING ABDUCTED BY ALIENS AS A DEVIANT BELIEF

## An Introduction

A married man claims to have two children with an alien being. "I know they're out there, and they know who I am." His wife is "confused, angry, and alienated." All of a sudden, she says, her husband "goes from being a normal guy . . . to being . . . well . . . kind of nutty, I guess. I don't believe him, but I don't disbelieve him either. . . . Would things have been different if we'd been able to have kids?" she asks herself. "Basically, I deal with it by trying not to think about it too much" (Clancy, 2005, p. 2).

The first widely publicized account of an extraterrestrial kidnapping was reported in the 1960s by Betty and Barney Hill. By the 1990s, a public opinion poll, conducted by the Roper organization, indicated that 3.7 million Americans believe that they have been abducted by space aliens (Hopkins, Jacobs, & Westrum, 1991). In the 1990s, Harvard psychiatrist John Mack (1995) lent academic respectability to such reports by arguing that he believed these claims to be true. The accounts, ranging from the look of the creatures to what they do with abductees, have by now become so standardized as to be eerily predictable.

What makes the claim of having been kidnapped by aliens a form of deviance? Mack's (1995) support of such claims produced stunned incredulity in his colleagues. Clearly, his endorsement of extraterrestrial kidnappings was deviant in the academic and psychiatric fraternity. The Harvard Medical School formed a committee, which spent over a year investigating Mack's research on abductees, eventually concluding that Mack had the right to reach his own conclusions on the matter. Still, academically respectable topics do not attract such skepticism; his colleagues wondered why a Harvard psychiatrist, a Pulitzer Prize winner, a physician at the pinnacle of his career would make such an unbelievable claim. Indeed, most people who believe they have experienced an abduction are reluctant to come forward and make what is clearly a deviant assertion. They know that it will be greeted by ridicule and stigma. And yet, in spite of the ridicule and the stigma, the skepticism and the incredulity, such claims are made and believed—and in abundance. What's behind them? What leads people to believe and make such an assertion?

At first glance, the claim of alien abductions does not seem outlandish. Most scientists—the late Carl Sagan perhaps most well-known among them—believe that extraterrestrial life exists *somewhere* in the universe. With billions of galaxies, says Sagan, each of which contains billions of stars, it is practically a certainty that at least one planet out there harbors some

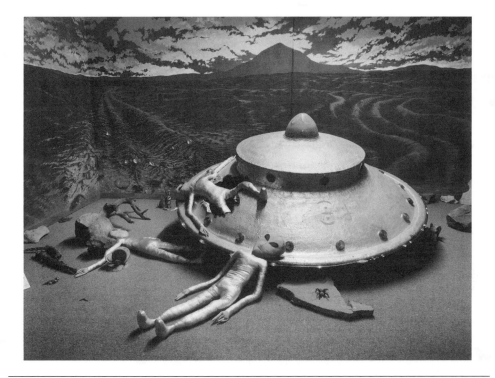

**Photo 2.1**    Roswell UFO Enigma Museum. Many Americans believe that a space ship with extraterrestrials aboard crashed in 1947 in the desert near Roswell, New Mexico. Actually, the available evidence indicates an Earthly origin for the debris, but the unofficial myth is more appealing—and more plausible—to much of the public.

SOURCE: Reprinted with permission from Douglas Curran.

form of intelligent life. Polls indicate that nearly half of the American public believes that alien space ships have visited the Earth (see Photo 2.1). Why, then, is the claim of alien abduction so strange?

Scientists are suspicious, skeptical, or dismissive of alien abduction tales because the evidence supporting such assertions is entirely anecdotal. What scientists refer to as "hard" data—physical evidence of any kind, artifacts, documents, anything that investigators can lay their hands on and analyze—is entirely lacking. In fact, according to Dr. Mack (1995), to insist on such evidence represents a bias in favor of "the physical laws set forth by Western science" (p. 17). The people he interviewed claimed that the extraterrestrials (ETs) they observed and interacted with were able to transcend the laws of nature: They passed through solid objects, used beams of light as energy sources, and performed mind-to-mind telepathic communication. Moreover, these aliens caused bodily transformations (such as scars and pregnancy and birth) that they then caused to disappear altogether (pp. 14–36). Clearly, given such assumptions, to call for physical evidence under such circumstances is futile. The fact is, claims of extraterrestrial kidnappings lie well outside the mainstream, as the reception to Dr. Mack's support of them indicates. And while scientists say they are dismissive of claims of first-hand ET contact because such assertions lack systematic, physical evidence, supporters of these claims argue that their assertions are dismissed out of hand because of social and cultural biases. Such assertions mark someone off as odd, eccentric, strange, even bizarre, a person who is likely to draw ridicule and stigma—someone whose stories are not to be trusted.

All available studies of abduction claimants indicate that these people are not mentally disordered. They are, in fact, as psychologically "normal" as you and I. And yet, they make claims that, in the absence of material evidence, are almost certainly false. How do perfectly normal people come to believe they were kidnapped by aliens? And how do they construct their stories? Why are these stories so invariant, so remarkably consistent with one another? What are the basic elements of such claims, the common themes, the justifications, the arguments? And what constitutes evidence to back up such claims? What satisfies these claimants that their stories are true? How do they come to accept as true what is almost certainly false?

In her book *Abducted*, Harvard psychologist Susan Clancy (2005) has interviewed and studied hundreds of people who believe they were abducted by extraterrestrials. They are aware of, and dismiss, explanations that attribute their beliefs to sleep paralysis, hypnosis, and suggestibility from science fiction films and television programs. They *know* their abduction beliefs are true because they *experienced* them as real. And how else, they ask, could so many others have had the same experiences? The many accounts from many and varied sources tell the same story: Intelligent creatures from another planet snatched them up, examined them, probed and poked at them, even subjected some of them to unusual sexual experiences. What's behind such experiences? How can so many people experience something that almost certainly never happened?

In this section, Christopher Bader provides an overview and history of the alien contactee/ abductee phenomenon, emphasizing the fact that it has evolved as a subculture with its own vocabulary and beliefs. Stephanie Kelley-Romano examines the contactee/abductee phenomenon from the point of mythology, emphasizing the sources of its appeal to believers. And while not a personal account, Susan Clancy's article asks the basic question every skeptic raises: "How do people come to believe they were abducted by aliens?" As she says, she takes alien abduction accounts seriously, but she does not believe them because they lack physical documentation. Clancy (2005) argues that the belief that one has been abducted results from a combination of a phenomenon called *sleep paralysis* and its accompanying "night terror" and culturally available explanations pointing to alien abduction. "At other times and other places in the world," says Clancy, "such night terrors have been interpreted as Satan, demons, witches, dragons, vampires, large dogs, and angels and erect gorgons. Today, it's extraterrestrials" (p. 49).

The belief that one has been abducted is likely to be met with derision by most Americans; it is, in other words, a form of deviance. Still, sociology demands an understanding of such a belief. Perhaps, however, nonbelievers will never find satisfying any answer to the question, "How do normal people come to believe that they were abducted by aliens?"

# REFERENCES

Clancy, S. A. (2005). *Abducted: How people come to believe they were kidnapped by aliens.* Cambridge, MA: Harvard University Press.

Hopkins, B., Jacobs, D. M., & Westrum, R. (1991). *Unusual personal experience: An analysis of the data from three national surveys.* Las Vegas, NV: Bigelow Holding Company.

Mack, J. (1995). *Abduction: Human encounters with aliens.* New York: Ballantine Books.

# Alien Attraction

## The Subculture of UFO Contactees and Abductees

### *Christopher D. Bader*

In the spring of 1983, a 50-year-old writer named Beth had her first UFO abduction experience. It was 2:25 A.M. Unable to sleep, Beth was tossing and turning in her bed when a bright light shone through a bedroom window. Beth stumbled to the front door and walked outside to see what was causing the glow. She was shocked to find a large, disc-shaped craft hovering above the front yard. After watching the motionless object for what seemed to be a couple of minutes, Beth retreated indoors, only to find her clock reading 5:30 A.M. Somehow, three hours had passed in the brief moments she had viewed the strange object. Beth fears that during this period of "missing time" she was abducted by alien beings who erased her memory of the incident.

After the experience, Beth suffered from severe anxiety attacks, had difficulty concentrating, and became extremely paranoid. Now estranged from her family, she has a short temper and experiences flashbacks of a "strange man" beckoning to her. Beth has come to believe that she is on a "special mission" but has no idea what that mission entails.[1]

John is a practicing psychiatrist in New Jersey. He began dating Betty in 1990 and the two quickly became very close. After they had been dating for some time, Betty confided in John about several encounters with what she believed to be alien beings. John was skeptical of her claims.

One evening, John dropped Betty at her house after a dinner date. He arrived at his home around midnight to find the phone ringing. Betty was on the line, hysterical, claiming that "the aliens" were at her home at that very moment. John jokingly suggested to Betty that the aliens should "come on over!" Betty simply replied, "They will."

John laughed, hung up the phone, and prepared for bed. As he entered his bedroom, he noticed a bright light shining through his bedroom window. Then the walls began to rattle. Objects fell off his shelf. A series of blinding balls of light danced around the room. Suddenly, it was morning. John was still standing in the doorway to his bedroom, clutching the doorknob. He cannot explain what happened during several hours of "missing time." After the experience, John attended meetings at a UFO encounter support group and has since

---

AUTHOR'S NOTE: Some sections adapted from Bader (1995).

become convinced that he was abducted by aliens that night.

## INVASION FROM OUTER SPACE

Accounts of strange, unidentified objects in the sky have a long history. The Biblical book of Ezekiel contains the sighting of a wheel-like object in the sky. In the late nineteenth century, people across the United States reported sightings of blimp-like airships. During World War II, pilots reported encounters with "Foo Fighters"— small globes of light that chased and circled their planes. In the Bible, strange objects were assumed to be the work of God or angels. The airships sighted in the 1800s were widely assumed to be the work of mysterious, but human, inventors. World War II pilots thought the Foo Fighters were secret weapons of the Germans or Japanese (Bader, 1995).

The first widely publicized claim of extended interaction with aliens was friendly in nature. In 1952, George Adamski collaborated with author Desmond Leslie on *Flying Saucers Have Landed*. The book told Adamski's "true" story of a series of contacts with men from Venus, Mars, and Jupiter. A short-order cook and self-proclaimed philosopher, Adamski had his first sighting of a UFO in October, 1946. He was peering through his telescope at a meteor shower when he spotted an object "similar in shape to a giant dirigible" (Leslie & Adamski, 1953, p. 172). After a series of progressively more spectacular sightings, Adamski started making trips out to the desert near his home in Valley Center, California. He believed the space ships might choose to land in less populated areas.

On November 20, 1952, Adamski and several friends were picnicking in a barren area near Desert Center, California. The group spent the day exploring and sat down to eat lunch about noon. At that time, a plane passed low over their heads, drawing the group's attention to a "gigantic cigar-shaped silvery ship without wings or appendages

of any kind" that was hovering nearby. A saucer-shaped craft emerged from the larger object and slowly settled into a cove about half a mile from the group. Adamski asked the others to stay behind, and he carefully approached the landing area. As he busied himself taking pictures of the vicinity, he noticed a man standing near the entrance of a nearby ravine. Upon approaching the man, Adamski realized that he was face-to-face with an extraterrestrial.

"Now for the first time," Adamski said,

I fully realized that I was in the presence of a man from space—A HUMAN BEING FROM ANOTHER WORLD!. . . . The beauty of his form surpassed anything I had ever seen. And the pleasantness of his face freed me of all thought of my personal self. . . . He was about five feet, six inches in height and weighed . . . about 135 pounds. . . . He was round faced with an extremely high forehead . . . and average size mouth with beautiful white teeth that shone when he smiled or spoke. As nearly as I can describe his skin, the coloring would be an even, medium-colored suntan. And it did not look to me as though he had ever had to shave, for there was no more hair on his face than on a child's. His hair was sandy in color and hung in beautiful waves to his shoulders, glistening more beautifully than any woman's I have ever seen. (Leslie & Adamski, 1953, pp. 194–195)

The being could not speak English, forcing him and Adamski to communicate through hand signals and "telepathy." The alien indicated that he was part of a friendly landing party from Venus that was visiting Earth out of concern about recent nuclear testing. The Earth, he warned, was in danger of destroying itself and surrounding planets. The being soon indicated that he had to leave and returned to his craft, which ascended out of sight.

Unfortunately for Adamski's tales, space exploration has taught us about the solar system, and so the veracity of his accounts suffered. His "eyewitness" descriptions of outer space did not match the experiences of astronauts: Venus, Mars, and Jupiter cannot support life. Moreover, photos included in his books proved easy to fake. Adamski's fortunes declined throughout the 1950s and early 1960s. He died of a heart attack in 1974.

## ABDUCTION

An equally pivotal, but significantly different, UFO tale appeared in the early 1960s. In September, 1961, Betty Hill, a New Hampshire social worker, and her husband Barney, a postal officer, were returning home from a vacation in Canada. At some point during their drive, Betty noticed a star-like object in the sky that appeared to be following the car. Barney finally stopped the car and got out to look at the object through binoculars. He was able to see a row of lighted windows behind which stood several figures wearing black uniforms and black caps. Panicking, Barney jumped back into his car.

The Hills' next memory is of finding themselves at a point further down the road. Once they reached home, they realized that their journey had taken a couple of hours longer than expected. After suffering nightmares about the experience for months, the couple sought help from Dr. Benjamin Simon, a Boston psychiatrist. Because the Hills were a mixed-race couple in the turbulent 1960s, Simon believed that Betty's nightmares stemmed from societal pressures on their relationship. He placed Betty into a hypnotic trance to probe her anxieties. Much to his surprise, Betty told him a bizarre story of alien beings taking her aboard a landed flying saucer. Once placed under hypnosis, Barney provided a similar account.

According to the Hills' story, the object they witnessed following their car had landed in the road, disgorging several creatures that escorted the Hills onboard. Barney described the creatures for Dr. Simon:

"[T]hey had rather odd-shaped heads, with a large cranium, diminishing in size as it got towards the chin," said Mr. Hill. "And the eyes continued around to the sides of the head, so it appeared that they could see several degrees beyond the lateral extent of our vision. . . . The texture of the skin . . . was grayish, almost metallic looking. . . . I didn't notice any hair . . . [and] there just seemed to be two slits that represented nostrils." (Fuller, 1966, p. 260)

Once aboard the craft, the Hills were subjected to a humiliating series of physical examinations. The creatures pulled at Barney's false teeth and seemed unable to fathom why Betty's teeth could not be removed. The beings pulled hair from Betty's head, took skin scrapings, and cut her fingernails with strange instruments. During a brief conversation with an alien who appeared to be the leader, Betty was shown a "star map" pinpointing the aliens' home planet. The abductors placed the Hills back into their car after somehow erasing their memories of the event.

Dr. Simon was skeptical of the Hills' story. He believed that the experience was a shared delusion based on Betty's fears that manifested itself under hypnosis. Nevertheless, he collaborated with the Hills and journalist John Fuller on a book about the experience, *The Interrupted Journey: Two Lost Hours Aboard a Flying Saucer*. The book was a bestseller, transforming the Hills into celebrities. The story was serialized in *Look*, a popular national magazine at the time. An NBC television movie aired in 1975. Unfortunately, Barney Hill died of a cerebral hemorrhage in 1969 and never saw the film. Betty Hill continue to speak about her experiences and published a book about UFOs in 1995; she died in 2004.

## CONTACTEES AND ABDUCTEES

The experiences of George Adamski and the Hills highlight a key distinction within the UFO subculture—contactees vs. abductees. The term *contactee* refers to people, such as Adamski, who report positive, consensual experiences with extraterrestrials. These stories typically mix sacred and space-age themes. Adamski's books used Christian symbolism extensively. Among other things, the aliens told him that Jesus was an alien "incarnated" on Earth to help humans learn to be peaceful and loving. The Biblical fallen angels are actually the universe's criminals whom the aliens had banished to Earth (Adamski, 1955). Further, contactee experiences usually involve trips on flying saucers to other planets or to mother ships hovering above the Earth. During their visitations, the aliens often impart a message of peace and concern for mankind's warlike ways.

There have been dozens of contactees since Adamski. Howard Menger, a New Jersey sign painter, claimed to have frequent encounters with the crews of flying saucers that landed near his home. *From Outer Space to You* (1959) outlines Menger's meetings with a gorgeous space woman and visits to an alien base on the moon. Contactee Gabriel Green ran for president in 1960 on the advice of his "space brothers." Frank Stranges claimed to have attended a meeting at the Pentagon with a Venusian named Val Thor (Stranges, 1991). The Aetherius Society (www.aetherius.org) was formed by a Londoner named George King, who claims to be in contact with a "cosmic master" from Venus. Now based in California, the group holds prayer sessions during which they charge "spiritual batteries" meant to cure societal ills. Unarius (www.unarius.org) is another California group founded by the late Ruth Norman and her late husband, Ernest. The group has purchased land near El Cajon, California in preparation for a mass landing by the "space brothers." Ruth, who also went by the name "Uriel," claimed to be the reincarnation of Confucius, Socrates, Henry VIII, and Benjamin

**Photo 2.2**    Betty Andreasson's Aliens. A substantial number of Americans have become obsessed with the idea of the presence of extraterrestrials on Earth, to the point where such an obsession has been incorporated into these people's everyday lives.

SOURCE: Reprinted with permission from Douglas Curran.

Franklin. Ernest claimed to be the reincarnation of Jesus. After his death, he became "Moderator of the Universe" (Curran, 1985).

The term *abductee* refers to people who claim to have had a negative, nonconsensual encounter with extraterrestrials. Following the prototype set by the Hills' experience, abductees believe they have been kidnapped by extraterrestrial beings and subjected to often humiliating medical procedures. Most abductions occur at night, while the victim is either in bed or driving down a lonely road. Unlike the Hill case, the majority of abductions involve one victim and no witnesses. Upon seeing an object in the sky or strange light outside his or her window, the abductee will then experience a period of *missing time*—a block of time during which the abductee cannot recall his or her actions. It is believed that the aliens erase the abductee's memories of the experience. Curiosity about this missing time, or sometimes strange nightmares, compel the abductee to seek help. A variety of UFO groups, abduction researchers, and independent therapists use hypnotic regression to recover the memories erased by the aliens. Under hypnosis, the abductee will recall the full details of the experience. As UFO experiences have become more common, a variety of UFO abduction and contactee support groups have appeared in the United States (Bader, 2004).

The contactee/abductee distinction is key within the UFO subculture. Someone who calls himself or herself a "contactee" is signaling an entirely different type of experience, and perspective on that experience, than someone who calls himself or herself an "abductee." Contactees enjoy their experiences and look forward to the next adventure. They feel privileged to have been selected for contact by the aliens. The contactee happily recounts his or her trips to other planets and the messages of peace received from the "space brothers." Although their stories continue to develop (as will be discussed later), abductees generally fear their experiences. They are not contacted, but *captured*. David M. Jacobs (1992), a history professor at Temple University, equates UFO abductions with rape:

> No matter how they handle the experience, all abductees have one thing in common: They are victims. Just as surely as women who are raped are victims of sexual abuse or soldiers can be victims of Post-Traumatic Stress Disorder, abductees are victims. (p. 257)

## NORDICS AND GRAYS

Over the years, UFO witnesses have reported a bewildering variety of creatures piloting the craft, from a "human-sized black figure, headless with webbed feet and wings like a bat" seen in Kent, England (Hough, 1989, p. 112) to a creature wearing a "black coat and wide-brim hat pulled down over a face that looked as if it had been covered with masking tape" witnessed in New Hampshire

(Randle, 1989, p. 140). However, abductees and contactees generally report encounters with two different types of creatures.

Contactees' description of the aliens is similar to Adamski's (1955). Called "Nordics," the aliens are human-like in appearance, of average height, and often have long, flowing hair. Contactees are typically struck by the beauty of the Nordics, as was Howard Menger (1959): "She seemed to radiate and glow," Menger explains,

> and I wondered if it were due to the unusual quality of the material she wore, which had a shimmering shiny texture not unlike, but far surpassing, the sheen of nylon. The clothing had no buttons, fasteners, or seams I could discern. She wore no makeup, which would have been unnecessary to the fragile transparency of her Camellia-like skin with pinkish undertones. (p. 26)

Abductees report encounters with creatures similar to those reported by the Hills. Dubbed "the Grays" by the subculture, the creatures are short in stature with white or gray skin; a large, egg-shaped head; enormous, cat-like black eyes; a slit for a mouth; small nostrils; and thin, sometimes clawed limbs. While the Nordics are very communicative and often speak English, the Grays rarely speak. If they do communicate, report abductees, it is typically through the use of short telepathic commands, such as, "Calm down and you will not be harmed." *The Alien Abduction Survival Guide* describes Grays thusly: "Small, thin beings with gray or ash-white skin color and large, almond-shaped eyes. Most are not much taller than three feet or so; others are notably taller and somewhat thinner. 'Greys' are the primary beings most people remember" (LaVigne, 1995, p. 108).

## IMPLANTS AND HYBRIDS

Since the mid-1970s, a New York artist and abduction researcher named Budd Hopkins has been a key figure in the UFO subculture. Through his books, such as *Missing Time* (1981) and *Intruders* (1987), Hopkins has advanced the theory that aliens are conducting a breeding experiment on Earth.

Hopkins' first revelation arose from hypnosis sessions in the 1970s with an abductee named Virginia Horton. Horton, it seemed, claimed two abduction encounters, which indicated that, for some reason, the aliens were following her life. The idea that someone might be abducted twice was entirely new at the time. Betty and Barney Hill, Travis Walton, and most other early abductees each had only one abduction experience. Abductees appeared to be people who were simply in the wrong place at the wrong time. The Horton case suggested that the "Grays" purposefully selected certain victims.

Horton's first strange memory was as a six-year-old on her grandparents' farm near Lake Superior in the summer of 1950. She had entered a barn to gather some eggs; suddenly, she found herself standing in the yard with a large cut on her leg. Then, when she was 16, Horton followed a deer into the woods. The next thing she remembered was coming out of those woods with a terrible bloody nose. Under hypnosis, she recovered memories of each incident, which involved examinations by gray-colored beings. During the second incident, the creatures inserted a "probe" into her left nostril that caused Horton's bloody nose.

Based on hypnosis sessions with people like Horton, Hopkins concluded that the majority of abductees showed evidence of having been abducted several times, including when they were small children. Furthermore, many of these cases involved the insertion of some sort of probe into a nostril or under the skin, believed to be a tracking device. The aliens use the device to locate the abductees when they are needed, for whatever mysterious reason. The UFO subculture uses the term "implant" to refer to these devices. Indeed, fear of implants is so prevalent within the subculture that some abductees have tried to locate their implants via x-rays, while others use special helmets in an attempt to disrupt the implant's signal (see www.stopabductions.com).

In *Intruders* (1987), Hopkins provides the reason behind the tracking of humans. The book centers on the experiences of Kathie Davis, who claimed upwards of a dozen abduction experiences since childhood. During Davis's experiences, the "Grays" performed repeated gynecological examinations. Under hypnosis, Davis eventually recovered memories of the aliens impregnating her and subsequently removing the fetus. In a later encounter, the beings showed her the result of this experiment: a half-human, half-Gray daughter. She described the being as having big, blue eyes; pale skin; a tiny mouth; and a head that was larger than normal (p. 223). Based on Davis's memories, Hopkins concluded that alien abductions are part of a long-term extraterrestrial breeding experiment.

The belief that one has been used to create half-alien, half-human children is common in the UFO contact subculture. In fact, the subculture uses the term "hybrid" to refer to these children. At a conference on alien abductions at M.I.T., Jacobs (1994) provided a detailed description of a hybrid:

> The offspring that abductees report look very much like a cross between alien and human. These apparent "hybrids" have hair on their heads, but it is often wispy and thin. They have a nose, but it is too small a nose for most humans. They have ears, albeit very small ones. They have a mouth and thin lips, but once again, they are small for the head. They have a pointed chin. They have very large eyes. (p. 87)

Recent years have witnessed an emerging literature about the hybrids. For example, *Raechel's Eyes: The Strange but True Case of a Human-Alien Hybrid* tells the story of a hybrid child living, and even attending college, in the U.S. while under government protection (Littrell & Bilodeaux, 2005). Meanwhile, *Star Kids: The Emerging Cosmic Generation* argues that the Earth is already home to children of advanced abilities, the result of interbreeding with the "star visitors" (Boylan, 2005).

## KINDER, GENTLER ALIENS

The UFO subculture has evolved over time. Understanding its members requires continually monitoring how their beliefs have changed. In recent years, abductees have started to question their relationship to the Grays. While most abductees still believe them to be abusers, a growing subset believe the aliens are misunderstood. Although terrifying at first, the "abduction" has turned into a positive experience. Such benign encounters are similar to the contactee tales and, indeed, some abductees now report experiences with both Nordics and Grays. As the ranks of these "new" abductees have grown, they have created the label "experiencers." Experiencers are people who have come to view as positive what was initially a frightening UFO experience. A quote from a recent therapy manual for experiencers provides a summary of this perspective:

> For most of us, the ETs who have contacted us have become interesting acquaintances and, in some cases, friends. After getting over our initial fright and upset, we have come to share a deep respect for them and the messages they have traveled so far to deliver. (Boylan & Boylan, 1994, p. 4)

## CONCLUSION

When I lecture about UFO beliefs, I am asked two questions more than any others. First, I am asked, "Are UFO abductions real?" This is soon followed by "Are these people crazy?" Both questions are based upon the same supposition: Unless these experiences really happened, there is something wrong with these people.

As a sociologist, I cannot answer (and frankly, I am not interested in) the question of whether UFO abductions and contacts are real or imaginary. If someone truly believes that he or she has been abducted by aliens and acts in accordance with that belief, does the reality of the event matter, from a sociological perspective? Rather than taking radiation readings or camping under the stars with a video camera, a sociologist with an interest in UFOs should spend his or her time trying to understand the subculture and its beliefs and examining societal reaction to those beliefs.

Through an anonymous survey of UFO abductees, I learned about the process via which people come to believe they have been abducted. Typically, an abductee has no memory of a UFO experience. He or she may be concerned about periods of missing time, strange nightmares, or bouts with depression or anxiety. Having heard of UFO abductions, either from the media or from a friend or family member, the person begins to contemplate a UFO experience as the possible explanation for his or her problems. Eventually, the abductee finds his or her way to a therapist with an interest in UFOs. The therapist uses hypnosis and encourages the recovery of UFO abduction or contact memories. Once the person believes himself or herself to be an abductee, he or she often seeks contact with like-minded people by joining a support group, browsing chat rooms, and so on. This tightens abductees' connection to the subculture and will help convince them that the vague memories they have are real. One does not have to be "crazy" to be an abductee. Rather, abductees are people with problems who, through sheer chance or through their network of friends and family, have found their way into the UFO subculture (see Photo 2.3). The key point is that once the abductee has entered the subculture, his or her beliefs become normative.

The stigma UFO abductees and contactees receive from wider society leads them to bond tightly to their subculture. Outside the realm of believers, those who report such experiences are considered frauds, deluded, or mentally ill. Abductees sometimes become estranged from their own families, as one discussed in her survey: "All family members with the exception of children feared, labeled, and ridiculed my . . . pickups. Their lack of understanding and fears of the unknown created a complete separation."

Wariness of outsiders has become a strong element in the subculture. Some believe that the U.S. government is in league with alien beings and engaged in a concerted effort to cover up abductions and ridicule UFO witnesses. Those in the UFO subculture who hold such beliefs see the dismissal of UFO contact and abduction tales as a consequence of this alien/government plan. One of the primary difficulties I encountered in researching contactees and abductees was convincing them I could be trusted. They were concerned I would either belittle their stories in the press or, worse, that I was a government agent seeking to infiltrate the group. This tendency of abductees to withdraw from the public reinforces their deviant identity.

With UFO believers, we can see that stigmatization can become a vicious cycle. When groups are stigmatized, they may retreat from the wider culture. This retreat often leads them to develop beliefs about the wider culture that reinforce that separation. As a consequence, they become further stigmatized, thus continuing the cycle.

**Photo 2.3**    Mt. Shasta Nights Dream. A substantial number of Americans believe that they have been kidnapped by extraterrestrials. Their descriptions of the experience usually include physical probing, experimentation, and often sexual assault. Most of the public finds such a belief peculiar, even deviant, but the people who hold it are not usually mentally disordered.

SOURCE: Mt. Shasta Nights Dream, by William L. McDonald © 2006.

## Note

1. Narrative from a survey the author conducted of UFO abductees. See Bader (2004).

## References

Adamski, G. (1955). *Inside the space ships.* New York: Abelard-Schuman.

Bader, C. (1995). The UFO contact movement from the 1950s to the present. *Studies in Popular Culture, 17*(2), 73–90.

Bader, C. (2004). Supernatural support groups: Who are the UFO abductees and ritual abuse survivors? *Journal for the Scientific Study of Religion, 42*(4), 669–678.

Boylan, R. J. (2005). *Star kids: The emerging cosmic generation.* Sun Lakes, AZ: Blue Star Productions.

Boylan, R. J., & Boylan, L. K. (1994). *Close extraterrestrial encounters: Positive experiences with mysterious visitors.* Tigard, OR: Wildflower Press.

Curran, D. (1985). *In advance of the landing: Folk concepts of outer space.* New York: Abbeville Press.

Fuller, J. G. (1966). *The interrupted journey: Two lost hours aboard a flying saucer.* New York: The Dial Press.

Hopkins, B. (1981). *Missing time.* New York: Richard Marek.

Hopkins, B. (1987). *Intruders: The incredible visitations at Copely Woods.* New York: Ballantine.

Hough, P. (1989). The development of UFO occupants. In J. Spencer & H. Evans (Eds.), *Phenomenon: Forty years of flying saucers.* New York: Avon Books.

Jacobs, D. M. (1992). *Secret life: Firsthand accounts of UFO abductions.* New York: Simon & Schuster.

Jacobs, D. M. (1994). Aliens and hybrids. In A. Pritchard et al. (Eds.), *Alien discussions: Proceedings of the abduction study conference* (pp. 86–89). Cambridge, MA: North Cambridge Press.

LaVigne, M. (1995). *The alien abduction survival guide.* Newberg, OR: Wildflower Press.

Leslie, D., & Adamski, G. (1953). *Flying saucers have landed.* New York: British Book Centre.

Littrell, H., & Bilodeaux, J. (2005). *Raechel's eyes: The strange but true case of a human-alien hybrid.* Columbus, NC: Granite.

Menger, H. (1959). *From outer space to you.* Clarksburg, WV: Saucerian Books.

Randle, K. (1989). *The UFO casebook.* New York: Warner Books.

Stranges, F. (1991). *Stranger at the Pentagon.* New Brunswick, NJ: Inner Light.

# Alien Abductions as Mythmaking

## *Stephanie Kelley-Romano*

It was spring of 1976. I was six or seven months pregnant and had been in bed asleep at night. I heard a hoarse whisper say, "Wake up." I opened my eyes just a crack but the bright light was painful so I closed them again. I tilted my head down before I opened my eyes again. When I did, I saw that I was naked and there was enough light to tell that I was standing outdoors. I raised my head and saw three figures in the bright light. In that instant I remembered having seen them before. I was afraid their abducting me might have an adverse effect on the baby and yelled at them about a doctor's appointment I had the next day, hoping they would fear discovery and let me go.

This story describes the initial stages of an alien abduction. It was told to me by "Emma" (all names here are pseudonyms), a self-professed abductee and, like most of the others I received narratives from, a fully functioning member of society. Although I remain skeptical of the empirical reality of alien abductions, invalidating the claims of these narrators is beyond the scope of my inquiry. Still, after reading Emma's stories and

hundreds like hers, I conclude that these people sincerely *believe* they have been kidnapped by extraterrestrial beings.

According to a poll conducted in the 1990s by Hopkins, Jacobs, and Westrum, 3.7 million Americans claim to have been abducted by aliens. A similar poll, conducted by the Roper organization, puts this figure at three million. More staggeringly, Scott Mandelker (1995) claims there may be as many as 100 million "sleeping" aliens among us, individuals who experience feelings of estrangement because they are "from elsewhere."

The abduction myth was first widely publicized in 1961 by Betty and Barney Hill, a middle-aged couple from New Hampshire. A close look at this phenomenon can inform our understanding of symbolic processes—exploring what it means to believe and how we come to know what we know. And unlike established, codified religious beliefs, the abduction myth is still in the process of developing. Over nearly half a century, believers have produced a body of narratives that continues to increase in complexity of form and function.

Believers and skeptics alike continue to attribute meaning to the abduction phenomenon and to struggle for legitimacy among the general public.

Abduction discourse—assertions about abductions—is a living myth, a body of stories making up a system of beliefs. This discourse is composed of four main story types that function in a progressively transcendent or spiritual fashion. Over time, the mythic system that makes up abduction beliefs builds a functionally more complete reality for adherents. To understand how the abduction myth functions for believers, I will define myth and explain how the formal elements of myth interact with its functions. Next, I'll explain the primary function each abduction narrative type serves and how these four narrative types differ. Finally, I will offer some conclusions about what this myth says to us.

## MYTHMAKING IN THE MODERN WORLD

Most of us today equate myth with falsehood. This belief fails to capture the importance and relevance of myth. In fact, myths are essential for productive, worthwhile living. Since ancient times, humans have told stories to explain the how and why of life. Myths are the glue of society that binds us to one another and to our traditions. They help us find significance in our lives. Far from being mere falsehoods, myths are essential truths that anchor members to their societies and the constituent members of the society to one another.

### Formal Characteristics of Myth

Mythic stories, like all narratives, have certain formal characteristics. Five basic building blocks construct a myth: narrative form, heroic characters, a special time, a special place, and archetypical language (Rowland, 1990). When these elements are combined, they create something larger than the sum of their parts; they create a myth.

Narrative form, the first of myth's formal characteristics, is simply the story-like quality of myths; that is, they have a beginning, a middle, and an end. As narratives, they provide a means of ordering events in a particular story-like sequence. Second, in myth, the characters are heroic. Typically, heroes undertake a journey into the realm of the supernatural, struggle with a source of power, and return to the world, victorious and changed. The heroic journey must be undertaken because of some fundamental deficiency in the individual or in the larger society; the hero's journey often represents an attempt to save the society, which is on the verge of ruin. In addition, the hero offers a role model to be emulated. The third and fourth components of myth address the setting of the story. The action takes place in a special time and a special place. Since the agents are heroic, they necessarily do battle in a consecrated, or otherwise sacred, place. Myths happen in a place and time of significance, which imparts "force and credibility" to the narrative (Rowland, 1990, p. 104). And finally, the narrator of myth uses archetypical language, a transcendent vocabulary that engages the emotions as well as the mind.

### Functional Aspects of Myth

Narratives assume a variety of forms, and many of them partake of the mythic qualities I just discussed: folk tales have heroes, fairy tales take place during a special time, and legends take place in a special place. How are myths different? They differ in two ways.

First, myths are accepted as true in ways that other cultural narratives are not. Myths represent a lived reality. Although empirically false in a number of respects, myths have the appearance of truth because they have widespread social acceptance; they are, above all, *believable*. And because myths are believed to be true, they are life-changing.

Second, myths are all-encompassing and sacred. They provide sacred beginnings, advice about the present, and hope and direction for the future. Mythic ideologies, when accepted, provide a way of living. The most obvious example of an encompassing, fully articulated, sacred myth is religion. Religious narratives, with their heroes, holy spaces, sacred times, and symbolic language, are myths in their most complete form. They function to provide believers with directions on how to live and justifications for their existence.

Myths offer three basic functions: pedagogical/psychological, sociological, and cosmological.

At their most basic, myths function pedagogically at the psychological level. They teach us skills essential for individual development and survival; how to act, accept, and change aspects of life; how to behave; how to evaluate behavior. They are stories that we use to see how we stack up against other people. They provide options for action by explaining what happens to characters who make certain choices. They also play an integral role in developing the self-concept by guiding listeners from their drab, routine, ordinary, everyday existence to a more spiritual, more transcendent place. Through myths, individuals contemplate their own image and possibilities for the future.

Myths also function sociologically. They allow people to identify with one another, to hive together to form societies. Myths are the sacred history that is passed down from one generation to the next. They establish what is acceptable and how people should act under certain circumstances. Myth promotes values and perceptions that are central to the community.

And last, myths function cosmologically. They explain the individual's place not only within humanity but within the universe as a whole. Myths situate the individual within the universe. The need for individuals to make sense of their place in the world has always been a main component of theological and mythological narratives and theologies. People need to have faith that there is meaning to life. Cosmologically, myth functions to give meaning to the seeming randomness and

absurdity of life. Ultimately, myth functions at the cosmological level as religion. Myths are essentially religious narratives.

We can see these three functions of myth as steps on the ladder to transcendence or spiritual communion. So, myths work to first provide the individual with a sense of self and then an understanding of cultural norms before finally making sense of the cosmological order.

## ALIEN ABDUCTION EXPERIENCES AS MYTH

This essay is based on the narrative testimony of 130 alien abduction experiencers (AAEs). An "abductee" is someone who is taken against his or her will, while an "experiencer" is a broader label and includes individuals who have had contact with, but may or may not have been taken by extraterrestrials. The four emergent narrative types are based on the motives of the aliens and illustrate the evolutionary nature of myth: physical salvation, hybridization, betterment of humanity, and cosmic community. Each story type builds on the next in the larger quest for transcendence.

### Physical Salvation: The Hero's Quest

Physical salvation narratives tell one of the most widely known stories of contact: Aliens are here to save us. This narrative type is an articulation of the hero's quest. Within narratives of physical salvation, and indeed most abduction experiences, individuals are taken against their will—literally carried away. Paul explains how he was captured:

> They [the ETs] were talking about me. The first one said that I had been able to overcome part of the sedative's effect and was now fully awake. He asked the second person if they should abort the operation since it appeared to be compromised. A large face appeared within the outer glow of the light beam.

I think I probably would have lost control of my bladder, had I not already been under the influence of some sedative.

Interestingly, Paul is special in that he is able to overcome part of the alien attempts to control him. Other experiencers, rather than fighting control, explain their complicity in the experience. For example, Mary claims, "I have personally agreed to this interaction. I volunteered to live this lifetime with a portion of my time spent with this civilization." She goes even further to correct my survey instrument, crossing out the word "abduction" and replacing it with "visits." She explains, "I hate the word abduction; it is not indicative of what is happening." Permission, ironically, is an important theme within this category of abduction. This renaming positions the "contactee" or "experiencer" as an agent who defines himself or herself. The discursive struggle that surrounds this fundamental label—abductee vs. experiencer—is one arena in which we can see competing mythic perspectives vying for dominance. Each claims the other has been "duped" by the aliens into thinking incorrectly about his or her abduction experiences. So, according to experiencers, abductees are presently incapable of recognizing the true benevolent aims of the extraterrestrials. Likewise, according to the abductees, extraterrestrials are fooling the experiencers into thinking their abduction is for the greater good of humanity.

The world the hero enters typically is intimate, yet strangely familiar. One way this intimacy is conveyed is through the presence of a "doctor" or "head alien" who is sympathetic to the plight of the abductee. The "head alien" often described by abductees is usually taller and often lighter in color than the typical gray alien. Interestingly, this head alien is usually of the opposite sex to the abductee. Josh regularly interacts with a "tall white" female alien and claims that he was selected for abduction because genetic engineering "has resulted in the ability for the whites to communicate with me and those like me much better." Like the traditional mythic hero, Josh possesses exceptional gifts that allow him to assume the heroic role.

The abduction itself, most often the physical examination, is the supreme ordeal the abductee must endure. As a result of this, however, a reward is gained and is brought back into the world. The boon brought back by the abductee most often comes in the form of a message for humanity. Abductees are given very specific tasks to perform upon their return or are told the role they will play during the upcoming merging of alien and human worlds. For example, Mary was told she would serve as a liaison between humans and aliens during a period of evacuation. She writes,

> I was standing on top of a hill, below me were many people, walking, carrying children and small parcels of personal belongings. They were all walking toward me. When I turned around there was a LARGE ship behind me and I knew the forms inside. We were waiting for these people to arrive.

Many participants are thrust into the role of mythic hero, in that they are taken aboard the ship, given knowledge or abilities, and returned ready to perform a special mission. They are further distinguished because they are the ones with whom the extraterrestrial "doctors" have chosen to develop a relationship. The focus of these narratives on the individual, as well as the specific reasons given for abduction, underscore that the individual is the focus of these stories.

Narratives of physical salvation function on the psychological level for those who believe. The missions these individuals are given lend significance to the life of the experiencer. They are chosen because they either are inherently/genetically better than others who have not been chosen or because they are advanced or intelligent enough to know to volunteer. The act of volunteering functions to give an appearance of personal empowerment. This empowerment, however, only goes so far; the extraterrestrials still exert total control during the abduction. Because of the importance placed on selection and the imparting of a mission, physical salvation narrators believe they are important within the larger population of people and are also special when compared with the smaller population of abductees. It is they, and not their extraterrestrial captors, who are the means to salvation.

## Hybridization: Narratives of Powerlessness

The second major narrative category is hybridization. In these narratives, extraterrestrials are using humans as host bodies to fortify their own species. Generally, these narratives express a fear of an overreliance on technology and a fear that they, as individuals, have no power over the medical advances of contemporary culture. Read at the most literal level, these stories express a fear of the technologization of procreation. Considering the prominence of reproductive issues such as abortion, in vitro fertilization, and stem-cell research, it is no wonder this living myth provides a space in which these issues can be played out and articulated.

In the hybridization narratives, as in narratives of physical salvation, humans are being physically kidnapped by extraterrestrials. Like narratives of physical salvation, these narratives place the abductee in the role of hero—albeit a different type of hero. As evidenced by the sexual and reproductive examinations, it is still the individual who is the focus of the abduction. The mere fact she or he is chosen points to her or his superiority. Despite the implicit superiority, the focus of this narrative category explicitly articulates a rhetoric of powerlessness, in that the focus of the stories told by abductees is their victimization at the hands of the extraterrestrials. These narratives work in opposition to the narratives of physical salvation, in that they express a lack of control and choice. These two story types provide alternative explanations of the motives of the aliens as well as different roles for the abductee/experiencer to occupy. They function similarly, however, in that they keep the focus squarely on the individual.

In these stories, aliens are visiting Earth with their own interests in mind. Christine states that the ETs are "cloning us and making their own breed of human/alien beings." Although extinction still seems to be central to the story, it is now the extinction of the extraterrestrials that becomes the motivating force. These malicious extraterrestrials have no desire to help humans. Kathleen writes, "I sense that they are here on their own agenda, and really don't give a SHIT about us."

A rhetoric of powerlessness is articulated through the theme of control, which is the most dominant theme within narratives of hybridization. Many experiencers explicitly acknowledge their lack of control. For example, Amy writes,

> You can be taken against your will, no one knows about it, you are treated like a lab rat, the entities involved don't care about you at all and you can be taken away at any time. And just about the time you think they won't do it anymore, it happens again. You feel totally helpless and used and don't even know why.

Interestingly, the theme of control is highlighted through the inclusion of outright defiance on the part of the abductee. Struggle on the part of the abductee is almost exclusively reported by hybridization participants. Although in most abductions individuals are paralyzed, cannot move, and oftentimes simply observe what happens, this is not the case for some of the narrators of hybridization stories. Mara describes,

> I woke up lying on my back on a table. It was cold. I tried to sit up but several hands gently tried to push me back down. I heard voices saying, "It's OK, just one more test, we have only one more test." I push them off and sit up, throwing my legs over the side of the table. I yell, "Get the hell off me! Fuck your tests, I want a human doctor!"

In addition to articulating an explicit lack of control, these narratives are also replete with examples in which information is withheld, arguably a more subtle narrative element evoking control. One particularly gripping account was submitted by Emma:

> Once I had come to rest on the table, I became aware of the tall yellow being; it was standing to my right, I could make out its thin torso. I said to it, "Please don't hurt the baby"; then I hear a high pitched voice say, "We won't hurt your baby." I saw a baby right on my chest, wearing a blue outfit, but I couldn't feel it there. As I turned my eyes forward again, I saw a yellow arm holding a tube that looked like it was holding a translucent emerald green liquid or gel. I became afraid as I tried to sit up and reach for it. I said, "What are you doing?" and became aware that I couldn't move anything but my eyes. I heard the high voice say, "You can't know that."

Clearly, in a culture in which knowledge is associated with power, the withholding of information by extraterrestrials is yet another way abductees are able to articulate feelings of powerlessness, particularly when it comes to reproductive technology and procedures.

Despite being thematically opposite—aliens are here to use us, not help us—narratives of hybridization are the rhetorical counterpart to narratives of physical salvation. Both articulate very similar stories and place the experiencer/abductee in the role of hero. Both are very much grounded in the physical description of the experience, as opposed to an exploration of the significance of the experience. These narrative categories both function on the psychological level. The blatant objectification of the human body as host and redefinition of person as resource is a plausible expression of how the individual feels. Articulations of physical control work to make this a disempowering rhetoric of victimization. Like other rhetorics of powerlessness, hybridization narrators fail to identify themselves as agents within these stories. The incorporation of a minimal amount of defiance functions to both allow the abductee to feel as if she or he has tried to exert herself or himself but is simply not able to overcome the aliens'

overwhelming force and to simultaneously reaffirm the absolute power of the extraterrestrials.

## Betterment of Humanity: Alien Self-Help

The third emergent narrative category type is betterment of humanity. In these narratives, the aliens act as a positive force in the lives of humans. Narratives of betterment of humanity work to convey social values through individual growth. The aliens described in these stories are concerned with the spiritual and mental evolution of humanity. Helen writes, "I believe that humans are being abducted/visited by aliens so they can teach us to use our hidden talents and to help ourselves in the future." The focus of the extraterrestrials, in this narrative category, has expanded to include all of humanity and has transitioned from the mere physical evacuation focus of earlier narratives to a more holistic focus and improvement of our species. Similarly, the form of these stories has transitioned from a detail-rich descriptive narrative to an explanation of why extraterrestrials are here.

Formally, narratives of betterment of humanity are less likely to be detail-rich. Because they are focused on justifying and explaining, there is often very little narrative description. In fact, the certainty of the level of reality on which these experiences take place is often called into question. Irving reports, "I believe I have experienced encounters with ETs on several occasions; however, it is difficult for me to know if these encounters have all been 'physical' face-to-face meetings, or 'out of body' experiences, or 'programmed' events." These narratives often include qualifying statements. For example, one experiencer writes they are here "to assist in our evolution, somehow." Others begin their explanations with phrases such as "Maybe all this. . . ." and "It is possible. . . ." and "I'm really not sure, but. . . ." Rhetorically, this is significant because the focus shifts from proving the reality of the experience to explaining the significance of contact.

A second significant formal change within betterment of humanity narratives is that the central agent of the narrative changes from the individual to the extraterrestrial. The aliens are here to impart wisdom and are benevolent, omnipotent beings. These narratives seem to serve as a bridge—both functionally and thematically—from the narratives of physical salvation to those of cosmic community. They begin to "float" possible explanations and motivations for abduction within the larger body of the abduction myth.

One of the most interesting developments within this narrative category is the inclusion of more species of beings. Betterment of humanity narrators include more diversity among races and are much more detailed in the characteristics and types of interactions between alien races. As in earlier narrative types, the dominant alien is the typical Gray alien. Ashley reports that these aliens are "tall and thin with large heads, and they had deep, large, oval black eyes." In addition to the Grays, betterment of humanity participants also report Nordic aliens. These aliens are very humanoid looking. They are commonly characterized as morally and intellectually superior, and more attractive, than the Grays. When describing a Nordic she saw, Nora writes, "He looked human. He had light blonde or white hair and blue eyes." The final alien species described in these narratives is the Reptilian. Reptilian aliens are emotionless, manipulative, and usually not acting in the best interests of humans. MaryAnne describes one Reptilian who had a "very powerful presence." She writes, "This being, now it is very hard to describe his face—almost reptilian? Faceted eyes, very deep and intense as he looked at me."

The relationships among these races are highlighted in betterment of humanity narratives. Gray aliens continue to be associated with menial tasks undertaken during typical abduction events. Their living spaces, as well as their bodies, are gray and featureless. They function to express the fear of what humans may become if they rely too much

on technology and continue to undervalue their emotional/creative natures. In their grayness— the blending of black and white—they also may articulate a fear of the loss of racial purity.

Nordic aliens, on the other hand, are idealized versions of humans. They are often associated with spiritual growth and love and act as protectors for the experiencer. The fact that white extraterrestrials are those that are most revered by (the overwhelmingly white) abductees further underscores the racial quality of the Myth of Communion. Nora's earlier use of "human" as interchangeable with "white" further speaks to the fact that this narrative assumes whiteness. To use the various species of aliens as a means of articulating racially based fears is consistent with the sociological function of this narrative category.

Finally, the sinister Reptilian aliens personify the fears abductees may have concerning the ability of outside influences to control their lives. The different characteristics of these species speak, in a very transparent way, a discourse on race and the unknown "other." It is the Caucasian aliens abductees/experiencers should emulate. They are the beings who, bathed in beauty and white light, possess the knowledge and compassion necessary to help the abductee/experiencer evolve mentally and spiritually. The less attractive Gray alien, on the other hand, because of its overreliance on technology and its inability to appreciate the more esoteric aspects of life, has been reduced to a physically weaker, bland being capable only of being directed. The racial markers of the beings, as well as the complexity of the interactions and relationships described in these narratives, indicate the polysemic (containing multiple meanings) nature of the Myth of Communion.

Betterment of humanity narratives play out racial tensions narrators may be reluctant to voice. Furthermore, they use extraterrestrials as the "unknown other" to serve key mythic functions. Although abductees explicitly articulate a narrative of caring and extraterrestrially motivated self-help, the implicit racial discourse is one of exclusion and hierarchy. Simultaneously, then, narrators are able to feel virtuous about their inclusiveness while continuing to discriminate against certain beings based on race. White/Nordic aliens continue to be morally and physically superior. They are the ones who are in charge of the Galactic Federation that ensures nasty Reptilian and Gray aliens stay in line.

## Cosmic Community: Sacred Community

The final narrative category is cosmic community. These narratives, certainly less common than any of the other narrative types, articulate the abduction myth in its most transcendent form. In these narratives, abductees begin to explain the sacred beginnings of the Myth of Communion. The Myth of Communion prescribes a set of virtues, which include humility, tolerance, and peace. In these stories, the tone is awe-filled and sacred. These narratives revolve around the common theme that extraterrestrials are visiting Earth to help integrate humanity into the larger cosmic community. To be allowed into the galactic community, the individual must have achieved some level of spiritual development and harmony. Marty writes, "It seems we truly are being nurtured toward full membership into the intergalactic, interdimensional community—those of us who are willing to make the sacrifices and advances."

Formally, these narratives continue the trend begun by betterment of humanity narratives in that they contain even less description of abduction events and more contemplation of the significance of events. For example, although "return" is a common abduction episode, in which abductees/experiencers describe their return to the location from which they were taken, only one cosmic community narrator includes it in her story. One way narrators are able to simultaneously claim to have been abducted yet not get bogged down in the

details is to make claims of "missing time." Abductees recall a bright light in their bedroom, perhaps become aware of a presence, and then wake with strange bruises on their legs. People who experience missing time do not have to describe awkward physical examinations or seemingly unbelievable reproductive or sexual encounters with extraterrestrials. Instead, they can make ambiguous claims of an anomalous experience, and then, by incorporating a few indicators of abduction, they can focus on the meaning and significance of the experience.

The dominant themes of these narratives are unity and transcendence. Narratives of cosmic community recognize the oneness of life—specifically, narrators report we are the aliens and the aliens are us. Jeff explains it all when he writes, "I am one of them—the human ETs—and they are in fact us, with a large-scale mission of guiding humanity into a new phase of cosmic awareness." Themes of unity and oneness are further reflected in the number of abductees who believe themselves to be part extraterrestrial; 25 out of my 130 interviewees believed this. This "hybrid link" works to further connect aliens and humans and to blur any boundaries that competing narratives of abduction may try to establish.

Thematically, these stories account for the earlier versions and explanations offered by narrators of physical salvation, hybridization, and betterment of humanity stories. As the myth incorporates more benevolent aims and aliens, it still must account for earlier stories of malevolent aliens. One way these narrators do this is to simply dismiss individuals who believe in narratives of hybridization. According to cosmic community narrators, they exist on a "higher vibration" and can see the true intent of the extraterrestrials. Yvette offers some retroactive definition as she describes different beings:

The malevolent Gray is a lower life form than the benevolent Gray. It looks a lot like the benevolent

Gray but the head is bigger, and they are not as refined physically or mentally. They came to the Earth in the 50s through 70s, but then they were barred.

Through this explanation, Yvette is able to account for all the stories of little gray aliens while at the same time advancing her more transcendent interpretation of the Gray aliens. This illustrates the changing nature of the Myth of Communion, in that abductees are able to redefine abduction elements and events to fit with contemporary values and culture.

An even more basic example of how the Myth of Communion adapts to stay alive and vital can be seen in the methods of sample collection. Whereas initially Gray aliens scraped fingernails, took vials of blood, and swabbed the inside of abductees' mouths, in the Myth of Communion, aliens simply snip a lock of the abductees' hair and are able to generate an entire genetic profile. If this myth is to continue to live and function in a vital way for abductees, it is necessary that the aliens reflect our increasing knowledge of technology and science.

Cosmic community narratives function at the level of the transcendent. The aliens could take the place of a traditional "God," and the experiencer fills the role of prophet and apostle. Although they advance the belief that there is a cosmic order that is morally good, these stories still revolve around individuals who are basically powerless over the extraterrestrials. Mythically, these stories work to explain sacred beginnings and instill social values. They also function to take alien abduction discourse to the next level—the cosmological level of myth—on which metaphysical questions of "why?" can be addressed.

## Conclusion

The Myth of Communion was born of a need to answer the same recurring human problems in a new way. This myth speaks directly to the human need for transcendence and significance. In a society where technology is a God term, the Myth of Communion emphasizes spiritual growth and emotionality. In a culture that has allegedly fixed the racial wrongs of the past, the Myth of Communion articulates fears through a thinly veiled white supremacist extraterrestrial hierarchy. The Myth of Communion shows us who we are, what we fear, and who we hope to become.

Aliens have infiltrated American culture and are here to stay. Regardless of the reality of what is happening to individuals who believe they have been abducted, mythic analysis of these stories is important and useful. Exploring the ways these extraterrestrial others are described reveals as much about us as it does about any potential visitors from space. The rise of this myth is also a disturbing indication of how quickly people may accept a new reality—even one that has such little evidentiary support.

The social space occupied by those who believe in UFO abductions has continued to move toward the center of mainstream culture. As it does, other realities are displaced or revised to assimilate the newer beliefs. Examination of the communicative practices involved in such a shift exposes the changing needs of the believer society as well as the linguistic strategies employed to gain legitimacy. This analysis only highlights some of the significant components of alien abduction discourse.

## References

Mandelker, S. (1995). *From elsewhere: The subculture of those who claim to be of non-earthly origins.* New York: Birch Lane Press.

Rowland, R. C. (1990). On mythic criticism. *Communication Studies, 41*, 101–160.

# How Do People Come to Believe They Were Abducted by Aliens?

## *Susan A. Clancy*

I once had this terrible nightmare—at least I think it was a nightmare. Something was on top of me. It wasn't human. It was pushing into me. I couldn't move; I couldn't scream; I was being suffocated. It was the worst dream I've ever had. When I told my therapist about it, she basically asked me if anything had happened to me as a kid. She was getting at sexual stuff, like if I had been abused. It took me off guard because I'd never thought about that before. Anyway, she said that sometimes memories that are really traumatic get pushed down by the psyche—it's like a protective mechanism—and that they can kind of "pop up" in dreams. I didn't . . . don't think I was ever abused—actually, sex is an area of my life that I pretty much feel in control of—but she made me think. Had something happened to me? Maybe something did happen. I wondered a lot because it seemed like my life wasn't going the way it should. Relationships were really hard for me. . . . Getting through graduate school seemed tougher for me than for other people. . . . I have a lot of trouble sleeping. It's so weird because I was such a happy kid. It was around the time I hit puberty that everything changed. For some reason, I started to have images of aliens popping into my head. Did you see that movie *Signs*—the one with Mel Gibson? The aliens looked more like those, not like the more typical ones. I'd be walking to school and then POP—an alien would be in my head. Sometimes I'd hit my fist against a wall because then the pain would help me think of something else. I really thought I was going crazy. After a while, I told a friend—Rob. I think you spoke with him; he's a graduate student at the Divinity School. He gave me a book to read. The book was called *Abduction* or *Abductions* and it was written by a famous psychiatrist at Harvard. It had lots of stories about people who'd been abducted. I read the book in one sitting. I couldn't put it down—it all clicked with me. I knew what the people were going to say even before they said it. I completely got what they felt—the feelings of terror and helplessness. I couldn't stop thinking about the book. Once I started thinking maybe I'd been abducted, I couldn't stop. Finally, I told my therapist about what was going on, and she said she couldn't help me with this, but she referred me to a psychologist in Somerville, someone who worked with people who believe in things like this. The first time I went to see him, he asked me why I was there. I opened my mouth to talk, but I started crying and couldn't stop. The tears were just pouring out of me. I'm not the kind of person who cries easily—I don't think I'm an emotional person. It was then I understood that there was something going on, that something had happened to me and I didn't know what it was. He said that I shouldn't be afraid, that this was very common, that it was the first stage of coming to realize what happened to me, that in some people the memories get only partially erased, and that those people can access them if they're willing to do the work, to undergo hypnosis and allow themselves to find out.

When I was first recruiting subjects for my study of alien abductees, I assumed that people wouldn't answer my ad unless they had actual memories of being abducted. I mean, the ad read, "Have you been abducted by aliens?" Why would you answer it if you didn't have any such memories? On what other basis would you think you'd been abducted? But as it turned out, most people who answered the ad merely *believed* they'd been abducted; in fact, they had no detailed personal memories of their abduction experience.

An initial phone screening would reveal that, yes, they thought they'd been abducted by aliens, so we would set up an interview at my office. The first question I'd ask would be, "How old were you when you had your first memory of being abducted by aliens?" "Oh, I don't have memories," they'd say. I was amazed. "You don't have any memories of the experience? Why not?"

Because, I was told, their memories had been rendered inaccessible. Some said the reason was that the aliens "erased my memories" or "the beings programmed the experience to be forgotten." A few believed (like some victims of childhood sexual abuse) that what had happened to them was simply too traumatic to be consciously available: The experience was "too awful for my mind to handle it, so I repressed it." Whatever the mechanism endorsed, the consequence was the same: There were no personal memories of the abduction.

But if they didn't have any memories of being abducted by aliens, then why did they believe they'd been abducted in the first place?

Everybody I spoke with had one thing in common: They'd begun to wonder if they'd been abducted only after they experienced things they felt were anomalous—weird, abnormal, unusual things. The experiences varied from person to person. They ranged from specific events ("I wondered why my pajamas were on the floor when I woke up") to symptoms ("I've been having so many nosebleeds—I never have nosebleeds") to marks on the body ("I wondered where I got the coin-shaped bruises on my back") to more or less fixed personality traits ("I feel different from other people, a loner—like I'm always on the outside looking in"). Sometimes they included all of the above. Though widely varied, the experiences resulted in the same general question: "What could be the cause?" In short, it appears that coming to believe you've been abducted by aliens is part of an attribution process. Alien abduction beliefs reflect attempts to explain odd, unusual, and perplexing experiences.

This search for causes was well-described by Terry, a 37-year-old elementary school teacher:

I went to dinner with some friends. We finished late and I was tired. But instead of just driving home, I felt compelled to drive south out of the city. I drove for like an hour, down Route 3, and then I turned around and came home. The next morning when I woke up, I turned on the news and found out that an unidentified flying object had been spotted south of the city, in the general vicinity of where I'd been driving.

Jon, a 39-year-old teacher, told this story:

I'd lived in the city my whole life, but moved to a very rural area in New York State for a new job. . . . I started to be afraid of being alone, especially at night. I'd been used to peace and quiet—but not anymore. I got, like, really scared to be by myself. I wondered why.

Here's Martha, a 27-year-old preschool teacher:

About a month ago, I started noticing this bruise on my thighs. I don't know what could be causing it. Every time I think it's going away, it gets dark again. It's really weird, not like a big deal or anything, but I want to know what it is.

And these are the words of a 63-year-old retiree named Renee:

Let me tell you—you're a shrink—I've been in therapy basically my whole life and nothing is helping me. I've tried psychoanalysis, medication, meditation, and I still feel depressed. I've been depressed since as long as I can remember. Something is seriously wrong with me, and I want to know what it is. I want to live a normal life.

For many abductees, the "I wonder why" stage begins after a frightening sleep experience. They wake up suddenly, terrified and paralyzed, sure that something is in the room with them, or that they're hurtling through the air, or being electrocuted.

Shawna, a 28-year-old bartender and graduate student, told me,

> One night I woke up in the middle of the night and couldn't move. I was filled with terror and thought there was an intruder in the house. I wanted to scream, but I couldn't get any sound to come out. The whole thing lasted only an instant, but that was enough for me to be afraid to go back to sleep.

Mike, a 44-year-old computer programmer, said,

> I woke up around three a.m. and couldn't move. I managed to open my eyes and there were creatures in the room with me. I saw shadowy figures around the bed. Then I felt this pressure like pain in my genitals. I must have fallen asleep again because the next thing I remember it was morning. I woke up in a state of shock.

And this is how James, a 50-year-old dermatologist, described it: "I found myself waking up in the middle of the night, seized with fear. There were beings standing around my bed, but I was totally paralyzed, incapable of moving. I felt surges of electricity shooting through my body."

Scientists have an explanation for these experiences. It's called *sleep paralysis*—a condition that occurs when our sleep cycles become temporarily desynchronized. Instead of moving seamlessly between sleeping and being awake, we find ourselves in a limbo where the two states briefly overlap.

When we sleep, certain neural mechanisms block motor output from the brain to the rest of the body so that we're essentially paralyzed. This is important because otherwise we'd be thrashing around, talking, shouting, and lashing out violently in our dreams.

But when sleep cycles overlap, it's possible to "wake up" before sleep paralysis has waned. If this happens, we'll be unable to move. And if we wake up while we're in the process of dreaming, dream material might linger into our waking state. We can find ourselves hallucinating sights, sounds, and bodily sensations. They may seem real, but they're actually the product of our dreams.

Despite the bizarre symptoms and effects, sleep paralysis is considered normal, not pathological. About 20% of the population has had at least one episode of this type, accompanied by hallucinations. We are particularly prone to such experiences during periods in which our normal sleep patterns get disrupted. People at risk include night-shift workers, travelers with jet lag, parents with newborns, and academics trying to finish grant applications. Though it takes only about half a minute for things to return to normal—for the perceptual, cognitive, and motor aspects of the sleep cycles to become resynchronized—this can seem an awfully long time to the victims. It is a truly frightening experience.

That sleep paralysis is "normal" might be comforting to those affected if they knew what it was. Almost no one does. There are no public policy programs to raise awareness of its existence, no feature articles in major magazines. Doctors don't mention it during checkups, and it's never been the topic of a talk show or popular book.

That being said, a *lot* of people in the world experience sleep paralysis, feel the urge to take long drives at night, are afraid of being alone in rural areas, find weird bruises on their bodies, have unexplained nosebleeds, or feel out of place in society. All of us, at some point in our lives, have symptoms, feelings, or experiences that we don't understand—but not all of us wonder deeply about them. This might be because we either don't care very much or don't think our experiences have a specific cause. Indeed, some people remain unconcerned in the face of anomalies that would perplex even the most complacent types. ("Yup, I got this rash all over me. Doc said it's something called purpura, pigmented purpura. . . . Nope, don't know how I got it. . . . Nope, not sure when it's going to go away. . . . Contagious? Don't think so. . . . What is it? I already told you; it's purpura!") But this isn't the case with abductees. For them, what happened *is* meaningful and they want to know the cause.

The search for meaning is the catalyst for alien abduction beliefs, but this quest hardly makes abductees unusual. Thinking about oneself, trying to understand why one has certain disturbing or baffling emotions, is a cultural preoccupation, and finding causes for personal experiences and feelings is a major industry. Open the phonebook and look at the lists of counselors, therapists, homeopaths, psychologists, and psychiatrists. Walk into a bookstore and check out the section on self-help and psychology.

Some people believe that if they understand *why* they feel the way they do, they'll be able to change things for the better. Others are greatly relieved to learn that their problems are caused not by their moral failings but by a psychological syndrome or a little-known disease.

But when there are so many available explanations—from excess carbohydrates to parental neglect, from insufficient Bikram yoga to too much Prozac—why pick alien abductions? What makes abductees unusual is not the perceived strangeness of their experiences, or their desire for explanation, but *the specific explanation they choose.* Why do some people come to believe that their sleep paralysis experiences, or their nighttime urges to take long drives, or the strange marks on their body are caused by extraterrestrials?

The answer is that their symptoms, feelings, and experiences are consistent with what they already know—or "know"—about alien abduction. In America today, few people are unaware of what aliens look like and what they supposedly do to the human beings they kidnap. Since the 1960s, we've been hearing widely publicized stories of alien abductions.

According to the standard script presented in books, TV shows, and movies, aliens come in the night. When they approach you, you cannot move.

You feel terrified and helpless. You levitate, feel vibrations running through your body, see shadowy figures. It's common knowledge that aliens leave strange marks on your body, such as bruises or scoop marks; that UFOs are seen at night from solitary cars on wooded roads; that when you've had an encounter with extraterrestrials, you're unable to account for a period of time; that afterward you feel anxious or depressed, different from other people and from your former self. For better or worse, alien abduction is one of our culturally available explanations for weird experiences like sleep paralysis and gaps of lost time. "I've had an encounter with aliens" went from being a sure sign of insanity to the subject of prime-time TV shows *(Mork and Mindy, Third Rock From the Sun, Roswell),* bestselling books *(Communion, Abduction),* blockbuster movies *(Alien, Predator, Close Encounters of the Third Kind, Men in Black, Signs),* and allegedly serious documentaries.

When you're looking for the cause of an anomalous experience, your search is limited to the set of explanations you've actually heard of. For most of us, the set of possible explanations is far from complete. We're unaware of the prevalence of sleep paralysis, sexual dysfunction, anxiety disorders, perceptual aberrations, chemical imbalances, memory lapses, and psychosomatic pain. But our set of possible explanations does include alien abduction because everyone knows about aliens and their modus operandi (they come in the night, fill you with terror, kidnap you, and erase your memories). "What happened to me is just like what everyone else says happened to them." "I'm not really into science fiction stuff. Before this happened, I never believed in aliens. But what I saw on that TV show is exactly like what happened to me."

Look at things from the perspective of 40-year-old Mike, who's had a frightening episode of sleep paralysis. He thought he was going to die. He's never had an easy time sleeping, and now he's absolutely terrified. He *has* to know what happened to him. Some possible explanations occur to him:

He's going crazy; he eats too much before going to bed; there are robbers in the house; he has brain cancer; he saw something supernatural, like ghosts or aliens. He's not sure. Okay, the supernatural explanations are unlikely, but the other ones just don't seem "quite right. . . . They don't fit what happened. . . . It was unlike anything that ever happened to me." Days later, browsing through the remainders in a local bookstore, he sees a book titled *Communion,* by Whitley Strieber. He leafs through it and discovers, on page 27, that the author once had a sleep experience just like his. And just like him, Strieber was freaked out and was afraid to go back to sleep. And just like him, Strieber always had a tough time sleeping, and relating to women, and figuring out what he wanted to do with his life. And it's a published book! A bestseller! Nonfiction! Mike buys it and keeps reading, and then, in a later chapter, he finds out that Strieber was prone to headaches and nightmares as a kid, just like him. All these coincidences are too much. Did what happened to Strieber happen to him? Could he have been abducted by aliens?

Another one of my abductees, 27-year-old Larry, had a weird dream in which he saw shadowy figures standing around his bed. He woke up with a stabbing pain in his genital area. It was a "terrifying experience." Familiar with *Close Encounters of the Third Kind* and other movies about aliens, he wondered whether he might have encountered extraterrestrials. Upon reflection, however, the shadowy figures seemed to him "too tall—I don't think aliens are that tall." Next, he considered the possibility that the groin pain stemmed from a repressed memory of childhood sexual abuse. He began to review family photo albums in an effort to retrieve memories of what might have happened to him. Because of the groin pain, the feeling that he was "somehow special, different from other people," and the "stealthy nature" of the experience, he briefly wondered whether a bio-tech firm in the area had sent employees into his home

to take sperm samples, but he quickly dismissed this as being "too unlikely." He considered the possibility that the experiences were spiritual in nature, but "I doubt that angels would wear hoods." He tentatively settled on the childhood sexual abuse explanation. Only after undergoing therapy and failing to recover memories of childhood sexual abuse did Larry conclude that he had been abducted by aliens.

Someone else I interviewed, a man named Paul, 41, was working for a resort in the Caribbean when he had two strange experiences. In one, he woke up naked on the couch, but he couldn't remember either lying down there or undressing. In the other, he dreamed he saw a small creature by his bed wearing a silver track suit, and he told the creature, "I hate what you're doing to me." After these experiences, he started to feel "vulnerable" when he went to bed. He stopped sleeping naked. He described himself as a "New-Agey" guy who believed that "Western science is very limited in its understanding of the universe; I'm open to things other people might not accept as being real." He had read widely about "past lives, ESP, spirits, and extraterrestrials." He also told me that he was very interested "in earth spirits that feature in native folk tales." He considered each possible cause, but "the only explanation that seemed to fit" was aliens. "I hear that they come into your bedroom and take you, and when they put you back it's in a different place."

According to Jon, the teacher mentioned above,

> Trouble sleeping could have a lot of causes. It could be stress. It could be that I'm not used to the new place yet. It could be something worse, like being contacted by aliens. Yeah, it sounds crazy, but who knows? The world is a weird place. . . . There's a lot we don't know. . . . I've been stressed before, but I haven't had trouble sleeping.

So people choose alien abduction as an explanation because they can. In the words of retiree

Doris, 73, from New Hampshire, "Why else would I wake up flying over my bed?"

"But it's so unreasonable!" one hardcore skeptic said to me. "There's no evidence that aliens even exist, never mind that they actually come to our bedrooms at night!" While this is true, it's not clear that the average person knows just how little evidence exists for extraterrestrial life or just how improbable visits from extraterrestrials are.

For most people, reports by other individuals count as evidence, especially if those others appear sane, attractive, and respectable. Betty and Barney Hill—the mom and pop of abductees—became famous in abduction history in the 1960s because, in the words of Seth Shostak, an astronomer associated with the SETI Institute, "they were more or less Mr. and Mrs. Front Porch." A number of equally sane, attractive, and respectable people have since produced bestselling books and popular screenplays about their abduction experiences, and many people view this large body of testimony as powerful evidence. But because the scientific community disagrees, abductees gripe that "scientists don't pay attention to our experiences."

To a scientist, anecdotes don't count as evidence. A thousand individual eyewitness reports are no more meaningful than one. This is because humans are fallible, and even with the best of intentions, we have limited knowledge and we all make mistakes. What we "think we saw" may not be what we saw at all. So from a scientific perspective, the only good way to validate a claim is to do so objectively. How do we know that Earth is round? Because the Earth's shadow on the moon is round, because photographs from outer space show that the Earth is round, because a ship's topmast is the last thing you see as the ship sails off toward the horizon. We don't know the Earth is round because your boss's cousin, who's a very respectable guy, said so. If anecdotal evidence or the words of attractive authorities could be relied on, we'd have to accept that Yeti and the Loch Ness Monster exist; that Elvis Presley, James Dean, and Jimi Hendrix are alive; that psychoanalysis cures schizophrenia; and that there were weapons of mass destruction in Iraq at the time of the 2003 invasion.

It's interesting that people seem to find anecdotal evidence compelling when the issue is alien abductions but not when the issue is, say, murder. Perhaps this is because there have been so many recent TV crime shows (such as *CSI: Crime Scene Investigation* and its offspring, *CSI: Miami* and *CSI: New York*) that clearly demonstrate what types of evidence are required to convict a suspect. In these shows, people are convicted on the basis of sperm samples, blood spray patterns, body temperature, and the type of bug crawling in the victim's nasal cavities, not because of what "Bob told my cousin Helen, and she never lies."

The possibility that aliens exist, and that they visit the Earth, doesn't seem all that implausible to many people. In fact, it seems quite probable. According to recent polls conducted in the United States, about 94% of respondents said they thought that intelligent aliens exist. In a more recent poll, conducted by CNN, 65% of respondents thought that UFOs had actually visited Earth.

In the words of 83-year-old Joe, a retired construction worker,

> I think ETs must exist. There are so many planets. . . . No reason to think it's just us out there. Hell knows, there's nothing special about us. Scientists don't know everything. No one can prove they don't exist. And it would make sense that something else is out there. Some kind of God, or something above us. . . . I like the idea that there's something magical out there. I have this buddy, and when he's had a few beers he talks about what happened to him. He was driving to Vegas one night and he saw something. A light in the sky. It followed him. He blacked out— and when he woke up, the car was in a ditch. He had no memory of what happened. Like I said, he don't talk about it much, but when he does he thinks something happened to him. He thinks something's

going on. Why else would all these people be talking about it? Why all the movies and books and all that? Where's there's smoke there's fire, I always said. And all those books written by military people. . . . I'm not saying anything for sure. I'm just saying there's a lot going on out there that people don't know about. What do we think—that we're alone out there? Then where do we come from? The Big Bang they talk about—well, what about before that? And everyone gets worked up about how they're taking people in secret, through walls. Why do we think that ETs, if they exist, would have the same laws of gravity or biology or whatever? Maybe another kind of being or life exists, one we can't even imagine. Anyway, all I'm saying is that anything is possible and that there must be something going on for all these people to be saying the same thing. Attention, the wife says— they're doing it to get attention. But who the fuck (pardon my language, little lady)—who the fuck would want to have that happen to them?

Many people would agree with some or all of what Joe says, but there are a lot of problems with it. For one thing, the "sheer number of planets" argument overlooks the fact that no matter how many planets there may be, they have to be hospitable to life, and, as we know just looking around at our own solar system, the right environment is not easy to come by. Is a certain planet just the right distance from its sun? Does it have the right temperature? Is there any water? Is it dense enough to support an atmosphere? If we consider all the prerequisites for life, this drastically reduces the number of planets available.

But let's say that some other type of life *does* exist somewhere in the universe. What are the odds that it evolved far enough to be intelligent? Evolution is opportunistic and unpredictable, and there's no inexorable path from one-celled organisms to intelligent, self-aware life. In fact, 99 out of every 100 newly arising species become extinct. Earth is a planet hospitable to life, and life did arise here. Since then, more than a billion species of animals have come into existence, yet only one possesses conscious intelligence. Humans *are* a miracle.

But let's say, for the sake of argument, that self-aware intelligent life *did* exist elsewhere in the universe. Why would those beings develop the fantastic technology they would need to get here across interstellar distances? Moreover, why would they want to? Why would such superior beings be interested specifically in us? Why would they be interested in egg harvesting and sperm sampling? Why would they be taking the same bits and pieces of people over and over again? The whole idea of aliens coming to Earth in UFOs and kidnapping humans for medical and genetic experimentation is not only extremely unlikely—it's downright silly. (Especially the part where the aliens wait nervously while you're getting undressed.)

But like many of us, believers don't think in terms of probability and don't habitually look for the simplest explanation. I always asked the abductees I met, "Do you think there's a better explanation for what happened to you?" And in essence, they always answered, "Maybe—but I trust my gut and my gut says aliens."

Even if people did know how to think probabilistically and parsimoniously, would they? Even if they understood that anecdotal reports don't count as evidence, that the probability of alien life is infinitesimally low (never mind alien life that defies all known laws of physics, biology, and chemistry to abduct you from your bedroom and mate with you), would they think any differently?

I doubt it. Lots of crash courses in scientific thinking might whittle down the number of people who "believe," but believers would still exist. When people are sorting through possible explanations for their anomalous symptoms and experiences, especially emotionally powerful ones, they rely not on abstract principles of parsimony or probability but on what "seems to fit" or "feels right" or "makes emotional sense."

Schizophrenia researchers know this. For almost a century, they've been trying to understand how patients form delusions. In psychopathology, the term "delusion" refers to a false belief that is strongly held despite outside evidence and that is entirely resistant to disconfirmation. Delusions are, along with hallucinations, one of the hallmarks of psychosis (colloquially referred to as "being crazy"). That being said, there is a good deal of disagreement in the field about what, precisely, constitutes the difference between a delusion ("I am the new Messiah") and a strongly held idea ("I have been abducted by aliens"). Brendan Maher, one of my teachers, used to say that "if the hair stands up on your arm" while a person describes what he believes, then you're probably dealing with a psychotic. Textbooks suggest that one can distinguish delusions from nonpathological beliefs according to the degree of conviction with which individuals hold to their beliefs despite clear contradictory evidence. One noted researcher on hypochondriasis taught that the distinction could be made on the basis of whether the individual is willing to entertain the notion that he might be wrong about his belief.

Today, "delusions" are generally understood as patients' best explanations for the odd sensory and perceptual experiences that are part and parcel of their disorders. According to this perspective, delusions reflect not disordered thinking, but normal thought processes that people engaged in to explain their perceived abnormal experiences (i.e., why they feel the way they do). Brendan Maher offered a memorable example in his "Psychopathology of Delusion" course at Harvard. He described the case of a woman who believed she had a hive of bees buzzing and stinging in her head; she complained about the bees for years. After she died, an autopsy revealed a brain tumor. It was the tumor that had almost certainly caused the weird sensations of buzzing and stinging that she'd felt and, quite naturally, tried to explain.

Though I was impressed with this theory of delusions—that they were people's explanations for their anomalous experiences—one thing bothered me. Why did the explanations have to be so weird? Why did the woman in Maher's example

speak of a beehive and not "side effects from a neurological condition that is impairing my sensory and perceptual systems"? Why would someone say, "The CIA is after me," rather than, "I'm losing my hearing"? I remember Brendan Maher looking at me across the room, smiling patiently, and saying, "Because that's what it felt like to them."

For a long time, I didn't really understand what he was talking about. But today, thanks to the alien abductees, I do. (Though I'm far from suggesting that alien abductees tend to be psychotic or otherwise psychiatrically impaired, they do hold false beliefs—ones that appear to be natural byproducts of their attempts to explain the unusual things that have happened to them. So, in that sense, research on the psychopathology of delusions extends nicely to nonpathological beliefs like alien abductions.) It baffled me that most of my abduction subjects had considered and rejected alternative explanations that were more reasonable and more probable than an explanation based on aliens. Why choose the outlandish explanation? Given all the available explanations for sleep problems, depression, and sexual dysfunction, why choose the weird and disturbing one, the one that was likely to stigmatize them and cost them their friends?

My interviewees answered this question for me and confirmed what Brendan Maher told me 10 years ago. Robin, a lovely and intelligent 21-year-old college student, said it best:

> I know you think it sounds weird. Everyone does. I do, too. But what you don't understand is that I know the abduction was real, so it doesn't matter what you think. What I felt that night was . . . overwhelming . . . terrifying. . . . There was something in the room with me. All I can say is that it happened to me; it didn't happen to you. . . . I felt them. Aliens.

What emerges again and again from the subjects' statements is that what happened to them *felt* alien. It didn't feel as if it could be explained in conventional, ordinary, mundane ways.

As Maher and others have argued, delusions (false beliefs) are people's best attempts to explain their anomalous experiences. And the vividness and immediacy of personal experience cannot be easily refuted. Assuring abductees that what they believe happened is infinitely unlikely, that there is no evidence to support it, is a waste of time. They have a different, more compelling kind of evidence: firsthand experiences are *real*. Any experience is accompanied by and dependent upon neural activity. Although neural activity is normally the *consequence* of external input, it can be created by direct activation of the neural substrate itself. Regardless of the source, instances of neural activity can all feel the same. Hence, the only way to distinguish between a "feeling" that an abduction occurred and its objective reality is through objective corroboration—something that, in the case of alien abductions, just doesn't exist.

So what are the kinds of things that feel so weird to abductees? Let me try to make this argument less abstract. As already described, sleep paralysis is an internally generated experience that is often attributed to something external: aliens. This is because it feels really creepy. Imagine this happening to you: After watching the evening news, you wash your face, brush your teeth, and go to bed. In the middle of the night, you suddenly wake up. You're wide awake. You open your eyes and try to get up, but you can't. You're on your back, completely paralyzed. There is a sinister presence in the room. Then you hear something. Footsteps? Something is padding softly through the room. Your heart is pounding and you try to scream, but you can't. Whatever is in the room moves closer. Then it's on top of you, crushing your chest. You glance to the left and see small shadowy forms in the corner. Your muscles are clenched and you're aware of electric sensations shooting through your body. Then the sensations stop. The experience passes and you can move again. Your heart rate slowly subsides and you begin breathing normally.

What the hell just happened? This is what most people who've had such an experience want to know. It's definitely what I wanted to know the first time it happened to me. And I had just written a paper on the topic! Although the phrase "non-pathological desynchrony in sleep cycles" kept running through my head the whole time, this certainly didn't alleviate the disorientation or the terror or the gasping for breath. The physicality of it was overwhelming.

It was an episode of sleep paralysis, an experience that's been scaring the living daylights out of people for centuries. And for centuries, normal people have been looking for an explanation outside themselves. A sensed presence, a shadowy creature moving about the room, a strange immobility, a crushing pressure, and a painful sensation in various parts of the body have been historically compatible with a host of improbable explanations. The phenomenology of the experience may be the same, but explanations differ depending on what the individuals—and the larger culture they live in—believe, expect, or infer could be possible. At other times and other places in the world, such night terrors have been interpreted as Satan, demons, witches, dragons, vampires, large dogs, and angels and erect gorgons. Today, it's extraterrestrials.

Yet although it's true that—phenomenologically speaking—sleep paralysis and alien abduction experiences have a lot in common, there is one important difference: Sleep paralysis is a fact; alien abduction isn't. So if you wake up in the middle of the night levitating above your bed and spinning like a chicken on a rotisserie, you should understand that the experience is roughly a billion times more likely to have been caused by something normal than by something paranormal. But be careful about telling this to an actual abductee.

| | |
|---|---|
| *Susan:* | You know, it's interesting. The experiences of sleep paralysis and contact with aliens have a lot |

in common. But the thing is that sleep paralysis is a well-documented medical experience, and so far as we know, there's no evidence that aliens exist. Don't you think that your experience is much more likely to have been caused by sleep paralysis?

*Abductee:*　No!

*Cell phone conversation overheard through the door a few minutes later:*　I'm totally pissed. Can you believe the nerve of that girl? She comes to me, like, "Oh, I believe you've been abducted! Let me interview you to learn more about the phenomenon!" And then she brings up this sleep paralysis shit. "Oh, what really happened is sleep paralysis." Riiight! How the fuck does she know? Did she have it happen to her? I swear to God, if someone brings up sleep paralysis to me one more time I'm going to puke. There was something in the room that night! I was spinning. I blacked out. Something happened—it was terrifying. It was nothing normal. Do you understand? I wasn't sleeping. I was taken. I was violated, ripped apart—literally, figuratively, metaphorically, whatever you want to call it. Does she know what that's like? Fuck her! I'm out of here!

You can't disprove alien abductions. All you can do is argue that they're improbable and that the evidence adduced by the believer is insufficient to justify the belief. Ultimately, then, the existence of ETs is a matter of opinion, and the believers have their own opinions, based on firsthand experience. They are the ones who had the experiences that require explanation. They are the only ones who can tell us which explanation seems to fit best.

All of the subjects I interviewed followed the same trajectory: Once they started to suspect they'd been abducted by aliens, there was no going back. (I have no idea what the turning point might be for those who start to believe and then are convinced otherwise. This would be an interesting area of research. Perhaps it would shed light on psychological and cognitive factors that are prophylactic against creating false beliefs.) Once the seed of belief was planted, once alien abduction was even suspected, the abductees began to search for confirmatory evidence. And once the search had begun, the evidence almost always showed up. The confirmation bias—the tendency to seek or interpret evidence favorable to existing belief and to ignore or reinterpret unfavorable evidence—is ubiquitous, even among scientists. Once we've adopted initial premises ("I think I've been abducted by aliens"), we find it very difficult to disabuse ourselves of them; they become resilient, immune to external argument. We seem to be habitual deductivists, rather than inductivists, in our approach to the world. We do not simply gather data and draw conclusions; instead, we use our prior information and theories to guide our data gathering and interpretation. Once abductees have embraced the abduction theory, everything else tends to fall into place. Alien abduction easily accommodates a great variety of unpleasant symptoms and experiences. It can explain anything and everything—"I always had nightmares as a kid"; "I had a troubled adolescence"; "I'm not interested in sex"; "I've been having stomach pains"; "I keep failing rehab." One subject, who was part alien, finally found an answer to a life-long question: "I look at my mother and I think to myself, 'I don't know you. Who are you?'"

Furthermore, once you believe, your belief becomes unfalsifiable. There is no way to prove that aliens *don't* exist. All you can do is argue that there's no evidence they do, that their existence is improbable. Abduction beliefs fall into Karl Popper's category of unfalsifiable propositions. These may be *scientifically* meaningless, but we don't live in a science lab. We live in the real world. In the real world, people don't ask whether there is enough evidence to justify their beliefs. They ask, What are the costs and benefits? Believing in aliens might cost them some friends. Relinquishing their belief would cost them a lot more. They would have to find another explanation and cast aside a compelling theory for their scary and unpleasant symptoms and experiences.

Nowadays, when skeptics say to me, "People must be really nuts to think they've been abducted," I disagree. First of all, coming to believe one has been abducted by aliens doesn't happen overnight. It's a gradual process. It progresses in fits and starts, through many stages in which the possibility seems more and more believable. Second, very few people are dead sure they've been abducted by aliens until they "get their memories." After that—well, if you had vivid memories of being sucked up into a tube of light, you'd probably be sure, too. Third, all people want to understand why weird and confusing things happen to them;

for better or worse, alien abductions have become one of the explanations culturally available to us. Fourth, very few of us are trained to think probabilistically and parsimoniously—and even if we were, we *still* couldn't refute belief in alien abduction. Finally, abductees generally entertain a number of possible explanations before embracing the theory of alien abduction. The reason they ultimately endorse abduction is actually quite scientific: It is the best fit for their data—their personal experiences. And skeptics can't critique those data because they have no access to them.

Abduction beliefs are natural byproducts of our attempts to explain the unusual things that can happen to us. Given that most of us want to understand our feelings, that very few of us think like scientists in our everyday life, and that alien abduction is a culturally available script, I often wonder why more people don't think they've been abducted. Today, confessing to such a belief doesn't make you "crazy"—it just puts you, in my opinion, a couple of standard deviations from the norm. Ten years from now, believing in aliens and in their presence among us will perhaps become as common as believing in God.

## Discussion Questions

1. The fact that abductees are statistically more likely to be better educated than the rest of the population may come as a surprise to some. The narratives told by abductees, however, make perfect sense of that unusual fact. How might education and the process of assigning meanings to one's experiences explain this seemingly unusual event?

2. People who claim to have been visited by extraterrestrial beings are often labeled as mentally unbalanced, but when "normal" people recount odd dreams to one another, very few would consider these dreamers mentally ill. In fact, if you were to recount an odd dream to a psychoanalyst, she or he might treat it as, in some sense, more "real" than your waking experiences. What is the sociological difference between an "abductee" and a "normal" person? Your answer should include a discussion of primary and secondary deviance and "master status."

3. The terms "experiencer" and "abductee" refer to people who claim to have been visited by extraterrestrial beings. Comparing those two groups with similar constructs in the tattoo world (either collectors or modern primitives, as compared with "people who get tattoos"), show how labeling becomes an issue of identity construction. Which labels, when applied to oneself, make a person's social activities seem more "legitimate," "real," or "acceptable"? How might these labels enable members of "deviant" social worlds to counteract the effects of stigma?

4. Good sociology, it is often said, either makes the familiar seem unfamiliar or the unfamiliar familiar. Explain deviance to someone who might find the topic odd, in a way that makes it seem less odd. How is your narrative similar to the narrative strategies employed by those who claim to have been visited by extraterrestrial beings? How is being a college student similar to being an "experiencer"?

5. Extraterrestrials come to visit you this evening. They bring you to their ship where they tell you that your experience in your deviance class has made you well-suited to save the world. What aspects of your course would fit well into your narrative as an "experiencer," and how will you communicate that information to get nonbelievers to take you seriously?

# PART 3

# BEING HUGELY OBESE

# OBESITY AS EXTREME DEVIANCE
## An Introduction

What makes the obese deviant?

In contemporary America, obesity is stigmatized. Fat people are considered less worthy human beings than are thin people. Goffman (1963) tells us that stigmatized persons are regarded as "not quite human" (p. 5) and, quite clearly, the obese are stigmatized. Oddly enough, even though the obese offer up a nearly perfect example of a "spoiled identity," in *Stigma*, Erving Goffman mentioned obesity only twice, and both times in passing. The first time, he sees obesity as the basis of one of a number of categories of stigmatized persons who form "huddle-together self-help clubs" (p. 22). In a second discussion, along with "the village idiot, the small-town drunk, and the platoon clown," he mentions the "fraternity fat boy," all of whom can serve as a "mascot for the group" (p. 142), even though "he is denied the respect accorded full-fledged members" (p. 141). Given obesity's nearly perfect applicability to most of the central concepts discussed in *Stigma*, one becomes curious that it does not play a more central role.

Obesity is an attribute that makes people different from the norm. Goffman (1963) describes "discrediting" differentness as attracting a "tainted, discounted" identity (p. 3). For the ancient Greeks, stigma attached to someone who became a "blemished person, ritually polluted, to be avoided" (p. 1). Men and women of average weight tend to feel superior to the obese, reward them less, punish them more, make fun of them; the obese may become targets of derision and harassment. What is more, thin people will feel that this treatment is just, that the obese deserve it, indeed, that such treatment is something of a humanitarian gesture because such humiliation will supposedly inspire them to lose weight. The nearly universal futility of such treatment may cause the observer to wonder about the purity of this motive.

The obese, in the words of one observer, "are a genuine minority, with all the attributes that a corrosive social atmosphere lends to such groups: poor self-image, heightened sensitivity, passivity, and a sense of isolation and withdrawal" (Louderback, 1970, p. v). They are subject to relentless discrimination; they are the butt of denigrating jokes; they suffer from persecution; it would not be an exaggeration to say that they attract a great deal of cruelty from the thin majority. Moreover, their friends and family rarely give them the kind of support and understanding they need to deal with this cruelty; in fact, it is often friends and family who are themselves dishing out the cruel treatment. The social climate has become

so completely permeated with anti-fat prejudice that the fat themselves have been infected by it. They hate other fat people, hate themselves when they are fat, and will risk anything—even their lives—in an attempt to get thin. . . . Anti-fat bigotry . . . is a psychic net in which the overweight are entangled every moment of their lives. (pp. vi, vii)

A substantial proportion of the obese accept the denigration thin society metes out to them because they feel, for the most part, that they deserve it. And few defend other fat people who are being criticized because they are a mirror of the very defects that are so repugnant to them. Unlike the members of most other minorities, the obese rarely fight back. In fact, they feel they can't fight back. Racial, ethnic, and religious minorities can isolate themselves to some degree from minority prejudices; the obese cannot. The chances are most of the people they meet in their everyday lives will be of average size; they live in a world designed for people with smaller bodies. The only possibilities seem to be to brace themselves—to cower under the onslaught of abuse—or to retreat and attempt to minimize the day-to-day abuse. Fighting back seems to be a rarely chosen path.

The fact is, to the thin majority, obesity is regarded as "morally reprehensible," a "social disgrace" (Cahnman, 1968, p. 283). Fat people are set apart from men and women of average size; they tend to be isolated from "normal" society. The single sin of obesity is rarely regarded as isolated. Hardly anyone who possesses one stigmatizing trait is thought to have only one. A single sin will be seen as housing a multitude of others as well, as the "tip of the iceberg." The one stigmatizing characteristic is a *master status*: Everything about the individual is interpreted in light of the single trait. "Possession of one deviant trait may have a generalized symbolic value, so that people automatically assume that its bearer possesses other undesirable traits allegedly associated with it" (Becker, 1963, p. 33). Thus, we raise the question when confronting someone with a stigma: "What kind of person would break such an important rule?" Typically, the answer that is offered is "One who is different from us, who cannot or will not act as a moral human being and therefore might break other important rules." In short, the stigmatizing characteristic "becomes the controlling one" (p. 34).

Although, strictly speaking, obesity falls into the type of stigma Goffman (1963) referred to as "abominations of the body," one of "the various deformities" (p. 4), in fact, it is regarded by the average-sized majority as a *moral* failing as much as a physical defect. Being fat indicates a *blemish of individual character,* more specifically, possessing a "weak will" and an "unnatural passion" (p. 4). The obese are overweight, according to the popular view, because they eat immoderately. They have succumbed to temptation and hedonistic pleasure seeking where other, more virtuous and less self-indulgent individuals have resisted. The stigma of obesity is, as with behavioral deviance, the outcome of a struggle between good and evil, vice and virtue. The obese must, therefore, pay for the sin of overindulgence by attracting well-deserved stigma (Cahnman, 1968). The obese suffer from what the public sees as "self-inflicted damnation" (Allon, 1982). In one study of the public's rejection of persons with certain traits and characteristics, one researcher found that the stigma of obesity fell more or less squarely in between that of physical handicaps, such as blindness, and behavioral deviance, such as homosexuality (Hiller, 1982).

So powerfully stigmatized has obesity become that a *New York Times* editorial argues that it has replaced sex and death as our "contemporary pornography." Our society is made up of "modern puritans" who tell one another "how repugnant it is to be fat"; "what's really disgusting," we feel, "is not sex, but fat." We are all "so relentless, so determined to punish the overweight. . . . Not only are the overweight the most stigmatized group in the United States, but fat people are expected to participate in their own degradation by agreeing with others who taunt them" (Rosenthal, 1981; Goode, 1996).

It is important to emphasize that deviance is only one way of looking at obesity. Many health experts also regard obesity as an unhealthy medical condition. Being hugely overweight increases the likelihood of a range of diseases, diabetes included, and, on average, shortens the life span, usually in direct proportion to the degree of overweight. While the health consequences of obesity are medically important, they have nothing to do with deviance. In the words of Marcia Millman (1980),

> The negative reactions and anxieties aroused by obesity cannot be adequately explained by the argument that obesity is unhealthy. Many other things we do to ourselves are unhealthy, yet they do not excite the same kind of shame, hostility, and disapproval. Furthermore, many people have strong reactions to weight even when a person is not fat enough for health to be affected. Clearly, obesity has become mythologized in our culture into something much more than a physical condition or a potential health hazard. Being overweight is felt to express something basic about a person's character and personality. . . . One need not deny that obesity may be unhealthy to ask why fat people are so stigmatized; people with other health problems are not condemned in the same ways. (pp. x–xi, xiii)

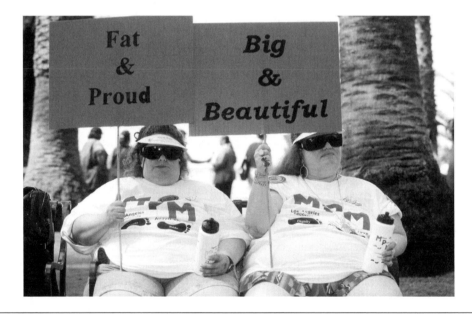

**Photo 3.1**    Condemnation and hostility from others for one's physical characteristics can result in a range of reactions, from internalizing one's inferior status to fighting against the system that puts one down. Here, fat people protest against size discrimination. John Kitsuse refers to the latter reaction as "tertiary deviance."

SOURCE: Gilles Mingasson/Getty Images.

To the extent that it fosters disability, illness has been discussed as a form of deviance (Parsons, 1951, pp. 476–477), but sociologically, deviance is conceptually, definitionally, and empirically separate from and independent of illness. Perhaps the most important theoretical development in the sociology of deviance has been to sever deviance from the illness or pathology concept (Matza, 1969, pp. 41–66). Efforts to define unconventionality—from atheism and interracial marriage to homosexuality and recreational drug use—as a form of pathology continue to be unsuccessful. More than half a century ago, sociologist Edwin Lemert (1951) argued that the time had "come to break abruptly with the traditions of older social pathologists and abandon once and for all the archaic and medicinal idea that human beings can be divided into normal or pathological." Moreover, Lemert stated, the term "pathological" must be divested of its "moralistic" overtones (p. 21). The fact is, the stigma of obesity is a moral, not a medical, issue; the compassion felt for the cancer patient, the blind, and the paralyzed is not, for the most part, extended to the hugely overweight.

In this section, Debra Gimlin, who is interested in how people react to, attempt to alter, and deal with their bodies ("body work"), assesses the efforts made by members of a self-help organization, the National Association to Advance Fat Acceptance (NAAFA), to reinterpret their hugely obese bodies. To mainstream American society, their bodies are an abomination, anathema, a disgrace. How successful are NAAFA members in inculcating the theme "fat is beautiful"? Not very, argues Gimlin. Her article points to the limits of the social construction of reality.

Goode's selection on the FA, the "fat admirer," the man who is sexually aroused by, dates, and has sex with fat women, highlights Goffman's (1963) concept of the "courtesy stigma," a form of deviance caused not so much by what one does but by whom one associates with. In this case, not only is it stigmatizing to *be* fat, it is stigmatizing to love fat women. Here we have a case of "guilt by association."

"Diane" explained to Goode how "Sally" reacted to the taunts she received from average-sized persons expressing their repugnance for her size. Sally is remarkably atypical of the obese. Diane goes on to describe the full spectrum of NAAFA members, however, and many of them, it seems, have internalized the stigma directed their way over the years. Most of them reject the defiant slogan, "I'm mad as hell and I'm not going to take it any more." Most, in fact, "just sit there and take it." This feature of internalization is one of the most interesting aspects of the stigma of obesity.

These selections focus more or less exclusively on obese women or, in the case of Goode's article, men who are attracted to obese women. This is true of the entire literature on obesity, especially with respect to stigma and deviance. Why? The answer we give is straightforward: Although men who are extremely fat will experience negative reactions to their weight, women are stigmatized far more for being overweight than are men. Physically, the ideal woman is very slim, in fact, slimmer than the average weight; women's magazines obsess about weight loss far more than men's magazines do; girls grow up being admonished for gaining weight far more than boys do; the diet industry is mainly addressed to women; women are less satisfied and far more self-critical about their weight than men are; and women are more likely to have what psychologists refer to as "disturbances" in body images— females are far more likely to develop neuroses such as anorexia as a result of these disturbances than men are. In short, being overweight is *more deviant* for women than it is for men

(Schur, 1980, pp. 70–72). Women tend to be judged "very much on the basis of physical appearance." Being fat "is considered such an obvious default or rebellion against being feminine that it is treated as a very significant, representative, and threatening characteristic of the individual" (Millman, 1980, p. xi). It seems reasonable, therefore, to devote a chapter to obesity as deviance by women.

# REFERENCES

Allon, N. (1982). The stigma of overweight in everyday life. In B. B. Wolman (Ed.), *Psychological aspects of obesity: A handbook* (pp. 130–174). New York: Van Nostrand Reinhold.

Becker, H. S. (1963). *Outsiders: Studies in the sociology of deviance.* New York: Free Press.

Cahnman, W. J. (1968, Summer). The stigma of obesity. *The Sociological Quarterly, 9,* 283–299.

Goffman, E. (1963). *Stigma: Notes on the management of spoiled identity.* Englewood Cliffs, NJ: Prentice Hall/Spectrum.

Goode, E. (1996). The stigma of obesity. In E. Goode (Ed.), *Social deviance* (pp. 332–340). Boston: Allyn & Bacon.

Hiller, D. (1982). Overweight as master status: A replication. *Journal of Psychology, 110,* 107–113.

Lemert, E. M. (1951). *Social pathology: A systematic approach to the theory of sociopathic behavior.* New York: McGraw-Hill.

Louderback, L. (1970). *Fat power: Whatever you weigh is right.* New York: Hawthorn Books.

Matza, D. (1969). *Becoming deviant.* Englewood Cliffs, NJ: Prentice Hall.

Millman, M. (1980). *Such a pretty face: Being fat in America.* New York: W. W. Norton.

Parsons, T. (1951). *The social system.* Glencoe, IL: Free Press.

Rosenthal, J. (1981, May 29). The pornography of fat. *The New York Times Online.* Retrieved from http://www.nytimes.com

Schur, E. (1980). *Labeling women deviant: Gender, stigma, and social control.* New York: Random House.

# NAAFA

## Attempting to Neutralize the Stigma of the Hugely Obese Body

### *Debra Gimlin*

Participants in the National Association to Advance Fat Acceptance (NAAFA) have bodies that fall outside the normal range, that are sufficiently aberrant as to induce abusive remarks from friends and strangers, to make finding a job difficult or impossible, and to block individuals from ever experiencing anything close to "normal" lives.

EDITORS' NOTE: From *Body Work: Beauty and Self-Image in American Culture* (paper) by Gimlin, D. L., copyright © 2001 by University of California Press–Books. Reproduced with permission of University of California Press–Books via Copyright Clearance Center.

NAAFA was created explicitly to contest popular notions of beauty. It was established in 1969 as a nonprofit civil rights organization seeking to increase the well-being of fat people. NAAFA policy documents charge mainstream or "thin" society with regarding its fat members as unsightly and undisciplined. According to NAAFA, members of the broader society attribute to fat people not only physical ugliness but also character flaws and immorality, clearly straddling two of Goffman's (1963) stigma—"abominations of the body" and "blemishes of individual character" (p. 4).

As a result of this stigma, NAAFA members argue, they are discriminated against socially and professionally; they are often unable to buy clothes, gain access to common spaces such as the theater and public transportation, or obtain health and life insurance. Fat people receive inferior treatment from health professionals and little understanding from their own families. They are frequently stared at and regularly victimized by tasteless jokes and verbal assaults. The result, according to the NAAFA home page, is often a poor self-image and feelings of worthlessness and guilt.

Members of NAAFA use the organization to construct an identity by renegotiating the relationship of body and self. They dismiss the notion that the stigmatized body implies a flawed character. On the one hand, the organization argues that the fat body and the self are unrelated. NAAFA thus denies the conventional moral implications of the fat body, including laziness, low self-esteem, vice, and stupidity. On the other hand, NAAFA also transforms the meanings of the fat body. In NAAFA social life, the fat body symbolizes a variety of positive identity traits, ranging from generosity to assertiveness to candid sensuality. Accordingly, NAAFA attempts to create a safe, sexualized social environment for its membership. Despite the group's considerable efforts, however, attempts to renegotiate self and body are limited in their success.

Reminiscent of Sykes and Matza's (1957) discussion of "techniques of neutralization"—in which even the most strenuous efforts to negate the meaning of deviant acts may fail in the context of internalized values and the reactions of conforming others—NAAFA's attempts to renegotiate meanings of the fat body rarely convert either outsiders or NAAFA members themselves. Because NAAFA exists in a social world that unwaveringly links body to self—and, by implication, connects the stigmatized body to a flawed self—the organization is unable to offer its members successful

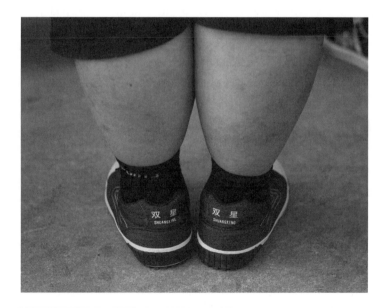

**Photo 3.2**   One means of dealing with anti-fat hostility is to lose weight—to alter one's physical appearance to conform to conventional standards. (With respect to obesity, health considerations also enter into the equation.) Here, a fat boy is attending a weight loss summer camp.

SOURCE: China Photos/Getty Images.

techniques for neutralizing the failed body. As products of the culture in which they live, NAAFA members may attempt to renegotiate meanings of the fat body. However, they are able to do so only within the insulation of the organization's social life. They are still bombarded with and influenced by broader cultural understandings of appearance, and they construct identities that are shaped by those understandings.

## The Women of NAAFA

Sylvia is a 45-year-old bookkeeper. She is 5 feet 8 inches tall, brunette, and around 350 pounds. A friendly person with a lively wit, Sylvia treats all members with warmth and caring, plans many of the group's social and political activities, and organizes much of her own life around her involvement in NAAFA. Obese even in early childhood, Sylvia recalls her experiences with weight. She told me that she was "fat from a little kid," describing herself as a "little, like, roly-poly." She explains, "I was 140 pounds in fifth grade and that was considered way too fat."

When she was 10, Sylvia's parents took her to a doctor for weight loss therapy. The physician prescribed amphetamines, which Sylvia took for several months, and she lost a considerable amount of weight. Because the pills eventually began to make her faint, Sylvia stopped taking them around age 11, at which point she gained "a tremendous amount of weight," all that she had lost and nearly 30 pounds more. By the time she entered junior high school, Sylvia weighed 200 pounds, where she remained for four years until, at age 16, she went to another diet doctor, who not only prescribed oral stimulants, but also gave her amphetamine shots. She notes, "Years later, we found out it was speed. . . . I lost 80 pounds."

Sylvia says that weight has affected nearly all aspects of her life, including her relationships with men and family members, education, and employment. She says, "I was accepted to three [nursing] schools and I knew I couldn't go to any of them because I had lied on the application, saying I was 180 pounds. That was the top weight that they would accept." Weighing 225 pounds, Sylvia knew that she would have to lose 45 pounds before the school physical, just three months away. Unable to reach 180 pounds, Sylvia instead attended the two-year nursing program at a local community college. While the program had no weight requirements, it provided training far inferior to that offered by the three schools that rejected her because of her weight. She eventually became frustrated with the program and dropped out of college. For the next 10 years, she worked in numerous odd jobs, eventually becoming a bookkeeper.

In addition to her struggles with weight and her educational and occupational challenges, Sylvia faced problems with her parents who were, she says, "always my worst critics." Sylvia's mother, a secretary, had been slightly overweight in her teens but managed to become and remain slender. Her father, a construction foreman, was quite thin until he entered his sixties, after which he gained approximately 15 pounds. By her account, Sylvia's parents attempted to manage her eating behavior throughout her life. Her mother "became totally obsessed with trying to control [Sylvia's] body," to the point of monitoring the contents of all the food containers in the home. Sylvia says, "She would have everything marked. She'd know how many cookies were in each box. She would actually put little tick marks on the milk carton, so that if I drank a glass of milk, she would know. . . . Eventually, it became a battle of wills of me trying to find more and more ways to actually get food." In Sylvia's recollection, her parents showed more or less affection for her depending on her eating behavior. She was required to lose weight "for the family, in order to . . . make them proud, to make them respectable. I was shaming the family by being fat. That's why I was good if I was going along with the program, and bad, unlovable, if I didn't."

Believing that her weight made her "unlovable," Sylvia's parents told her she would never find a husband. Nevertheless, Sylvia married when she was 21. Her husband, a successful engineer from an upper-middle-class family, had shocked Sylvia's parents by falling in love with her. She recalls that several months before her wedding, Sylvia's mother convinced her father to tell her,

> "We don't think you should wear white to your wedding." I said, "Why?" and he said, "Well, because you're not a virgin," and I said, "You are so full of crap. Mom doesn't want me to wear white because it makes fat girls look fatter. . . . Well, I'm wearing anything I want." So I cut my parents out of my wedding plans completely.

Sylvia's marriage ended after two years, during which time she gave birth to a daughter. Several years later, she received a telephone call from an old friend. Mary, who is also a fat woman, had gone through a Weight Watchers program with Sylvia, and together they had lost—and regained—more than 80 pounds each. Sylvia recalls the telephone conversation:

> Mary goes, "What are you doing?" I said, "I have a three-year-old daughter and I'm sitting home on the weekends." She said, "Do I have a place for you! What if I told you there's a place you could go and dance and the men want to dance with you because you're fat?" I said, "Right."

Despite Sylvia's initial hesitation, she decided to attend a NAAFA dance with her friend. "I never looked back. I embraced this thing totally." For the first time in her life, Sylvia found herself in a social group in which she was considered attractive because of her body rather than, at best, in spite of it. Even if only in a small, isolated group, Sylvia was recognized as a sexual person. The organization provided her with a sexual outlet, a place where she could pursue men openly without fearing rebuff of her stigmatized body.

Five years later, Sylvia met her current boyfriend, with whom she has now lived for three years. She explains that at the time she met Mark, her interactions in NAAFA had helped her come to terms with being fat, stop dieting, and feel she was "a whole person" without a man in her life. Sylvia learned to see herself as "completely there" explicitly through her involvement in NAAFA.

Many of the members of NAAFA told me that before joining the organization, they had never been in a social group that had welcomed and accepted them. The women described childhood homes that provided little comfort: They were often chastised for their weight, tormented by their siblings, and neglected by their parents. For example, Terry, a 34-year-old student and member of the local chapter, discussed numerous battles with her mother, who controlled her eating and punished her for not caring more about her appearance. She describes one revealing incident in her childhood:

> I couldn't find my bike. I ask my mom, and she says, "I gave your bike to the moving man. His little girl didn't have a bicycle." We had this terrible fight. So finally she says to me, "I gave your bicycle away because I don't want the new neighbors seeing your fat ass riding up and down the block."

Terry's story resembles the experiences endured by many NAAFA members. Diane, a 36-year-old receptionist, remembers her mother saying, "Opportunity knocks once, and you'll be too fat to open the door." Diane says,

> That's one of my favorite quotes, and, "Don't bring any of your boyfriends home because we don't want to meet anybody that would date you." Or, "Men only date you because you have a car." These were words of wisdom, you know.

For many of these women, NAAFA becomes a new family. During one meeting of the Fat Feminist Caucus (FFC; the political arm of the organization), much of the conversation focused on the importance of the group as an environment in which the women's experiences of victimization were recognized, their feelings of need and loss validated. At this particular meeting, a first-time attendee tearfully spoke of her gratitude for a place where she could feel like she was "okay." Several other women said that they hated to think about "where [they] would be" without the group. Two others joked that they had to hold each other down because their happiness lifted them up into the air.

In addition to having poor family relationships, many members of NAAFA remember having few friends while they were growing up. Many were teased incessantly, often to the point that they would skip school to avoid other children's ridicule. Terry recalls,

> I was new to the neighborhood, and a guy in my French class would start yelling things about me being fat and making jokes and getting his buddies to all laugh with him, and I started sneaking into class early and getting way in the back, because we had these, like, booths. . . . I knew if I could get into the last row, then Philip wouldn't see me.

And Katherine, 51 years old, told me that she grew up feeling as if she had no place in which to feel sheltered or secure. She "didn't feel safe in school" or "in the streets" or even when she went home. Based on these experiences, Katherine says that she views the world outside NAAFA as "basically threatening."

NAAFA provides its members with a safe harbor. It also becomes one of the only places where fat women are considered sexual beings. Indeed, many of the women I interviewed told me that they had never felt attached to their bodies as objects of sexual desire or attraction until they came to NAAFA. Tamara, a 32-year-old engineer and member of the FFC, explained that fat women separate themselves from their bodies because they, like other members of the society, come to believe that their appearance is unacceptable.

Before becoming involved in NAAFA, many of the group's members had few romantic involvements;

their interest in men or boys was often ignored or even ridiculed. Sheila recalls a particularly humiliating experience:

> When I was in third grade, I told my girlfriend that I liked one of the little boys in class and he caught up with me in the back of the school yard and punched me in the arm and said, "Don't you ever tell anybody you like me," you know, and I knew it was because I was a fat kid.

Others described themselves as being sexually disinterested before they encountered an environment that acknowledged them as desirable women. Amy, a 28-year-old student and member of the FFC, told me that before learning about fat pride ideology, she believed that her life would be void of sexuality. She described herself as having always been "neuter," and exclaimed her shock on first encountering men who sought her out as a sexual partner.

Many of the women said that even though they had been sexually active and romantically involved with men before entering NAAFA, their partners often criticized their bodies and showed them little respect. Karen told me that before joining NAAFA she had repeatedly involved herself with men who treated her cruelly. In one such instance, she discovered that her partner had been lying to her about his involvement with another woman. When she confronted the man about his lie, he said that she "was not attractive enough to tell the truth to."

Rose, a 38-year-old secretary and member of the local chapter, told me about a particularly sadistic man whom she lived with for four years: "He said, 'I'd rather put my foot in a snake pit than make love to you.'" Rose left this man and became involved with her first "Fat Admirer" or "FA," who appreciated her fat body and respected her. Because the FA "didn't have much upstairs," however, their relationship soon ended.

NAAFA offers members a welcoming social environment, potential friends with similar experiences of size discrimination, and an opportunity for sexual and romantic pursuits. Within the organization, NAAFA women do not need to fear that their sexual interests will be ignored or, worse, despised. NAAFA members also gain access to seamstresses and clothing manufacturers who produce lingerie and evening wear for fat women, and they often dress up for the first time at the group's social events. Within NAAFA, fat women can flirt openly, flaunt their sensuality, and openly pursue men without fear of disdain.

## ATTEMPTS TO NEUTRALIZE THE DEVIANT BODY

NAAFA, an organization of stigmatized individuals, attempts to offer its members what Erving Goffman (1959) has called "advocated codes of conduct" for dealing with themselves and the "normal" world (p. 111). These codes provide members with alternative techniques for neutralizing the fat body and constructing normal identities. Within its formal doctrines and more informally in group interactions, NAAFA prescribes particular approaches to self and body. Specifically, NAAFA members come to the group to learn methods of dealing with the self that are more positive than those offered by the larger society. They seek out constructive ways of incorporating the stigmatized body into identity—of not equating a failed body with a flawed self. The political strand of the group argues that fat women are no different from "normals," while the local chapter links fatness to a specific conceptualization of self—the sexualized, feminized self. NAAFA thus understands or formulates or constructs the body-self relationship in two distinct—and somewhat contradictory—ways. This "self-contradiction," to use Goffman's terminology (p. 108), means that for NAAFA members, the body is simultaneously the self and not the self.

### Fat Is Meaningless: The Fat Feminist Caucus

The political segments of the organization see the self and body as separate entities. Time and time again in its formal statements, political activities, and member newsletters, NAAFA claims that the traditional moral implications of the fat body—including sloth, ignorance, and self-hatred—are not, in truth, associated with fat. NAAFA's members argue that they are as capable, intelligent, and worthy as average-sized members of the society and so should be granted equal rights and respect. Furthermore, with assurances that "it's not your fault that you're fat," NAAFA's literature claims that fat individuals are not personally responsible for their weight. Instead, NAAFA cites medical literature pointing to the influence of genetic predisposition and the limits of restrictive dieting on body size.

In this conceptualization, the fat body has no implications for identity. However, because society discriminates against fat people based on a single, effectively accidental, characteristic, the organization recommends specific tools for building self-esteem. These tools include facing, to quote the *NAAFA Workbook: A Complete Study Guide*,

> our whole, complete selves and loving all our parts, not just the nice sides but the complete package, "warts" and all. . . . Take a good look at yourself, take stock, and begin to affirm what is good, and love and accept the rest. (NAAFA, 1993)

According to NAAFA, fat people are just like everyone else. While their negative characteristics may very well deserve assessment, self-esteem requires that they also be accepted. In NAAFA's formulation, these negative qualities do not include fatness. Fat is unrelated to the inner person; therefore, it is not necessarily bad to be fat. Fat, according to the *NAAFA Workbook*, "is not a four-letter word." In keeping with Goffman's (1959) argument, the group suggests that stigmatized individuals define themselves as "no different from any other human being," even as those around them define them as deviant (p. 108). Although the outside world may ascribe specific identities to fat persons, NAAFA members themselves contend that the self is independent of the body.

In the FFC, group members rely on notions of the disembodied self as they negotiate their political activities and their individual attempts to come to terms with being fat. Women who come to this group (usually after they participate in one of NAAFA's local chapters or its national convention and dislike the sexualized environment) are primarily interested in political activity and community building rather than in romantic liaisons or a fat-centered social life. The FFC stresses that personal and political empowerment is possible through a shared understanding of each other's experiences and the bond of shared oppression.

## Fat and Beautiful: The Local Chapter

The local chapter of NAAFA uses a different strategy for neutralizing the fat body. This strand of the organization, rather than conceptualizing the self and body as distinct, attempts to transform the meaning of the fat body and, by implication, its significance for the self. The men who come to NAAFA dances and parties do so specifically to meet fat women. As other authors have commented, it is the fattest of the NAAFA women who are most highly prized and sought after by FAs (Millman, 1980, p. 4). In the economy of NAAFA social life, the fat body is a valuable resource.

At one dance and lingerie fashion show I attended, the women's clothes were quite revealing— short, tight, or low-cut—and were clearly intended to show off every bulge, roll, and jiggle. The members of NAAFA reveled in their fat, revealing their flesh to an audience that would, presumably, appreciate it. The women's positive attitudes about themselves and their appearances were obvious from their efforts to call attention to their bodies. The fashion show featured clothes by a local seamstress who sells moderately priced apparel for fat women. The woman who made these clothes described each item, usually making a comment about the new styles now available to the "full-figured."

After the regular clothes had been displayed, the lingerie and sleepwear portion of the show started. These clothes ranged from typical pajamas to completely sheer red nighties, "upstairs maid" fantasy teddies, a see-through outfit of red camisole and tap pants, and a sheer white nightgown and robe. The outfits were modeled by NAAFA women who had been dancing with their friends just moments before; most left little of their bodies to the imagination. Judging by the catcalls from the crowd, all of the lingerie—and by association, the women's bodies and their candid sexuality—was accepted with enthusiasm.

The dance provided a glimpse of NAAFA's idealization and sexualization of fat. At least in this isolated setting, NAAFA members could embrace their bodies as objects of sexual desire and enjoy the ramifications that being desired has on their understanding of themselves. At the local level of the organization and within this insulated space, the meaning of the fat body is transformed.

Importantly, the group's capacity to renegotiate the understandings of fat is dependent on its ability to separate itself from the cultural significance of NAAFA members' stigmatized bodies. However, even in such a setting, participants are aware that their fat bodies—or their attraction to fat bodies—deviate from mainstream understandings of the significance of fat. When the fashion portion of the evening began, Sylvia announced that the show would be videotaped for a local television station. When I asked her why she had made the announcement, she responded that many of the FAs would want to leave the dance rather than risk being seen on television. Clearly, the men recognized that the safety of NAAFA social life, as well as the organization's ability to construct its own understandings of the fat female body, relies on the group's separation from the broader culture. They realize that the group appears markedly deviant to the outside world. In turn, the organization recognizes many FAs' desire to hide their attraction to fat women. NAAFA's literature suggests that society, peer, and parental pressure may lead many FAs to stay "in the closet" about their preference rather than face the ridicule it would engender.

Members of NAAFA attempt to negotiate self and body in a culture that equates fat with disease, sin, ugliness, and deviance. And this negative identifier has obvious ramifications for the character attributions that others make about fat people and FAs. Because of the enormous social pressure to the contrary, NAAFA members are predictably unable to sustain at an individual level the group's understandings of the fat body or its implications for identity construction. At the broader culture level, in the world outside, the body and the self are too closely and profoundly linked.

## WHERE IT FAILS

While the two strands of NAAFA—the Fat Feminist Caucus and the local chapter—approach the relationship of the self and the body somewhat differently, both of their strategies aim to reduce the negative implications of the fat body. However, even though the group attempts to reconceptualize fat, few of the NAAFA women I interviewed perceive fat as attractive or desirable. Although many of the fat women longed to be involved in intimate relationships with men who appreciated them physically, none were involved with fat men. Moreover, this lack of sexual interest in fat men suggests something of a disingenuousness on the women's part: They want to be considered sexual beings but do not see fat men in the same way. Furthermore, more than half the women I interviewed were, despite innumerable failed attempts, trying to lose weight, often at the same time that they criticized others' (and even their own) efforts to do so. NAAFA provides reasons for its members to stop dieting, arguing that the behavior is destined to failure and so hints at self-deception. While many of the women I interviewed recognize NAAFA's "party line" as valid, they nevertheless

provide counterarguments, most commonly in the form of reasons why specific efforts to lose weight have proved unsuccessful. More than half of these women told me that their past diets failed primarily because they required unrealistic eating regimens: They were too restrictive of calories or food varieties; relied on drug treatment instead of behavior modification; or occurred at a time when the women were not, for some personal reason, "ready" to lose weight. Despite NAAFA's argument that fat people are fat because of genetic predisposition, the women often blamed specific—but not all—diets for their failure to lose weight.

Many NAAFA women have experienced short periods of being at average weight. Importantly, all of them say that they were not truly "themselves" during these periods of thinness; they behaved in ways that they would not normally behave, were sexually promiscuous, acted haughty, and treated fat people unkindly. Describing herself when she was slim, Sylvia says, "Man, I thought my shit didn't stink. I was another person." And Terry recalls, "When I got thin, I would go out to bars and pick up guys. I had never been promiscuous before." They now suggest that they feel ashamed of their behavior and of deluding themselves that they could "pass" as thin. And still, members of NAAFA continue to invest enormous amounts of time and energy in ridding themselves of their fat.

Although they may welcome sexual attention, few of the women in NAAFA trust or respect FAs. Most are suspicious of the men's motives and accuse them of pursuing fat women because they are looking for "mommies," need to feel physically overpowered, or are so insecure with their own attractiveness that they imagine only fat women are desperate enough to date them.

NAAFA women often told me that they were not entirely comfortable with the fact that men in NAAFA regard them as attractive because of their body types. Not unlike other women who feel that they are valued solely for their appearance, NAAFA women resent FAs' attraction to body type rather than to their unique emotional, physical, and intellectual traits. Many NAAFA members dislike the association of their fat bodies with particular— primarily sexual—characteristics. They question both the attachment of fat to sexual desirability (and, perhaps, sexual appetite) and the men who find them sexually attractive. In effect, they reject the local NAAFA chapter's transformation of the meaning of fat.

Even the members of NAAFA, then, fail to accept the organization's reconceptualizations of fat. Instead, these women continue to regard the fat body as significant for self and consider the stigmatized body as indicative of a self that is, in some way, flawed. Evidence for this failure is members' continued attempts to change their bodies, their rejection of fat men as sexual partners, and their scorn for FAs. Put succinctly, NAAFA members (just like the rest of the society) hate fat.

Attempts to negotiate normative identities are not always successful, particularly in the context of stigma (Levi, 1981). NAAFA women's bodies prohibit them from living "normal" lives. The bodies NAAFA women inhabit not only depart from the cultural ideal, they also deviate strikingly from the "failed" bodies most women have. Essentially, the women in NAAFA spurn fellow members of their stigmatized group. In so doing, they reinforce rather than undermine the cultural fear and repudiation of fat.

## REFERENCES

Goffman, E. (1959). *The presentation of self in everyday life*. Garden City, NY: Doubleday-Anchor.
Goffman, E. (1963). *Stigma: Notes on the management of spoiled identity*. Englewood Cliffs, NJ: Prentice Hall/ Spectrum.
Levi, K. (1981, April). Becoming a hit man: Neutralization in a very deviant career. *Urban Life, 10,* 47–63.
Millman, M. (1980). *Such a pretty face: Being fat in America*. New York: W. W. Norton.
NAAFA. (1993). *NAAFA workbook: A complete study guide*. Sacramento, CA: Author.
Sykes, G., & Matza, D. (1957, December). Techniques of neutralization: A theory of delinquency. *American Sociological Review, 22,* 664–670.

# The Fat Admirer

## *Erich Goode*

Two of the more fascinating issues regarding human sexuality are how and why we *eroticize* particular persons or categories of persons as sexual partners and how and why social norms *condemn* us for making certain sexual choices and, contrarily, encourage and idealize making others. An enormous volume of intellectual and scholarly work has been devoted to addressing these two questions with respect to the sex or gender of our sexual partners. Why homosexuality? And why does society *condemn* homosexuality? Or, contrarily—and much more recently— why *heterosexuality*? And why doesn't society condemn heterosexuality? (Foucault, 1978; Gagnon, 2003; Greenberg, 1988; Stoller, 1979). But very little work has raised these questions with respect to the *size* of our sexual partners. How do we come to be attracted to partners of a certain degree of corpulence? And why does society condemn us if our sexual partners are too fat?

There are perhaps millions of men in the United States who have a sexual preference and engage in sexual practices that run so sharply against the grain of conventional taste and behavior that most Americans would either refuse to believe in their existence or would regard their sexuality as "sick"—a kind of "fetish." Further, the predilections and experiences of these men are so well concealed that they have almost totally escaped serious study by sociologists and psychologists. The men to whom I refer have a strong erotic desire for obese women. Within the circles of men with this preference, and among the women who attract the sexual attention of these men, they are referred to as "fat admirers" or, simply, "FAs."

To be plain about it, these men prefer their sexual partners to be fat. They do not date fat women in spite of their size but, in part, because of it. The vast majority of all men, FA and non-FA alike, choose their sexual partners partly—and at first, mainly—because of how pleasing their partner's looks are to them. "It's a matter of chemistry," one man explained. "I simply can't start a relationship unless the woman turns me on physically." However, the features of a woman's body that "turn on" the FA are quite different from those that excite his non-FA counterpart. The FA is excited by the softness, the roundness, and the weight of women, their curves and bulges. "After all," one man I interviewed asked rhetorically, "who wants to impale himself on a bag of bones?"

Men who are attracted to fat women reject the charge that FAs generally and "mountain men" (men who are attracted to hugely obese women) specifically have a fixation or a "fetish." Millman (1980) quotes an FA who responds to the charge that he is attracted to women who have a "specific body type" in the following words: "I actually have less specific physical criteria than most men. I'm attracted to women who weigh 170 or 270 or 370. Most men are only attracted to women who weigh between 100 and 135. So who's got more of a fetish?" (p. 24). The fact is, the American ideal female body type falls within an extremely narrow weight range. In contrast, FAs tend to be sexually interested in women across a very broad spectrum of weights.

Anti-fat prejudice has its origin in two sources. Certainly, our current obsession with good health must be counted as one of these sources. But the second, I submit, is surely our puritanical heritage. As we cast aside traditional sexual restraints, certain other sources of guilt remain. Today, self-indulgence is more likely to be equated with an immodest appetite for food than for sex. Gluttony, it seems, is one of the last remaining taboos. Indeed, even sexual license makes it obligatory that one look good when naked. And today, that means being thin. Thin people believe that they have the right to feel more morally virtuous than fat people: They have resisted the temptation to gluttony to which the overweight have clearly succumbed. Fat people invite, or so the "thin chauvinist" ideology would have it, well-deserved *retribution*: They are derided and humiliated because they are self-indulgent and lack the willpower of righteous, temperate, upstanding souls. The fact is, most men and women of average size find fat people esthetically unappealing, and a major part of the reason for this is that the obese are regarded as having given in to the siren song of self-indulgence. The stigma of obesity is interlarded with a vein of smug, self-righteous moralism.

The current prevailing aesthetic standards in this society dictate that women should be thin. Moreover, standards here require women to be thinner than do standards in some other societies of the world, and today women are required to be thinner than they were in past generations. The trend in the size of the ideal American woman is, perhaps, reflected by the evolution of the models for the "White Rock Girl," the symbol of a soft drink company. In 1894, she was 5'4" tall, measured 37-27-38, and weighed 140 pounds. In 1947, she was 5'6", 35-25-35, and weighed 125 pounds. Today, she's 5'8", 35-24-34, and weighs 118 pounds. (Today's American woman is closest in dimensions to the 1894 model.) White Rock's representatives comment on this trend, in a leaflet titled "Psyche, Cupid, and White Rock," in the following words: "Over the years, the Psyche image has become longer legged, slim hipped, and streamlined. Today—when purity is so important—she continues to symbolize the constant purity of all White Rock products." The equation of "slim" with "pure" is a revealing comment on the Puritan attitudes that prevail toward the fuller-figured woman. The same trend prevails for *Playboy* centerfolds: Over time, models have become thinner, slimmer-hipped, less busty, less voluptuous, more angular, and more "tubular" in appearance (Polivy, Garner, & Garfinkel, 1986, pp. 89–90). The same is true of contestants in the Miss America Pageant and is even more the case for contest winners. It is interesting to note that, during the past generation, American women have *gained* an average of 30 pounds.

The FA's distribution in the population is probably impossible to determine with any accuracy. William Fabrey, founder of the National Association to Advance Fat Acceptance (NAAFA), a civil rights organization dedicated to the elimination of prejudice and discrimination against fat people, estimates the FA's extent in the population at one in 20, or some two to three million men. For a variety of reasons, there are relatively few female FAs—women who have an erotic desire specifically for fat men. In fact, nearly all the women I interviewed in NAAFA had conventional standards regarding the size of their preferred partners, desiring men with an average or muscular build. Hence, here, I will concentrate exclusively on the male FA and the obese women to whom he is attracted.

Considering that the ideal of feminine beauty as represented in the media and in advertising, and as translated into choices men make in their actual behavior, is extremely slender, a man's preference for considerably larger women is likely to be met with disbelief and derision. A great deal has been written on the "stigma of obesity" (Braziel & LeBesco, 2001; Cahnman, 1968)—the condemnation that fat people experience for being overweight. However, only a small proportion of the men I interviewed were themselves fat. One of the issues I'd like to deal with here is the role that social stigma plays in the lives of men who are not fat but find themselves irresistibly attracted to women who are. In other words, these fat admirers face *stigma by association*.

In *Stigma* (1963), Erving Goffman argues that a person's identity can be discredited as a result of associating with stigmatized others. The relationship causes wider society, Goffman says,

> to treat both individuals in some respects as one. Thus the loyal spouse of the mental patient, the daughter of the ex-con, the parent of the cripple, the friend of the blind, the family of the hangman, are all obliged to share some of the discredit of the stigmatized person to whom they are related. (p. 30)

Goffman refers to this as a "courtesy stigma" and states that "the tendency for a stigma to spread from the stigmatized individual to his [or her] close connections provides a reason why such relations tend either to be avoided or to be terminated" (p. 30). The fat admirer provides a living illustration of the fact that though relations between non-stigmatized and stigmatized persons can be sustained to the mutual benefit of both parties, they tend to be fraught with conflict, contradictions, and dilemmas.

An assistant (Joanne Preissler) and I conducted formal interviews with 15 men in NAAFA. In addition, for two years, both of us conducted participant observation of NAAFA activities and functions, such as meetings, conventions, and dances and parties, and conducted both formal and informal interviews with the female members of NAAFA. And lastly, as a comparison, Preissler conducted some informal interviews with fat women who were not members of NAAFA. We found that FAs are varied, but most can be characterized by their position along three dimensions: "closet" versus "overt," "exclusive" versus "preferential," and "mountain men" versus "middle-of-the-roaders." And lastly, we found that few women, whether members of NAAFA or not, were able to accept that "fat is beautiful" or accept the normality of the FA's preference for sex with fat women. Hence, NAAFA's attempt to construct obesity as acceptable has to be regarded as a partial failure (Goode & Preissler, 1983).

## CLOSET VERSUS OVERT FAS

As with homosexuals, some FAs are overt and open about their preference; they are "out of the closet" in expressing their desire for obese women. In contrast, others are "closet" FAs: They don't want anyone to know that they date extremely fat women. An overt FA is willing to be seen in public on a date with a fat woman; to acknowledge his preference to friends and family; and, if he is dating a fat woman on a regular basis, acknowledge that the two are a couple and that he prefers his partner at her current weight. An overt FA can easily imagine being married to a fat woman; indeed, he relishes the idea.

A "closet" FA does not wish to be seen in public with his fat date and will usually not accompany her to a restaurant or a movie. He does not acknowledge his preference to friends or family and will minimize the importance of his relationship with fat women should others find out about it. Some closet FAs may even "keep a thin girlfriend on the side" as a cover. A common lament by closet cases is "I love the way you feel in bed, but I can't stand the way you look on the street." Sally, a 385-pound woman, told us about her own experience with dating a man who was fearful of being seen in public with her.

You know what he told me? He said, "I can't afford to be seen in public with you, in my position. My peers would ostracize me." He rarely took me out. When he did, if we went to a restaurant, he'd pick the darkest corner. I had to eat quickly and slink out of there. . . . The man skulked from corner to corner, like some kind of a rat in a sewer. For many FAs, dating fat women is only for the sex. It's not supposed to be public knowledge.

Here's a portion of the interview Preissler and I conducted with Allen, a 36-year-old bookkeeper:

*Q:* What's the weight class of your strongest sexual preference?

*A:* 350 to 500 pounds.

*Q:* Are you comfortable with the fact that you're interested in overweight women?

*A:* No, I don't even want it known.

*Q:* Do you openly acknowledge a preference for big women?

*A:* No, God, no.

*Q:* Have you ever been embarrassed by your partner in public?

*A:* I would never be seen in public with a big, fat mama.

*Q:* Why do you prefer large partners? What is it about them?

*A:* It's just a turn-on—all that fat. It's like the forbidden apple.

*Q:* What type of relationship do you usually form with your fat partners?

*A:* Sex. Only sex.

*Q:* Could you compare a heavy woman with a thin one in terms of personality?

*A:* Oh, I don't know. I don't get to know most of them—I just screw them.

*Q:* Would you ever marry a fat woman?

*A:* Absolutely not.

*Q:* What would you do if you got fat?

*A:* I would never get fat.

John is a 35-year-old social worker. His appearance is one of rugged masculinity; he works out in a gym and is extremely muscular. He wears tight-fitting clothes that accentuate the bulge of his chest, shoulders, arms, and thighs. He tentatively agreed to be interviewed, depending on whether he liked the questions. He read them over and handed back the interview schedule, refusing to participate in the study. When asked why, he replied that although he likes big women, he isn't really an FA, whom he regards as "sick and dirty." When questioned, he became cold and defensive, even hostile. "Look," he explained, "for me, a fat woman is strictly a sexual thing. I haven't got any other interest in them."

John attends social activities, such as dances and parties, at which fat women appear. He does not approach any of the women, expecting them to approach him. He spends nearly all of his time at these functions with a frozen smile on his face, drinking and staring at the participants. The observer's impression is that he has a thinly disguised feeling of contempt for these people, fat women and FAs alike, and that he is laughing at them inside. When asked why he attends these social events, he replied, "Sure, the last couple of things, I showed up, took in all the people, watched all the women and men, had my six-pack, and split, then I go party with my friends." Since he is regarded as so physically desirable, he has dated a few of the women we interviewed, and he is described as an enthusiastic, passionate lover of fat women. He is, however, incapable of admitting it to himself.

A contrary case is presented by Fred, an overt FA and a 40-year-old scientist. Women describe Fred's appearance as that of a "cuddly teddy bear." He has always preferred and dated fat women, even in high school and college. He married a large

woman about 15 years ago. They had a child and are now divorced. When asked about how he feels being an FA, Fred answered, "I feel fine about it. It is normal for me. I have always been attracted to large, soft women, so for me it is just part of my sexuality." Fred is very overt about his preference. Everyone involved in his life is aware of it. He freely explains to anyone who is interested exactly what turns him on about large women. "Look," Fred explains, "I'm a jiggle junkie. I love to play with unsupported flesh, I love curves and roundness. Nothing compares with the body of a fat woman—their flesh yields to my touch."

When asked whether he ever felt uncomfortable about being an FA, Fred replied, "Of course not. A strong part of my identity is the FA part, and I like my image." He admits that being an overt FA does have its difficulties.

> The hardest part for any FA is the parents. The parental stuff you get is unbelievable. Typical American parents all want their sons to marry the girl-next-door type. Some finally accept the departure of the FA from the ideal type, and some can't. With time, mine did. Regardless, you cannot live your life to please others. If you're an FA, you might as well face it—and enjoy it.

## EXCLUSIVE VERSUS PREFERENTIAL FAs

A second dimension that distinguishes different types of FAs is the *exclusive-preferential* spectrum. The attraction of nearly all of our informants was of the "preferential" variety; that is, they dated both thin or average-sized women and fat women. Some had been involved with women who were not overweight, but preferred that their partners weighed more; some even encouraged them to gain weight. Several said that they discontinued the relationship because their partner's slenderness was a problem for them. We talked to only a few men who said that they had difficulty achieving an erection with an average-sized woman, or enjoying sex with one if they were erectilely functional. The men we interviewed, with only a small number of exceptions, had a preference for larger women that ranged from slight to great, but nearly all of them would choose sex with an average-sized attractive woman to no sex at all, or a relationship with her to no relationship at all. Only two men with whom we conducted a formal interview said that they had only experienced intercourse with fat women.

Samuel is in his early forties and is a high school teacher. He has a trim, athletic build. Most women of his approximate age would find him attractive in appearance. He is of average height and weight. At the age of 19, he attempted intercourse with a prostitute of average size, but, he explained, "I was not fully functional with her." A brief time after that, for a year, he lived with a young woman, also of average weight, with whom, again, he was "not totally sexually functional." After this relationship ended, all of the women he dated and with whom he had intercourse were fat. His former wife's weight fluctuated between 180 and 220 pounds when they were married, and her lack of size was one of the major reasons for their divorce.

Samuel refers to women who weigh between 225 and 250 as "thinner heavy women." With them, he explained, "sometimes I get an erection, but I just can't carry it through to climax. I can't get into it. I keep thinking about how *thin* and *hard* they are." On the other hand, with "much heavier women," who weigh more than 300 pounds, "I have multiple orgasms—four or five times in a night." Samuel currently lives with a woman who weighs more than 400 pounds. They engage in intercourse "at least twice a day." Almost all of his sexual partners have weighed between 300 and 500 pounds. "I could like thinner women as friends," he told us, "but I would never be sexually functional with them." The physical feature that he likes most about fat woman is their softness, their "rolls of flesh." Samuel is, in short, an *exclusive* FA.

In contrast, Jim is a "preferential" FA. He is 29 years old and works as a commercial artist. Jim's looks have been described to us as striking. He is tall, with a slim, lanky, although athletic body. He has a strong-looking face with bright eyes and a cleft chin. Attracting women has never been a problem for him. Jim's sexual and romantic interests range from average-size women to those weighing more than 400 pounds. He explained,

I like women. I am a very sensual man. I love the feel of a woman's body. I love sex. I love the movement of a woman when she walks. With a big girl, there is a lot of movement. Their bodies shake as they move, and that appeals to me. But you can find this in women of all sizes. Some women of average size will walk in a way that I find sexy, too. It's not the weight as much as the other qualities I look for. It doesn't matter how big she is. . . . I just like them all.

Jim could be described as a *preferential* FA.

## Mountain Men Versus Middle-of-the-Roaders

Closely related to, but not identical with, the exclusive-preferential spectrum is the *size* of the ideal sexual partner a man envisions. As part of the interview, Preissler and I handed each respondent five different cards with an illustration on each one outlining the body of a woman in one of five different weight categories. Card 1 depicted a woman who would weigh about 150 to 175 pounds, if she were of average height. Card 2 was that of a woman who weighed between 200 and 225 pounds. Card 3 represented a 250- to 275-pound woman. Card 4 portrayed a woman well over 300 pounds. And Card 5's figure was in the over-400-pound range. We asked each respondent to choose which figure he would prefer to make love with. Three of the 15 men we interviewed said that they couldn't choose, that they would enjoy having sex with a 150-pound woman as much as with a 400-pound woman. Their preference for fat women was only slight, and they enjoyed sex with an average-sized woman almost as much as with a fat woman. I concluded that FAs exhibit a considerable range in their size preference. Some unequivocally chose Card 5, the over-400-pound woman. I call them *mountain men*. Others picked Card 1 as depicting the body of their physical ideal; they could be called *middle-of-the-roaders*.

Hence, at one end of this spectrum we find the man who prefers his sexual partners to be "chubby," "pleasingly plump," or "voluptuous." He prefers and is attracted to women who are more fuller-figured than the American ideal, but considerably more petite than is true of the mountain man's preference. The middle-of-the-roader most decidedly likes fat women, but they must be "smaller" fat women—in the under-200-pound category. Most of these men said that they would prefer being with an average-size woman who is shapely to the ones depicted on Cards 4 and 5.

Rick is 42, an instructor of English literature at a local community college. He is of average height and build. Rick unhesitatingly chose Card 1. When asked if there were any "famous women or celebrities" who approximate his physical ideal, he said "Dolly Parton—if she gained about 25 pounds and her ass was a little bigger." He has had sexual experiences with perhaps a dozen women who would be classified as medically obese; the heaviest weighed about 300 pounds. He has also made love with many more who were merely "overweight," that is, 10% to 20% above the medically recommended ideal. He describes his ideal woman as being short, weighing 150 to 160 pounds, with a small waist, heart-shaped derriere, full legs, fleshy thighs, and large breasts. She should be curvaceous, he explained—soft, round, and definitely on the plump side. Rick is not uncomfortable about being classified as an FA, and he is completely open about his sexual preference, but he is not certain that he is a "true" fat admirer because he finds himself drawn to the slimmer women at NAAFA dances and parties. One woman we talked

to, however, described Rick as "a flaming FA—but at the lowest end of the spectrum."

The most clear-cut case of a mountain man we interviewed was Samuel. Only one interviewee (Fred) rivaled him with respect to the heaviness of his ideal sexual partners. One of the questions our interview dealt with was the respondent's sexual fantasies. The first one Samuel mentioned was having intercourse with a circus fat lady. He described very large women with a quality that approximated reverence or awe. Samuel is a true mountain man. Fred, like Samuel, is both an exclusive FA and a mountain man. The woman Fred lives with weighs more than 400 pounds. The sexual fantasy Fred mentioned first involved living with a woman, encouraging her to eat, and feeding her more and more so that she became enormously fat. Fred and Samuel adhere to the axiom, "the bigger, the better."

## STEPPING OUT OF THE CLOSET

As with homosexuality, stepping "out of the closet" is a crucial step in the development of one's sexual identity. Accepting that one is an FA is the first step; it determines how a man will treat the fat women he dates, as we can readily see if we compare the behavior of John with that of Samuel. The next step, making a public acknowledgment of his preference, is also crucial in the social and emotional development of the fat admirer. Both these steps are difficult to make, given society's stigma toward the obese and the man who chooses and prefers obese women as sexual and romantic partners. All of the men we interviewed (except one) related embarrassing or humiliating experiences they suffered from people with more conventional views of the appropriate size of one's sex partners. These incidents were instigated by friends, relatives (especially parents), and even perfect strangers. Consequently, the overt FA must either be an inner-directed, unconventional person, an individualist unconcerned with the opinions of others, or be willing to confront or otherwise deal with the taunts he will inevitably face as a consequence of his size preference.

It is not surprising that only a minority of the men we interviewed were completely overt concerning their preference for fat women. One man we interviewed recalled an experience at a NAAFA convention in Atlantic City. Three NAAFA women (who were not companions of this man) stepped into an elevator clad in swim suits. Another man turned to his companion, giggled, and said, loudly enough for all the occupants of the elevator to hear, "What—is the circus in town?" The fact that our informant was sufficiently embarrassed to remain silent is significant. It takes a nonconformist to be able to stand up and be counted in such a humiliating situation, and very few people possess that quality.

One of the factors of "stepping out of the closet" is living in a community large enough to support an organization like NAAFA that is designed to facilitate social contact between fat women and FAs. When they first realize their preference, most FAs believe that they are the only men in the world who love fat women. Initially, they are usually mortified, embarrassed, ashamed. They attempt to explain it away. When they can no longer do so and must face the implications of their desires, they may feel they are psychologically abnormal. The realization that other cultures or other periods of history have rhapsodized larger women—as exemplified, for example, in the work of Rubens and Renoir—may give the FA an inkling that his taste in women is not so bizarre, after all. Meeting and talking with other men who feel the same way, especially at social gatherings attended by dozens of fat women and FAs eagerly pursuing them, is likely to be a major factor in "coming out." (Although it is not necessarily decisive, as John's case reveals.) A common reaction to such an experience is "I realized that I wasn't alone, that I wasn't some sort of a freak, but there are lots of men out there just like me."

## FAT WOMEN VIEW THE FA

Most obese women have not gained a sense of self-acceptance regarding their weight. Most feel self-conscious about being overweight, and some even feel disgusted with themselves because of it. They feel that their current size is temporary. "I'm not fat," they will explain, "I'm on a diet." At one extreme, some will put off dating, wearing a bathing suit, buying clothes, or even appearing in public beyond the bare minimum for survival— until they shrink down to an acceptable size. Several women we interviewed discouraged suitors altogether, and one had not been to bed with a man for more than 10 years. "I just can't take my clothes off in front of a man the way I look now," she explained. A very high proportion of the women we interviewed became divorced as a consequence of gaining weight after bearing children, followed by their husband's sexual rejection of them. Their sexual modesty is, therefore, not surprising.

More commonly, fat women will date men but feel uneasy about these men's sexual interest in them. Since they are unable to view themselves as sexually desirable, they will feel extremely uneasy, even anxious, about men who adore and are excited by their bodies, feeling that "there must be something wrong with them if they like me the way I look." These men are attracted to the very physical aspects that these women find most repulsive. Consequently, the self-rejecting fat woman finds it difficult to enjoy sex with the FA. Many FAs complained to us that most of the women they dated could not deal with the lavish praise they showered upon them. "You *know* I hate my thighs," a man quoted one of his dates—who was under 200 pounds—as saying. "Take your hands *off* them!"

Eileen weighs 200 pounds. She is married to a very large man—6'6", 380 pounds. She was married at the age of 17 and weighed only 125 at the time. She has two children and is a full-time homemaker. Eileen is disgusted with the way she looks and makes critical remarks about fat people, especially women, wherever she sees them. She has a habit of buying expensive dresses that are four sizes too small for her. She hangs them in the closet and never wears them. "Isn't that beautiful?" she exclaims, showing an expensive dress to one of us. "It's a size 10. I'm going to wear it to the party next month." To the objection, "But you've got to lose 50 pounds to fit into it," Eileen replies, "I'm on the egg and spinach diet. I can do it." When the date of the party arrives, she is still fat, and she refuses to go to it. She wants as few people as possible to see her at her current weight.

Eileen does not shop in the stores in her home town, but in communities nearby because she is afraid that someone she grew up with will see that she has become fat. She refuses to attend business dinners with her husband, which is expected in his firm, because his associates and their wives will see her and think she's fat. She refuses to be seen in public in a bathing suit or revealing shorts. She won't even walk around the block with her children because her neighbors will notice how much she weighs. Eileen leaves the house as little as possible. Almost all of her fantasies revolve around the exciting things she will do when she becomes thin. Eileen has put off living today for an imaginary future. Her obsession with her weight, and the way she has chosen to deal with it, creates a major strain in her relationship with her husband; it continually endangers the viability of her marriage. Eileen is acquainted with members of NAAFA, but she would never join such an organization, she says.

Self-loathing fat women such as Eileen, who feel strongly negatively about their weight, find it alarming that FAs are attracted to them, in part, because they are overweight. One of Millman's (1980) informants expresses this view in the following words: "Personally, I think a man who would go to a dance only looking for a fat woman is deranged" (p. 21). The obverse of this, the fact that the overwhelming majority of all American men will only look for an average-sized woman, in part "because" of her weight, without being labeled

"deranged," indicates the lopsidedness of our society's definition of the appropriate size of partners. While everyone wants a partner "who likes me regardless of my size" (p. 21), the fact is, no man—FA or non-FA alike—and very few women are attracted to a partner regardless of his or her looks, and size is a major aspect of looks. The negative feelings that most fat women have about their bodies translate into an even stronger negative feeling about the men who are attracted to them because of this undesirable and undesired feature. "There must be something wrong with him if he likes me the way I am," was a common statement the women we interviewed made. Many FAs, therefore, face stigma not only from conventional society, but from a high proportion of the very women they date and whose size preference these women cannot accept.

It is difficult to escape the stigma that accompanies being fat in this society. Very few overweight people, especially women, are able to say, "Fat can be beautiful." The women who join NAAFA typically enter with a wounded self-image. Usually, the new member knows very little about it beyond what one new member told us: "I heard there's a club where there are men who like to go out with fat women." She is likely to regard the attentions of these men with a mixture of contradictory feelings: excitement, puzzlement, disbelief, and alarm. It is as if the traditional standards concerning the aesthetics of weight that everyone has been exposed to have been turned upside down.

A naïve woman with an ego bruised from a lifetime of insults and social isolation may be susceptible to flattery from an articulate, eager FA. One man we interviewed was admonished by a female member of the organization in the following words:

> You meet these insecure fat girls who come here [to NAAFA social functions], you take them home, you make them feel good, they fall in love with you, and you never call them again—you're breaking their little hearts. You ought to be ashamed of yourself, mistreating them like that!

Hence, conventional wisdom would predict that persons with a low sense of self-esteem would enter into a dating relationship—almost any dating relationship—more readily with someone who shows interest in them than those who feel positively about themselves. As a result, chances are, all other things being equal, they would be more available for sexual exploitation.

On the other hand, the men we talked to were split down the middle on the issue of whether fat women would be more—or less—eager to enter into a sexual relationship than women of average size. One man, Dennis, a popular and distinguished-looking gentleman in his forties, expressed the following complaint regarding the impact of the fat woman's lack of self-confidence (FAs and NAAFA women use the word "thin" to refer to women who are not fat): "Fat women are harder to take to bed than thin women," Dennis explained, "because of their lack of self-confidence. They just don't believe that a man really likes them the way they are, and they are self-conscious about being naked in front of a man." In contrast, he said,

> Thin women are more sexually aggressive and self-confident. I do worry that fat women I want to date and go to bed with will think that I only want to go out with them because they're going to be "easy"—but that doesn't apply to me at all. There are some guys who do go out with heavy women because they think they'll be "easy." But in my experience, that's a myth.

## CONCLUSION

A sizeable but unknown proportion of American men can be regarded as "fat admirers": They are sexually attracted to obese women, in part because these women are fat.

Independent of its medical causes or consequences, being overweight in America today is *stigmatizing*. Obesity is not merely unfashionable—it is considered deviant, a blemish of individual character. Heavy people are ostracized, humiliated,

made fun of, and discriminated against for their size. They have been described as the "last minority in America" toward whom prejudice may be expressed with impunity (Louderback, 1970). Children are reluctant to accept a fat child as a friend; adolescents keep more social distance between themselves and their fat peers than they do others of average weight; elite colleges discriminate against fat applicants; and job discrimination against the obese, which is routine, is justified by invoking insurance risks or impaired job performance. The unrelenting rejection on both the organizational and the interpersonal levels generally results in the internalization of stigma. Characteristically, fat people come to believe themselves to be an inferior form of humanity, deserving of society's contempt and scorn (Cahnman, 1968; Maddox, Back, & Liederman, 1968).

It is possible that in no other area of life is this rejection so powerful and pervasive as in the aesthetic and erotic sphere. Commercials advertising weight loss products to women claim that a thinner figure will induce one's husband to be more affectionate and more sexually turned on, or, if one is unmarried, will attract more romantic interest from a greater number of men. The men we interviewed violate this expectation. While the overwhelming majority of American men—and women—consider fat unsightly, for the FA it is the reverse. Since these men reject dominant aesthetic and erotic standards, they are regarded as deviant by the conventional members of society—and even by some fat women themselves.

For the FA, the stigma of obesity represents "guilt by association"—to be more specific, guilt by preference—or, in Goffman's (1963) terms, a "courtesy stigma" (pp. 28–30). Dating fat women attracts almost as much scorn (in addition to bewilderment) as being fat does. Consequently, the majority of FAs remain distinctly covert in their preference. Many refuse to escort their dates to a public place, don't admit their preference to friends, and may even keep a thin girlfriend on the side. They are, in short, *closet* FAs. The majority of completely "overt" FAs tend to be unconventional, inner-directed individualists. Some of the men we interviewed were exclusive FAs; others had a mild preference for fat women. And some were "middle-of-the-roaders" (they preferred chubby but not fat women), while others were "mountain men": They had a strong erotic desire for hugely obese women.

Fat is, as one observer has written, a "feminist issue" (Orbach, 1980). Unfortunately, Orbach's analysis is based on the assumption that fat women are physically unappealing to men—perhaps to all men—and this is why women become fat: to avoid becoming sex objects to men in a sexist society. None of the women we interviewed became fat to avoid the sexual attention of men; indeed, all expressed interest in that attention.

But fat *is* a feminist issue because women's physical desirability is judged to decline more precipitously for each pound above a specific ideal figure than is true of men. It is clear, then, that sexism is inherent in society's anti-fat prejudices because women are more strongly and frequently ostracized for being overweight. Standards of what a woman should look like are more exacting—and more weight-oriented—than is true for men. Women are forced to be more concerned with their body image than men are; a virtual obsession seems built into our culture's ideal women's body size. The stigma of obesity falls far more heavily on the shoulders of women. Although some—a few—of the women we interviewed came to see themselves as "big, beautiful women," most fat women have internalized this sense of stigma and see themselves as less worthy human beings overall than their "thin" sisters do. One indication of this: When Richard Troiden and I asked a sample of 150 gay men whether they would take a magical pill to make them straight, almost no one said "yes." (See Troiden, 1988.) But when Carol Sternhell (1981), a journalist, asked female NAAFA members "if they could swallow a 'thinness pill,'

most said they would—but only because being fat in our culture is so damned painful" (p. 15).

## REFERENCES

Braziel, J. E., & LeBesco, K. (Eds.). (2001). *Bodies out of bounds: Fatness and transgression*. Berkeley: University of California Press.

Cahnman, W. J. (1968, Summer). The stigma of obesity. *Sociological Quarterly, 9,* 283–299.

Foucault, M. (1978). *The history of sexuality, volume I: An introduction* (R. Hurley, Trans.). New York: Pantheon.

Gagnon, J. H. (2003). *An interpretation of desire: Essays in the study of sexuality.* Chicago: University of Chicago Press.

Goffman, E. (1963). *Stigma: Notes on the management of spoiled identity.* Englewood Cliffs, NJ: Prentice Hall/Spectrum.

Goode, E., & Preissler, J. (1983, January–March). The fat admirer. *Deviant Behavior, 4,* 175–202.

Greenberg, D. F. (1988). *The construction of homosexuality.* Chicago: University of Chicago Press.

Louderback, L. (1970). *Fat power: Whatever you weigh is right.* New York: Hawthorn Books.

Maddox, G. L., Back, K. W., & Liederman, V. (1968, December). Overweight as social deviance and disability. *Journal of Health and Social Behavior, 9,* 287–298.

Millman, M. (1980). *Such a pretty face: Being fat in America.* New York: Norton.

Orbach, S. (1980). *Fat is a feminist issue.* New York: Berkley.

Polivy, J., Garner, D. M., & Garfinkel, P. E. (1986). Causes and consequences of the current preference for thin female physiques. In C. P. Herman, M. P. Zanna, & E. T. Higgins (Eds.), *Physical appearance, stigma, and social behavior* (pp. 89–112). Hillsdale, NJ: Lawrence Erlbaum.

Sternhell, C. (1981, October 6). Big girls don't cry. *The Soho News,* pp. 14–15.

Stoller, R. J. (1979). *Sexual excitement: Dynamics of erotic life.* New York: Simon & Schuster/Touchstone.

Troiden, R. R. (1988). *Gay and lesbian identity: A sociological analysis.* Dix Hills, NY: General Hall.

# Living in an Extremely Deviant Body

## *A Personal Account Contributed by "Sally" and "Diane"*

Sally, a manager of a small business office, is married and in her early forties. She is emotionally estranged from her husband, and they have no children. She weighs 385 pounds and is distinctly bottom-heavy. Diane manages a retail store, is in her thirties, and is divorced with one child. She weighs about 250 pounds. Most average-sized people would use the stereotypical phrase "such a pretty face" (Millman, 1980) to describe their appearance. Sally and Diane are members of NAAFA—the National Association to Advance Fat Acceptance. For NAAFA's members, the term "fat" is descriptive, not pejorative. They reason that fat people have an abundance of fat, and there's nothing wrong with fat. NAAFA, ostensibly a civil rights organization dedicated to fighting discrimination against fat people, is, for most of its members, a kind of "love boat" for fat women and their male admirers. Referred to as "fat admirers" or FAs, these men, mainly of average size, are erotically and romantically attracted to heavy women. The organization's main purpose is to facilitate liaisons between these two symbiotically connected social categories.

"Let me tell you about something that happened just the other night," Diane tells me.

It illustrates what I'm talking about. Sally and I were standing outside the American Legion hall during a NAAFA dance. We were taking a break, getting some fresh air, gossiping about people we know, things that had happened to us. There were several other NAAFA women there, Betsy and a couple of her friends, standing near us. And Sally and I were engaged in deep conversation. Well, a van full of kids—they weren't kids, they were men in their twenties, and one young woman—drove by and stopped at a light. They started to *howl*. They went "*Hee-hee-hee-hee-haw-haw-haw-haw!*" They laughed and pointed, and yelled things at us, as if we were *pigs*, animals without feelings, just like we were the *elephant man* standing there, a *freak* to be made fun of without restraint. I think that if they had a *squirt* gun or a *fire*cracker or something to *throw*, they would have *thrown* it at us. People I've never seen before pulled up in traffic and started *screaming* at us. The other fat people who were outside on the sidewalk near us, I looked at them and thought they were all going to start *crying*. They were all, it just so happened to be, a bunch of soft, Betsy-type women standing out there.

Diane pauses to formulate how she should relate this experience.

So, Sally and I turned around and began *yelling* really, really *nasty* things at these young men in the van. I yelled—excuse my English—*You ugly, fucking son-of-a-bitch! Shut your ugly, ignorant, fucking mouth, you ill-mannered bastard! Look at your face, you're as ugly as shit! Shut your mouth or I'll have you arrested for being ugly! Get out of your truck, you ugly son-of-a-bitch and come on over here!* I tore into them! I completely went wild! But *Sally* went wild also. We were *screaming* at them. "You're dumb and ugly; only a dumb, stupid son-of-a-bitch would open your mouth like that. Look at your face, you're so goddamn ugly and dumb! Your mother should have used birth control!" I mean, I *really* went wild. Both of us did. Well, dead silence. The truck went dead silent. They sat there and stared at us, *stone*-faced. How *dare* we—pigs, their whipping dogs—turn around and yell something like that back at them? And it just so happened two were very ugly. How *dare* I mention that? And so I yelled, "You with the big nose! You keep your goddamn mouth shut!" We screamed at these people horribly, like we were screaming at a pack of dogs to run away from us, leave us alone! They just fell silent. One started giggling again. They were made very uncomfortable by our aggressive reaction. They never anticipated it. Nobody would have believed that we had that in us. The people in the cars around took all this in. And it was *dead silent*. The light changed and they just left.

All right, I yelled something really coarse. Whether I was right or wrong, I can't say. The point is, I couldn't stand it another minute. I am a success, I am bright, I am attractive. I *will not* be yelled at and insulted like that. You yell at me, I'm going to scream at you. So help me, they're lucky I didn't blow their fuckin' brains out, that's how furious I was. I would have struck 'em if I could have gotten over the cars in between me and them. All I could see when they started this was, all these people at the NAAFA dance, they have to run and go to this secret hall, slinking around, hidden away from society, just so they can have a *dance*, just so they can relax and have a good time. So, these people at the dance, they *hurt*, they were yelled at, insulted, they were being hurt by a bunch of ignorant *shitheads!* I tell you, if I had had my gun in my hand, I would have at least blown out their tires. I will start doing push-ups again to build up my arms so I can knock the mouth off of anybody who ever does it to me again. I *refuse*. I can't stand silent any longer. Not everyone in that dance hall was strong enough to defend themselves or was willing to take the risk of defending themselves. And I'm sure that my destiny is to do it for them. But I won't take it any more. I'm mad as hell! [Laughs]

Diane [she is not in Sally's presence]: No matter where Sally goes, she is stared at. She is stared at as a freak so often that I guess, out of survival, she chooses not to notice it. Sally's attitude is—and of course, she doesn't believe it, but she uses it, 'cuz what else has she got?—she says the reason why they stare at her is because they've never seen a big

woman as beautiful as she is. If you see Sally, with her filthy, greasy, orange hair and a horrible sun dress on, no stockings and no bra, and every bit of her shaking, walking along with those huge, enormous hips and those fat legs—what are you going to think? I have seen people turn around and just openly *stare* at her, and it certainly isn't because she's the most beautiful woman you have ever seen. She chooses to ignore this, but it's impossible to ignore. I've been with her so many times when people are just *staring* at her. And she blocks it out. It's a survival technique. If she doesn't do it, she will *crack*. I mean, you can't *stand* being treated like a *freak* the way she is. Every time you went some place, if you were stared at like a freak, you would *break*. So she has built walls. She completely ignores it. And if somebody is nice to her, immediately she figures it's because they think she's so beautiful and they want to sleep with her. I mean, even just common courtesy is twisted and turned by Sally. It's absolutely *heartbreaking*.

Being with Sally in public is a unique experience because I cannot get over society. You know. . . , people do not often stare at me. I mean, they may look at me and notice that I'm a fat woman, or look me up and down once or twice. But it's no big thing, there are *many* people my size. Until you go with Sally, you cannot understand the *amount* of *cruelty* and *hostility* towards her simply because of her size. I *cannot* understand, in society, why someone would just stand and *stare* at someone because they are different. I do not stare at cripples, I do not stare at somebody because maybe they have one arm, because I have compassion in my soul. If I can do this and many people I know can be that way. . . , why are there so many people—I mean, this is my own confusion—why are so many people so cruel that they just stand there and *stare* at these large women—and men, of course. But when I've been with Sally, people *go out of their way*, they punch each other on the arm and say, get a load of *that* woman, and they stare at her, they'll turn around and do triple-takes, they burst out laughing, *loudly*, so she can hear it, they *want* her to know that they are looking at her and not approving. *That* is the thing I want to put my finger on.

What is it with society that when they see somebody like a Sally that they have to make a gesture or a remark or cause an incident so that their disapproval is *recognized*? Why can't they just look at her and maybe think to themselves, "I'm glad I'm not like that," or, "Boy, that one is big"? Why does there have to be a forced *recognition* that they don't like her which causes her such *enormous pain* that the woman has become bitter, suicidal, terribly sad, and overpowering with people she is involved with? *Why* is it? Is it the need to have somebody to be better than? Is it the need to have somebody to beat down? A whipping dog? What is that *terrible need* in society to pick on fat people? It's unbelievable. And the *effect* on the person who *gets* this reaction is devastating. I just don't know what to say.

Sally had an experience recently. It was a good one. She went into a bakery to buy some bread. And the girls in the bakery laughed out loud at her and were pokin' each other and lookin' at her and being really *rude*. And so Sally walked over—waddled over—to the counter and said, "Excuse me, but which would you rather be—fat or stupid?" And the girl behind the counter says, "Stupid." And Sally says, "Congratulations, you got your wish." Those girls behind the counter were struck *silent*. They were *stunned* that *she*, a lowlife, a second-class citizen, would have had the *nerve* not to take their harassment. They just didn't know what to say. I wonder what it is in society people have this feeling that fat people are *subhuman*. And when a fat person sticks up for themselves they are *so* stunned that they don't know how to deal with it.

This is true even of the family. You would think the family would be like a refuge, a place where you are loved and protected. But what does a fat person do when their family members are just as cruel as people on the outside? It happens to us all the time. I mean, when Sally tells the story about how her brother used to have friends over and she would be *locked* in her room; can you imagine how her self-esteem would suffer? I mean, the woman *has* no self-esteem. She feels little better than *slime*. It's so sad. There's no way in hell anybody will ever convince me that being fat deserves *that* type of treatment. There's something very wrong here. I mean, would

she be locked in her room if she was six foot four? Or four feet tall? Or really ugly? Or walked with a limp? What is it about being fat that causes people to treat her that way? I just don't understand it.

This isn't just Sally. [All the other members of NAAFA]—all of them have had serious, *serious* breaks with their families, *entirely* on the basis of their fatness. Beverly's . . . mother has, like, *disowned* her because she won't lose weight and, you know, hasn't straightened up. [She] does not deserve to be disowned. That is an absolutely stunningly *beautiful* girl. That's pure insanity. Susan's parents refuse to talk to her any more because she's so fat. They completely broke ties with her. She tried to call her father on Father's Day and he just hung up on her. He doesn't even want to bother with her any more because she's just too fat. And the reason for this break is that, previously, at Christmas, her parents were absolutely harassing her. "How can you *live* with yourself? You're so fat! *Do* something about it! You're disgusting!" In front of the whole family, her parents went on and on about this to Susan. And her husband stood up for her, but her parents were so disgusted that it turned into a big family row, and they broke off with her about it. There isn't any family relationship any more.

Beverly's family broke up with her because of her weight, Susan's family refuses to talk to her, Evie's . . . father would just torture her daily about dieting. Her mother did not want her at the same dinner table with them. She made her eat an hour earlier than the rest of the family because they were so revolted seeing her at dinner. Three Thanksgivings ago, Evie's family went to a restaurant and the father ordered the turkey dinner for the whole family, and he ordered a *broiled fish platter* for Evie. And no dessert, just the fruit cup appetizer. Since then, her family has had a complete break with her. Eve. . . . comes from a family that constantly harasses her about her weight. Her brother, whom she loves dearly and was very close with, is getting married. She has two brothers and two sisters. Every single other brother and sister was asked to be in the wedding party with the single exception of Eve. They wouldn't *allow* her to be in the wedding party because she's *fat*. This is a girl who's a professional *model*, with a professional modeling agency in the City, and she's rejected from some little *shithead*'s wedding because of her *size?* It broke her heart. It's such a horrible life to lead, this being fat. I just can't understand how society can punish fat people the way it does. I especially don't understand why family members do it to their own. . . .

There are no photographs, no pictures of Betsy in her parents' home because she's *fat*. We took a bunch of pictures of her at one of the NAAFA events and some of them look *lovely*. And Sally said to Betsy, now get these [pictures] developed—you know how Sally is—and get this one framed, put it in your house. And Betsy said, "I can't, my parents refuse to allow pictures in the house because I'm *fat*." Not only do they reject her fatness, they are rejecting that she even *exists*. She's not even allowed to have a photograph of herself around the house. Also, her father doesn't allow her to wear a dress or shorts in front of her brothers-in-law because they would see her legs and be so *revolted* that they wouldn't come back into the house. So she's paranoid even about putting on a dress, this poor woman, because if someone sees her legs, God would strike them dead, 'cuz she's so disgusting, you know, looking at her legs is *sudden death*. [Laughs] So I said to Betsy, well, that's ridiculous, how do your brothers-in-law feel about that? So she said, well, my one brother-in-law took me aside and said, well, your father's crazy about this fat thing, I think your legs are great, don't worry about it, you wear whatever you want around me. But her *other* brother-in-law is married to her very thin, *thin* sister and he *does not* want to look at Betsy. All he does is constantly *harass* his wife not to eat. If she picks up something, he says to her, put that down, you don't need this, you don't need that, he's made her *terrified* that she would get fat like Betsy. . . .

Diane's interview with Sally, conducted several days after she tape-recorded the above statement, illustrates many of the principles that run throughout this book.

*Sally:*    I think NAAFA is a very good organization. I think it's kind of like going to church. It gives you support and self-esteem. It gives you a place to let your hair down and be yourself and not have to put on airs and not have to be something that you're not. And it gives you a chance to be beautiful. Away from the maddening crowd.

*Diane:*    What is your overall opinion or assessment of the FAs that attend NAAFA activities?

*Sally:*    Well, I think that it's just like any place else, whether in the straight world or the gay world or whatever. It has its good and its bad. I've met some very nice FAs and I've met some jerks. But you meet those in everyday life, too.

*Diane:*    How would you describe the way that FAs act at a NAAFA activity?

*Sally:*    It goes to the last question. Some act like normal human beings and some are very comfortable with the situation. And some don't really know where they are or who they are. Some of them are just as bad off as some of the fat women who don't have any self-esteem. I've met men in NAAFA who have no self-esteem at all. I think some of them are worse than the women as far as self-esteem is concerned.

*Diane:*    Can you give me an example of that?

*Sally:*    Well, you get men that, you know, they see you and they want to take you out and they wait—I've had men call me up two weeks after a dance and say to me, gee, I met you at the dance, I'd love to take you out, well, I reply, why didn't you ask me at the dance? They say, I didn't ask you at the dance 'cuz I didn't think you'd want to bother with me.

*Diane:*    Pitiful.

*Sally:*    Sure it is. That's what I'm talking about, the self-esteem. There's such a lack of self-esteem in a lot of these men. I think a lot of men get hooked up in NAAFA not really because they're so enamored with fat women but because they think that fat women are hard up and an easy mark. It's easier to get a fat woman in bed than a thin woman because there's more competition for the thin woman. I mean, I'm not saying that this is true in all cases, but I'm sure that happens, you know.

*Diane:*   Is there anything different about the FA's conversation, compared with men who are not FAs?

*Sally:*   Oh, yeah, well, being with an FA is more comfortable. A lot of men who are not FAs are not as *comfortable* with the fact that you're fat. They're not as comfortable saying to you, gee, you're pretty. An FA who's together finds it very easy to say to a pretty fat woman, you're very pretty. A man who's what I call a "straight" man [a non-FA, a man who is attracted exclusively to thinner women], he finds it very *difficult* a lot of times to tell you you're pretty. Or he'll paraphrase it by saying, ah, gee, you have a pretty *face*. You know, not so much *you're* pretty. Whereas an FA looks at you and, to him, you're pretty *all over*. Whereas a straight man looks at you and says, you've got a pretty *face*. You know, that's basically the difference.

*Diane:*   What about the activities that an FA suggests for a date, are they any different from that of a non-FA?

*Sally:*   I don't think so. The only thing is that, with an FA, he's more aware of *seating*, you know, if you go into a restaurant, whether you can fit into a booth or a chair or go to the theater. Most FAs are more attuned to whether you can fit in a chair or he asks himself, do I want to take her there because she'd be comfortable? Whereas a straight guy, it never even *dawns* on him to think about something

like that, he would never even think about it. *You* have to tell *him* that.

*Diane:*   Do you think that FAs treat heavy women the way that most men treat women of average weight? Any differences you can think of at all?

*Sally:*   Well, I think, the only thing I can think of is that a lot of FAs treat women very badly sometimes. And I think a lot of men treat women on the outside very badly, too. I hear stories all the time about how thin women—even pretty thin women—get treated so badly by these guys.

*Diane:*   OK. How would the FA treat fat women badly?

*Sally:*   Well, some FAs will gravitate toward a fat woman mostly because he figures she's hard up, she's desperate, she'll do *anything in the world* to get herself a decent guy. I mean, I've heard stories that'll curl your hair.

*Diane:*   Like what? Give me a couple of examples.

*Sally:*   Well, I'll give you an example. I was going to a motel with somebody one night and he said to me, am I paying for the room or are you? And I said, well, if you're *not*, we're not going. I mean, that's how simple that was. But I'm sure there are plenty of fat women out there who would say, OK, I'll pay for the room. My belief is that a woman gets treated the way she expects to get treated. If she expects to get treated poorly, that's *exactly* how she's going to be treated. The guy's going to pick up on it and treat her whatever way she expects. He's going to treat her just as badly as she expects to be treated. I mean, if you have low self-esteem and you're out in the world, men are going to treat you rotten because they can feel it, they can pick up on it that you lack confidence. If you have a lot of confidence in yourself, *everybody's* going to treat you fairly decently. At least, that's what I've found to be true. My experience has been that as long as I have confidence in myself, mostly everybody treats me fairly good.

*Diane:* Do you believe that FAs have a stereotype of heavy women?

*Sally:* Well, it goes back to the same thing, they see us as needy and grateful. Some FAs have a lot of respect for fat women, but I think a lot of them have this stereotype. You can tell the type, you can look at an FA and tell by the type of a woman that he goes with. You find an FA who picks on the women who are sloppy and unkempt, who don't take care of themselves. You find a woman who looks good and who's attractive and keeps herself nice and you find an FA who gravitates toward them, he's an FA who respects a woman.

*Diane:* Do you think that one aspect of the stereotype is that heavier women are *easier* sexually than women of average size?

*Sally:* I think that's part of it. I've heard FAs say that: "The only reason I go for fat women is because they're easier. I don't really care for fat women, but they're easier to get."

*Diane:* Do you believe that most men hold this stereotype?

*Sally:* I would say it's about 50 percent. I mean, there are the men who just happen to prefer the fat body, you know, and they're together, but there are men who have their own problems who cannot function in a straight world. So they come into what they think is a *disabled* group of people. They're more comfortable because they don't have to knock themselves out, they don't have to *try* as hard to get a woman into bed, they can just be their own raunchy self and you know, not worry about it.

*Diane:* Do you think that most FAs are interested in dating heavier women pretty much solely for sexual reasons?

*Sally:* I would say a good 80 percent, yes. . . .

*Diane:* How do you think fat women feel about that?

*Sally:* I'm sure it depresses them, a lot of them. . . .

*Diane:* What is different about being in bed with an FA versus a non-FA?

*Sally:* When you're with an FA, he *appreciates* your body. When you're with a straight guy, he accepts it, but he's not overwhelmed. An FA's *preference*—I mean, that's like saying, well, I like a tall girl or a thin girl or a blonde girl, or I like a guy with blue eyes. Of course, if you find someone you're *particularly* interested in, you're going to enjoy it even more. It's a lot more *comfortable* to be in bed with an FA than it is with a straight guy, especially the first time. The first time going to bed with a straight guy is *really rough*. Because you don't know whether he's going to look at your body and be *repulsed* by it or turned *off* by it, or even be able to *function*. But with an FA, it's a *lot* more comfortable.

*Diane:* What is different generally about dating an FA versus dating a non-FA?

*Sally:* Well, it depends on the FA. Some FAs are very uncomfortable with fat women. They're OK in bed, but they don't want to be seen on the *street* with a fat woman. So, an FA who's confident and certain of himself, he doesn't really care about what other people or his peers think. It's very nice to be with an FA because he's proud of you. But you can't be with an FA who's just like a straight guy and doesn't want anybody to know he's dating a fat woman. . . .

*Diane:* Do you think that the quality of men who are interested in dating you would be any different if you were of average weight?

*Sally:* I would imagine if I weighed 120 pounds, I could go out with Prince Charming, sure. . . .

*Diane:* Do you feel reluctant to go to a public beach or a swimming pool in a bathing suit because of your weight?

*Sally:* Yeah.

*Diane:* If you did go onto a fairly crowded beach or a swimming pool in a bathing suit, do you think that most people's reaction would be different compared with if you were of average weight?

*Sally:* Oh, sure. I think they would be *amused* and I'm sure there would be plenty of heckling and making fun of me, nudging the buddy next door to take a look. . . .

*Diane:* When you see a slim model in a magazine advertisement or on TV, what are your feelings and thoughts? Do you think, "I wish I looked like that"?

*Sally:* No.

*Diane:* Have you ever experienced a stranger making a remark on your size in public?

*Sally:* Oh, sure.

*Diane:* Can you tell us about some of these experiences?

*Sally:* I just had one yesterday. Two little old ladies walked out of a restaurant and they went to get on the elevator in my office building and one saw me and she nudged the other one to turn around and look at me and I ran up behind her and said I'd

rather be *fat* than *old*. I've had many of those.

*Diane:* Have there been situations in which you felt that you were ignored or left out because of your weight?

*Sally:* Not so much in my adult life. As a teenager, yeah, sure. I'm sure every fat person has. Anybody who's different. You know, it's not only the fat kids. It's the *short* kids, or *super-tall* kids, or *black* kids—or whatever. All kids, anybody who's different. If you're not normal, so to speak, mainstream, not like everyone else, you're left out of a lot of things.

*Diane:* Have members of your family felt ashamed because of your weight?

*Sally:* Yeah, all of them. My brother hasn't talked to me for 27 years because of my weight, and my stepmother still doesn't talk to me today because of my weight. When my sister was in the hospital, my father wouldn't stay in the house alone because of my weight. He didn't want to be alone with me; he might *catch the fat*, you know, he was afraid. He would *never* introduce me as his daughter. I picked up some things for my stepmother, and my dad and my husband and I drove to her apartment and I said, "Daddy, let's drop these things off for her." So, when we got to the apartment, my stepmother was standing in the lobby, talking to a bunch of women. Well, when she saw me, she almost *died*. When my husband and I walked into the lobby, my stepmother introduced me and my husband to these women as Mr. and Mrs. Simon. Not as my *daughter,* but just Mr. and Mrs. Simon. And she says, "Go on upstairs." So we walk upstairs and my husband says, "Why didn't she introduce you as her daughter?" I said, "'Cause she doesn't want anybody to *know* that I'm her daughter."

*Diane:*  That's horrible. Have you had any direct personal experience with size discrimination by doctors?

*Sally:*  Sure. The ridicule. Once, I called up a doctor's office. A chiropractor. I said, "Do you take fat patients?" And he said, "What do you consider fat?" I said, "I weigh 350 pounds," and he laughed and said, "Of *course* not! There's *nothing* I can do with a 350-pound person!"

*Diane:*  You should have called up a professional association and complained.

*Sally:*  Who you gonna call? He's a chiropractor; he is not even a medical doctor.

*Diane:*  Yeah. They must have some kind of a professional association you can complain to. Jesus, that's terrible.

*Sally:*  It's like a dog pound, the animals, you know, that's the way we are treated.

*Diane:*  That's horrible. Hiring and promotion on the job? Have you ever experienced discrimination because of your weight on the job?

*Sally:*  Not promotion. I missed out on a good job one time—as a matter of fact, two good jobs—because I couldn't pass the physical 'cause of my weight.

*Diane:*  Just the weight?

*Sally:*  Just the weight. I passed everything else.
. . .

*Diane:*  If you could swallow a magic pill and wake up in the morning weighing 125 pounds, would you do it?

*Sally:*  I might. I don't know; that's something I'll really have to think about. I'm not sure.

*Diane:*  What do you think your ideal weight is?

*Sally:*  I'd like to be about 285. Between 285 and 300. About that magic pill, I say no. But if

you asked me whether I'd like to wake up weighing 160–180 pounds, yes; 125 pounds, I wouldn't *know* that body. I couldn't *relate* to it. If you start out at 125, it would be no time at all before you're 180.

*Diane:*  If you could take a magic pill that would *keep* you down to 125, would you do it?

*Sally:*  Oh, well, to *keep* you at 125, that's different, yeah. But if I were going to get down to 125, believe me, in three weeks' time, I'd be up to 180, so it really wouldn't make any difference.

*Diane:*  What do you think the reason is why you weigh more than average?

*Sally:*  Psychological. I think, basically, my problem is just bad childhood. My childhood was so bad that it changed my eating patterns, and as a child, I ate out of frustration, and that just stayed with me. And with the fat on, I could never get it off. The fat's *there*; it's not going to go anyplace. I think the weight's going to be there forever.

*Diane:*  Have you tried dieting or any weight loss programs?

*Sally:*  Yep. In Nassau Medical Center, I had the bypass surgery done and went on their 500-calorie-a-day diet. I went on the diet where you get injections of a pregnant woman's urine and you eat 500 calories a day, and that's supposed to make you lose weight.

*Diane:*  How'd you do?

*Sally:*  I didn't lose anything [chuckles]. I looked just like this. [They both laugh.] The bypass, I lost 150 pounds, which I put right back on. And the *pills,* which I got from a pill doctor, I lost 225 pounds, which I put back on.

*Diane:*  What are your feelings about these weight loss programs?

*Sally:*  I think it's worse to lose weight and gain weight and lose weight and gain weight than to stay at the same weight. I think it'd be nice to be at a particular weight and to be able to *stay* there. I mean, whether it's 350, 250, or 150, or whatever. I think it would be nice just to be able to *stay* at that weight without having to worry about gaining. . . .

*Diane:*  Were you heavy as a child?

*Sally:*  I weighed over 400 pounds when I was 14 years old.

*Diane:*  Growing up, what was the reaction of your parents to your weight?

*Sally:*  Bad. My father used to buy cake and ice cream every day and then make fun of me if I ate it. But I ate it anyway. I was so used to him making fun of me, it didn't make any difference. My brother always made fun of me. He wouldn't bring his friends in the house because of me. He used to tell my father to lock me in my bedroom or he wouldn't bring his friends in the house.

*Diane:*  They didn't lock you in your bedroom.

*Sally:*  Yes, they did.

*Diane:*  They locked you in your bedroom so your brother could have his friends in the house?

*Sally:*  Yes, that's right.

*Diane:*  What did you do in there?

*Sally:*  Played, sewed, read comic books. Whatever.

*Diane:*  Oh, my God.

*Sally:*  I knew that was my place.

*Diane:*  How old were you when this was going on?

*Sally:*  Till the time I was about 16 years old. Once, I jumped off my balcony.

*Diane:*  Did you? Good for you!

*Sally:*  But I got the *shit* beat out of me for doing it. [Chuckles.]

*Diane:*  What did you think—you'd go in the room, now your brother can have his friends over?

*Sally:*  Don't come out until your brother's friends are gone.

*Diane:*  That's one of the most horrible things I've ever heard.

*Sally:*  Oh, that was *light* stuff. My father beat me every day of my life. From the time I was two years old till I was 17. Because I was fat.

*Diane:*  Well, what about your brother? Did he beat your brother? What about your little sister?

*Sally:*  No, no, no.

*Diane:*  Growing up, what was the reaction of your friends, your playmates, your schoolmates, to your weight?

*Sally:*  I didn't have too many friends growing up. I always had plenty of boyfriends, but I didn't have too many girlfriends.

*Diane:*  How about teachers?

*Sally:*  I had *one* nice teacher who really took pity on me. Because she knew the situation. Only one teacher that I can remember who was really nice to me.

*Diane:*  Did you feel different when you were in high school, or set apart?

*Sally:*  Sure. Just being *different* makes you different.

*Diane:*  Have you ever *refused* to date a man because he was too heavy?

*Sally:*  A couple of them. Maybe two.

*Diane:*  Do you feel that, for you, there's a point at which a man becomes too heavy to be desirable?

*Sally:*  Yes. That occurs at maybe 100 pounds over the average weight.

*Diane:*  Can you picture yourself in a long-term relationship with a very heavy man?

*Sally:*  No.

*Diane:*  Can you picture yourself married to a man over 100 pounds overweight?

*Sally:*  No.

## Reference

Millman, M. (1980). *Such a pretty face: Being fat in America.* New York: Norton.

## Discussion Questions

1. Deviance is an extremely broad umbrella, covering, as it does, a variety of forms and manifestations. How does obesity differ from other instances of deviance, such as extreme tattooing and homosexuality? Be specific and detailed. How does being an FA (fat admirer) differ from being obese? How would Erving Goffman conceptualize the FA?

2. All forms of deviance are accompanied by attempts to neutralize the stigma that accompanies them. How is obesity different from most other examples of deviance with respect to the success of this effort, and why?

3. What is it that the "thin" majority finds "morally reprehensible" about obesity? Why are the obese stigmatized and regarded as "not quite human"?

4. According to the authors, obesity straddles two different kinds of stigma. What are they and what makes obesity unique in this respect?

# PART 4

# BELIEVING IN WHITE SUPREMACY

# WHITE SUPREMACY AS DEVIANCE
## An Introduction

While leaders of racist movements—Matthew Hale and Tom Metzger are offered as examples here—reject the label "supremacy" and instead, they say, support racial "separatism," they do strongly believe in the natural superiority of whites and the inferiority of non-whites. They don't want to live in the same society with nonwhites because they regard them as their inferiors. And if these "inferiors" don't wish to abandon the society in which they live? Well, these leaders hint that terrible things will happen to them. Hence, in spite of their objections, the term "white supremacy" seems to us distinctly and almost uniquely applicable.

What makes white supremacy a form of deviance—of *extreme* deviance? There are at least two answers to this question. The first is that someone espousing such views would be rejected, condemned, denounced, and stigmatized by most (although, unhappily, not all) audiences nearly everywhere in the United States. And the second is that its ideology clashes with mainstream American values.

Try to picture a person such as Matthew Hale or Tom Metzger, whose articles follow, being hired as a public school teacher; being a professor at a mainstream college or university; as a physician or lawyer, attracting and holding a clientele; being a successful salesperson, executive, or office worker; or even simply getting along with his or her peers. The fact that Matthew Hale was excluded from the Illinois Bar Association because of his racist beliefs and his association with known supremacists—in spite of the fact that he holds a law degree from an accredited law school and he passed the Illinois bar exam—is one indication of the racist movement's deviant status. Expressing the views of extreme racists, in the form enunciated by leaders of white supremacist organizations, stirs up a scandal in practically all settings we might imagine. Such reactions constitute the very embodiment of deviance; they are one aspect of any definition of deviance.

Some observers might object, claiming that America is a "racist" society. As Kathleen Blee explains in her article, *some* aspects of white supremacist belief are simply an exaggerated version of beliefs held by a substantial proportion of the white majority. To turn the equation around, diluted forms of racism are common among American whites. So, what makes white supremacy deviant? Is this a matter of mere degree—that movement activists are simply *more* racist than the typical American white person? Or is there something qualitatively and distinctly different about the beliefs held by the members of white supremacist organizations?

White supremacist movements attempt to recruit members to their cause by invoking values that many whites support. Consider the fact that in the twenty-first century, Caucasians and persons of African descent are strongly demographically segregated in the United States and the fact that most Americans oppose any form of government intervention to change that segregation. Consider, too, that most whites oppose affirmative action—programs designed to redress systemic discrimination against minorities in college admissions and in employment. Over three-quarters of white respondents surveyed oppose preferential treatment for minorities in college admissions, and nine out of 10 oppose it in hiring and promotion (Schuman, Steeh, Bobo, & Krysan, 1997, pp. 174–175). Hence, affirmative action (commonly, and mistakenly, referred to as "reverse discrimination") is a "wedge" issue for racist movements when they appeal to whites. As Matthew Hale, active in the World Church of the Creator, claims when he talks to college students whom he wants to join his organization, blacks receive scholarships because of their race, and he knows many whites resent that.

Another issue of overlap between the white majority and white supremacist organizations is immigration. Many whites approve of restricting the flow of immigrants—particularly illegal aliens—into the United States (mainly from Latin America; most Americans do not object to illegal immigration from Canada or Europe). A Zogby poll found that two-thirds of Americans disagree with amnesty for illegal aliens. Six in 10 agreed with the statement the United States should "admit fewer immigrants each year." (Only 6% wanted more immigrants.) And two-thirds agreed with using military troops along the Mexican border to "curb illegal immigration." Hence, racist movements use this as a selling point to encourage potential members to join.

In spite of some parallels between the ideas of many whites and those of racist movements, the differences vastly outweigh the similarities. One clue to white supremacy's estrangement from the American mainstream is found in numbers. Rarity is not a *definition* of deviance—rare qualities aren't necessarily deviant—but it does *suggest* non-normativeness. No, it's not "deviant" to be a billionaire, but yes, most forms of deviance are, in the words of Edwin Lemert (1951), "differentiated behavior [and beliefs and characteristics] which at a given time and place [are] socially disapproved" (p. 22). Kathleen Blee, whose article follows, estimates that there are fewer than 50,000 "racist activists" in the United States, "with as many as 200,000 sympathizers." Moreover, these figures suggest sharp declines from the early twentieth century, when millions of Americans joined white supremacist organizations, including the Ku Klux Klan, and a decline, too, from the 1980s, when their numbers were several times higher than what they are today. If racist ideas are as appealing as the above parallels suggest, then why are so few Americans members of white supremacy organizations (see Image 4.1)? One answer is that the ideology of white supremacy is repugnant to the vast majority of white Americans. Here are a few of the tenets of today's racist organizations that clash almost violently with mainstream values.

*The Inherent Superiority of the White Race.* All white supremacists argue that whites are genetically superior to nonwhites, specifically persons of African descent. In this belief, the movement's supporters disagree—sharply and radically—from the white American mainstream. A minuscule percentage of the white population believes in the inherent or inborn superiority of the white race. In 1968, only 6% of whites surveyed said that inferiority in innate ability explained why blacks were less successful economically and educationally (cited in

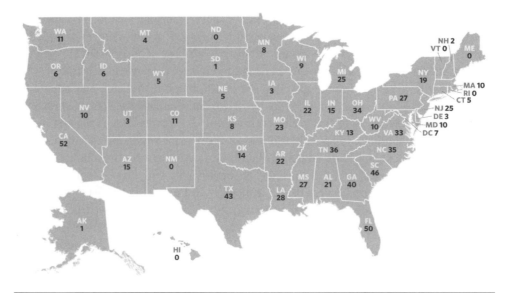

**Image 4.1**    Number of Active Hate Groups by State, 2005. Although racist and anti-Semitic hate groups are spread across nearly the entire United States, they tend to be more common, especially on a per-population basis, in some states than others. The overt expression of strongly racist views is non-normative, even though more subtle forms of prejudice and discrimination are widespread in America.

SOURCE: Southern Poverty Law Center.

Schuman et al., 1997, p. 153). Since that time, this position has become so rare among American whites that it is almost never included in public opinion polls. *The Bell Curve* argued that blacks were genetically inferior to whites (Herrnstein & Murray, 1994). Only a few scholars agreed with the book's position; the vast majority of researchers were unanimous in their denunciation of its claims.

"*Ethnic Cleansing.*" Like the German Nazis during World War II who advocated, and brutally attempted to implement, a *Judenrein* Germany (a Germany free of Jews), white supremacists argue that America should be completely white. Indeed, they believe the U.S. should be not only all-white, but free of Jews as well as Latin Americans and "race traitors" (whites who do not agree with them). The desire for a "pure" white population is so rare among the American public that public opinion polls do not even include a question on the issue. The percentage that supports the white supremacist's view is minuscule.

*Hostility Toward Race "Mixing."* One of the pillars of the white supremacist's ideology is that race "mixing"—mainly, but not exclusively, interracial dating and intermarriage—is the downfall of the white race. (This view does not address the issue of the slave owner's illicit sexual relations with his female slaves, which resulted in a substantial racially mixed African American population.) The majority of the American population disagrees. In a poll conducted by the Pew Research Center, over three-quarters of the respondents said that they agree with the statement "It's all right for blacks and whites to date each other." Among whites, this figure was over seven in 10; over nine in 10 blacks agreed. As recently as 1987, public opinion was more or less evenly split (48% agree, 46% disagree), indicating a substantial increase in the past 20 years in the acceptability of interracial dating and, presumably, marriage. In the past 30 years, the percentage of married couples made up of spouses of a different race has increased five times, again, indicating the growing legitimacy of intermarriage (*The Washington Post*, March 31, 2006, p. A2, based on U.S. Census figures). These statistics would be greeted by the white supremacist with horror.

*Extreme Anti-Semitism.* According to Kathleen Blee, while racist organizations in the past, such as the early Klan, were mainly concerned with persecuting African Americans, their principal contemporary enemy is Jews. American Jews have too much power and influence, white supremacists argue, and have led blacks around by the nose, encouraging them to make demands they otherwise would not have made. Hence, Jews are their main target rather than African Americans. Some white supremacists argue that Jews are not human beings but descendants of Satan. Most white supremacists also argue that anti-Semitism is the Jews' own fault because they "manipulate and control the finances, the government, and the laws of the people," to quote Matthew Hale. While white supremacy has become more directly hostile toward Jews, anti-Semitism among the American population has declined sharply and dramatically. (A survey conducted in 2002 by the Anti-Defamation League, "Anti-Semitism in America," indicated that American anti-Semitism has increased somewhat since the 1990s.) For instance, between 90% and 95% of respondents to polls taken in recent years say that they would vote for a Jewish candidate for president—a position that white supremacists find repugnant.

*Sympathy for German Nazism.* White supremacists often cite the Third Reich as an example of a regime to be emulated; Hitler's *Mein Kampf* is frequently mentioned as a book that stimulated them to become white supremacists and from which they draw ideological inspiration. Most supporters of white supremacy regard historical accounts of the Holocaust as exaggerated or a hoax and downplay Jewish deaths as being the result of conditions that befell everyone during wartime (see Image 4.2). In sharp contrast, most Americans regard German Nazism with hostility, view the Holocaust as a tragic historical event, and cannot disassociate the Third Reich from Allied deaths during the Second World War.

*Sympathy for Violence Against Enemies of the White Race in the "Race War."* As Matthew Hale argues, white supremacists believe that the white race is being "raped, pillaged around the world, and we therefore hate those who are engaging in this." The recent successes of African Americans, and the historical successes of the Jews, have been obtained at the expense of whites, these ideologues claim. What blacks, Jews, "and other races" want is supremacy, not equality. Nonwhite races (including Jews) are the "biological enemies" of whites, just as a shark is the enemy of a human swimming in the ocean. This calls for geographical and national separation or retaliation in kind; if we don't fight back, "our race will become extinct." Neither Hale nor Metzger specify exactly what violent behavior supporters of white racism should resort to,

**Image 4.2**    Cover of *Intelligence Report,* Spring, 2006. White supremacists argue that Jews, persons of African descent, and Latino immigrants should be excluded from the United States—or, at the very least, segregated from white Christians in a few states of their own. Most white supremacist groups take their inspiration from German Nazism and accept violence as a means of advancing their goals.

SOURCE: Kevin Scanlon, Photographer.

but both have incited or expressed sympathetic views on specific violent acts against Jews and nonwhites. The vast majority of Americans reject racist-inspired violence and its basis; most would regard Hale and Metzger's analysis of racial warfare as deranged.

Why look at extreme racism in a deviance course? In a nutshell, because we learn the lesson that it is possible for mainstream cultural values and behavior, if pushed to their logical extreme, to become transformed from conventional to deviant. As we saw, a substantial proportion of American whites feel uneasy about taking steps toward full racial and ethnic equality. But this is a long way from saying that racism is a mainstream American value, and even further from accepting the view that most Americans are sympathetic to the white supremacist's methods and goals. White supremacy, as it is expressed by movement organizations such as the Ku Klux Klan (KKK), Christian Identity, World Church of the Creator, militant skinheads, and Idaho militias, is anathema to the vast majority of Americans. The constellation of supremacists' beliefs, as spelled out above, sets them apart from the American mainstream and marks them off as deviant—*extremely* deviant (see Image 4.3).

**Image 4.3**   Most Americans would view a man whose body is covered with racist and anti-Semitic tattoos with alarm. They would agree that he is an "extreme" deviant and would be unwilling to interact with him in the usual manner.

SOURCE: Southern Poverty Law Center.

The example of white supremacy teaches us that determining what's deviant is not a mere academic exercise but a real-world, blood-and-guts struggle with how an activity, a belief, or a condition fits into a society's cultural and interactional mix. It is about what real people do when confronted with what they don't like. And as it is constituted, the vast majority of Americans most decidedly *don't like* the values, the goals, and the methods of white supremacy; it is, in short, a form of extreme deviance.

One last point. As we emphasized earlier, nearly 30 years ago, David Matza (1969) argued that in order to *understand* deviance, we must *appreciate* it (pp. 15–40). Like most academics, taken as a whole, sociologists detest racism and find nearly all of the views expressed by white supremacists repugnant. It strains the concept of appreciation nearly to the breaking point to say that Matthew Hale's and Tom Metzger's ideology must be appreciated. It is no contradiction to say that to understand these views, one must adopt a relativistic and value-neutral stance *and* to say that, personally, we abhor such views. Giving a soap box to Hale and Metzger does not represent an endorsement of what they say. Indeed, reading their statements is a lot more likely to turn the reader away from their views than toward them. Still, these views are social and cultural products, however extreme and distorted, of our society; they reflect a social place in that society, and they represent an attempt to socially construct the racial situation in a certain way. Mere denunciation of white supremacy will not stamp it out, but a thorough understanding of it necessitates understanding where its advocates are coming from, and this task, however repellent, demands getting inside the mind of its advocates.

## REFERENCES

Herrnstein, R. J., & Murray, C. (1994). *The bell curve: Intelligence and class structure in American life.* New York: Basic Books.

Lemert, E. M. (1951). *Social pathology: A systematic approach to the theory of sociopathic behavior.* New York: McGraw-Hill.

Matza, D. (1969). *Becoming deviant.* Englewood Cliffs, NJ: Prentice Hall.

Schuman, H., Steeh, C., Bobo, L., & Krysan, M. (1997). *Racial attitudes in America: Trends and interpretations* (Rev. ed.). Cambridge, MA: Harvard University Press.

# White Supremacy as Extreme Deviance

### *Kathleen M. Blee*

The statements that follow this article, by Tom Metzger and Matthew Hale—self-proclaimed leaders of high-profile racist groups—give a glimpse into the extremist ideologies that exist in the contemporary U.S. white supremacist movement. In his statement, "What We Believe as White Racists," Metzger fuses racist and anti-Semitic beliefs and hostility to nonwhite anti-immigrants with an attack on the military and the economic system of capitalism in order to create what he describes as a "Third Position" for the modern white racialist movement. The Third Position blends ideological principles from World War II-era German Nazism, in particular support for a white working class understood to be facing economic destruction from corporate power and monopoly capitalism and obsessive attention to purported Jewish conspiracies, with standard white supremacist philosophies that are broadly shared by a number of organized white supremacist groups in the United States today. These

include Metzger's emphasis on racial separatism (an attempt to suggest that the Third Position is not a racial supremacist movement) and his insistence that white "race suicide" will be the inevitable effect of higher birth rates among nonwhites than whites.

Metzger's extensive diatribe against organized religion and the U.S. government is particularly noteworthy because it represents a distinct shift in white supremacist beliefs today as compared to the past. For most of U.S. history, racist movements were fervently nationalistic, exemplified in the self-characterization of earlier Ku Klux Klans as "100% American." Earlier racist movements were also generally vocal in their support for mainstream Protestant religions, which they regarded as under attack from the corrupt theologies and politics of Catholicism, Judaism, and atheism. Rituals of cross burning and depictions of the "fiery cross," for example, have long been used by the Ku Klux Klan to equate itself with the principle of militant Protestantism. Today, however, many racist groups have revised their views on Christianity and patriotism and regard both Protestantism and the U.S. federal government as irredeemably tainted by the influence of Jews, Israel, and Judaism. (Racist groups generally distinguish between federal and lower levels of government, the latter considered to be less likely to be under the control of Jewish influences.) They term the U.S. government as a "Zionist Occupied Government" (ZOG) and denounce all organized Christianity as a tool of Zionist interests.

In his interview, Matthew Hale reveals a philosophy similar in many aspects to that espoused by Tom Metzger, especially the disparagement of Christianity and nationalism ("We do not pay homage to Christianity or to the Constitution or even to America") and antipathy toward Jews and nonwhites. Like Metzger, Hale claims to promote racial separatism rather than white supremacy, although this is belied by his assertion that whites are genetically destined to be the elite race. One aspect of Hale's discussion is particularly significant: his reversal of the roles of racial victim and perpetrator (Berbrier, 2000). Although he acknowledges that Jews have been persecuted historically, Hale argues that this is the result of actions taken by Jews themselves. Jews, Hale insists, practice a "religion [that] is extremely hostile to those not Jewish" and "have made themselves disliked" by working "to manipulate and control the finances, the government, the laws." Hale's arguments are fairly typical of a broad range of activists in modern white supremacy who assert that their anti-Semitic beliefs are no more than a reasonable response to Jewish hostility, aggression, and domination of the major institutions of modern society.

Metzger and Hale rose to public prominence as racist spokesmen after traveling through a number of different racist and right-wing groups. Metzger was a member of the ultra-conservative John Birch Society in the 1950s before moving into racist extremism. He served as Grand Dragon of the Knights of the Ku Klux Klan, flirted with electoral politics with a run for U.S. Senate from California, and was involved in the White American Political Association before founding a viciously racist and anti-Semitic group he named "White Aryan Resistance" (WAR). Although never a large group, WAR has garnered attention in the white supremacist movement as well as from the mainstream media for its tactical innovations. Foremost, WAR has been adept at using media outlets to promote Metzger's racist ideas to the public. WAR's newspaper and, later, Internet Web sites stand out as extreme, even among racist groups, for their explicit and highly violent racist and anti-Semitic caricatures, jokes, commentaries, and cartoons. In addition to these conventional forms of media, Metzger has experimented with new ways to reach an audience. He has distributed online videogames that feature attacks on racial minorities and Jews, such as "Nazi Duck Hunt"; "Shoot the Blacks"; and "Kaboom," a game in which players control a suicide bomber that they try to position as close to as many Jews as possible before detonating the explosives. Through WAR, he also has produced *Race and Reason,* a series of television shows modeled after late-night interview programs, which he was able to market successfully to cable public-access stations in a number of locations around the United States.

Metzger also gained prominence as a racist leader because of his advocacy of two structural changes. The first is commonly termed "leaderless resistance," an organizational strategy that has been adopted by much of the white supremacist movement. The strategy of leaderless resistance is based on the belief that organized racism has been hampered historically by its structure: As a network of public groups, white supremacists can relatively easily be identified, and then prosecuted, by law enforcement. Instead, Metzger argued, the racist movement could better evade surveillance if it was organized as small covert cells of highly committed activists connected to each other, if at all, only through their common reliance on Internet postings.

Metzger's second structural innovation was his insistence that the white supremacist movement will secure its long-term future by recruiting teenagers and young people. In particular, Metzger worked to create alliances between adult racist groups and the young neo-Nazi skinhead gangs who began to appear in the United States in the 1980s. His creation of WAR Youth and the Aryan Youth Movement were aspects of this agenda. Ultimately, this effort would prove to be Metzger's undoing. In 1990, he was ordered to pay a $12.5 million judgment for inciting the murder of Mulugeta Seraw, an Ethiopian student, by a Portland, Oregon skinhead gang with close connections to WAR. Metzger also has been active in the effort to recruit women to white supremacism. WAR-affiliated groups like Aryan Women's League (associated with Tom's daughter, Lynn) have created videos and Internet sites to broaden the appeal of organized racism to women.

Like Metzger, Matthew Hale drifted through various racist groups, including the National Association for the Advancement of White People (NAAWP), before discovering a small white supremacist religion called Church of the Creator that would make him famous. This group, later renamed the World Church of the Creator (WCOTC), proclaimed Hale its *pontifex maximus* or high priest and provided him a vehicle by which to distribute his views. The propaganda of WCOTC, full of hatred for Jews and nonwhites, is circulated through conventional means, generally by dropping pamphlets with titles like "Facts That the Government and the Media Don't Want You to Know" on driveways in white neighborhoods. The propaganda is also circulated on WCOTC Web sites and through its public access television shows. Like Metzger, Hale has worked to broaden the scope and tactics of organized racism, particularly by recruiting young men to the cause of racist extremism. Hale has also been active in trying to appeal to women through his affiliated Sisterhood of the WCOTC and Women's Frontier. Although WCOTC claims to have chapters

in a number of places in the United States, it is unclear whether even the largest WCOTC chapters contain more than a handful of members.

There is another similarity between the racist careers of Tom Metzger and Matthew Hale: Both came to prominence through the violent actions of another racist activist. Just as Metzger's fame grew with his association with the Oregon skinhead murder, so, too, Hale became well-known to the public in the wake of the murderous rampage of Benjamin Smith, honored in 1998 as WCOTC's "Creator of the Year," who killed two people and wounded nine in a 1999 multi-city shooting spree targeted at Jews and racial minorities (Anti-Defamation League of B'nai Brith, 2006).

## THE LANDSCAPE OF ORGANIZED RACISM

Matt Hale and Tom Metzger and their groups have received significant media attention as racist spokespersons, but they represent only one aspect of organized white supremacy today. To understand the broader landscape of extremist racism and how it intersects with and deviates from mainstream beliefs and ideologies, it is necessary also to look at other racist leaders and organizations (Dobratz & Shanks-Meile, 1997; Potok, 2004).

The U.S. white supremacist movement today encompasses a variety of groups that pursue similar agendas of white racial superiority; increasingly, these groups target Jews as the principal enemy and consider nonwhites offensive and dangerous, but ultimately manipulated by Jewish overlords. Despite its ideological commonalities, white supremacy is splintered into different factions that compete for members, resources, and media attention. There are four kinds of racist groups, of which the Ku Klux Klan, the neo-Nazis, the white power skinheads, and the white supremacist edge of patriot movements are the most active.

The Ku Klux Klan is the oldest and most widely recognized group of white supremacists in the

United States, tracing its roots to the loosely organized confederation of white rural men who inflicted savage violence on African Americans, Northerners, and their supporters in the former states of the Confederacy in the immediate aftermath of the Civil War. Although modern Klan leaders work to portray the KKK as having been in continual operation since the 1870s, the Klan is actually historically discontinuous, with waves of activity arising and then collapsing in the 1870s, 1920s, 1950s, and 1980s. Ideologically, the Klan is the most traditional major racist group today, with about 100 Klan chapters promoting America-first and xenophobic agendas, like restrictions on immigration. Today, the Klan is in serious disarray, with a scattering of often-antagonistic chapters, relatively few members (no more than several thousand) or new recruits, and little success in expanding its base beyond lower-middle- and lower-class white Southern rural men and women.

A more vigorous segment of U.S. white supremacy is the various neo-Nazi groups that take their ideological inspiration from resurgent Nazi and fascist movements in Europe and the former Soviet Union. These often advocate acts of cataclysmic violence to destroy Jews and others under the control of Jews, like the U.S. federal government, the United Nations, major national and international media, and the U.S. judiciary. Although there are substantial differences in structure and actions among neo-Nazi groups, many are actively recruiting women and youths and, as a result, are growing or stable in size while other aspects of organized white supremacy decline. Structurally different, but sharing some ideological features with neo-Nazis, are Holocaust-denying groups, which style themselves as scholarly associations and promote "revisionist" ideas about World War II through professional-appearing journals. These groups deny that Hitler made a deliberate effort to destroy European Jewry, arguing instead that the number of Jewish casualties was exaggerated to secure the postwar political interests of Israel or gain reparations for diasporic European Jews and that, in fact, the number of Jewish deaths was small and primarily the result of normal wartime deprivations.

Ideologically close to neo-Nazi groups are racist skinhead groups, which have increased in membership somewhat in recent years. These generally recruit young adults and teenagers, often through white power music concerts and a racist skinhead subculture of partying and violence (Futrell & Simi, 2004). Although the fluidity of racist skinhead groups and the transience of their members makes estimates of size difficult, it is likely that several thousand youths may participate in racist skinhead gangs in a variety of states, under names like East Coast Hate Crew, Hammerskins, White Wolves, and Keystone State Skinheads (Anti-Defamation League of B'nai Brith, 2006; Blazak, 2001). Racist skinheads tend to favor street-level violence ranging from minor crimes to murder and organized terrorist attacks on synagogues and racial minority and homeless persons.

Finally, there are a scattering of hyper-nationalist militia and neo-Confederate groups that embrace tenets of racism and (often) anti-Semitism along with a militant patriotism and support for paramilitary action by concerned white citizens (Aho, 1990; Gallaher, 2003). Generally concentrated in Southern and Western states, these try to organize whites against what they perceive as attacks on their positions and privileges through the immigration of nonwhites, government policies that promote nonwhites in the workplace and in education, and the endorsement of civil rights agendas such as the adoption of Martin Luther King Day as an official government holiday. In the twenty-first century, militia groups have declined dramatically, although racist anti-immigrant groups appear to be growing (Southern Poverty Law Center, 2006).

In recent years, the distinctions among racist groups have blurred as leaders have tried to create alliances and forge a "Fifth Era" of U.S. racism and, increasingly, because of the widespread adoption of "Christian Identity" (CI) beliefs by members and leaders in many racist groups. Christian Identity cobbles together a variety of theological elements from Christianity, Judaism, and racism in a convoluted and distorted fashion, as, for example, in the claim that Aryans are the real lost tribe of Israel. There are several active versions of CI, but the most common form among racist activists includes the belief that white Aryans (i.e., whites who are not Jewish) are the only actual humans. Jews, they argue, are descendants of the serpent in the Garden of Eden (thus, literally children of the devil). Nonwhites are said to be descended from lesser races of beings that pre- ceded Adam and Eve or from animals and are thus better characterized as "mud people" than as human (Barkun, 1994). There are a handful of Christian Identity groups and sects (which they call "churches") across the United States, but CI's greater impact on the racist movement is through the propagation of its doctrines by Klan, Nazi, and white supremacist leaders. Indeed, it is common for racist leaders in a variety of groups now to denote themselves as CI "ministers."

The size of the racist movement is difficult to estimate because no groups maintain public mem- bership rosters, all wildly exaggerate their member- ship, and many operate underground or with great secrecy, but most knowledgeable observers estimate the number of committed racist activists at fewer than 50,000, with as many as 200,000 sympathizers. This is a considerable number of people committed to an extremist racial agenda, but it represents a decline since the recent peak in the 1980s and a considerable reduction from the millions recruited into racist agendas in earlier decades of U.S. history.

## THE IDEAS OF ORGANIZED RACISM

The ideas and agendas of organized white supremacy are not simply more extreme versions of racist or anti-Semitic ideas and actions that could be found among mainstream whites. Rather, white supremacist groups inculcate their members with distinctive sets of beliefs and a particular form of reasoning in order to generate commit- ment to the dangerously violent agendas of white and Aryan supremacy (Ezekiel, 1995). Although racist groups differ somewhat, the general ideol- ogy of most organized white supremacy groups today includes a set of ideas, some surprising, about *race, Jews, gender, religion,* and *patriotism.*

Racist groups insist that human *races* are bio- logically and genetically distinct and organized in hierarchical fashion. White supremacists thus argue that nonwhite persons are inherently and definitively different from—and inferior to— whites in intellect, morality, industriousness, and overall human value. Racist groups have been able to convince their recruits that groups of people vary in their worth by race because such ideas overlap significantly with the beliefs that many ordinary U.S. whites continue to hold (Feagin, 2001), despite decades of scientific evidence that the actual distinctions among races are minimal, arbitrary, and culturally variable (Gould, 1996). With such an amenable foundation in the general white population, racist supremacists need only to *elaborate* ideas about nonwhite inferiority and threat that their recruits already hold and motivate them to activism in defense of the white race. Despite considerable similarity between the ideas of race held by racial extremists and those of many ordinary whites in the United States, however, there is also one area in which they sharply diverge. Mainstream whites generally pay little attention to whiteness as a racial category, separat- ing, instead, all whites from various categories of nonwhites (Frankenberg, 1993; Ignatiev, 1996). White supremacists, in contrast, distinguish care- fully among whites, separating those who they consider to be "true whites" (i.e., those who advo- cate racial separation and the superiority of the white race) from "race traitors" or "apathetic whites," who permit erosion of white privileges by their support for or lack of action against the agendas of nonwhites (Blee, 2002).

*Jews*, who have long been a target of racist groups in the United States and elsewhere, are now considered the primary enemy by many of today's white supremacist groups, in large part because of the increasing ties between U.S. racists and Nazi groups in Europe and elsewhere and the influence of the deeply anti-Semitic philosophies of Christian Identity. Yet, the widespread adoption of an ideology based on the obsessive hatred of Jews by U.S. white supremacists—including young recruits—also is perplexing because over time, anti-Semitic attitudes have declined significantly in the U.S. population at large (Dinnerstein, 1994). Moreover, World War II-era German Nazism is widely deplored in the United States because it is associated with an enemy government and tremendous loss of lives in the Holocaust and the War. Thus, there is no platform for the obsessive anti-Semitism of white supremacy that is comparable to the way racist beliefs of mainstream whites make possible the virulent racism of white supremacist groups. To create the toxic anti-Semitism that is characteristic of white supremacist groups today, racist leaders thus need to *transform*, rather than—as in the case of race—simply elaborate the pre-existing ideas of their recruits. They do so by invoking conspiracy theories, teaching their recruits that Jewish control of the international economy, world politics, and even day-to-day life of non-Jews is both complete and carefully hidden. Appearance, white supremacists insist, is deceiving; it is only racist groups, recruits are instructed, that have managed to pierce the veil of misunderstanding and expose the reality of Jewish control. Such conspiratorial logic is difficult to counter because the absence of evidence—in this case, evidence of Jewish manipulation of society—is regarded as evidence of the effectiveness of the conspirators' disguise (Blee, 2002; Brustein, 2003; Smith, 1996).

Few ideas in organized white supremacy have varied over time as much as those pertaining to *gender*, reflecting larger societal changes in what are considered appropriate roles for women and men. With the notable exception of the massive 1920s Ku Klux Klan, in which women constituted a significant and very active proportion of members (Blee, 1991), most U.S. white supremacist groups before 1980 regarded white women as *symbols* and *carriers* of the race rather than as potential racist activists. Images of white women victimized by racial minority male rapists or exploited by Jewish male business owners—a common message of propaganda by all racist groups—pointed to the need for white Aryan men to become involved in racist agendas while white women were encouraged to bear large numbers of white babies to preserve the numerical superiority of their race. Racist groups routinely denounced feminism and gender equality as an assault on the white race, insisting that efforts to create gender equality would necessarily undermine their efforts to sustain racial inequality. White women, they argued, should support male racist activists but should do so in the background (Ferber, 1998).

Since the 1980s, however, a new idea of gender has percolated into white supremacy, supplementing, although not replacing, the emphasis on white women as victims. This new view posits white women as potential race warriors, fighting for white privileges alongside their male comrades while retaining their role as racial mothers. A common image in this motif is that of a young, attractive white woman with a baby strapped on one side and an assault weapon on the other. This peculiar mixture of ideas about women and gender in white supremacy reflects the decision of many racist groups to allow women to join, both to strengthen the racialist movement and to lure the boyfriends, husbands, and children they assume will follow these women (Blee, 2002; Ferber, 2004). It also accounts for the great inconsistency in how white supremacist groups handle some issues of gender.

For example, Tom Metzger's group advocates abortion rights for nonwhite women while many racist groups oppose abortion for all women.

Racist groups have also changed considerably in their ideas about the role of *religion* in the white supremacist movement. Earlier, as we saw, most U.S. racist groups drew on symbols and beliefs of Protestantism, particularly conservative and evangelical Protestantism, to justify their support of white superiority as consistent with Christianity and to differentiate themselves from Catholicism and Judaism, which they regarded as inferior and dangerous religions. The long-time symbol of the Ku Klux Klan, for example, is the fiery cross, displayed as a patch on a Klan uniform and used in rituals by lashing logs together in the form of a cross and setting it ablaze; it is meant to invoke a sense that the Klan is enacting a Christian agenda (Blee, 1991). Today's racist leaders, as evidenced in the statements by Metzger and Hale, are less likely to embrace Christianity (Southern Poverty Law Center, 2000) and, indeed, often explicitly denounce organized Christian denominations as being under the sway of Judaism. Some white supremacist groups declare themselves to be atheistic; others style themselves as followers of racially interpreted pre-Christian religions like Odinism (Gardell, 2003), and most have some allegiance to the precepts of the deceptively titled theology of Christian Identity.

Finally, white supremacist groups increasingly reject the *patriotism* that is a widely held value among mainstream Americans, in favor of what they term a "pan-Aryanism" or worldwide Aryan supremacy. Although twentieth-century racist movements have generally cloaked themselves in the garb of nationalism and patriotism, claiming, in the self-description of the 1920s Ku Klux Klan, to be "100% American," today's white supremacists are less likely to express unabashed support for the U.S. government, particularly the federal government, which many perceive to be dominated by Jewish conspirators. Racist movements continue to embrace some xenophobic ideas, particularly opposition to unrestricted immigration into the United States, but they also direct their antipathy at what they regard as undesirable efforts by the government to bolster multiculturalism and reward undeserving racial minority persons with access to desirable jobs, schools, and political appointments.

## THE AGENDA OF ORGANIZED RACISM

It is not only the ideas of white supremacy that separate its adherents from the mainstream population. The goals of white supremacist groups also are extreme and generally violent, although many groups try to suggest otherwise in public. Some racist leaders, like Thom Robb of the Knights of the Ku Klux Klan and David Duke of the National Association for the Advancement of White People and the European-American Unity and Rights Organization, work to present themselves as moderate advocates of the rights of white persons rather than as racists, a tactic that Matthew Hale also uses to deny that he should be labeled as a "white supremacist." Such leaders frame their discussions in terms that they think will resonate with the mainstream population (Berbrier, 1998), arguing, as does Tom Metzger, that they are simply advocating "freedom of choice for all concerned" and that fairness requires that the gains of the twentieth-century African American civil rights movement be expanded to advance the forgotten cause of white people. Although some groups proudly characterize themselves as racists or racialists, others insist that they are only interested in racial separation, not racial supremacy, and that their goals are fully compatible with those of other racial separatist groups, like black or Chicano/a nationalists.

Examination of the internal documents of racist groups or the conversations among their activists indicates that many of them are less benign than they publicly suggest (Blee, 2002).

Regardless of difference in their specific and immediate agendas, most white supremacists encourage "race war" or cataclysmic conflicts between whites and nonwhites; seek to erode what they see as a Jewish-controlled federal government; and make various efforts at low-level terrorism by circulating images and descriptions of graphic violence against racial minorities, Jews, white "race traitors," and other target groups.

How white supremacists should regard and treat Muslims is highly contested in today's groups. Some now routinely include Muslims among their enemies on the grounds that Muslims (whom, they erroneously assume, are all Arab) should be regarded as nonwhites. Others are willing to overlook such racial categorization to allow the possibility of allying with violent Islamic militants based on a mutual antipathy toward Jews and Israel.

## THE ADHERENTS TO WHITE SUPREMACY

White supremacist leaders wildly exaggerate their success at recruiting people to their cause. Matthew Hale's statement that his church has "experienced such growth these past few years" is an indication of how he would like the public to regard the state of the WCOTC, but it is not a statement of fact. The same is true for all racist groups, which routinely overstate the size of their membership as a way of bolstering their stature in the mainstream media and the white supremacist movement, as well as creating fear among the groups that they target as their enemies.

Groups also give misleading information about who joins and how they are recruited. It is common for racist leaders to insist, as Hale does, that the WCOTC is recruiting multitudes of new members through their Internet site. In fact, no white supremacist group recruits effectively through the Internet; most rely on personal contacts and referrals in order to reduce the chance of inadvertently bringing police informants into the

group. Moreover, although Hale's claim that the WCOTC is attracting college students from Ivy League colleges is wildly exaggerated, it is true that the recruits to many white supremacist groups, especially neo-Nazi groups, are increasingly young and from the middle class.

There is one aspect of Hale's commentary on recruitment that is worth noting: his claim, largely accurate, that today's white supremacist groups draw members from mainstream segments of the population rather than from those who are socially disaffected or politically marginal. Indeed, studies of those who join racist groups find that most have quite ordinary lives before they come into contact with racist recruiters. Most come from rather average families, not particularly racist or dysfunctional. Many are well-educated and hold steady, even professional-level jobs before they enter racist groups. They are lured into organized racism by a variety of factors. For some, especially those lured into white power skinhead and neo-Nazi gangs, it is a sense of community, identity, and affirmation that they find attractive about white supremacist groups. The pervasiveness of violence within these groups can also be appealing to young recruits who perceive such violence as a route to increasing their power and status among their peers. For others, especially those who join groups like the Ku Klux Klan and older recruits, the racist movement promises a simple solution to the frustrations of daily life. For many recruits, therefore, the virulently racist and anti-Semitic ideas of white supremacy are learned from contact with racist activists, not from beliefs that cause them to seek out racist groups (Blee, 2002, 2003/2004).

In white supremacist groups, racial minorities, Jews, and other enemies of white supremacists are identified as the cause of nearly all problems that confront white Aryans, from unemployment or problematic workplaces to political inefficacy and crime. As a conspiratorial form of anti-Semitism has gained ascendancy, many now blame Jews for a wide range of personal problems as well. It is not uncommon, for example, for racist activists to insist that Jews have developed secret means of transmitting their agendas into the brains of unsuspecting Aryans, so that even such things as conflict with a lover, failing an examination, or having an automobile accident might be the effect of Jewish domination (Blee, 2002).

## CONCLUSION

The white supremacist movement in the United States is not growing. In fact, most segments of the movement may be shrinking. But it continues to pose a serious threat because its adherents hold extremist ideas about racial groups and are dedicated to acting on those beliefs. For some groups, these actions are the traditional tools of racial supremacy, creating a sense of vulnerability and fear among their enemy groups by spreading hateful messages and asserting the strength and inevitability of white supremacy. For a small but dangerous set of groups, however, defense of the white race increasingly involves more profound and spectacular acts of violence to undermine their enemies and solidify the position of white Aryans. Racial extremism can only be countered through intensive efforts to monitor and prosecute those who practice violence and to undermine the ability of such groups to find recruits and audiences among the mainstream population.

## REFERENCES

Aho, J. A. (1990). *The politics of righteousness: Idaho Christian patriotism.* Seattle: University of Washington Press.

Anti-Defamation League of B'nai Brith. (2006). Extremism in America. Retrieved from http://www.adl.org/learn/ext_us/default.asp?LEARN_Cat=Extremism&LEARN_SubCat=Extremism_in_America

Barkun, M. (1994). *Religion and the racist right: The origins of the Christian identity movement.* Chapel Hill: University of North Carolina Press.

Berbrier, M. (1998). Half the battle: Cultural resonance, framing processes, and ethnic affectations in contemporary white supremacist rhetoric. *Social Problems, 45,* 431–450.

Berbrier, M. (2000). The victim ideology of white supremacists and white separatists in the United States. *Sociological Focus, 33*(2), 175–191.

Blazak, R. (2001). White boys to terrorist men: Target recruitment of Nazi skinheads. *American Behavioral Scientist, 44*(6), 982–1000.

Blee, K. M. (1991). *Women of the Klan: Racism and gender in the 1920s.* Berkeley: University of California Press.

Blee, K. M. (2002). *Inside organized racism: Women in the hate movement.* Berkeley: University of California Press.

Blee, K. M. (2003/2004). Positioning hate. *Journal of Hate Studies, 3,* 95–206.

Brustein, W. I. (2003). *Roots of hate: Anti-Semitism in Europe before the Holocaust.* New York: Cambridge University Press.

Dinnerstein, L. (1994). *Antisemitism in America.* New York: Oxford University Press.

Dobratz, B. A., & Shanks-Meile, S. L. (1997). *White power, white pride! The white separatist movement in the United States.* New York: Twayne.

Ezekiel, R. (1995). *The racist mind: Portraits of neo-Nazis and Klansmen.* New York: Viking.

Feagin, J. R. (2001). *Racist America: Roots, current realities and future reparations.* New York: Routledge.

Ferber, A. L. (1998). *White man falling: Race, gender, and white supremacy.* Lanham, MD: Rowman & Littlefield.

Ferber, A. L. (Ed.). (2004). *Home-grown hate: Gender and organized racism.* New York: Routledge.

Frankenberg, R. (1993). *White women, race matters: The social construction of whiteness.* Minneapolis: University of Minnesota Press.

Futrell, R., & Simi, P. (2004). Free spaces, collective identity, and the persistence of U.S. white power activism. *Social Problems, 51*(1), 16–42.

Gallaher, C. (2003). *On the fault line: Race, class, and the American patriot movement.* Lanham, MD: Rowman & Littlefield.

Gardell, M. (2003). *Gods of the blood: The pagan revival and white separatism.* Durham, NC: Duke University Press.

Gould, S. J. (1996). *The mismeasure of man.* New York: W. W. Norton.

Ignatiev, N. (1996). *How the Irish became white.* New York: Routledge.

Potok, M. (2004). The year in hate, 2004. *Intelligence Report.* Retrieved from http://www.splcenter.org/intel/intelreport/article.jsp?aid=529

Smith, D. N. (1996). The social construction of enemies: Jews and the representation of evil. *Sociological Theory, 14,* 203–240.

Southern Poverty Law Center. (2000). Pagans and prison. *Intelligence Report.* Retrieved from http://www.splcenter.org/intel/intelreport/article.jsp?aid=270

Southern Poverty Law Center. (2006). The nativists. *Intelligence Report.* Retrieved from http://www.splcenter.org/intel/intelreport/intrep.jsp

# Interview With Matthew Hale

## *Russell K. Nieli*

Matthew Hale, who goes by the title of pontifex maximus of the World Church of the Creator, first came to national attention in late 1998 when a panel of the Illinois Bar Association's Committee on Character and Fitness voted to deny him a license to practice law in the state of Illinois. This action was taken by the panel despite the fact that Hale had received a law degree from the Southern Illinois University School of Law at Carbondale, had recently passed the Illinois bar exam, and had complied with most of the requirements usually associated with character and fitness. In denying Hale a license, the panel based its judgment on Hale's active advocacy of overtly racist and anti-Semitic views. "While Matthew Hale has not yet threatened to exterminate anyone," the panel wrote, "history tells us that extermination is not far behind when government power is held by persons of his racial views." Those seeking to deny Hale a law license became even more determined after Benjamin Smith, a friend of Hale's and former member of Hale's church, went on a racially motivated shooting rampage in July 1999 that, before it ended with Smith's suicide, left nine people wounded and two dead. In the following interview, Hale explains some of the basic principles of the Creativity religion that are propagated by his organization. Creativity, Hale explains, is a religion that is not based on supernatural revelation, as Christianity is, but draws its inspiration from the eternal laws of nature itself. These laws, he says, can be determined through close observation and reasoning. Nature, says Hale, decrees that every species of living thing must look out for its own kind or it will be eliminated in the struggle for existence. Conflict, competition, and struggle are ineradicable elements of human nature and life itself, Hale argues, and white people must wake up to the fact that the other races of the globe constitute their biological rivals and potential enemies. If white people don't wake up to this hard fact of life, Hale claims, they will be dispossessed and eliminated by the nonwhite races from the territories they inhabit. Blacks and other nonwhite races, says Hale, claim to support equality, but in reality what they truly want is racial supremacy and racial

EDITORS' NOTE: From Nieli, R. *Contemporary Voices of White Nationalism in America,* copyright © 2003. Reprinted with permission of Cambridge University Press.

privilege. Jews, too, Hale claims, seek domination and supremacy over other races, and it is because of this fact that they have universally provoked such hostility wherever they are encountered. Hale explains how his organization has been particularly successful in recent years in attracting young people and especially young college students. Although whites from many different demographic groups join his organizations, the World Church of the Creator, Hale says, is particularly interested in appealing to "the best and the brightest" among the youth in order to form a racially conscious white leadership class for the future.

## THE INTERVIEW

*Interviewer:* You are the head of a white, racially based group called the World Church of the Creator. Could you explain the nature of this organization? We would like to know particularly what is its underlying philosophy, what are its goals, and what activities does it engage in to further these goals?

*Hale:* The World Church of the Creator is a pro-white, racial-religious organization which is dedicated to the survival, expansion, and advancement of the white race and the white race alone. We are not a Christian organization. Instead of basing our views, our ideology, our religion, on Christianity, we base it on the eternal laws of nature as revealed through science, logic, history, and common sense. We believe that in a natural state, each and every species looks out for its own kind. Each and every subspecies looks out for its own kind. This being the case, it follows that we, as white people, should look out for our own kind. We should not care about the other races—they can do what they will—but we should focus on our own. The World Church of the Creator, in this respect, is certainly a very radical organization, and we do not pay homage to Christianity or to the Constitution or even to America. We are an international organization in scope—we consider all white people, wherever they may be, to be our brothers and sisters.

The techniques we use for getting our message out, for winning white people over, include many things, such as the Internet. We have a large Internet presence; we have a Web site that is a general Web site, we have a Web site that's specifically for kids, we have a Web site specifically for teenagers, and we also have a Web site specifically for women. Also, the World Church of the Creator passes out a lot of literature around the country and around the world. I can safely say that at any moment in time, there's a member somewhere passing out our literature. Another technique we use is using the mass media, or at least utilizing the media, to reach our people. I do a lot of interviews myself. I'm on a lot of programs and I reach a lot of people that way. Also, we distribute our books, namely *The White Man's Bible* and *Nature's Eternal Religion*—those are the two main books of Creativity. We pass them out around the world, and people read of our religion that way, too. We really are the only religiously-based racist organization that is not based on the Christian religion or based on an idea of a deity. I think that's one of the reasons why our church has experienced such growth these past few years. We have no real rivals; we have no real competitors. When people reject belief in Jewish Christianity or the idea of the supernatural, they naturally gravitate our way if they have racial beliefs.

*Interviewer:* How would you characterize your membership in terms of its demographic characteristics? What sorts of people join your organization, and what are their reasons for joining?

*Hale:* We particularly attract the youth. In fact, I can say that probably half of our members are younger than 25 years old—we are a very youth-based organization. As far as income is concerned, I would say that we attract a lot of people of higher financial status. We are considered by many in the white racial movement to be the elite. For example, we do not welcome people who are irresponsible; we do not welcome people who are prone to criminal activity. We encourage responsibility and knowledge in each and every member. Unlike other organizations, we have our own books; we expect our members to read these books and to know them thoroughly, and certainly we have attracted a lot of college students. College students have been really the bulwark, I guess you could say, of our church, the vanguard of our church. I, myself, graduated from two colleges, so this is the type of person that we attract.

*Interviewer:* Could you elaborate further on your strategies for recruiting college students? Do you actively recruit on college campuses? Do you have auxiliary college organizations? What sort of campuses do you go to? What sort of college students join the World Church of the Creator?

*Hale:* We attract college students mainly through the Internet. Many college students use the Internet, and they are attracted to us by that manner. We also have members that go on college campuses and distribute literature, members who will also simply talk to people on campuses. They will see a group of people, and they will walk up and say, "Hey, have you heard about Creativity?" And a lot of people have not heard of the name per se. They have heard of me, or perhaps even heard of the church, but when asked have you ever heard of Creativity, a lot of people still say no to that. And then the member will explain what our Creativity religion is all about. We generally reach out to the private colleges and universities, and indeed to the best schools, though not through any intentional design or disregard of the other schools. We find, however, that people at many of the best private schools . . . at . . . Princeton or Harvard or Yale or Northwestern . . . people at these schools seem to be a little more open-minded and able to grasp more thoroughly where we are coming from. This cause that we represent is by no means a cause for dummies or a cause for those who accept things blindly. We have a lot of evidence behind our views. We have a lot of history, a lot of facts, statistics, and everything else to buttress our claims. Another reason why we go after the private schools is because we want to have the elite. We are striving for that, focusing on winning the best and the brightest of the young generation.

*Interviewer:*  What is the attraction of your organization to college students, and especially to "the best and the brightest"?

*Hale:*  Well, oftentimes, they are very idealistic students, very idealistic people, and certainly, they are not going to accept anything that they are told without some reason behind it. We find that college students, in general, are more receptive to new ideas; they're more open-minded, and they are willing to get involved in our church with less worry about peer pressure or what their parents may think. In a sense, it is an act of rebellion, and even students at Princeton or other prestigious universities still have the capacity to rebel.

*Interviewer:*  What exactly are they rebelling against?

*Hale:*  Well, they're rebelling against the prevalent notions of our time, notions such as that all men are created equal, notions such as that we're simply all Americans, or that we all should just get along, things of this nature. These are really notions that no one ever tries to provide any proof of, or any evidence for. And when we question these assumptions and beliefs, it is often young

bright college students who are most receptive to what we say.

*Interviewer:*  To what extent have government policies and programs, in your view, contributed to racial tensions in America? What government policies or programs would you like to see changed and which ones retained?

*Hale:*  That is a very good question because oftentimes it is assumed, for example, that we are strongly opposed to affirmative action. Well, in a sense we are, and in a sense we aren't, because affirmative action brings more people into our cause. Blackness America pageants bring more people into our cause. Black Entertainment Television brings more people into our cause. The more that the other races obtain, the more white people feel that it's being obtained at their own expense. Take college scholarships . . . I've had so many students say, "Hey, wait a minute! Why can't I get a scholarship because I'm white . . . there are blacks that get them because they're black?" And, of course, my answer to that is, well, the blacks don't want equality. The other races don't really want equality—they talk about equality, but it's really just a smokescreen. What the blacks and other races really want is supremacy, and when I tell that to people who feel aggrieved, they are very interested and they take notice.

*Interviewer:*  And those who take notice are often college students?

*Hale:*  Oh, yes! College students are the most upset about the governmental policies.

*Interviewer:* How about your general views on race in America? Could you describe your vision for the racial future of America?

*Hale:* The Creativity religion holds, first and foremost, that multiculturalism breeds racial violence. We believe that as long as people are forced together in one big melting pot, as it is called, there will be all kinds of violence and tension. The only way to end the violence and the tension between the races is to have separation. Separation between the races—that's the first point. Second of all, we believe that as the white race becomes more of a minority in this country, this country will lose all stability and essentially it will become like a Yugoslavia. Hopefully, there will not be the violence that we have seen in what was once Yugoslavia, but, in any case, there will be ethnic enclaves forming in America, and the country will essentially break apart. We believe this development is inevitable and should not be resisted or opposed.

*Interviewer:* So you don't think that multiracial or multiethnic cultures can survive in any kind of peaceful manner? You don't believe that people of different races and ethnic groups can get together and form a multiracial, multiethnic society that's cohesive and stable?

*Hale:* No, not ultimately, and the history of the world has proven that. No multi-cultural society has ever survived for any length of time. Egypt, which had many cultures and races at one time, eventually fell. India fell. Certainly Central and South America, which are multicultural, have been stagnant as far as economic development is concerned. They have all kinds of natural resources, but they are way behind the more advanced nations economically. So yes, we do believe that no multicultural society can endure in peace and prosperity for very long.

*Interviewer:* In America, we celebrate annually the birthday of Dr. Martin Luther King, Jr. What is your opinion of Dr. King and the black-led civil rights movement of the fifties and sixties in which he played so prominent a role? Is America a better place or a worse place because of that movement and the philosophy of nonviolent mul-tiracialism that he supported?

*Hale:* Well, I think America is far worse than it was before he began his crusade. Certainly, it's worse for white people, and quite frankly, that's the only people we care about. It might be better for blacks in some ways, or it might not. I mean, I talk with blacks who feel that separation is good for their race, too, that they don't want to have schools that are integrated because black and white students have different needs. King's philosophy may have been a philosophy of nonviolence, but he used force to intimidate people. He used at least shows of force constantly. When you have people marching by the thousands down your street, if you're a homeowner, you feel a little intimidation. So he wasn't above using that kind of pressure, just as

Jesse Jackson uses it today. As far as Martin Luther King himself, I think that one of the worst things that happened was that he was assassinated. I think that if he had not been assassinated, his statements and views concerning the Vietnam War would have led to his downfall and perhaps even the movement that he represented. I would much rather see a Malcolm X-type solution to the racial problem than a Martin Luther King-type solution.

*Interviewer:* By a Malcolm X-type solution to the racial problem, do you mean a separatist solution rather than an integrationist one?

*Hale:* Yes, that's right.

*Interviewer:* Many people would characterize your organization as a racist group or hate group. How do you respond to such characterizations?

*Hale:* Well, we certainly are racists, and we accept that label just fine, as a badge of honor. We believe that a racist is a person who loves his own race, and that is the epitome of good, as far as we're concerned. Now, as far as being a hate group, that's certainly some people's characterization of us, but we are no more of a hate group than the NAACP is a hate group or than the Republican and Democratic Parties are hate groups. What I'm getting at is that everybody basically hates; everybody has things that they love and things that they hate, and it's only natural to hate what is happening in this country to our white race.

*Interviewer:* But can't people love one thing without hating something else? If a man loves his wife and children, it doesn't necessarily mean that he hates his neighbor's wife and children.

*Hale:* I'm glad you said that because that is an analogy I use quite often. If you love your wife, you would hate the rapist of your wife, and that's what's happening to white people today. The white race is being raped, pillaged around the world, and we therefore hate those who are engaging in this. We even hate those white people who are consciously doing this.

*Interviewer:* But is it inevitable that people of differing races or ethnic groups are going to rape and pillage each other? Can't people respect each other's rights?

*Hale:* Well, I think we have to understand that war and struggle is a fundamental part of the human psyche, just as much as it is in animals, so we have to determine where and to whom we are going to divert our energy and our hostility. We submit that the other races are biological rivals; they are biological enemies. A shark is not our natural enemy, as long as we're not swimming in the water. A giraffe is not our natural enemy. A bear isn't even our natural enemy! But the other races are capable of dispossessing us of our territories, of our lives, and therefore they are our natural enemies.

*Interviewer:* Could you explain how you came to your current views on race? Did you have any early experiences with white supremacist literature or white supremacist organizations?

*Hale:* I really didn't have any early experiences of this type. I wasn't raised in a racist household either—and racist is the term I would use here, rather than white supremacist. White supremacy is not a label that I accept, for the simple reason that it connotes an idea of holding others down or reigning over them, which we do not want. We want separatism. I guess you could say the first racial piece of literature I ever read was Adolf Hitler's *Mein Kampf.* I read it when I was 12 years old. I was interested in history and wanted to read about the man who had made such a mark on the Second World War. But I came to the views I hold today primarily by observation of the world around us. By observing the world, we can discover the laws that guide all life. Human beings, just because they may be more intelligent than other animals, or because they can wear fancy clothes, or drive nice automobiles, cannot divorce themselves from the laws of nature. If we follow the laws of nature and take care of our own kind, then our race will be secure, we'll be prosperous. But if we ignore the laws of nature, then our race will become extinct, and that's, unfortunately, what's happening today. The whole purpose of the World Church of the Creator is to straighten out the white man's thinking so that he can become the elite, as he was really destined by nature to be.

*Interviewer:* You think that the white race is destined by nature to be an elite race?

*Hale:* Genetically, yes. I mean genetically we are the elite. If you look at any encyclopedia, 99.99 percent of the contributions listed within it are from white people. I don't think this is because whites wrote the history books or the encyclopedias. I think it's because white people have a genetic edge—intellectually, anyway—over the other races.

*Interviewer:* What was the late Benjamin Smith's relationship to your organization? What attracted him to the World Church of the Creator, and do you have any explanation for his descent into murder and mayhem?

*Hale:* Yes, Ben Smith joined the church . . . I think he was a member from May of 1998 until April of 1999. He joined the church, to my knowledge, because he believed in the racial struggle, and he did not believe in Christianity— that was something that attracted him, that we were not a Christian group. We feel that, as much as we respect our white racist Christian comrades, that it's simply a contradiction to believe in racism and believe in Christianity. The two do not go together. Ben Smith—it's hard to say exactly why he did what he did. I have surmised all along that it was because of the denial of my law license. I will never know, probably, the full reason why he did commit crimes. I'm concerned, though, that as white people feel more dispossessed, feel that they are without recourse, that violence will increase.

*Interviewer:* Where do Asians and Asian Americans fit into your racial scheme of things? If high achievement in areas like science, technology, and economic organization confer upon white people some claim to preeminence or elite status, it would seem that Asians, in recent years, have an even greater claim. Asian Americans, for instance, have shown very high levels of academic achievement. They have higher scores than whites on many standardized tests. They are vastly overrepresented in such intellectually demanding fields as physics, engineering, and computer science, and they have much lower rates of many social pathologies, including out-of-wedlock births, crime, and welfare dependency. How would you assess the position of Asians in America and the world?

*Hale:*    Well, I think that the Asians are a good example of hard work. They work very hard; there's no question about that. But I think if white people worked as hard, they would surpass the Asians, without question. After all, most of the creative technological achievements of the world have come from our white race. The Asians are good at copying and expanding upon things that white people already created. If we were to go back 150 years, back before Commodore Matthew Perry sailed into Tokyo Bay, we would see that the Asian culture was extremely stagnant. There were almost no technological achievements there at all. So what we have seen is the Asians looking towards the Western white world and choosing to adopt a white culture, to adopt white technology and a white mode of achievement. And they have taken this white technology and run with it—there's no question about that. But if white people spend a little less attention on drinking or partying, I think that they would be able to replicate, indeed surpass, what the Asians have been able to accomplish recently.

*Interviewer:*    And what about the Jews? Jews are white, and they have also made outstanding achievements in all sorts of intellectual fields. They are disproportionately represented among Nobel Prize winners, among prize winners in many sciences, and they are certainly vastly overrepresented in many academic fields. What are your attitudes on this? Why do you display such hostility towards Jews in your published literature?

*Hale:*    Well, to your first question, I would answer very similarly to the situation with the Asians. The Jews work hard, and it's very much part of their religion to work hard. They work very late into the night; they see work as really being important for their ethic. As far as contributions, though, creatively, the Jews, once again, are not a very creative people. I mean, they're good at some things. They are certainly found in large numbers in the science field, in medicine, and in law, but generally speaking, they have not been a creative people. For example, if you were to look back into the classical period of time in Palestine, the Jews created almost nothing. There's a museum of ancient art, I believe it is at the University of Cairo, and when you walk by the exhibits, you find things from the Phoenicians, you find things from the Sumerians, etc. But when it comes to the Jews, you find nothing because the Jews did not create anything at that time.

As far as why we have antipathy towards the Jews, it is because of their religion, largely. Their religion is extremely hostile to those not Jewish. The Talmud is replete with hostility towards non-Jews, calling us cattle, saying that we're created by God so that Jews would not have to be served by beasts. The Talmud condones the rape of three-year-old girls, for that matter. It says that a girl three years of age may be violated. This is a religion that has some serious problems with it, and it's because of their religion and because of their attitude towards non-Jews that Jews have been persecuted for so many years. They have not been hated for no reason at all, and that's one of the things that I thought about when I was 11 to 12 years old. "Why are the Jews hated so much?" I asked. I mean, why would people seek to exterminate them? Was it for no reason? And I found in my readings that the Jews have made themselves disliked, and that's the reason.

*Interviewer:* Don't you think that jealousy is a big factor here, since the Jews have been so economically successful?

*Hale:* That's just a cop-out. That's the Jews trying to erect a smokescreen over what they've been doing. I'm not jealous of Jews. I don't care how much money a Jew may have. I feel I have more character and more going for me than they do, and I think it's really another kick in the teeth from the Jews for them to say that the reason why anti-Semitism exists is because we're jealous of them. The reason why anti-Semitism exists is because Semitism exists, because of Jews trying to manipulate and control the finances, the government, the laws of the people. They have done this from time immemorial. They were kicked out of Egypt because of it. Of course, the Jewish version is that they wanted to go and the Egyptians wouldn't let them go, but that's not the Egyptian version of events. They caused problems in Germany and caused the rise of Adolf Hitler. They were a problem in ancient Rome; they've been a problem throughout Europe. And it was not because of jealousy.

*Interviewer:* If your opposition to Jews has much to do with their religion, what is your attitude toward secularized Jews, particularly secularized Jews who don't identify with the Jewish religion, as many of them don't?

*Hale:* Well, it's certainly true that there have been some Jews that have taken that position, but what we call upon them to do is to repudiate publicly Judaism. And if they are unwilling to do this, we still consider them our enemies.

*Interviewer:* You would consider them your friends if they would repudiate their religion? Let's say a Jew even married a Gentile and didn't identify with Judaism as a religion at all; that sort of person would be welcomed into your organization?

*Hale:*    Well, I'm not saying that. I don't think it's an either/or. There is somewhat of a middle ground here, and what we're saying is that while we do not want the Jews as part of our white culture, part of the society that we are struggling to create, if Jews will repudiate the Talmud, repudiate the Jewish aim to control the world—the Jews have incredible control in the world—then we would not consider ourselves as much an enemy of those particular Jews as those who do not repudiate the Talmud.

*Interviewer:*    In the past, white racist and white supremacy groups have generally drawn both their leaders and followers from the ranks of the least educated and poorest of whites. You obviously don't fit this mold, and your organization doesn't seem to either. You are college educated and have now a law degree. Do you think racist and white supremacist thinking is gaining ground among the better-educated middle classes? Is this a trend in the future that you see developing?

*Hale:*    Yes, I do. I see the white middle and upper classes certainly seeing the handwriting on the wall, seeing that a multiethnic society is a mistake, that integration has not been a pie in the sky, that it has not been wonderful for white people. On the contrary, it has harmed us immensely—harmed our public schools and made our neighborhoods unsafe. I have talked to many white people who feel this way. In fact, in the nine-and-a-half years that I have been a public activist, I've seen a great change for the better for our cause. I've seen a lot more people express interest, and I've seen the intellectual quality increase dramatically of those who express interest. Obviously, we have a lot of poor members, a number of them anyway, and we have members who are not very educated. We welcome all white brothers and sisters to our cause, but at the same time, we realize that in order for our movement to succeed, we have to win the best, and that's what we are trying to do.

*Interviewer:*    Well, that's the end of the formal questions. Is there anything else that you would like to tell us that you haven't so far, either about your own views or about your organization?

*Hale:*    Well, one thing I would like to say is that for me, the most powerful book I have ever read is *Nature's Eternal Religion.* This is a book available through our organization. I first read it in 1990. To all white men and women I offer this challenge: Read this book cover to cover and see if you don't come to the same conclusions that we have. Read this book and judge for yourself the soundness of the principles we espouse. I invite anyone to do this.

*Interviewer:*    Thank you.

# What We Believe as White Racists

*Tom Metzger*

## IMMIGRATION

There are now, by statistics, 14 million Mexicans and Latin Americans in the United States. That is a terrible guess, since the Iron Heel government, in Washington D.C., has no real idea of how many there are. Consider this: The United States border control says that they may stop 10% each day. That, in itself, represents thousands each day. Now simply multiply that amount by ten.

Even beyond immigration, legal or illegal, the very numbers of nonwhites already here, and their high birth rate, are enough to plunge North America into a banana republic status within two decades or less.

On the other hand, imagine a separatist state or region in the Southwest that could see the impact each day of thousands of immigrants, climbing on board each day, with no hope of a federal solution. Of course, they would do what tribes have done since the dawn of time. They would rally their forces and stop it with a force of arms. How? The same way Syria has no drug problem. Violators are executed. There go the "coyotes" and others that would destroy living space for a quick buck.

For example, if an area like Florida wanted to accept the dregs of the Caribbean, let them, with the understanding that the second this mud flood oozed into the sovereign state of Georgia, it would be "lock and load" time. Now, isn't that simple? It's freedom of choice for all concerned. The Floridians are free to swamp their state and exhaust their natural resources and infrastructure. The Caribbeanites are free to try the border of the sovereign state of Georgia. However, the sovereign citizens of Georgia are free to stop them, using any method

necessary, and stop the invasion of their sovereign state.

Those that await a Big Brother Washington D.C. or Los Angeles Cesspool Grande solution wait in vain, since their solutions are either not forthcoming or are much worse than those that we propose.

Separatism is a state of mind whose time has come. The superstate is the enemy of racial and cultural self-determination. It is also the extreme enemy of man's environment. That is enough reason for us.

Good hunting and keep preying!

## ABORTION

The white separatist movement today has no logical or coherent position on abortion.

A majority in the right wing-oriented racialist movement rightly perceive massive abortion as further impacting the survival of the white race. Unfortunately, this position is more tied to those with a religious position, usually Christians. These same people are usually silent on how the increased birth rate among nonwhites is just as deadly to our race's survival, especially in North America. Even if they do speak about this issue, they do not address the obvious logic, which is that abortion and birth control among nonwhites should be a major project.

On the other extreme, many support abortion as a means of helping to limit an explosion of massive proportions among nonwhites already living in North America. These people do not address the fact that future leaders and thinkers of our race are

EDITORS' NOTE: Reprinted with permission of Tom Metzger.

being destroyed by the millions. What is worse is that it is self-induced.

The logic is perfect. Very little abortion should be tolerated among our white race, while at the same time, abortion and birth control should be promoted as a powerful weapon in the limitation of nonwhite birth. Overt support of both nonwhite population control and non-support of abortion for whites has the same desired effect.

Promoting this Third Force position confuses and angers the churches, with their anti-abortion position, and at the same time angers and frustrates the abortion proponent's position, as well. The Third Force position on pro-white life is played on with demonstrations and well-written handouts. This will raise the tempo in this hot issue.

Imagine a few large signs showing up at anti-abortion demonstrations. For example, a sign which boldly states, "Support White Life" or "Stop White Genocide." That would create an all-new debate. At the same time, signs for a pro-abortion demonstration might state, "Free Choice For Nonwhite Abortion" or "Minorities Have Abortion Rights."

Covertly invest into nonwhite areas; invest in ghetto abortion clinics. Help to raise money for free abortions in primarily nonwhite areas. Perhaps abortion clinic syndicates throughout North America that primarily operate in nonwhite areas and receive tax support should be promoted. At the same time, issue stock. This will help whites raise their standard of living, in two ways.

A note of caution: Both sides in this issue have a propensity for violence. When you join in a demonstration, on either side, have back-up with you. This is just in case the peace-loving Christians or Jews get hysterical.

## MILITARY WARFARE

There has been no military war in modern history that promoted the general welfare of the white race. As the great general Smedly Butler lamented,

"war is a racket." Only in limited cases, where war has temporarily slowed the birthrate in nonwhite areas of the world, would war be considered even slightly positive. However, when the destruction of resources and pollution are taken into account, even that method of birth control is like "cutting your nose off to spite your face." Remember, after every such economic adventure, the "spook in the sky" people quickly move in to patch up the nonwhite populations, to begin anew the cycle of birth, poverty, and death.

So, why are so many so-called white racists military or war oriented? Why do healthy white people salivate while waving the system's flag and run off to participate in these slaughter games?

Robert Audrey wrote the great trilogy *African Genesis, Territorial Imperative,* and *The Evolution of Social Contract.* He put it this way: "Men are motivated by three things: (1) Stimulation, (2) Identity, and (3) Security." It seems that modern warfare appeals to all three.

What, then, causes a trained killer to go from an unstoppable predator in war (who is prepared to carry out any order) to become a cowardly wimp in the civilian life, in defense of his race or family? Is it the great psychological control by the media, churches, or education, which are controlled by occult forces?

White men and women cannot be totally snivelized when they are capable of rising to primordial brutality under certain conditions. War is economic for a few and also a way for many white men to release their natural aggression. Is this the reason that our jails, prisons, and mental hospitals are full, due to the white man's straight-jacketed and unnatural society? I think that it is.

The mystics will not admit, and be proud of, man's animal nature. Almost all religious beliefs promote the idea that natural aggression is evil and that straight-jacket demotions are good. One thing that we know for sure is that military promotes more race mixing than any other area of society.

All modern warfare has been at the expense of our white gene pool. All modern institutions are designed to stifle white racial aggression, to the betterment and expansion of lesser races. War breeds phony patriotism of a non-nation nation. The diverse races and religions of North America will ultimately sink into Third World poverty and disease, if internal white aggression is not released from its men and women.

In short, military warfare benefits a very few, at the expense of the many. This warfare destroys needed natural resources and diminishes the best breeding stock of our race. It promotes hyper-patriotic race mixing and racial pollution. Other dangers are that all sophisticated spy satellites and Star Wars-style weapons can and will be used, ultimately against those that were bankrupted paying for them.

Make no mistake. The so-called end of the phony Communist struggle marks the beginning of "Operation Mop-Up" by transnational financial cartels and the occult forces behind them.

Among our enemies, white racism or separatism is about to become the new crusade. If need be, the same polyglot forces and weapons tested on the "terrible" Saddam Hussein and Iraq will be used against you.

Logic: War is a racket. Support at least a 75% cut in defense, not only in this country, but in every country in the world. White separatists must oppose system-controlled warfare!

## LAWMAKERS

Otherwise known as legislators, these men and women are held in high esteem, for the most part. The reason is that there is a myth that is perpetuated by the media. That myth is that your lawmakers are your friends, due to the number of bills that they successfully push through into laws. Those that are unable to create bills and push them through the hoops into laws are looked on as ineffective and even called lazy. When it comes election time, woe be it to a lawmaker that has been unable to enact new laws.

In California, as an example, over 1,000 new laws went into effect in January, 1992. White voters ignorantly think that massive creation of new laws may afford them new and better protection. What does it really bring to you? It brings you more control, less liberty, and higher taxes.

What an amazing and deceptive machine. The slaves, in the name of law and order, are actually manipulated into believing that more laws means more liberty and more security. The slaves (or zombies, as I like to call them) cannot be excused, for they have a vast history that will plainly show that legislators are not the friends of liberty or of the peasants (as we are commonly referred to by the legislators, in their private circles).

"So," you ask, "what, then, is the answer?"

It is simple. There are more laws on the books in the United States than ever before in history. At the same time, the standard of living has dropped like a rock. Nonwhite crime has gone through the roof. In fact, in all areas where white working people are impacted, most new laws have not helped at all. In fact, most laws are very expensive and just open up new problems, requiring by system logic, more laws.

The answer is obvious. We need thousands of lawmakers that will become law eliminators. In other words, a WAR on laws. Repeal should be the word for each new election. Legislators should be judged to be a greater friend of the people by battling entirely for the elimination of costly and ineffective laws.

The greatest help for the white race today would be state and national legislators that run on a platform of no new taxes, coupled with no new laws. For if you enact more new laws, this guarantees more new taxes. Do you see how simple it would be?

Your enemies control the law-making machinery. They also control the unequal application of these laws that help their friends and destroy their enemies. So, get smart, you young, white Americans!

Run for office, but on the basis of spending your entire effort in repealing laws. Couple your arguments with the obvious. Most laws cause higher taxes and usually don't solve a problem. In fact, they actually appear to call for even more laws to correct the evils of the law that you just enacted.

Whites who love liberty cannot love the great OZ, the great and deceptive lawmakers.

## TAXES

*Fact:* Virtually all taxes today are directly, or indirectly, used to control and destroy the future of our race. *Logic:* Any program or method that circumvents taxes is a white revolutionary act. This even applies to tax avoidance by those that you perceive as your enemies, who are doing it purely for personal financial greed or advancement. In the past, tax avoidance movements were preoccupied with some obvious or special gripe. In the right wing, it was many times controlled by arguments such as abortion protest or certain anti-war activity.

Overt methods are not important when you understand that all tax enforcement today is directly, or indirectly, supporting your destruction as a white separatist. All tax avoidance, in any way, helps to bleed and weaken the Beast. Your sweat and hard-earned wages are the only source of power that is used against you. In short, the old adage applies: "The power to tax is the power to destroy."

There are thousands of ways to play this game. For our more well-off friends, you are probably well aware of many ways to fight this game of financial warfare. To our lower, middle-class and poor whites, there are also hundreds of easy methods. Try not to buy new when better-quality used merchandise is available, with no taxes involved. Flea markets or shopping through the miscellaneous for-sale columns, or in newspapers and throwaways, are great ways to avoid tax. Buy your fruits and vegetables from open-air, non-tax-style markets or direct from the farmer, whenever possible. The prospects are endless.

The underground economy is a fabulous mechanism and well-suited to our purpose. There are also a vast number of books on the subject.

Remember that the underground economy is seditious to our enemies but a great weapon for white racial advancement. Again, bleed the Beast. Spread these ideas among even your non-racial contacts, since all tax avoidance and underground economic activity directly helps our case. It is easy and it is fun! Use your imagination, and start your war today.

Good hunting!

## WOMEN

There has always been a strain, in all of the races throughout time, that has overdone the male dominance habit. For very early man it must have been such, since much activity was largely compiled of brute strength. However, even then, the logic and reasoning of women must have played a part in man's evolution. I cannot picture any advancing tribe or race in which women not only gave birth to the future, but also kept the fires burning and the food coming. Living in a hunter-gatherer society, it would be impossible for women not to be thrust, from time to time, into combative positions.

As white settler women in early America, they had to shoot or drive off Indians or wild animals. Thus it must have been with early man, except for the use of the gun. It is illogical to think that as ancient tribes came under attack by others, women did not join in the fight for survival.

The role of women seems to have been altered between goddess and warrior, to outcasts in their own homes, throughout history.

No intelligent white man or woman would deny the physical, biological, and chemical differences between the two sexes. No intelligent white man or woman would believe that women, in general, are capable of matching men as power lifters or in areas of brute strength. There are, however, always exceptions to almost every rule that is known to man. Generally, on the other hand, men are not able to replace the special bond of a mother and her child. This, again, is not to say that there are no exceptions.

In relatively modern times, within a few hundred years, what has been man's approach to the women of our race?

The invasion of Rome by occult Judaism, and the later revolution of occult Christianity, perpetuated some of the worst stereotypes of women. The Judeo basis for Christianity, through the writings of the Old and the New Testaments, is still the worst detractor of women. Jews, in particular, operating in Western society, brought in the very worst oppression of women. Christianity simply promoted the same negative regard for women. Even worse are the Jew's Talmudic teachings, perpetrated right up to the present day. These ideas, even in the late twentieth century, through Hasidic and Orthodox Judaism, are the most ridiculous attitudes ever put to paper about women. To observe the extremes of such activity, simply travel to New York City, or any large American city, and visit a Hasidic Jew or hard-line Orthodox Jew neighborhood to check it out for yourself. To save time and money, simply read the book *Hole in the Sheet,* written by a Jewish woman, about the sick and perverted treatment of Hasidic and Orthodox women by Jewish males.

These attitudes have had a strong influence on white European and American civilization. For example, in many Northern areas, blacks received the right to vote before white women. Even today, our white women are put at the same level as the nonwhites, in civil "wrongs" legislation. These events at the end of the twentieth century are counterproductive to our race's survival and advancement.

Understand that a majority of the nation's views on the relationship between men and women have their origins in Judeo-Christianity. The same religion that wrongly promotes the myth that all men are created equal also promotes a negative attitude toward our white women.

The right wing or conservative movement, and the racial elements thereof, have perpetuated some very negative attitudes, also. These positions have caused, in part, the political flight of many capable women into the arms of the extreme left, which includes lesbianism and race mixing. WAR believes that an equal percentage of women are as concerned over our status racially as the men are. Many women put the men to shame in their work and in their sacrifice for the benefit of the white race. When you look around at the weak and wimpy status of a large percentage of white men, it is obvious that millions of hard-working, hand-fighting, and hard-mothering women are needed in this great struggle.

Throughout our travels as a race, there have been exceptions to the Judeo-Christian idea of women. Historically, women have been proven to be great leaders, warriors, thinkers, scientists, and so on.

Our views must be futuristic and not tied to myths of Asiatic cult religions. Imagine determining today's actions by adhering to the maniacal ramblings of ancient religious dervishes who sat in the desert, babbling at the moon. It is simply not productive.

I must add that there is wisdom in the studies of the ancients, along with idiocy. One must carefully screen out the nonsense. You will recognize nonsense, since it is both illogical and irrational.

White women of our race must be rated by several criteria. One criterion is ability in whatever area that they wish to work in. If they are capable and are able to show that ability, then forget all of the artificial barriers. At the same time, just because a man is white and male, this should carry no special ticket to our struggle. Our most dangerous spies, informants, and Iron Heel supporters, at this time, are men. As white motherhood becomes more and more threatened, the number of females entering our ranks may outnumber the males.

Let's not help our enemies by putting up Middle Eastern- and Asiatic-based roadblocks to male/female unity.

## AMERICA FIRST OR RACE FIRST

WAR and Tom Metzger were probably the first to coin our ideological struggle as white separatism. Even though our economic determinist enemies continue to simplistically label us as white supremacists, our message is slowly getting through. There surely are white elitist supremacists; however, they operate in the economic determinist camp while pretending to fight "naughty" racism (belief in one's own race).

From the recent re-emergence of breakaway republics in the Soviet Union, to the Northern Indian colony of Kashmir or even closer, Quebec in Canada, ethnicity and culture are again gaining their proper place on the world stage.

Extremists on the left rail against the re-emergence of nationalism, while the right wing rails for America first. The left continues to support the idea of suppression of nationalistic moves, preferring the failed "bigger is better" attitude of the last several decades. The so-called right has correctly argued against a world-class Big Brother, while at the same time they have supported an equally dangerous transnational economic program, which falsely equates capitalism with free enterprise. When discussing the right and the left, however, things can become very confusing, in this age. The majority of the right has followed the lead of the left into programs and laws suppressing discrimination. Discrimination and property ownership are the two issues that separate all mankind from slavery. Without the ability to discriminate, ethnic and racial protection is impossible. Anyone who advocates laws against discrimination, coupled with private ownership of property, becomes your enemy, no matter what racial group they belong to or which flag they happen to wave.

One must remember that forced integration and the outlawing of discrimination increased at the same rate as state control of private property. These anti-separatist ideas were enacted under the various flags of the so-called Democracies. Under Old Glory and the Pledge of Allegiance, our race became enslaved. Remember those anti-separatist words, "one nation indivisible, with liberty and justice for all." Separatists are not nationalists. For the most part, a separatist sees national borders as lines drawn arbitrarily, to the tune of economic guidance, not for racial or cultural best interests.

For today, what is this nation? It is certainly no longer an identifiable, homogenous, racial or cultural group. What, in some cases, may have had its beginnings as race and culture, today is simply an economic outline that encloses any combination of races and beliefs. This, of course, is not a real nation. This is a bastard nation, with almost no roots, where millions of nonwhites can claim only one generation on the land. That land usually being the asphalted big metropolis. These sad places cannot, without tongue in cheek, be called cities or city-states. They are like overnight mining camps that rise in population until they suck out the environmental resources and then collapse to resemble the early cities of Iraq. The metropolises being the gaping anal cavities of a sick and dying nation. To those unclean places flock the worst of all races. Only the most degenerate of the white race struggle to stay on top of the maggot pile in such unnatural settings.

In the face of these twin monstrosities lie the bastardized metropolis of "Blade Runner" fame and the artificial rainbow nation. Separatist movements, worldwide, are truly a renaissance of natural logic.

The drastic differences between a real racist, which is a white separatist, and a white nationalist of today are very important. To a white separatist, the overriding importance is race, not what we have known as nation, in this century. The white separatist, by his or her very nature, must applaud racial and cultural separatism worldwide. White separatists are not interested in attempting to build another Tower of Babel. It is discernible in all the cities of North America. Yes, the babble of languages, dialects, and people, all of whom are called Americans.

Your masters do not fear you as an economic segregationist; however, they do fear you as a true separatist. For if the Soviet Republics have the ethnic and cultural right of self-determination, why do not the states of the United States? When the economic determinists applaud the various separatist moves in other areas of the world, why not in North America? Some would say that this is a return to state rights, while in fact it is an advance to state sovereignty. There should follow a competition of the states. The states or regions that are convinced that their future is best protected by the advancement of the black race should openly advertise that fact. Those states or regions that desire a homogenous Euro-American or white population should advertise as such. Those states or regions that believe that the Mexican and Central American population would provide the future with the most healthy environment should advertise as such. In other words, total freedom of choice. We hear a lot about freedom of choice lately, don't we? When was the last time you heard of freedom of choice on the subject of race or racial separation? The press has, in the last 12 years, for the most part frozen out any portion of an interview that outlined or even mentioned the idea of separatism. No matter what you label yourself as, the press always uses the terms "white supremacist" or "NEO-Nazi." These terms are then predigested, as to what Pavlov's sheep are in turn supposed to say and do, in reaction to those few brave enough to even mention the possibility of separatism.

Smaller racial and cultural states (if you will) tend to move away from arms races and nuclear war, due to the lack of resources. The only small states that get into the armaments race are those that are being supplied with weapons from larger states. The environment would certainly benefit, since a people more aware of their smaller amount of resources could not be "hoodwinked" by political economic shell games that make it seem that there are unlimited resources. Much of what I am

saying is found in the writings of well-known writers, not only of our race, but also from other races around the world. Smaller states or regions follow a more Jeffersonian ideal of government, also.

What of population? Today's idea of population control is no control at all. North American politicians today look at immigration in a nineteenth-century context. They see unlimited land and unlimited resources, with racial homogeneity being of no or questionable value. This is like running a large 1992 airport with a 1950 schedule. It will not work and it is not working. The faster we can careen to a pluralistic society, the faster the quality of life erodes. The larger the size of government, the greater the mistakes that are made. Population in a smaller state or region is more easily controlled. It is much easier to see the overall problem when you are closer to the problem.

## RELIGION

Religion is a subject that has existed for thousands of years and has caused more blood to flow than almost any other human pastime.

It is my view that the subject must be divided into two parts: the strong belief in something (which could be almost anything) and having faith in something that is not provable by any present-day logical and rational facts or evidence.

It is the opinion of many that religion, in a modern sense, must have had its greatest push forward at a time when a hunter-gatherer society changed to an organized agricultural way of life. Our best evidence would tend to indicate that religion of that day was a method of organizing people and, in short, controlling larger and more complex social structures. It would also seem that this was a "chicken or the egg" proposition. The perceived need for people to control gave birth to the age-old query, "Why?" The answer, which was simply given by someone who was perceived to be smarter than the rest, was that "God told me so." Out of fear of death and the unknown, men created abstract gods to help them control men, for good or bad, take your pick. In the early stages, these manufactured gods took the form of symbols of reality such as the Sun, the seas, the weather, war, and a host of other realities. Although these beliefs were highly misused by many a witch doctor or tribal leader, in general, the reality behind the symbolic gods and what they represented was very real and natural.

As the great power of a religion based on faith and not fact emerged, flocks of would-be Jimmy Swaggarts swarmed over the populations. From then until now, what is broadly recognized as religion is entirely based on faith in leaders that are speaking to a monotheistic god, and that god speaks to them, or so they claim. Our studies show that Christianity, Judaism, and Islam all spring from a common occult force, which was Egyptian in origin (other material on that subject is available through WAR's national office).

Faith religionists of today mock the reverence that was held for the Sun by ancient societies. In fact, a religion based on the Sun was both factual and provable, while the God of Christianity, Judaism, and Islam has no basis in fact, whatsoever. The historical myth of Jesus has been promoted at least 16 times by much older civilizations. Jesus is just an updated version of the same myth.

The Sun was reality. All could easily see the Sun as both a benefactor in the northern and southern hemispheres and a much more cruel reality at the equator. A man thirsting at the equator at high noon would cry, "Why are you punishing me?" while our Nordic ancestors would ask the same question in the coldest times of winter.

It is plain to see that Judaism could never have gained a large following in Europe. This occult society had its limitations in overt activity; however, it did well as a covert occult society.

Since Christianity is, in fact, a slave religion, it is satirical at least to see the negro adopt a slave religion after chattel slavery was ended. It simply underlines the fact that consciously or unconsciously, weak humans desire the status of sheep, no matter what they say. For example, take the pecking order of the barnyard chickens: Very few are able to, or have the desire to, break free. Through fear, men are controlled by occult religious forces. If you would listen to those that are obvious front men for such drivel, they will tell you that "it is for your own good," of course.

The natural control of white tribal society was through natural ways, for the most part. Through the leadership principle, right of combat, and natural selection, the weak are weeded out and the fabric of the race is strengthened.

If Aryan white man is unable to confront the enemy within the gates of Christianity and Judaism, then there is no hope. We must prepare our dwindling numbers to move toward a combination of technological and natural barbarianism if we are to survive and expand as a race. The medicine men and the witch doctors of our race must be thrown down. You cannot serve two masters, one being the Judeo-Christian myth and the other being in favor of the white eugenics idea. For yet a little while, we must have patience with those among us that have been unable or unwilling to throw off the subversive Middle Eastern cult religions. However, time is running out, and the albatross of Christianity will surely destroy our reformation, if not subdued.

Remember the likely evidence that life on this planet, and especially man, may simply be an aberration in the vast universe.

Those of our race, and a few from Judaism, created Christianity to carry forward occult control into pagan Europe. Actually, evidence shows that mythical Jesus was created by the Niciani Council in about 300 A.D.

As white racists, any religion must be based on the real preservation and advancement of our race on the Earth today. No faith promises of heaven or hell need apply. One need not have faith that race exists; it is plain for all to see.

Christianity, so far, is the dominant occult faith religion of western white man. Thus Christianity, even more than Judaism itself, is more destructive to our race. Those that would rise in anger at that suggestion need to observe our society more closely. Every destructive idea to our race can find its basis in Christianity. Without the occult Judaism, it is very likely that Christianity would never have appeared in Europe. However, once Christianity was entrenched, it dragged occult Judaism right along with it. In North America, there would be no Judaism if there had not been Christianity. Since these are both occult control mechanisms, they tend to, from time to time, heed the other. However, both Judaism and Christianity spring from the same roots, and their "marriage" is one of convenience. Not to realize that the front for these religions is just faith and to refuse to see the reality of this age-old control mechanism is to live in a fog.

Perhaps this is it: "What you see is what you get," nature screams out to us. If that is so (and I see nothing to disprove that), then that makes our adventure even more spectacular. One of those millions of mathematical and chemistry combinations that led to you and I. By the first law of natural selection, we are truly a "bootstrap" race. We may choose the control of this planet and the unlimited possibilities of space, or we may decide to sink into the dysgenic failure of cultures and societies that now flourish mainly because of faith religion and greed that threaten to drag us down and out.

Break out of your death cell, white man! Your race, and only your race, must be your religion.

## GOVERNMENT

Government is the euphemism for the modern state. Since government denotes the perennial lie, "of the people," it is used to mislead those that should know better.

All governments are oligarchies, which are ruled by the few. Some oligarchies have facades,

such as the Congress and the Senate. This method of illusion has become quite popular, even in openly straight dictatorial countries. Example: the People's Republic of China, or India's late Ismira [*sic*] Ghandi's oligarchy, which she named "a guided democracy."

Even so-called dictatorships are, in reality, oligarchies and are run by the few. The modern oligarchy, which refers to itself as a democracy, is the most deceptive. That is because democracy is a fraud today, just as it has been throughout history.

Many have said that the government or the state is theft. This is true. Even the best of states are a protection racket. These rackets are far more dishonest than unlicensed organized crime (the mafia, etc.). For example, the state takes $1.00 in tax, and you are lucky to receive 20% of that in services. These services are then usually redirected to people not of your race. The hold-up man on the street takes all that you have at the time. The burglar carries off all that he can from your house. However, rarely do these men make regular demands upon you, such as the state does, by robbing you and always claiming to be doing it "for your own good" or "for your general welfare." You may rob and kill without worry of punishment if you are licensed by the state. The state police kill quite regularly, as do the military, the F.B.I., and the C.I.A. These people are allowed to. Most of us travel through life unlicensed, unless it is perhaps a license to drive or to run a business. Should we attempt to operate anything without the proper license, we are sent to jail or possibly executed.

Much of this con game comes from the historical fraud known as God-directed government, or the divine right of kings. In the modern time, it is referred to as the divine right of the state. Millions believe in this totally baseless conception and chain their offspring from birth with this emasculating idea.

The religious zealot promotes the nonsense that a mythical Abraham came down from a mountain with a code of laws from the great spook in the sky. The politician says that the great emissary of God or the state, such as a Congressman or a Senator, comes down from "the hill" in Washington, D.C. with laws for the people.

In general, those Christians, Jews, or humanists (Christians without a Christ) superstitiously believe in this myth, unless they are part of the bureaucracy of small-time licensed criminals who believe out of greed of being part of the mob. In other words, national states are gangs; no less, no more. The gangs, by their nature, strive to become larger by gobbling up smaller gangs (smaller states) on their way to becoming syndicates (or as we know them to be now, transnational corporations). Remember that the goal of international socialism and international capitalism was to destroy smaller states or to absorb them into the "Super Gang." Soviet Russia was a good example, and the term "the West" as opposed to "the East" was another. The result, in that case, was the "Cold War." The "Cold War" gobbled up nations into the specter of the "one big fight." Using this as an excuse, the natural resources of the world were squandered along with the death of millions. All in the name of peace, brotherhood, and national defense. At the same time, unlicensed gangs did the same thing. Instead of small gangs controlling small amounts of turf, the idea was to have one big gang control it all. First in one major city, then in another, until we have national organized crime, complete with Governors and the Board of Directors. Finally, the unlicensed gang power becomes so great that in many cases it overlaps into, and becomes a part of, licensed gang activity (the Iran Contra Affair, etc.).

Street gangs are the lowest common denominator, and in reality, the most sensible of all gang activity! Most street gangs today are satisfied with control of a few blocks of turf and a financial cut. These gangs are somewhat beneficial since they, in some ways, erode the confidence in the "Big Gang," which supplies protection. However, the "Big Gang" tries to use this as a method of gaining tighter controls of the white non-gang populations. Enters: drunk driving, road blocks, helmet laws, and seat belt enforcement as an example of seemingly "good" plans. These so-called "good" plans guide the sheep (that's you) to a more total control by the "Big Gang" in Washington, D.C.

In summation, international gangs lead us into far more dangerous wars, more dangerous population increases, more dangerous destruction of the environment. All of this is of the greatest threat to the white race.

Not even the wars between the smaller white states (gangs) have had the effect that transnational gangs, with open borders, have had on white nations. In this case, smaller is better. Besides being better, the smaller white state is raised by natural leaders and those that can be dealt with, should they get out of control.

The international-style state is inefficient, to the maximum. Perhaps we are moving toward a time of city-states. All-white city-states would be desirable and efficient, plus they would be culturally strong. As an example, the greatest time of culture and art on the Italian Boot was in the time of the city-states. Italy has not since demonstrated anything that comes close. Greece, at its Aryan peak, comprised city-states.

Perhaps the white idea of the Northwest or Southeast solution is more than can be expected. As smaller becomes more beautiful, why not city-states with satellite village states? By effective immigration, this is a reachable goal.

However, a war against the Super State must be fought to the finish. Your ammunition is readily available. Cut economic support for the Beast. In short, starve the bureaucrats out. All of their international gang plans are based on sheep that will finance them. Without your cooperation, they are dead.

Think about it, and then join the hunt and the underground economy.

## Discussion Questions

1. Some people believe that America is a racist society. If so, does this mean that white supremacy is *not* a form of deviance? Why or why not?

2. Advocates of deviant belief systems argue for the validity of those beliefs in specific and distinctive ways. How do racists validate and justify white supremacy? Are these arguments persuasive to most whites? Why or why not?

3. Racists claim that they are not white *supremacists* but white *separatists*. Is that assertion convincing? Why or why not?

4. The belief that one has been abducted by aliens and the belief that white gentiles are genetically superior to and should live separately from Jews and nonwhites are both regarded as seriously deviant in this society. Draw some parallels between these two belief systems. How do they differ?

# PART 5

# HAVING AND ENDORSING ADULT-CHILD SEXUAL CONTACT

# ADULT-CHILD SEXUAL CONTACT
## An Introduction

"Pedophilia" is defined by the American Psychiatric Association's (1994) *Diagnostic and Statistical Manual* (DSM-IV) as "recurrent, intense sexually arousing fantasies, sexual urges, or behaviors involving sexual activity with a prepubescent child or children (generally age 13 years or younger)." For such a diagnosis to be made, the DSM-IV adds, such urges must cause "clinically significant distress or impairment in social, occupational, or other important areas of functioning." Moreover, the manual warns, an individual should not be included if he or she is in late adolescence and is involved "in an ongoing sexual relationship with a 12- or 13-year-old." Specifying its definition even further, the DSM-IV requires that for the diagnosis to be valid, the adolescent must be at least 16 years old and at least five years older than the child. To narrow matters down even more precisely, the DSM-IV requests the clinician to specify which *type* the pedophile falls into—the *exclusive* type, who is attracted only to children, or the *nonexclusive* type, who is attracted to adults as well as children (p. 528).

Most, if not all, true pedophiles, say Davison, Neale, and Kring (2004) are interested in youngsters specifically *because* they are sexually immature. But does that mean that the pedophile can be clearly and unambiguously demarcated from the adult who does *not* experience sexual urges toward children? Yes and no, say Davison et al. As it turns out, roughly one-quarter of the adult population is aroused at the sight of nude pictures of children. Moreover, their arousal is significantly correlated with conventional arousal: The more aroused subjects are by adult heterosexual pictures, the more likely they are to be aroused by pedophile pictures. This might seem a disturbing finding, say Davison et al., but it emphasizes the difference between fantasy and reality. Another way of saying this is that although a substantial proportion of the adult population is sexually aroused by, and has sexual urges toward, prepubescent children, relatively few act on those impulses. Studies suggest that pedophiles, compared with adults who do not approach children sexually, rank low on social maturity, self-esteem, impulse control, and social skills (Finkelhor & Araji, 1986).

The DSM-IV's definition is psychiatric and clinical, not sociological. Hence, it is inadequate for the sociologist's needs. This does not mean that it is wrong so much as it addresses a distinctly different set of issues than the ones in which we're interested. In this chapter, Keith Durkin and Steven Hundersmarck distinguish the pedophile from the child molester; pedophile is a psychiatric term, while child molester is a legal term. Not all child molesters are true pedophiles, and not all pedophiles are child molesters. Many men who molest children do not report recurrent or intense sexual urges toward them. Moreover, the men who do report such urges and act on them, but experience no distress or dysfunction as a result, would not be included in the DSM-IV's definition. And lastly, by this definition, adults who are in their twenties, thirties, and older may engage in sex with girls in their teens yet be excluded from the DSM-IV's definition, and yet, such men are clearly engaging in what most of us—clinicians and the general public alike—would regard as sexual exploitation and abuse (Witt & Greenfield, 2001). Clearly, the *clinical* definition of pedophilia is narrower than the public or popular—or *social*—definition. Hence, sociologically, it is likely to be inadequate.

The DSM-IV's attempt to define pedophilia, compared with our brief excursion into the problems such a definition raises, reminds us that adult-child sexual contact is partly a matter of definition—a social construction, if you will. It raises a host of questions: What is a child? What is an adult? What sort of age difference between the adult and the child does there have to be? How much contact does there have to be? How fixated on children does the adult have to be? How much resistance does there have to be? (And *legally*, an underage child—defined differently in different jurisdictions—is not competent to grant sexual access, although the *public's* conceptualization of the meaning of "resistance" may differ from the law's.) How much harm does the adult inflict on the child? What constitutes sexual contact? Is the child aware that such contact constitutes abuse? How do our relevant and significant audiences judge such behavior? And, relevant for many observers, is the sexual contact heterosexual or homosexual? Certain adult-child sexual contacts would be *universally* regarded as abuse, as pedophilia—as deviant and reprehensible—while others would generate more divided opinions and muted condemnation. In other words, adult-child sexual contact is a category that is clearly defined at the extremes but fuzzy around the edges.

For instance, most of us would not see a consensual affair between an 18-year-old man and a 16-year-old girl as pedophilia or as sexual abuse, and yet in some jurisdictions the law defines it as statutory rape. But if the girl were, say, 12 rather than 16 and the man 21, nearly everyone would agree that it should be illegal and it is a form of sexual abuse. Again, we have a social construction on our hands, although the law's definition and the public's may not always agree.

The social constructionist nature of what constitutes adult-child sexual contact emphasizes the role of audiences, the law and law enforcement and the general public being only two such audiences. Howard S. Becker (1963) reminds us that *moral entrepreneurs* may be central in any definition of behavior as deviant. Becker defined a "moral entrepreneur" as someone who either *creates* a new set of moral rules or who *enforces* moral rules (pp. 147–163). Moral entrepreneurs may be officials (politicians, lawmakers, judges, the police) or unofficial (friends, relatives, neighbors), and in the matter of sexual contact between an adult and a child, moral entrepreneurs may include a child's parents (pp. 147ff.). Clearly, the parents of a 16-year-old girl are likely to have strong reasons to object to their daughter's affair with an 18-year-old man: He belongs to the wrong ethnic group, the wrong social class, he's not college-bound, he uses drugs, he drives recklessly. Or, they simply

**Image 5.1**   Many forms of deviance have generated organized societal responses that attempt to protect victims or presumed victims. A very tiny proportion of child kidnappings are perpetrated by strangers or other non-relatives (most are perpetrated by parents engaged in custody battles); nonetheless, stranger abductions elicit enormous public concern. "Amber alert" is the public notification of the kidnapping of a child. It was named after a 1996 child kidnapping and murder victim, Amber Hagerman.

believe that a 16-year-old girl—*their* 16-year-old girl—is too young to have sex. Hence, what would, under many circumstances, have been an acceptable relationship becomes redefined as deviant, not only because of the ages of the parties in question but because of ancillary characteristics of the participants. As Becker says, to define behavior as deviance, an act of *enterprise* is necessary—"somebody blows the whistle" (p. 122). Becker's point is that what makes an act deviant is not solely a function of the behavior in question but also a consequence of whether someone *reacts* to that behavior. In the case of our hypothetical 16-year-old girl and 18-year-old man, such a reaction is not always automatic. But in the case of an adult having sex with a younger child, the reaction is likely to be immediate and intense. Some cases of deviance are socially constructed with respect to where we draw the age line.

In *Odd Man In*, Edward Sagarin (1969) chronicled the rise of "organizations of deviants" whose goal was to redefine their unconventional, despised, or outsider status. Thus, we find that pedophiles, like alcoholics, homosexuals, drug addicts, dwarfs, ex-convicts, and transvestites, have banded together to neutralize or reverse the enterprise of deviance-defining moral entrepreneurs. NAMBLA, the North American Man-Boy Love Association, is one of several organizations whose goal is to define adult-child sexual contact as acceptable, nondeviant, even conventional behavior. NAMBLA's goal is to abolish the laws against age of consent and against child pornography and to create a climate of opinion favorable to "man-boy" sexual expression. "We seek freedom from the restrictive bond of society which denies them [children] the right to live, including to live as they choose," declares a NAMBLA bulletin. It is the organization's position that noncoercive sex between an adult and a child is not abusive or inherently injurious. NAMBLA uses strategic alliances with humanitarian and progressive causes and organizations—gay rights, the women's movement, and pro-choice—to create for itself a climate of respectability and legitimacy. In "The World According to NAMBLA," Mary de Young explains the organization's strategies for attaining its goals. Readers are likely to find NAMBLA's arguments distressing and its conclusions repugnant.

In his personal account, "From Victim to Offender," "Dave" (a pseudonym) describes his experiences with molesting children. After two prison sentences, Dave is convinced that sexually molesting children is harmful to the victims. In contrast, "jay_h," the pseudonym for a spokesperson for man-boy love, offers a personal statement of his views. Jay_h believes that the laws setting a legal age limit on sex are wrong and should be abolished and that boys should be allowed to have sexual experiences, including with adults. Nearly all of the rest of us disagree and hence are likely to react to this "love manifesto" with moral outrage, even anger. In fact, most of us regard jay_h's advocacy as a form of deviance—*extreme* deviance. As with white supremacy, it is extremely difficult for most of us to step back and be the complete sociologist and "appreciate" such a position. Again, we argue that our position toward extreme deviance can run along two tracks simultaneously. One track says, "I have a right to my position; I find such a belief, and the behavior that expresses such a belief, abhorrent, morally wrong, repulsive in the extreme." The other track insists that advocates of adult-child sexual contact have to be understood and that simple condemnation obliterates our capacity to get a sense of what these people are doing and why. This moral dualism is one of the things that makes deviance one of the most fascinating of sociological topics we might encounter.

# REFERENCES

American Psychiatric Association. (1994). *Diagnostic and statistical manual of mental disorders* (4th ed.). Washington, DC: Author.

Becker, H. S. (1963). *Outsiders: Studies in the sociology of deviance.* New York: Free Press.

Davison, G. C., Neale, J. M., & Kring, A. (2004). *Abnormal psychology* (12th ed.). New York: John Wiley & Sons.

Finkelhor, D., & Araji, S. K. (1986). Pedophilia: A four-factor model. *Journal of Sex Research, 22*(2), 145–161.

Sagarin, E. (1969). *Odd man in: Societies of deviants in America.* Chicago: Quadrangle Books.

Witt, P. H., & Greenfield, D. (2001). Pedophilia. In C. Bryant (Ed.), *Encyclopedia of criminology, Vol. III: Sexual deviance* (pp. 217–220). Philadelphia, PA: Brunner-Routledge/Taylor & Francis.

# Pedophiles and Child Molesters

## Keith F. Durkin and Steven Hundersmarck

The articles in this book represent a diverse array of extreme forms of deviance, ranging from racial supremacists to the morbidly obese. However, for many observers, the concept of "extreme deviance" is likely to evoke images of the most disvalued forms of sexual expression, such as sadomasochism and bestiality. Arguably, the best examples of this phenomenon are pedophiles and child molesters. Those individuals who have sexual relations with children are undoubtedly extremely deviant. Such contacts are illegal everywhere in the United States. Individuals who engage in such behavior (or even possess such an orientation) enjoy little social support. Not one of the 2,753 respondents to a recent national survey on sexual behavior indicated that they believed it was "normal" or "all right" for adults to have sexual contact with children (Janus & Janus, 1993). The thought of adults engaging in sexual activity with children is simply disgusting to most people. These people are thought to be among the most despicable of all deviants. In fact, such individuals are even disvalued by other deviants. In jails and prisons, pedophiles and child molesters occupy the lowest rung of the inmate stratification system and are often kept in protective custody for their own safety.

The purpose of this essay is to discuss pedophilia and child molestation as extreme forms of deviance. First, we examine the often overlooked and frequently misunderstood conceptual distinctions between pedophiles and child molesters. Second, we discuss the social organization of pedophilia. There are voluntary organizations for even the most disvalued forms of deviant behavior. For instance, the Diaper Pail Friends cater to those interested in infantilism, and the Zoophiliac Outreach Organization is an organization for people interested in bestiality. Several organizations for pedophiles are addressed in the following discussion. Also, we explore the rationalizations and justifications given by pedophiles and child molesters. Given the strong societal condemnation and stigma associated with this behavior, it is important to understand how these individuals attempt to protect their self-image and identity in the face of such strong social disvaluement and normative prohibitions. Finally, we consider the recent societal reactions to these individuals, which manifest in legislation and even vigilantism.

## PEDOPHILES AND CHILD MOLESTERS

There are a veritable plethora of definitions of pedophilia and child molestation in the professional literature, and often the terms are incorrectly used interchangeably. However, pedophilia typically refers to a sexual orientation or preference, whereas child molestation normally refers to an actual behavior. Pedophilia is normally defined as the sexual preference for children. A pedophile is conceptualized as an adult whose erotic images and sexual fantasies focus on children (Lanning, 2001). A pederast is an adult male who is sexually attracted to boys. Pederasts sometimes refer to themselves as "boy-lovers." On the other hand, a child molester is any adult who engages in any type of activity of a sexual nature with a child. Not all individuals who molest children are pedophiles. However, even if a pedophile does not engage in sex with children, he may participate in related activities that are unlawful, such as the possession of child pornography.

There are three types of child molesters described in the professional literature. The first type is called a situational or regressed child molester. These particular individuals would not be classified as pedophiles. Their sexual orientation is for adults, and they normally engage in sexual relations with age mates. There is typically some stressor in the individual's life, such as alcohol abuse, drug abuse, or social maladjustment, which precipitates this behavior (Mayer, 1985). This is probably the most common type of child molester (Lanning, 2001), and their victims are typically female (Holmes, 1991). The second type of child molester is the preferential or fixated molester. These individuals are classified as pedophiles. Mayer (1985) argued that the preferential or fixated molester has a "habitual compulsion to molest children of a certain age, comparable in some ways to the compulsion of alcoholics to drink" (p. 28). They are usually single men who have little or no contact (either social or sexual) with age mates (Lanning, 2001). This type of molester often uses child pornography. Although they are much less common than the situational or regressed child molester, they have the potential to molest a tremendous number of victims (Lanning, 2001). The final type of child molester is the mysoped. Although they are the rarest type of child molester, they are greatly feared because of the brutal nature of their attacks. These offenders "are intent on molesting children with the expressed desire to harm their victims physically" (Holmes, 1991, p. 36). They typically abduct their victims, who frequently are mutilated and murdered during the attack (Mayer, 1985).

There is a large body of literature that indicates that children who are molested experience a wide variety of problems as a result of their victimization. They may suffer physical difficulties such as sleep disorders. These children may also experience affective problems such as fear, anxiety, depression, and low self-esteem. They may also experience post-traumatic stress disorder and behavioral problems such as poor academic performance and aggressive behavior, as well as inappropriate sexual acting out.

## SOCIAL ORGANIZATION OF PEDOPHILIA

In recent years, pedophile organizations have formed and become increasingly vocal about their support for adult sexual behavior with children. At times, these groups have been rather militant in their rhetoric and have even attempted to proselytize their carnal ideology. For instance, there have been several European groups that advocated adult sexual contact with children. Perhaps the best known is an English group called the Pedophile Information Exchange (PIE). PIE was founded in 1971 to advance the cause of adult-child sex and was politically active in lobbying for the end of laws against "consensual sexual acts between adults and minors" (de Young, 1988, p. 583). This group had advocated that the age of consent be lowered to four years old (Mayer, 1985). Pedophile groups have been active in other European countries as well. They include Norway's Amnesty for Child Sexuality and Norwegian Pedophile Group, as well as the Studiegroep Pedofilie in Belgium.

There have also been pedophile organizations in the United States. There were two organizations that advocated adult sexual activity with children, the Rene Guyon Society and the Childhood Sensuality Circle, which are currently inactive. The Rene Guyon Society, founded in 1962, once claimed a membership of 8,500 persons (Mayer, 1985). This group's slogan was "sex by eight or else it's too late." The now defunct Childhood Sensuality Circle, formed in 1971, advocated abolishing the age of consent laws. This group promoted the "exchange of information and child pornographic materials including tapes, films, and photographs" (Mayer, 1985, p. 9). Both of these groups ceased their organizational activities by the mid-1980s.

The only major pedophile group currently active is the North American Man-Boy Love Association (NAMBLA). Founded in 1978 after the arrest of 24 Massachusetts men for having sexual contact with adolescent boys, this group advocates the abolition of laws regarding the age of consent, as well as the release of all men incarcerated for noncoercive sex with minors. NAMBLA has its organizational headquarters in New York City and local chapters in Boston, Los Angeles, San Francisco, and Toronto (Holmes, 1991). The group publishes a newsletter called the *NAMBLA Bulletin*. This organization has received a great deal of publicity and even had a spokesperson appear on the *Larry King Live* television program.

With the advent of the Internet, pedophiles have a new avenue for organization. The Internet can function as a social consolidation mechanism, bringing together like-minded individuals, such as pedophiles. They can use the Internet to communicate with each other as well as to trade pornography. There is a vast array of Web sites, newsgroups, chat rooms, and discussion forums related to pedophilia and adult-child sex. One example would be the Usenet group alt.support.boy-lovers. Existing organizations such as NAMBLA have a strong Internet presence. There is also a wide variety of literature available online that supports the pedophile viewpoint. This includes titles such as *The Boylove Manifesto*. There is also a new project called BoyWiki, which is modeled after the exceptionally popular online interactive encyclopedia Wikipedia.

## RATIONALIZATIONS AND STIGMA MANAGEMENT

A review of the relevant academic literature suggests that pedophiles and child molesters employ a variety of strategies in an attempt to rationalize, justify, and otherwise normalize their deviance. Mayer (1985) noted that "one striking characteristic of pedophiles is the ability to minimize or rationalize his activities" (p. 21). In his classic paper on child molesters and drinking, McCaghy (1968) found that many child molesters engaged in deviance disavowal. He interviewed 158 males who were convicted of having sexual contact with

children and found that about one-third attributed their sexually deviant behavior to alcohol:

> I was drunk and I didn't realize their age, I was half blind [note the victims in this case were six and seven years old]. . . . Drinking is the reason. I could always get women. I can't figure it out. A man's mind doesn't function right when he's got liquor on it. (p. 48)

By blaming their deviant behavior on alcohol consumption, these men were seeking to disavow the identity of a child molester. McCaghy (1968) concluded that by using deviance disavowal, the offenders "can avoid the self-concept of (a) child molester" (p. 48).

Based on his extensive experience in law enforcement investigating cases of child molestation, Lanning (2001) observed that "many child molesters, especially preferential child molesters, spend their lives trying to convince themselves they are not immoral, sexual deviants, or criminals" (p. 129). He provided several examples of these justifications. For instance, the offender may claim that he cares more for the children than their own parents do. He may rationalize the activity as merely being a type of "sex education" for the child. Lanning also found that these individuals frequently "blame the victim." For example, they may assert that the child initiated the activity or enjoyed the activity. They may also claim that the child was "promiscuous" and "seduced" them.

De Young (1989) examined the publications of NAMBLA and found that they often contained "accounts" that attempted to justify pedophilia. An account is "a linguistic device that is employed whenever an action is subjected to a valuative inquiry" (Scott & Lyman, 1968, p. 46). They are a type of exculpatory mechanism used by individuals to explain deviant behavior, and they serve as a type of stigma management technique to protect the individual's identity from being damaged. De Young (1989) found *denial of injury* was a prevalent theme in NAMBLA literature:

For NAMBLA, this justification involves the admission that the organization advocates adult-child sexual behavior, and that its members engage in the behavior, and the justification that neither the behavior nor the philosophy is in any way injurious to children. (p. 116)

De Young (1989) also discovered the publication of young boys' alleged descriptions of the benefits that they have experienced from engaging in sexual relationships with adult men. A second type of justification used in the NAMBLA publications was the *condemnation of condemners*. Law enforcement officers and social workers are typically the targets of diatribes that accuse them of engaging in a variety of unscrupulous practices including the brainwashing of children and "persecution" of "boy-lovers." De Young concluded,

> The intent of this justification strategy is both straightforward and clear: If the condemners can be reconceptualized as engaging in the same or even more victimizing or exploitative acts as those for which NAMBLA members are accused, then their censure of members is irrelevant at best and hypocritical at worst. (pp. 119–120)

More recently, Durkin and Bryant (1999) examined one month's worth of postings from 41 admitted pedophiles to a computer forum for "boy lovers." They found that the most common form of account offered was *denial of injury*. This involved the contention that sexual contact with adults is not injurious to children. Others took this a step further by offering a *claim of benefit* account. They asserted that sexual contact with adults is actually beneficial to children. Another account offered in these Internet postings was *condemnation of condemners*. These posts closely resembled the material found in NAMBLA publications that was discussed above. Frequent targets of condemnation were law enforcement, psychologists, psychiatrists, and social workers. One other account offered was *BIRGing* (basking in the reflected glory of related others). This consisted of the assertion that "great men" such as Socrates, Plato, and Oscar Wilde were also pedophiles.

Durkin (2004) explored the use of stigma management techniques in virtual communities (e.g., computer forums, Web pages, discussion groups) frequented by pedophiles. Aside from the use of accounts, he documented three other stigma management techniques. First, pedophiles attempt to provide validation to each other for their disvalued sexual identity via the Internet. For instance, they assure each other that they are not alone and share similar experiences and issues. Many of the computer postings involved providing support "to pedophiles that were facing personal problems related to their orientation or behavior" (p. 135). Second, pedophiles engage in semantic manipulation of the deviant label. This appears to be a cognitive mechanism for self-enhancement. In the larger society, pedophiles are called "perverts," "sex offenders," and "baby rapers." In virtual communities, pedophiles refer to themselves as "boy lovers" and the children they have illicit contact with as "loved boys." This semantic manipulation may allow pedophiles to conceptualize themselves as men with a "romantic" interest in children. Finally, pedophiles engage in deviance disavowal in these virtual communities. They seek to minimize the most negative aspect of their identity—the desire for sexual contact with children. This is portrayed as being of peripheral significance. Instead, their concern for the general welfare and betterment of youth is presented as the most important part of their identity.

## SOCIAL REACTION

Over the last dozen years, sex offender legislation has evolved and expanded as a result of high profile cases that have resulted in the passage of proactive and preventative laws in response to public fear of and outrage against sexual offenders. The targets of these sex offender and sexual predator laws are typically pedophiles and child molesters. For instance, registry laws have evolved from a tool used to assist law enforcement officers into a method of accounting for and controlling where convicted sex offenders live and work. Current state laws regarding registration of sex offenders are the result of federal guidelines as outlined in the Wetterling Act and more restrictive state-sponsored legislative actions such as Jessica's Law. The Wetterling Act (known more formally as The Jacob Wetterling Crimes Against Children and Sexually Violent Offender Registration Act) was passed as part of the Federal Violent Crime Control and Law Enforcement Act of 1994. The law is named after Jacob Wetterling, an 11-year-old who was abducted in 1989 by an unknown assailant while riding his bike one evening. It required states, for the first time, to implement registration of sexual predators, of individuals convicted of criminal offenses against minors, and of individuals convicted of sexually violent offenses. States were given three years from September 1994 to comply with the new law or risk losing federal grant money.

In 1996, Congress amended the Wetterling Act with Megan's Law, which was signed by President Clinton. Megan's Law was enacted in response to public outrage over the rape and murder of seven-year-old Megan Kanka. Megan was enticed into a neighbor's house with the promise of a puppy. Once inside the house, Megan was raped, then strangled. Her body was stuffed into a chest and dumped in a park. It was learned that the neighbor was a two-time sex offender who was living in the house with two other sex offenders he had met in prison. Megan's Law expanded the scope of the Wetterling Act in that it required states to release relevant information that is necessary to protect the public concerning a specific person required to register under this section. Since the law was enacted in 1996, all 50 states have adopted the basic tenets of the law, varying only in the procedures required for offender registration.

The Jacob Wetterling Improvements Act of 1997 further strengthened the law regarding sex offenders who maintain multiple residences or move across state lines. The law requires convicted sex offenders who are college students, military personnel, and other convicted sex offenders to register their primary and secondary places of residence, school, and work. In 2000, the Campus Sex Crimes Prevention Act was passed, further amending the Wetterling Act, "requiring offenders to report information regarding any enrollment or employment at an institution of higher education and to provide this information to a law enforcement agency whose jurisdiction includes the institution" (U.S. Department of Justice, 2003, p. 34). This Act went beyond prior Wetterling amendments in that the focus involved registry beyond the primary home. Most states have continued to expand registration laws beyond the requirements set forth by the amended Wetterling Act. A majority of these states have extended the recommended 10-year period an offender must register and have added to the list of offenses for which an offender must register.

Even more sweeping changes are in store for child sex laws. In March 2005, nine-year-old Jessica Lunsford was abducted from her bedroom in Florida, then raped and murdered by a registered sex offender who lived nearby. Her body was buried near the sex offender's residence. He had not registered his change of address with the Florida registry. Legislators in that state began action on new legislation almost immediately. The legislation was put on the fast track when 13-year-old Sarah Lunde was murdered in the state and another registered sex offender was charged with her murder in April 2005. In May 2005, Jessica's Law was passed in the State of Florida. This law contains components of laws passed in other states and goes beyond any action taken at the state or federal level before. The main emphasis of the law in Florida is the establishment of a mandatory sentence of at least 25 years for offenders convicted of certain sex crimes against children 11 years old and younger, with life-time tracking by global positioning satellite after they are released.

Because each state has discretion in adopting laws to curb sex offenders, there are a number of laws that fall outside those already discussed. For instance, in New York State, sex offenders are prohibited from working in ice cream trucks. In California, sex offenders cannot run massage parlors, and Kansas legislators are considering giving sex offenders pink license plates (Matthews, 2006). As lawmakers and the public continue to search for answers and the means to control sex offenders, there will continue to be novel and diverse legislation to address sex offenders.

Recognizing the high recidivism rate for sexually violent predators, a number of states have enacted legislation that allows for commitment in a treatment facility after an individual's prison term. In 1990, the State of Washington passed the Sexually Violent Predator Act, which allows for special commitment and possible life commitment of sexual predators with a mental or personality defect (Cohen, 1998). Under the law, sex offenders are evaluated at the end of their prison sentence to determine whether or not they are sexual predators. If they are determined to be sexual predators, they may be held in a high security treatment facility until they are no longer a threat. An individual can be classified as a sexual predator on the basis of the nature of the offense and not necessarily on the basis of a preexisting and defined mental disorder. At least 16 states have adopted similar civil commitment laws (Matthews, 2006). It is estimated that about 2,200 "sexual predators" were held using civil commitments in the late 1990s (LaFond, 2003).

Currently, eight states allow for chemical or surgical castration of sex offenders. At least two other states are considering legislation to allow castration as a treatment option. Chemical castration involves giving sex offenders weekly injections of Depo-Provera (a form of birth control for women) or another form of antiandrogen to reduce the amount of the male hormone testosterone in their system. Surgical castration is the removal of the testicles. There has been limited success with both forms of castration with a certain class of offenders. In Texas, as in other states, castration must be voluntary. However, there is movement toward requiring surgical castration as an involuntary treatment, as well. Chemical castration is used as a treatment option in Sweden, Germany, Denmark, and, more recently, France. In France, chemical castration was introduced in order to address an alarming increase in sex crimes. It is estimated that almost one-quarter of male detainees in French jails (8,200 people) are sex offenders, and nearly three-quarters of those have raped children (Laurenson, 2005).

There is evidence of vigilante action taken against registered sex offenders. In 2001, a Texas judge ordered 21 registered sex offenders to post signs on their homes and automobiles warning the public of their crimes. Immediately there were repercussions against a number of the offenders. One attempted suicide, two were evicted from their homes, several had property damaged, and one had his life threatened (Milloy, 2001). The most obvious case of vigilante action against registered sex offenders occurred recently in Bellingham, Washington. On August 26, 2005, an ex-convict named Anthony Mullen, who claimed to have been sexually abused as a child, killed two registered sex offenders who lived together in the same house. Mullins posed as an FBI agent and entered the home of the registered sex offenders. After questioning them at length, he shot them both in the head execution style because, in his words, they did not seem remorseful for their past crimes (O'Hagan & Brooks, 2005). Mullins admitted to using the registry to locate his victims. Complaints of lesser forms of harassment against registered sex offenders are common in the literature.

## Conclusion

Pedophilia and child molestation are among the most extreme forms of deviance that occur in our society. Moreover, pedophiles and child molesters are probably the most socially disvalued of all deviants in America. Nonetheless, these behaviors share some characteristics with other forms of deviant behavior, namely, the tendency of participants to attempt to organize themselves, and the tendency of the deviant to attempt to rationalize or otherwise justify his actions. Because of our societal concern for the safety and welfare of children, a number of laws have been enacted in an attempt to control the actions of pedophiles and child molesters. These include offender registries, community notification, civil commitments, and even castration. In the future, there will be a continuous challenge related to balancing community safety with protecting sex offenders from being the target of vigilantes.

## References

Cohen, F. (1998). *The mentally disordered inmate and the law.* Kingston, NJ: Civic Research Institute.

De Young, M. (1988). The indignant page: Techniques of neutralization in the publications of pedophile organizations. *Child Abuse and Neglect, 12,* 583–591.

De Young, M. (1989). The world according to NAMBLA: Accounting for deviance. *Journal of Sociology and Social Welfare, 16,* 111–126.

Durkin, K. F. (2004). The Internet as a milieu for the management of a stigmatized sexual identity. In D. Waskul (Ed.), *Net.SeXXX: Sex, pornography, and the Internet* (pp. 124–139). New York: Peter Lang.

Durkin, K. F., & Bryant, C. D. (1999). Propagandizing pederasty: A thematic analysis of the on-line exculpatory accounts of unrepentant pedophiles. *Deviant Behavior, 20,* 103–128.

Holmes, R. M. (1991). *Sex crimes.* Newbury Park, CA: Sage.

Janus, S., & Janus, C. (1993). *The Janus report on sexual behavior.* New York: Wiley.

LaFond, J. Q. (2003). Outpatient commitment's next frontier: Sexual predator. *Psychology, Public Policy and Law, 9,* 159–182.

Lanning, K. V. (2001). *Child molesters: A behavioral analysis* (4th ed.). Washington, DC: National Center for Missing and Exploited Children.

Laurenson, J. (2005, January 13). French test "chemical castration." *BBC News* [Electronic version]. Retrieved from http://news.bbc.co.uk/2/hi/europe/4170963.stm

Matthews, M. K. (2006, February 2). Molesters confined even after jail time is up. *Stateline.org.* Retrieved from http://www.stateline.org/live

Mayer, A. (1985). *Sexual abuse: Causes, consequences, and treatment of incestuous and pedophilic acts.* Holmes Beach, FL: Learning Publications.

McCaghy, C. H. (1968). Drinking and deviance disavowal: The case of child molesters. *Social Problems, 16,* 43–49.

Milloy, R. E. (2001, May 29). Texas judge orders notices warning of sex offenders. *The New York Times,* p. 10.

O'Hagan, M., & Brooks, D. (2005, September 7). Man says he'll plead guilty to killing sex offenders. *Seattle Times.*

Scott, M. B., & Lyman, S. (1968). Accounts. *American Sociological Review, 31,* 46–62.

U.S. Department of Justice. (2003). *Office of Justice Programs annual report: Fiscal report 2001–2002.* Washington, DC: Author.

# The World According to NAMBLA

## Accounting for Deviance

### *Mary de Young*

Look tenderly on little boys

Their softness as fleeting as a flower,

The cheeks like petals such a little hour,

The deepest dimple theirs so transiently

Look tenderly on little boys.

The transience of childhood innocence is an enduring theme in literature and poetry; however, the "Little Boys" poem from which these lines are taken did not appear in a literary anthology, but in the monthly *Bulletin* of NAMBLA—the North American Man-Boy Love Association. Organized in 1978 in the wake of the arrests of 24 prominent Revere, Massachusetts professional and businessmen for sexual activities with adolescent males, NAMBLA is a political, civil rights, and educational organization that advocates and promotes adult sexual behavior with male children. The taboo against adult-child sex, indeed, is consistently and ardently held in this and other cultures (Murdock, 1949), yet when NAMBLA was formed, there already was an international network of organizations of self-proclaimed pedophiles that served as organizational models.

Inspired by their European predecessors, two pedophile organizations that predated NAMBLA also were formed in the United States. The Rene Guyon Society, created in 1962 by a group of seven laypersons after attending a conference on sexuality in Los Angeles, took its name from the French jurist and Freudian psychologist who had been an outspoken advocate of adult-child sex. It also adopts his motto as its slogan: "Sex by year eight, or else it's too late." The Society advocates the abolition of statutory rape and child pornography laws and encourages its purported 5,000 members to give their own children, and others, early sexual experiences with loving adults (O'Hara, 1981). Although it still maintains a mailing address in the Los Angeles area, the Society is no longer politically and socially active in promoting its cause. Believing that affection transcends age differences, the Childhood Sensuality Circle was founded in San Diego in 1971 to champion sexual self-determination for adults and children. It also advocated the abolition of age of consent laws, promoted the early initiation of young children into sexual behavior with family members, and encouraged children to use their own standards in the selection of adult sexual partners (Davilla, 1981). The organization stopped publishing and mailing its *Nusletter* in 1984 because of the failing health of its elderly founder, Valida Davilla, a former student of Wilhelm Reich.

NAMBLA, then, is the only pedophile organization that remains active in this country, and it has withstood the legal harassment that has closed down many of its European counterparts. Due to their beliefs and practices, all of the pedophile organizations, in fact, have experienced a considerable amount of legal interference, ranging from searches of their headquarters and their members' homes, to seizures of materials for evidence, to the arrest and incarceration of their members. Social

EDITORS' NOTE: From de Young, M., "The World According to NAMBLA," in *Journal of Sociology and Social Welfare, 16*(1), copyright © 1989. Reprinted with permission.

stigma also has been sustained by organization members. Some have lost jobs when their organizational affiliation was discovered; others have been forced to use pseudonyms to protect their identities; and still others have been ostracized by their professional colleagues and social companions (O'Carroll, 1982).

These pedophile organizations and their members consistently have come up against an unusual degree of consensus on the part of the larger society that adult sexual behavior with children should be taboo, that it is victimizing and exploitative, and that its redress properly falls within the purview of the law. Although not uniform in extent, the strength of the consensus that does exist should not be underestimated. It continually has been demonstrated in studies of attitudes toward crimes and the law conducted by various ethnic and socioeconomic groups in this country (Finkelhor, 1984; Rossi, 1974; Sellin & Wolfgang, 1964), as well as in cross-cultural surveys (Newman, 1976). It may very well be that in the consciousness of the larger society, nothing is more repugnant than the sexual abuse of children (Finkelhor, 1984).

And that raises an important question. In the light of that strong consensus that adult sexual behavior with children is victimizing and that it is reprehensible, *how does NAMBLA justify and normalize its philosophy and practices?* In other words, how does NAMBLA account for its deviance? It is the purpose of this article to explore an answer to that question by reviewing the 1982 through 1985 newsletters, booklets, and brochures published for public dissemination by NAMBLA. This article does not provide a systematic analysis of the content of these publications; rather, it utilizes a data-reduction technique (Weber, 1985) by which textual material is classified into content categories generated by a larger theoretical framework. For the purposes of this article, that framework will be Scott and Lyman's (1968) theory of accounts.

## ACCOUNTING FOR DEVIANCE

Sociologists have long noted that individuals and groups can and do commit acts and hold beliefs they realize are considered wrong by others, and that in doing so, they create a problematic situation that calls for resolution, or at the very least for explanation. The problematic nature of the situation arises because the behavior or the beliefs of these individuals deviate from the expected, the routine, or what the larger society may even consider the normal. In that problematic situation, then, the deviating individuals or groups are motivated to avoid or to reduce public censure and stigma by engaging in behavioral or verbal conduct that justifies and normalizes their deviance vis-à-vis the expectations of others and the norms of the larger society (Mills, 1940; Scott & Lyman, 1968).

Psychologists would refer to this verbal conduct as rationalization, but sociologists offer a broader framework for its interpretation. Such verbal behavior, or its correlate in written form, is considered an "aligning action" (Stokes & Hewitt, 1976). That metaphor of alignment is both descriptive and explanatory. By examining various techniques and strategies, it describes how deviating individuals and groups attempt to align their lines of conduct with others and with the norms of the larger social structure, and it explains *why* they do so. The techniques of alignment are varied, but the motivation for engaging in them is consistent: Successful alignment will justify and normalize the deviant behavior or belief, thus reducing, if not eliminating, social censure and stigma.

Scott and Lyman (1968) refer to these various aligning actions as "accounts," those "linguistic devices employed whenever an action is subject to a valuative inquiry" (p. 46), and they propose two different types. The first, *excuses,* are those accounts in which the individuals or group admit the behavior or the belief in question is wrong, bad, or inappropriate, but deny full responsibility for it. Excuses generally take the form of "appeals." An "appeal to accident" redefines the offending conduct or belief as the product of unforeseen or uncontrollable circumstances; an "appeal to defeasibility" insists that it occurred only because the individuals or the group were not fully informed or fully aware. An appeal to "biological drives" presents the deviant behavior or belief as the product of innate drives that cannot be predicted or controlled; and an "appeal to scapegoating" blames others for it.

The second type of accounts, *justifications,* are those in which the individuals or group accept responsibility for the deviant behavior or belief, but deny the pejorative or stigmatizing quality of it. This category of accounts has generated a great deal of research within the sociology of deviance. Based as it is upon the criminological concepts of "techniques of neutralization" (Sykes & Matza, 1957), it has been used as a theoretical framework for analyzing the verbal accounts of compulsive gamblers (Cressey, 1962), social dropouts (Polsky, 1967), moral offenders (Hong & Duff, 1977), and murderers (Levi, 1981). And in recent years, it also has been used to analyze the verbal and the written accounts of sexual deviants. In two interesting studies, Scully and Morolla (1984, 1985) used the concept of accounts to examine the justifications and excuses of convicted incarcerated rapists; a similar framework was used by McCaghy (1968) with child molesters. Writings by sexual deviants also have been scrutinized through this particular theoretical lens. Taylor (1976) reviewed the works of the so-called "Uranian poets," those pedophilic writers whose ranks included such notables as F. E. Murray, W. B. Nesbitt, and Ralph Chubb, and discovered examples of the "uses of artistry as a motive-formulation resource for the justification and possible enactment of guilt-free sex" (p. 100). In a content analysis of the publications of the three pedophile organizations in this country, de Young (1988) found persistent themes that could be categorized as justifications.

Justifications, then, as a category of accounts, have demonstrated considerable utility as a theoretical framework for the analysis of the language and writings of deviant individuals and groups. It is this framework that will be used in this article's examination of the publications of the NAMBLA organization. Justifications generally involve six different strategies (Scott & Lyman, 1968), four of which will be used in this article: denial of injury, condemnation of the condemners, appeal to higher loyalties, and denial of the victim. The style and intended purpose of each of these will be explained and will be illustrated with selections from the publicly disseminated literature of NAMBLA.

## Denial of Injury

Using denial of injury, the individuals or the group acknowledge responsibility for the deviant act or belief but insist that it is permissible because no one is injured or harmed by it. For NAMBLA, this justification involves the admission that the organization advocates adult-child sex, and that its members engage in that behavior, and the claim that neither the behavior nor the philosophy is in any way injurious to children.

This assertion is contrary, of course, to the strong consensus that adult sexual behavior with children is, indeed, harmful. The child sexual abuse literature is rife with empirical research and case studies that bolster that consensus (de Young, 1985, 1987). Even the language that is part of the lexicon of both the lay public and professionals in the field—words like "abuse," "victimization," "exploitation," and "trauma"—attest to what most people believe are the deleterious effects on children of adult sexual behavior.

In the face of that strong consensus, then, NAMBLA must redefine the impact of both its philosophy and its members' behavior to stress the positive, rather than the injurious, effects of adult-child sex. Its publications, therefore, are filled with anecdotal accounts, letters, poetry, and articles that proclaim the benefits and advantages to children of having a sexual relationship with an adult male. Some of those advantages are very specifically detailed. Accounts of children having been rescued from lives on the streets, of children finding a loving alternative to an abusive home, or of discovering in the pedophile someone to talk to or to help them during periods of distress are prominently featured in every NAMBLA publication. Yet, when examples of the benefits to individual boys are set aside, the more general advantages of "man-boy love" are much less clear. The rather esoteric tenor of these explanations is illustrated by the following examples from NAMBLA (1985):

> Man love is also something which has helped thousands of boys discover their own sexuality and get in touch with what they really feel (Lotringer, 1980: 1). If sex is an expression of shared love (as man/boy love is), then it is beneficial to both partners, regardless of age. . . . Nothing is more beneficial than to feel a sense of security in the love of another. It creates a euphoria. The [pedophile] takes the young boys from the streets, give them a good home and material needs, and loves them. (p. 6)

NAMBLA, however, does acknowledge that harm may follow the adult-child sexual encounter; in the face of such overwhelming clinical and case study evidence, it can do little but acknowledge that. The organization, however, is quick to place the culpability for that harm on others who, it insists, respond inappropriately or prejudicially to adult-child sex. By displacing that blame, NAMBLA implies that there is nothing deviant about the sexual behavior, per se, but only about the public's reactions to it.

> Why can't we here in America do as those in the Netherlands have done? That is, EDUCATE the public to see that, in proper context, a man/boy relationship can be of benefit to the boy and the trauma that the police so quickly point out as connected to such relationships are caused not by the relationship, but by what the police themselves subject the boy to? (1984b, p. 4)

In no study known to us is there any suggestion that pedophile contacts are harmful in themselves. But in

our culture we usually cannot consider just the actual contacts. If they lead to other things there might well be a lot of damage that can be done by the parents of a child who had contact with a pedophile. On discovery they often react in panic. They become furious or outraged. Such a reaction . . . is very harmful to the child. . . . Then there is the damage caused by contact with the police and the courts. . . . The reactions of society can cause great damage to the child. (deGroot, 1982, p. 6)

Another tactic for denying injury is the publication of [alleged] youngsters' accounts of the benefits they have experienced from sexual relationships with adult males. Here are the very persons the larger society views as victims adamantly disavowing that label and, at least by inference, rejecting the care and protection that would be afforded them because of that status. The NAMBLA *Bulletin,* for example, for some period of time featured a column by "The Unicorn," allegedly an 11-year-old self-described "faggot" whose column was a testimony to the erotic superiority of sex with adult males as he described his various lovers and the positive effects each has had on his physical, emotional, and even spiritual development (1983e, p. 10). The organization also published a pamphlet, "Boys Speak Out on Man/Boy Love" (NAMBLA, 1981), which features short anecdotal accounts by boys of the positive effects of their sexual experiences with adult males. A perusal of the titles of the selections in this pamphlet suggest the tone of the testimonials: "Thank God for Boy Lovers," "If It Weren't for the Mark, I'd Probably Be Dead Today," "I Need My Lovers," and "The Best Thing That Ever Happened to Me."

The NAMBLA *Bulletin* also publishes letters [purported to be] from youngsters that describe the benefits they receive from sexual relationships with men.

> I am a boy of 13 and I hope you will read this letter. The spelling and stuff isn't too good. . . . I wish I was one of the kids [in the stories featured in the *Bulletin*] with someone to love me like that. . . . And

I think it's wrong for people to bother men and boys who just want to love each other. (1983b, p. 3)

There are enough of us young people in the country to stand up and put our foot down. To tell our feelings in the way we want to be understood and the way we want to be loved. . . . What we need is communication, peace, love, joy in our hearts, and happiness for people we are in love with. [Signed] Lover Boy Joe, age 13. (1984a, p. 5)

The denial of injury, then, is a justification that redefines adult sexual behavior with children in positive terms. As a rhetorical strategy, it is used to convince those of the larger society who will read its literature that contrary to popular belief, no injury or harm is incurred by children from engaging in sex with adult males; that the harm that has been stressed by other sources is really due to the inappropriate and prejudicial reactions of ignorant people and systems; and that even the children who have experienced this behavior will eschew the label of victim and proclaim the beneficial effects of sexual behavior with adults, if only they are asked. The insistence of this justification is that there is nothing really deviant in adult-child sex; therefore, any censure of the NAMBLA organization and its membership is undeserved.

## Condemnation of the Condemners

The second justification is the condemnation of the condemners, a rejection of those who would reject. The utility of this strategy is that in redirecting the condemnation and censure it has received from the larger society back on the society itself, NAMBLA can normalize its philosophy and the behavior of its members by demonstrating that they do not differ noticeably from the larger society. The condemners, real and potential, are thus characterized as hypocritical and as deserving condemnation themselves.

Since the censure of adult sexual behavior with children is so strong, the condemnation of the condemners found in the publications of NAMBLA is

equally strong. Much printed space is taken up with what are often sustained polemics against professionals in the field of child sexual abuse and against the criminal justice and the mental health systems. Individuals are listed by name, cases are dissected and analyzed, and flaws in decision making and errors in judgment are highlighted, all in a tone that is more often mockingly derisive than not. The following illustration demonstrates the breadth and the depth of that condemnation:

Con men who once made their living selling snake oil are now surfacing as "experts on child sexual abuse." They have deliberately confused expressions of love and affection with violent physical abuse. . . . Police departments suffering from a bad public image due to internal corruption, excessive use of force, and for poor management have turned to boy-lovers as easy prey. . . . District Attorneys needing a dramatic case for the voters to remember and psychiatrists needing public funds to build a private practice have turned to boy-lovers as the answer to their prayers. Demagogues in state and federal legislatures have also found the anti-boy-love hysteria tailor made for raising campaign funds and increasing name recognition through the sponsorship of laws pandering to the public's misconceptions. (NAMBLA, 1983c, p. 4)

[The children] continue to seduce adults and call those who reproach them for it "silly fools." The children had learned a bit about psychoanalysis. They said, "For every objection they were forced to abandon, these funny ladies and gentlemen immediately produce another. Could it be that they are really only unconsciously hiding the secrets of their own inner souls? Isn't it just that they are a little bit afraid of sex itself?" But nobody bothered to listen to what they said, for how could the truth ever be heard from the mouths of children? (NAMBLA, 1983a, p. 9)

The intent of this justification strategy is both straightforward and clear: If the condemners can be reconceptualized as engaging in the same or even more victimizing or exploitative acts as those for which NAMBLA members are accused, then their censure of the members is irrelevant at best, and hypocritical at worst. The sting of any subsequent criticism from them, then, is effectively precluded.

## Appeal to Higher Loyalties

The third justification that can be found in the publications of NAMBLA is the appeal to higher loyalties, a strategy by which the organization and its members normalize their behavior and philosophy by insisting the interests of a higher principle to which allegiance is owed is being served. That higher principle, for NAMBLA, is the liberation of children from what it characterizes as the repressive bonds of society; the sexual liberation of children, then, is presented as a necessary step for achieving the larger goal. The following excerpt illustrates that point:

> Members of NAMBLA are committed to the protection and development of the young. Our beliefs and activities have their foundation in values which say that all people are important and should have the inherent right to conduct themselves as they wish as long as the rights of others are not abused. Children are our special concern. We seek their freedom from the restrictive bonds of society which denies them the right to live, including to love, as they choose. (NAMBLA, 1984b, pp. 6–7)

> We recognize that children need more than sexual freedom and self-determination; they need economic self-sufficiency and the right and power to control all aspects of their lives, with help from but without interference by adults. NAMBLA favors the empowerment of young people in our society. Children should be treated as full human beings, not as the private property of their parents and the state. (NAMBLA, n.d., p. 1)

This espoused higher loyalty has the character of what Hewitt and Hall (1973) refer to as a quasi-theory and "ad hoc explanation brought to problematic situations to give them order and hope" (p. 367). Because it has structure and consequence,

a quasi-theory permits otherwise deviant situations and philosophies to be perceived by others as meaningful and even normal in light of common sense notions of human behavior and social arrangements.

That children need to be treated "as full human beings," that their protection and development are preeminent concerns, falls well within the rubric of common sense and common interest. It is both meaningful and normal to hold such an ideal, and on these issues alone, NAMBLA would not expect disagreement from the larger society. That larger society also may agree on some of the fundamental objectives that must be accomplished in order to achieve that goal, such as the empowerment of children, but when NAMBLA adds what would be considered a deviant objective, the "sexual freedom" of children, to that logic, the appeal to higher loyalty takes on the character of a quasi-theory. It espouses a hopeful goal, the development of children into "full human beings," and develops a structure, that is, a set of objectives for achieving that goal, and includes within that set an objective that the larger society would not, under other circumstances, accept.

Another facet of this appeal to higher loyalties involves the affinity NAMBLA has with the goals of other, nonstigmatized organizations and with social welfare concerns. The organization, for example, has expressed a great deal of sympathy and support for the women's movement as well as loyalty to the gay rights movement and views its own struggle for credibility and acceptance as analogous to their struggles. NAMBLA has also taken on such social welfare concerns as sexism, ageism, racism, nuclear warfare, abortion, unemployment, and the military draft, as well as esoteric concerns such as circumcision and clitoridectomy (NAMBLA, 1983f, p. 3). This partnership with other legitimate organizations and with social issues that are concerns of the larger society as well is a strategy for aligning the organization of NAMBLA and its membership with that larger society.

These appeals to higher loyalties, and the affinity with the goals of other legitimate organizations and with pressing social welfare concerns, allow NAMBLA to assume a mantle of legitimacy. That mantle, if successfully worn, further protects the organization and its members from the censure of the larger society.

## Denial of the Victim

The final justification found in the publications of NAMBLA is denial of the victim. Here, the victim, the child in this case, is reconceptualized as having deserved or brought on the deviant behavior; due to the victim's culpability, therefore, the responsibility of offending individuals for the behavior and its consequences is diminished.

This justification involves the conceptual transformation of children from victims of adult sexual behavior into willing partners. This transformation can only occur if NAMBLA is able to convince the disbelieving larger society that children are able to give full and informed consent to sexual acts with adults. But this issue of consent is a thorny one. Long after the debate about the morality of adult-child sex has been aired, and long after the uncertainties about the effects of such behavior on children have been satisfactorily addressed, the issue of consent will remain the most basic and fundamental problem that larger society has with adult sexual behavior with children (Finkelhor, 1984).

And it is a persistent and difficult problem for the NAMBLA organization as well; NAMBLA has made such general statements on the consent issue as these: "If a child and adult want to have sex, they should be free to do so. Consent is the critical point . . . force and coercion are abhorrent to NAMBLA" (1984b, p. 3); and "NAMBLA is strongly opposed to age of consent laws and other restrictions which deny adults and youth the full enjoyment of their bodies and control over their lives" (1984a, p. 7).

The problem, however, is not really with the definition of consent—the law spells that out quite clearly—but with the *age* at which it can be given in a free, knowledgeable, and informed manner. NAMBLA asserts that the current age of consent laws in this country, which pro forma make its members' sexual behavior with youngsters illegal, are anachronistic and repressive. It strongly advocates for their repeal, as the following excerpt illustrates:

> NAMBLA does not simply wish to repeal age of consent laws; rather, we have never accepted the validity of the frame of reference on which such laws are based. Under the circumstances, we cannot name an age of consent. . . . NAMBLA will not participate in abstract, narrowly defined and ultimately pointless games of "pick an age." . . . Sex does not require highly developed "cognitive tools"; it ought to come naturally. (1983b, p. 1)

Does sex require highly developed "cognitive tools"? If the act itself does not, the consent to engage in the act certainly does, so despite the organization's resistance to engage in a game of "pick an age," the age at which a child can give full and informed consent to sexual acts must be determined if this justification is going to be successful in normalizing the behavior of NAMBLA members and avoiding public censure.

And the very debate over that age is still waged within the ranks of NAMBLA. In a position paper created by the steering committee of the organization, consent was defined as both informed (understood and accepted in advance) and with the intent and spirit of love. Because understanding and acceptance at least imply some "cognitive tools," the committee backed off from its original insistence that it would not pick an age and selected nine as the age of consent. Some members argued that it should be lower. One insisted that "a five-year-old aware of sexual feelings can act upon them at any time of his choosing. There are many five-year-olds who understand the meaning of sex more than many 35-year-olds" (1983d, p. 4). Other members, perhaps predicting how the larger society would respond to these proposed ages, advocated that the age be raised to 13 or 14. Even while the NAMBLA organization vehemently argued this issue, one of its founding members went on record to defend all consensual sexual relations, "regardless of the age of the partners" (Lotringer, 1980, p. 21).

Obviously, the issue of consent and the age at which children can freely and intelligently render it continues to be a problem for the NAMBLA organization. It is for the larger society as well, as evidenced by the fact that the age of consent established by law tends to vary from one state to another. While the larger society may find some value in debating whether that age should be uniform across the country, and may find some interest in deciding what that age should be, the same attitude studies that demonstrate such a strong consensus that adult sexual behavior with children is harmful and exploitative also show an increase in that consensus where very young children are concerned. In other words, the debate about whether the age of consent should be 13, 14, or 15 may be lively, but there is little demonstrated acceptance of lowering that age, and virtually none for removing it.

Denial of the victim, predicated as it is upon this issue of consent, is unlikely to be a successful justification; indeed, it may be this single issue of consent and the failure of this justification that will always keep the deviant label on this organization and its members, therefore keeping them out of alignment with the larger society.

## CONCLUSION

In the face of a strong consensus that adult sexual behavior with children is abusive and exploitative, and that its effects are negative at best and traumatic at worst, the North American Man-Boy Love Association has a vested interest in justifying, and thereby normalizing, its philosophy and its members' practices. This article has utilized the sociological framework of accounts, with a special reference to justifications, to examine how that process is accomplished in the publications of NAMBLA.

The use of accounts by deviant individuals and groups is an area of research that has the potential to generate insights into deviancy. And in the area of sexual deviancy, where myth and misunderstanding abound, the study of these aligning actions may increase knowledge of how individuals and groups labeled deviant attempt to negotiate and reconceptualize their beliefs and their behavior in the face of society's censure.

If the imputation of deviance is indeed a product of interactive process between the individuals or group so labeled and the labelers (Schur, 1979), then the study of accounts may also lead to an understanding of that process. How accounts are given, in terms of their manner and their style, and how accounts are accepted and the consequences of their acceptance are researchable hypotheses, and studies designed to address these issues and others will make rich contributions to the sociology of deviance.

## REFERENCES

Cressey, D. R. (1962). Role theory, differential association, and compulsive crimes. In A. Rose (Ed.), *Human behavior and social processes* (pp. 443–467). New York: Houghton Mifflin.

Davilla, V. (1981). *CSC position paper* (2nd ed.). San Diego, CA: Childhood Sensuality Circle.

deGroot, D. (1982). *Paedophilia*. Boston: NAMBLA.

De Young, M. (1985). *Incest: An annotated bibliography.* Jefferson, NC: McFarland and Company.

De Young, M. (1987). *Child molestation: An annotated bibliography.* Jefferson, NC: McFarland and Company.

De Young, M. (1988). The indignant page: Techniques of neutralization in the publications of pedophile organizations. *Child Abuse and Neglect: The International Journal, 12*(4), 583–591.

Finkelhor, D. (1984). *Child sexual abuse: New theory and research.* New York: The Free Press.

Hewitt, J. P., & Hall, P. M. (1973). Social problems, problematic situations, and quasi-theories. *American Sociological Review, 38,* 367–374.

Hong, L. K., & Duff, R. W. (1977). Becoming a taxi-dancer: The significance of neutralization in a semi-deviant occupation. *Sociology of Work and Occupations, 4,* 327–343.

Levi, K. (1981). Becoming a hit-man: Neutralization in a very deviant career. *Urban Life, 10,* 47–63.

Lotringer, S. (1980). Loving boys. *Semiotext(E) Special, 1*(5), 20–30.

McCaghy, C. H. (1968). Drinking and deviance disavowal: The case of child molesters. *Social Problems, 16,* 43–49.

Mills, C. W. (1940). Situated actions and vocabularies of motive. *American Sociological Review, 5,* 904–913.

Murdock, G. P. (1949). *Social structure.* New York: Macmillan.

NAMBLA. (n.d.). *What is NAMBLA?* New York: Author.

NAMBLA. (1981). *Boys speak out on man/boy love.* New York: Author.

NAMBLA. (1983a, March). *Bulletin, 4*(2).

NAMBLA. (1983b, April). *Bulletin, 4*(3).

NAMBLA. (1983c, May). *Bulletin, 4*(4).

NAMBLA. (1983d, July/August). *Bulletin, 4*(6).

NAMBLA. (1983e, November). *Bulletin, 4*(9).

NAMBLA. (1983f). *NAMBLA Journal, 6.*

NAMBLA. (1984a, September). *Bulletin, 5*(7).

NAMBLA. (1984b, December). *Bulletin, 5*(10).

NAMBLA. (1985, April). *Bulletin, 6*(3).

Newman, G. (1976). *Comparative deviance: Perception and law in six cultures.* New York: Elsevier.

O'Carroll, T. (1982). *Paedophilia: The radical case.* Boston: Alyson.

O'Hara, T. (1981). *Rene Guyon Society bulletin.* Los Angeles: Author.

Polsky, N. (1967). *Hustlers, beats and others.* Chicago: Aldine Press.

Rossi, P. (1974). The seriousness of crime: Normative structures and individual differences. *American Sociological Review, 39,* 224–237.

Schur, E. (1979). *Interpreting deviance.* New York: Harper and Row.

Scott, M. B., & Lyman, S. M. (1968). Accounts. *American Sociological Review, 3,* 46–62.

Scully, D., & Morolla, J. (1984). Convicted rapists' vocabulary of motive: Excuses and justifications. *Social Problems, 31,* 530–544.

Scully, D., & Morolla, J. (1985). Riding the bull at Gilley's: Convicted rapists describe the rewards of rape. *Social Problems, 32,* 251–263.

Sellin, T., & Wolfgang, W. (1964). *The measurement of delinquency.* New York: John Wiley and Sons.

Stokes, R., & Hewitt, J. P. (1976). Aligning actions. *American Sociological Review, 41,* 838–849.

Sykes, G., & Matza, D. (1957). Techniques of neutralization. *American Sociological Review, 22,* 663–670.

Taylor, B. (1976). Motives for a guilt-free pederasty: Some literary considerations. *American Sociological Review, 24,* 97–114.

Weber, R. P. (1985). *Basic content analysis.* Beverly Hills, CA: Sage.

# From Victim to Offender

## *"Dave"*

I spent my childhood growing up in what would now be termed a dysfunctional family. My father had been married previously and retained custody of his two daughters. My mother became my father's housekeeper. They began a sexual relationship some time later and I was the product of their union. I loved my mother immensely but she suffered extreme mood swings. She would be all over me giving me kisses and cuddles one minute, and the next, she would belt me and put me on a shelf in the linen cupboard with the door closed. When I was three, my uncle began fondling me, giving me lots of affection and attention, telling me that I was his special boy and that what he was doing was our little secret and that I shouldn't tell anyone, least of all my mommy or daddy. My mother had taught me to keep secrets, especially family secrets, so I understood.

When I was six or seven, my mother gave birth to my sister. I heard my parents arguing about who the father was. One day when my baby sister was about six months old, my mom and dad were arguing late at night. The noise woke me up. I went into their bedroom to see what was going on because I could hear my mom screaming at Daddy to stop it. When I got to the bedroom door I could see Daddy holding a pillow over mom's face. I ran into the room and began hitting and kicking my dad, telling him to let Mom go. I was very distraught and needed to be quieted down. I heard Dad tell my mom that she had to leave and take my baby sister. He said that as he was not her father, he didn't want her in the house, but because I was his son, he would keep me. When I woke up the next morning my mom and baby sister were gone. I was absolutely devastated at losing both of them at once.

Dad found a new housekeeper in a very short time. At some point during the next few weeks, my mother came past when I was playing in the front garden. As soon as I saw her I ran to her, crying tears of both sadness and joy. Mom took me out that day and many other days thereafter. Sometimes we went to her home where I could spend time with my baby sister. I hated having to return to Dad's house, but I had no say in the matter. I longed to live with Mom despite her moods. Quality time with Dad was minimal because he worked 16 to 18 hours a day, and I only saw him when he came home from work, and that was usually to say goodnight before I went to sleep. Sometimes we had Saturday afternoons or Sundays together, and then I realized that I loved him dearly, too.

When I began school, my uncle and aunt invited me to spend holidays at their home. Uncle's

holidays always coincided with school holidays, and on every occasion he could be alone with me, he removed my clothes and did whatever he wanted to do. He would run his hands all over my body, fondling me while giving me kisses and cuddles. He always put my penis in his mouth and sucked it, then asked me to reciprocate. If I said no, he would try coaxing, then bribing me. He was never angry nor did he ever use force. His bribes were very attractive; for example, he let me drive his car when we visited his beach property or he bought me gifts that were special and expensive. I usually cooperated because I was desperate to please him given that he was the only one to consistently give me attention and approval. He would have me bathed and dressed before my aunt arrived home from work.

From the age of three, I wandered around the streets alone and talked to people. I was always a happy-go-lucky child; nothing ever seemed to bother me nor did I have any fear of anything (people, animals, or traffic). This was how I met my first friend who was the same age as I was. When I was aged 5 or 6 years, I needed money to buy cigarettes and matches and I'd already learned that people who knew me would give me a few cents to pull out some of the weeds in their gardens. This soon became a regular job that I enjoyed doing.

My parents taught me "Always do what grown ups tell you to do" and "It's naughty to say no to an adult. You are only a child and adults have been around a long time. They only do or tell you to do things for your own good." As a consequence, I spent the biggest part of my childhood being physically, sexually, and psychologically abused and even tortured by many different adults. One day, some of my regular gardening customers were not at home or didn't need any help and so I decided to knock on other doors to offer my services. As I walked along the street, I saw a house with a lot of weeds in the front garden. I walked up the driveway and knocked at the door. The occupant eyed me up and down. Although almost eight, I was probably smaller than the average five year old. I had big blue eyes, white blonde hair, and a very fair complexion. The man asked me whether I could wash dishes. I'd seen my sisters wash them and it didn't look hard, so I said "yes" (even though I'd never washed a dish in my life). He said, "Well maybe I do have a job for you, so come inside."

It turned out that my new employer was a member of a very sadistic pedophile group that included both men and women. I was soon to find that they brought children from other states and sold them to pedophiles as sex slaves. State wards were brought from a children's home by staff, but the majority were the pedophiles' own children. When sex slaves became adults, they often remained under the group's control. When the young women gave birth, their babies were taken from them to be used for sex and pornography. The women didn't know where their children were. All of these children lived with their abusers and were shared among their friends at any time of night or day. Many of these abusers were accompanied by their sons and daughters, who were instructed to abuse us physically and sexually while the adults watched. Over the next eight years, I was taken in the trunk of a big black car to many different locations to be used for their sadistic sexual pleasure.

Sometimes I was anally and orally raped by five or six adults. At other times there could be up to 20 adults and as many children being used for sex. However, it wasn't just the sex that was damaging; we were also degraded, humiliated, and forced to be subservient in every possible way. We had to thank the adults for everything they did to us, regardless of how painful or physically damaging it was. Lots of money changed hands between the adults, although it was years later before I realized that the organizer was being paid for our suffering. These sexual predators were adults in responsible professional positions: men in police uniforms, teachers, priests, judges, doctors, lawyers. Two of the abusers were a husband and wife team who

managed a state children's home and often brought children with them. I always had to refer to the man who had hired me to wash his dishes as Master. I was a good boy and did what I was told to do. Over the next few months I was put on display for many of his pedophile friends.

By the time I was nine I had been taken to many different houses, either naked or in various manner of dress. I was so small that the men sometimes transported me in a suitcase, overnight bag, a cardboard box, or a sack, and sometimes in a small wire cage normally used for carrying pets. The wire cage was mostly used for their night-time country sessions. My master would either deliver me to the house or he told me to knock on the front door and do whatever the person or people in the house told me to do. He said that he would be able to tell if I had been a good boy by what was in the envelope when he picked me up two or three hours later. During those eight years I was continually told that what was happening to me was my own fault, that I only had myself to blame. After all, didn't I beg them to rape, torture, and degrade me? I even thanked them for whatever they did—as if I had some sort of choice.

The other victims' ages ranged from 6 months to adolescence. The most popular victims seemed to be from 8 to 10 years of age. Remarkably, some who had been abused throughout their entire lives were still under the control of these sex offenders when in their twenties. They were mostly females who had spent their childhood as "sex children" and were kept by their masters as slaves or servants, child bearers and prostitutes, as well as being used by group members to clean their houses and do the laundry. Occasionally men would strip, degrade, humiliate, and use the adult victim for sex with everyone else watching. These women were also beaten and treated cruelly by their masters.

The reader will no doubt be wondering why I returned to my master's house, knowing what would happen to me there. He controlled me by telling me that I was a bad kid and would be in "big trouble" if I didn't return when instructed to do so. We children were trapped by these predators and were programmed to believe the things they told us. We knew that if we told anyone what they did to us, they would know and punish us even more, so we couldn't trust or talk to anyone for fear of their reprisals. We were made to feel dirty, degraded, and worthless. We were told that we were useless, hopeless, and could do nothing right. We were often belted, caned, kicked, punched, strapped, and whipped; sometimes they used the buckle of their belts. The abusers would often grab one of us by our wrist and kick or punch us in the side of our ribcage. They also bent children over a coffee table with their legs wide open or had them crawl around on hands and knees with legs apart and kicked or punched them between their legs, sending them reeling across the room from the force of the blows. Then the children had to thank their abusers, no matter how much pain they were in. I suffered less than the others because I was returned to my home each day, so the abusers couldn't leave bruises or scars that couldn't be explained as a fall from a tree, a bike, or a cart crash and may have led to them being suspected.

One of the houses had a large room where all of the sex children took turns being tied or strapped by the ankles and wrists to a long rack or bench-type fixture, where they would be whipped or belted. Attached to another corner of the room was another rack that a child would be tied to. This rack had some sort of electronic machine with a voltage regulator that had wires coming out of it. One of these wires had a metal cylindrical bar about the thickness of a broom handle and about six to eight inches in length. This was inserted in a boy's anus or in either the anus or vagina of a girl. Then they had at least two other wires with alligator clips attached to them. They were connected to other parts of the victim's body, such as armpits. The power was then switched on, and the current was gradually increased. As we jerked and

screamed with pain, the adults laughed and jeered and humiliated us. The racks had provisions to stretch our bodies either straight or with our arms and legs spread-eagled. This was achieved by using ropes that were tied to our limbs. By adjusting the settings, they were able to open and close our legs, giving them easy access to our genitals to intensify our pain. Other times, we were drugged to such a state that we were unable to do anything other than lie down, enabling them to do whatever they wanted to our bodies. I was usually aware of what they were doing, but I was unable to move or talk. When the men had finished with us, we were given to their wives and natural children to torment and abuse. We then had to be obedient to their offspring, who were sometimes even younger than us. They enjoyed abusing the power that their parents gave them.

Terrified that my father would discover what was happening, I would crash my cart or bike into walls and trees to hide the belt-buckle marks, whip marks, and bruises. As time went on, the crashing became more serious. I wanted to end my life simply because the pain and torment were just too much to bear.

At the age of 12, I started babysitting for neighbors on Fridays or Saturday nights. This was when I first became a sex offender. Most of my offences involved touching, caressing, fondling, looking at children (boys and girls) in various stages of dress and undress, and performing oral sex with young children. As an adult offender, I had children reciprocating. In my life I have been charged with numerous counts of child sex offences including indecent sexual assaults, indecent acts, sexual assaults, aggravated sexual assaults, incest, attempted sexual penetration, anal penetration and attempted vaginal penetration, and aggravated rape. Now, I am deeply ashamed of my offending behavior, but at the time I regarded it as normal. It never occurred to me that it was wrong or that I might be arrested and jailed, which of course I was. That took me completely by surprise. After all, police and judges had been my abusers and no one protected me, so how could I have taken the law seriously?

Now that I am in my late forties, I can see the psychological damage that was inflicted on me and that I, in turn, replicated with my own victims. I am not intending to justify my crimes; I accept full responsibility for my own actions; I had a choice and, having experienced victimization, should have known better than anyone that abuse can ruin lives.

By now I had a nephew and a niece, and my stepmother and the children's mothers would let them run around naked. My stepmother sunbathed topless in the back garden (unlike my real mother, who always kept her body and her children's bodies modestly covered). I took my niece or nephew out for walks as soon as I was permitted. From the day they came home from the maternity hospital, I was taught to change their dirty diapers, and toilet training gave me plenty of opportunities to fondle their genitals.

My first babysitting jobs involved two young girls and one boy. Even though I had by now seen many naked girls and boys, in many different positions, and had even at times been told by my abusers to lick the girls' genitals or the boy's penis, I had never been able to have a really close look at a vagina. I had a very strong desire to examine one of the girl's genitals more closely and achieved my objective, licking and kissing and cuddling her. I later committed sexual offences with that girl's brother and sister also. I was often left to bathe and change children into their pajamas, so I had plenty of opportunity to both look at and fondle them. I played "tickles" and sometimes licked or sucked the children's genitals. I turned my abuses into a game, which made the children more receptive to my advances.

When I was 14 and people had gotten to know me and learnt by word of mouth that I was available for babysitting, they would ask me to take care of their children when they wanted to go out for

the evening. I now regularly cared for children aged from six months to about 10 or 11 years old. The usual age group of my victims was between 8 and 11 years.

I did not molest every child that I took care of. Not every child interested me sexually, but babysitting gave me the opportunity to abuse many victims in a relatively short period of time. Some I found attractive but sensed that they were out of bounds and I couldn't touch them. Sometimes parents made comments that I interpreted as permission to molest their children. Abusing children was easy! I reminded them of something that their parents said as they were leaving the house, such as, "Be a good boy and girl and do whatever David says. If you don't behave he has our permission to pull your pants down and smack your bare bottom." Another said, "David, will you make sure they wash themselves properly in the bath?" or "Would you mind washing them and make sure they are properly dried?" I saw all of these comments as an open invitation from the parents to abuse their children. Also, it was easy to say to the children that they had been naughty and have them pull their pants down so I could have a look or feel their genitals instead of giving them a smack. They were grateful for the lesser of two evils, although I never intended to smack them. The children I was asked to bathe and dry off were up to 7 and 8 years old and, at the time, I couldn't believe my luck.

Some of the children were in the bath when I arrived, and parents left them in my hands as they were getting ready to leave. I always enjoyed bathing and drying the girls, and I would pay a lot of attention to the genital area. I deliberately dried boys first so that they returned to their rooms to don their pajamas, leaving me with the girls. I dried them in such a way that I had a good view, and this satisfied me for several weeks until the children trusted me and I was confident that I could carry out my offences with little fuss. At no time did I ever sexually penetrate any of my victims, simply because I did not want to hurt them as I had been hurt by my abusers. I didn't abuse children frequently; sometimes weeks or even months passed between offences. What I am saying is that I had committed sexual crimes with children for many years right up until the time that I married my first wife.

My first prison sentence was for sexually assaulting my stepchildren. As a family unit we did occasionally take care of friends' children, but I didn't abuse them because there was no need; I had victims readily available in my own home. Louise, my future wife, was 13 years older than me. At the time that we met I was helping at a church boys' club. As one of two leaders, I would drive the boys to their homes after the club meeting. It was through the boys' club that I first met Darren, who eventually became my oldest stepson. I enjoyed his company from the very beginning. He told me he lived with his mom, a single parent; a brother; and four sisters. Darren also said they had no contact with their father. Once I'd developed a relationship with Louise and her family, the children began taking turns to stay at my place for a weekend. On each occasion I said to Louise that I would make a bed for them on the sofa. She always replied that I shouldn't go to any trouble, just "bunk them in your bed." Before the visits, Louise routinely told them to behave and do everything that I told them to do, adding that if they misbehaved I had her permission to smack their bare backsides. Once again, I interpreted her replies as permission to molest the children and I used her statements to advantage. On most occasions, the children complied with my wishes.

I sexually assaulted all of Louise's children from their very first weekend at my house. Usually I would begin with fondling, and then I would either remove their clothes or ask them to get undressed. Then I would perform oral sex on them. I would put them in the bath with me and during the night I would have them in bed with me. Later, when we moved into a house together, Louise told me that she and I would not be sleeping together until after we were married. Her parents would disapprove,

she said. When I asked where I was supposed to sleep, Louise replied, "Bunk in with one of the children." Some of the children were complaining that I always slept with the same child. They viewed her as being privileged and were jealous. They said they wanted to have their turns, so we created a roster for every child to sleep with me excepting the two youngest.

Sometimes I would molest the children individually in their beds, but mostly it would happen when their mother was either watching TV in another room or she was out playing bingo. It happened, too, if the children and I were out visiting one of my friends at night. I committed offences in the car on a vacant lot along the way to or from my friend's home. When I was committing offences, all five children would often participate. There were a number of times that I anally penetrated them, but I told myself that the children enjoyed it. Now, I realize that they participated in order to please me. When necessary, I used bribery, coercion, trickery, or emotional blackmail to have my needs fulfilled. I continued my offences with the children after Louise and I were married and until I was eventually charged with these crimes and jailed.

I was thrilled when Louise gave me the news that she was pregnant with my child. She assured me that I didn't have to marry her but she would appreciate me being there to support my child. Louise said how much her children thought of me and that she could see the close bond that existed between us. I talked with Louise about marriage and told her that I wanted my child to have my name and not be born a bastard, as I was. Louise said, "I am not like your other girlfriends. I don't care if you have long hair or a beard and I don't care if you don't get a job because I accept you for who you are. The only thing that I do want is for you to give up taking drugs." It took time but I have never looked back. I've stayed clean ever since and will be forever grateful to her for that.

The fact that she was now carrying my first child (and I was convinced that I loved her children) made marriage seem right. I loved Louise for her special qualities, but looking back, she was more like a mother, sister, or close friend than a wife and lover. We talked about a wedding and the children agreed that we should marry and wedding plans were made. For the first time in my life I felt alive, loved, and needed.

Quite often, Louise would watch an evening show that the children and I didn't wish to see, so four or five of the children would watch TV or videos in one of their bedrooms. During this time I often molested them. It was easy to do at any time, even when the younger children were sitting on my knee in the chair right beside their mother. At the time, I always convinced myself that they enjoyed what was happening. They would reciprocate the acts at my request and often without me even asking. Looking back, I now see that they did this not because they enjoyed it, but to please me. I am not sure when it happened, but at some point in time I anally penetrated each of four of the children on several occasions. I honestly don't know why. I still don't understand.

Alex, my firstborn, was born the following October. It was one of the happiest days of my life. He arrived prematurely and I delivered Alex at home. Louise and I then took him to the hospital. I adored my child and used to take him for long walks on most days. This gave Louise time to do her housework and gave me quality time with my son. Jack, a second son, followed.

Just prior to my marriage to Louise, a young lady came to the house selling encyclopedias. I took one look at Laura and fell madly in love with her. The tragedy was that both she and I were about to get married. Andrew, her husband-to-be, worked a night shift and Laura didn't like being alone at night, so I began staying with her. Some of the children often came with me, and soon Laura and I were having an affair. This began about the time that I got married. Four of the children knew what was happening, and I presumed that they all approved because no one told their mother. James,

one of Louise's children, summed it up one day by saying that I should divorce his mother and marry Laura, then he and the other children could come to live with us. This continued for several years. Laura had a child; I still don't know whether it was mine or her husband's.

## PRISON, RELEASE, AND REIMPRISONMENT

On November 10, 1983, I was arrested and later imprisoned for molesting the children. Initially, there were many charges, but they were reduced to 17 including indecent assaults and incest. I received a six-year prison sentence with a five-year minimum. I had my initiation to the prison system by receiving a beating from other prisoners within seconds of my arrival in the exercise yard, thanks to a comment made by the senior prison officer. From there I was placed on a 23-hour lockup. I wasn't coping at all well in the prison's D wing and made my third suicide attempt. I was then sent to a division that had a much higher level of security; it was a psychiatric unit. That is where I first met Morrison. He was to become a co-offender for my next offences and was a major influence on my life thereafter.

I take full responsibility for all that my children suffered at my hands and the hands of my co-offenders. What grieves me most is that, given my own damaging experiences, I should have known better. I cannot forgive myself for allowing either my co-offenders or myself to ruin my children's lives. I was and still am an insecure person. Morrison and I built up a friendship; he was able to convince me that there was nothing wrong with what I did. He was a lot stronger than me and he became my protector during my first prison sentence, keeping me safe from other prisoners who believed that they had the right to bash, mutilate, and even rape child sex offenders. With his convincing manner, I readily believed all that he told me. This doesn't justify my crime in any way, nor am I making excuses or laying blame, as I am totally responsible for what I did. I mention it merely as an explanation. I think that it was really Morrison the other convicts hated most. What they hated about me was the fact that I was perceived as his friend. Because of that, they stopped speaking to me. They engaged in name-calling and threatened me, which in turn made the friendship between Morrison and me even closer.

Louise and the children began coming to the prison to visit me. They all seemed to have forgiven me and we looked forward to visiting days.

The first night that I was released from prison, I spent time with my wife and children. I was asked by Louise to put my son Jack to bed in his cot. Upon entering the bedroom, I found a pile of dirty diapers and a mattress that was literally dripping urine onto the floor. I was really so disgusted by the way that Jack had been treated in my absence that I felt very guilty for not being there to care for him. I made up my mind there and then that I would do everything in my power to have as many of the children as possible to live with me, starting with Alex, my other son with Louise, and Jack.

I found my former mistress, Laura, within three weeks of leaving prison, and I moved into their house to live with her and my children. As soon as I was settled, Louise allowed me to have Alex and Jack for weekends. Soon after that, my sons were spending more time with me than with their mother. So I spoke with Louise about getting the boys into school and kindergarten where I was now living with Laura. Louise agreed, saying that she had done enough child rearing while I was in prison so now it was my turn. Louise also said that I could have Alex and Jack; however, she would not part with the government child support that she was receiving for their care. I told her that regardless of that, I wanted them and that I would be happy to support them with the government benefit that I was now receiving. Laura, the children, and I could not have been happier. Now we were a family.

My divorce and Laura's went through at about the same time. At some point, Harry, Laura's ex-husband, came to live with us. I was having a rest on my bed. Alex was with me and he was providing oral sex when Harry walked in. I was caught in the act. Harry responded by saying that he wanted Alex to do the same for him. My immediate reply was negative, but Harry threatened to call the police if I didn't cooperate. I said he wouldn't dare. Harry said he would, and I eventually believed him and capitulated. Looking back, I think Alex only responded to Harry's wishes to protect me, as he had already lost me once and didn't want to lose me again. Alex ended the argument by saying that he would do it as long as he didn't have to tell the police. I told Alex that he didn't. He said he knew that, but did it anyway. As for Laura, I was able to convince her that what I was doing was normal.

I began to visit Morrison, initially on my own but later with Laura and the children. Laura's husband Harry had, by this time, moved out. Laura had suffered his violence for far too long. One evening, I caught him physically abusing Laura and one of the children. I belted the living daylights out of him. I told him if I ever saw him hurt Laura or the child again, I would kill him—and I meant it.

Laura became my wife in 1988. I loved Laura then and I love her now. She was my life and my world, yet I destroyed Laura's life as I destroyed the lives of my children. Within two years, Laura gave birth to a son and a daughter. However, I know that because of my evil crimes I will never be able to see them again, and that hurts far more than being in prison.

I have always loved Laura and all my children. I truly wanted to give them a better life than the one that I had as a child. I wanted them to have a good education and proper medical attention and a good, happy, and stable home full of love and affection that I never received in childhood from anyone other than my uncle, the child abuser. I felt that if I modeled myself on my uncle and spent as much quality time with my children and gave them as much physical affection, I would be a good father. That was my intention. However, I failed them miserably. My need for acceptance was paramount and the children accepted me.

As I grew up I equated love with sex, modeling myself on the uncle I once adored. With poor communication skills coupled with mood swings (like my mother), I used emotional blackmail and coercion (like my uncle) to get whatever I wanted. Paradoxically, I needed to be there for my wife and children and give them a normal life, a life that I never had. But how could I do that when I had absolutely no idea what normal meant? I never, ever wanted to harm children in any way. I never wanted to become anything like my abusers, but it happened. I want so much to change, learn, and understand what normal is, and then live as normal a life as I possibly can. In those days, whenever I got close to someone, they either hurt me or my own self-destructive mechanism switched on and I pushed them away. Then, in turn, I end up hurting the people I care most about.

My most recent offences, for which I was jailed a second time, began when two of Louise's boys came to live with Laura and me on a permanent basis. I managed to convince Laura that there was nothing wrong with what I was doing. The offences that I committed consisted mostly of fondling and oral and anal sex and later having my children reciprocate. These offences were all very much in line with my earlier sexual offences, excepting the anal rape that I committed on Alex. Except for the crime of rape, the rest of my offences differed little over the years, except that I was now offending within the family to which I was supposed to be a father figure. The most recent crimes were far worse than any of their predecessors because I had three co-offenders also committing the offences on my children with me. One of them was my wife. The fact that I committed the offence myself was bad enough, but much worse was the fact that I allowed other people to use my children for sexual gratification. Not only had I become very dangerous, but

I had created an even greater betrayal of trust to my children than anyone else involved. This not only intensified the enormity of the crimes but added to the horrific pain and fear to which the children were subjected.

I remember the look of distress on the faces and the trembling bodies of my wife and children as my children were being taken away by the child protection workers, a sight that I will never forget. Just prior to being arrested, vigilantes came to our house and beat my wife and me as a result of the media coverage we had received. I was questioned for several hours and beaten by the police. I felt very ashamed, scared, embarrassed, confused, and very alone. Once inside prison, I remained very confused about everything that had happened. I had abused and lost those who mattered most to me in life. Why had I done it? Now I had not only lost my wife and children but my mother as well—all of whom I loved dearly. Now I felt that I had nothing left; I had destroyed the lives of the people I most cared for and felt that I deserved all that was happening to me. I felt so guilty and unworthy that I just wanted to curl up and die.

The years I spent in prison were extremely difficult to bear, but at least now, I can see the light at the end of the tunnel, and with the education and living skills that I acquired, I now feel that I will have a better chance to lead a crime-free life and, for the first time in more than 40 years, become a useful member of society.

In my early years, I don't think I had any guilt or fear relating to my offences as I didn't see that I was doing anything wrong. From about the age of 17 or so, I would sometimes feel some fear of rejection and guilt about what I did, but I still viewed the behavior as a normal and acceptable part of life. I was still carrying the guilt, shame, and fear from my own childhood abuse.

However, it wasn't until I had been caught for sex offences on a 13-year-old girl that any real guilt, fear, and shame entered into the equation in relation to my own crimes. I think this was because I had both used force and frightened myself and saw that I was becoming like my own abusers. I didn't like the thought of that. Until that particular offence, I hadn't seen myself as a bad person. After that offence, despite the fear, I continued offending in the same way that I had previously. I was wracked and plagued with the guilt of my crimes. I was feeling guilty when I went to prison for the sex crimes that I committed on the children from my first marriage. At the same time, I feared for my life from other bigger and violent inmates. It helped when Louise and the children visited and forgave me, assuring me that I had not harmed them. It helped when they said they still loved me. They unwittingly reinforced the messages I was receiving from other convicted child sex offenders who confirmed my distorted way of looking at things. I continued to believe that there was really nothing wrong with what I did, that there was nothing wrong with me, that the law was the problem. I began to feel less and less guilty about what I had done to them.

After my release from prison and with my sons now living with Laura and our children, the cycle of offences started all over again, and it wasn't long before I was again out of control. Guilt and fear re-emerged and began to take over my life again, particularly after Harry began using Alex and even more so when Morrison came on the scene. By now, the guilt, fear, and shame became prevalent immediately after each offence, but I was out of control and only thinking of my needs. I had become a tyrant to my family and I had trapped them into being used by Morrison, Harry, and my own pleasure and sexual gratification. Although I showed proper fatherly care for my children in all the other areas of their lives, I had now become what I had detested most in my life, a serial pedophile. I resembled my own abusers, albeit on a much smaller scale. The only difference was that I would not tolerate violence or torture. Nevertheless, with the benefit of hindsight, I realize the offences I committed were no less harrowing to the children than the offences committed on me, and I was infinitely worse than my uncle because I had exposed the children to abuse by men they detested.

## FACING THE OUTSIDE WORLD

When I eventually left prison, I had served 14 years of a 20-year sentence. My former wives and their now-adult children were notified of my release. Within the first week, my first wife went to the media to warn the world that this dangerous pedophile was now free. Television showed photographs of me but, of course, they were 14 years out of date. She was very angry and said that I should not have been allowed parole; I should have completed my sentence. She and her children did what they could to have me returned to jail. First, she said that I was driving my car around her house, harassing her. After 14 years in prison, I had neither car nor license to drive and had no idea where she lived. Luckily, I was able to prove my whereabouts when I was alleged to have been miles away. Then, she tried other tactics. She and most of the children from that marriage went to court for a violence intervention order, which, theoretically, should have sent me straight back to jail. They claimed that I had been phoning, stalking, and harassing them from the day that I was released. One of my trained volunteer support workers contacted the chairperson of the parole board and suggested that police should ask them to provide a description of me. Needless to say, they gave the description of me as I was 14 years earlier. In the years in jail, everything about me had changed. However, despite the fact that they had clearly lied under oath, no action was taken against them.

Finding living accommodations was a nightmare. Although I had only offended against children in my immediate family, I was not allowed to live near a school, kindergarten, bus stop, railway station, church, park, or other venue where children might congregate. I was banned from attending a church because there was a school next door. I was banned from having contact with other convicted criminals. I was not allowed to have a pet or even an aquarium because "some pedophiles use them to attract children into their homes." Nuns helped me to find second-hand furniture and learn how to use public transportation and ATMs.

By now, I was so sick from Hepatitis C and liver damage that I was unable to work and had to rely on a government disability pension. Although I am only in my forties, I find it difficult to breathe and walk, and I'm told that I don't have long to live.

I was placed on the sex offender's register and a uniformed police officer was assigned to me. I learned that these officers were untrained for this work and their hatred of child sex offenders was immediately apparent. The officer walked into my apartment when an elderly neighbor was present. He announced that he had come to search my home for child pornography and that he was authorized to walk in at any time of the night or day. He searched through my cupboards and drawers, and I realized that this was just another form of bullying because he neither examined my computer nor my video collection.

I have no intention of ever hurting another child or human being for the rest of my life. I just wish to enjoy what life I have left. I am fortunate to have a good psychiatrist whom I see regularly, and I'm prescribed what is commonly called "chemical castration" but is really a drug to keep my sex drive under control, which, along with the understanding and knowledge that I gained from the therapy program, should enable me to live a crime-free life.

Does treatment work? In my case, I think I can say that it did. I know of others who made the decision not to re-offend. However, I tend to think that it is only effective if you want it to be, if you are sick of the guilt, fear, and shame. Some abusers went through the process and said all the right things, but intended to re-offend within the first week of their parole.

At times, my home seems like a jail without the company of others. I have no friends. Life is very lonely. After all, what decent person would want to befriend me if he or she knew my history? The parole board eventually agreed that I could have an aquarium. I spend hours watching the fish. I gave them all names.

I don't feel sorry for myself, but sometimes I think it might be better if I were dead, or better still, if I'd never been born. If only it could be unraveled and we could start again. I would tell the truth and say, "No, I can't wash dishes." How different everything would have been!

# The Boylove Manifesto

## *"jay_h"*

### WHO ARE WE?

Boylove is a worldwide phenomenon that does not recognize the boundaries of gender, race, nationality, age, religious beliefs, or philosophy. Boylove describes a special kind of relationship between human males. Boylove has always been with us, exists among us today, and will always continue to exist.

A boylover is commonly referred to as a "pedophile." Since boylovers can only speak for themselves, the feminists' viewpoint cannot be expressed as part of this document. For the same reason, you will not find a treatment about the love of women to boys, nor the love of men to girls as part of this discussion. The aim of this document is to explain the love between human males.

As boylovers, we distance ourselves from the current discussion about "child sexual abuse." We are not willing to participate in a confrontational discussion that does not even take into account the variety of sexual relationships between various age groups.

This document represents the views of the author. The stereotyped boylover does not exist. There are as many different opinions among boylovers as there are men who love and admire boys.

## Who Should Read This Document?

This document was written for all boylovers, their friends, their boyfriends, and their girlfriends. Further, it was conceived for those children who have been, or may someday be, confronted with this subject. It is aimed at parents, counselors, teachers, and everyone whose life is touched, privately or professionally, by children. Hopefully, it will be read by some who deal with children, youths, and boylovers as part of a therapy program. Finally, this document is a resource for those who may have kept an open mind and are genuinely interested in learning more about the difficult subject of "boylove."

This document hopes to assist the reader in shaping his or her own opinion. While we are not hoping to gain any supporters for our opinions, we would like to be afforded the opportunity to submit our point of view to the current debate.

## Why Was This Document Published?

The discourse about sexual contacts between different age groups, particularly those that take place between children and adults, has reached a dead end. The parties on either side of the argument are no longer on speaking terms. Those who have taken it upon themselves to protect every boy from

every boylover place the blame squarely on the boylover. To further their cause, these people do not bother to separate fiction and hearsay from the alleged facts. Their doctrine still nourishes from several centuries filled with repressive sexual standards. When child sexuality became taboo, the thought spread through our collective conscience that a child is simply not a sexual being. Sigmund Freud ventured past this taboo. Since that time, the attempt has been made to restrict the newly discovered sexuality of children by means of legislation. The imbalance of power that governs the relationship between adults and children was swiftly expanded to include the subject of sexuality. The adult members of our society mandate how a child is to cope with his or her own sexuality. The attempt to employ restrictions and punishment as a means of child rearing often causes the child to experience serious conflicts. While it may traumatize the child, it will certainly do nothing to further his or her natural development in the future. The discrepancy between the desire a child may experience and the restrictions placed upon these desires by society harms the natural and healthy development of his or her own sexuality. As a result, these children will suffer from some psychological damage even as adults.

This document presents the opposing point of view. At the same time, it attempts to liberate children and adults from many false premises which govern our relationships and our sexuality. In view of the social and cultural position of a boylover, an attempt will be made to present his fundamental ethics—particularly the rights of the boy and the boylover's responsibilities.

## What Is Boylove?

It is not possible to reduce or limit boylove by focusing only on the sexual aspects of an intergenerational relationship. Human sexuality plays the same part in a boylove relationship as it undoubtedly does in any relationship between human beings. Therefore, it may not be present, only slightly present, or explicitly present in any given relationship. A relationship that is based on sexual contact alone is not really part of boylove because this term includes far more than that.

A boylover desires a friendly and close relationship with a boy. This relationship will not necessarily include any sexual intimacy, nor will it necessarily exclude it. A boylover's fascination focuses primarily on the "boyish" and "childish" traits that are particular to any boy. The physical traits of the boy and the boylover's sexual desires, which may or may not be present, are quite secondary to that fascination. A boylover will go to great lengths to protect a boy from negative influences or any physical and emotional harm. Further, a boylover will not resort to threats, nor will he show any signs of aggressive or even violent behavior as part of a relationship.

## The Boylove Relationship

In most cases, the attraction between the boylover and the boy is mutual. The boy is drawn to an adult who takes him seriously and treats him respectfully. The boylove relationship is void of the demeaning power struggles and restrictions that are customarily a part of any child/adult relationship. In a boylove relationship, the boy is afforded the chance to experience himself as a person. A person who may have and express his own opinion, without running the risk of having it cast aside as unqualified or even "childish." His spirit, as well as his body, are seen as a whole. Not as something that is still in the process— a developmental stage on the way to adulthood.

A child is commonly viewed as someone who needs to grow up in order to become a person. Society applies adult standards in order to shape and mold the child. Personality traits that may be considered undesirable or inconvenient are often removed in the process of child rearing and education.

As part of a boylove relationship, the older partner accepts and nourishes the spirit of the child. The boylover doesn't try to apply adult standards of behavior in order to force the boy's spirit to fit the mold. The boy experiences this acceptance of his own unique character as something very special and pleasant. He feels free to develop and grow because his partner treasures his personality and takes it seriously.

Although the adult partner is always in a position to exercise power over the child, the boylover tries to avoid any power struggles within the relationship. However, the boylover must be aware of the fact that an imbalance of power is present in any adult/child relationship. Therefore, a situation may arise where he may need to raise this topic with his partner.

## What Are the Rights of the Boy?

First and foremost, it is the right of the boy to develop his personality and his sexuality freely. This rule must govern every boylove relationship, and it does. Any physical or psychological pressure inherently infringes upon this precious right. Further, any restrictions that may interfere with the development of his personality, or those that may prohibit him from experiencing his sexuality without restraints, may also be considered an infringement of his rights. It is the boylover's responsibility to shape the relationship in order to comply with the wishes and needs of the boy. It is also his responsibility to ask questions and listen carefully. Most importantly, the boylover must not interfere with the autonomous development of the boy.

The boy has the right to be protected against physical or psychological abuse. It should also be considered a form of abuse when a boy is prohibited from exercising his rights to experience a loving relationship, or if he is not allowed to experience and develop his own sexuality. The rights of the boy should be respected in this regard, too.

## WHAT ARE OUR DEMANDS?

We demand the freedom of individual sexuality for boys and for boylovers.

We demand that current standards of sexuality are reconsidered. These standards infringe upon basic human rights because they prohibit children and those who love them from even thinking about engaging in any sexual intimacy.

We demand that any medical, psychological, or religious notions that are preconceived against child sexuality be exempted from a discussion about new sexual standards.

We demand that children as well as boylovers be included in the current debate concerning sexuality between children and adults. At this point, the "experts" are people who have gained their knowledge about intergenerational relationships from books and statistics. It sounds incredible: There are people who are defending the best interests of an age group and they haven't even bothered to ask members of this age group if this representation is desirable or in their best interests.

We demand our freedom of speech in the media. The Internet is being targeted as the forum for boylovers. We demand to be held to the same standards as every other participant in the Internet: If there is nothing illegal being published on a "boylove site," then this site may not be shut down or censored at will.

We demand a forum for open communication between boylovers. A forum that is entirely free from repression. This discourse, support, and a sense of community is important. It is a place to discuss sexual ethics and a forum that will be reached by boylovers from around the globe.

We demand that society reconsider the status of the child. This is our most important demand. Since children are not granted their own personality, and since they are not being taken seriously, there are "experts" who may represent their "best interests." And as long as we allow this representation to take place, children will be denied their right to develop their own personality, as well as their own sexuality.

---

### Discussion Questions

1. How are the pedophile and the child molester different? Why is this distinction sociologically relevant?

2. In *Outsiders*, a book on deviance, Howard S. Becker emphasized that *moral enterprise* is central to labeling behavior as deviant. Why is this principle especially crucial in defining sex between an adult and a minor?

3. How does NAMBLA (the North American Man-Boy Love Association) "justify and normalize its philosophy and practices"?

4. How are the sociological and the psychiatric perspectives toward adult-child sexual contact different?

# PART 6

# EARTH FIRST!

Going to Extremes to Save the Environment

# EARTH FIRST!
## An Introduction to the Radical Environmentalist Movement

Co-author Angus Vail began a small research project recently that involved Community Emergency Response Team (CERT) training at the local fire department. During the first class, after covering basic principles of triage, evaluating a disaster scene, defining the term "emergency," and so on, the instructor turned to the topic of terrorism. This discussion was not especially long, but it ended with some interesting speculation about whom the CERT members should fear. In the words of one of the instructors, "The ones that're gonna attack us are the environmentalists." It would appear that the U.S. Department of Justice agrees: Attorney General Alberto Gonzales recently mentioned radical environmentalists as one of the primary domestic terrorist threats to this nation. The FBI's zeal in going after these "terrorists" bore fruit on January 20, 2005, when they announced a 65-count indictment against 11 members of Animal Liberation Front (ALF) and Earth Liberation Front (ELF). If we are to take the Justice Department at its word, as clearly some do, environmentalists pose a clear threat to the safety of this nation. But how did the Justice Department come to that conclusion?

Earth First! is probably the most widely known radical environmentalist organization and it was founded by a few self-professed hippies living in Wyoming who thought the billboards that dotted the highways of their county represented a blight on the natural landscape. One Sunday night during the 1970s, after the bars closed at 10 PM, these same hippies cut down one of those billboards, and thus was born the radical environmentalist movement. After addressing the billboard problem, they next took on a proposed oil field by pulling up surveyors' marking stakes. Eventually, the organization would protect old-growth forests and endangered species around the country, always by nonviolent means. This seemingly innocuous behavior would not seem to qualify for inclusion in a book titled *Extreme Deviance*. So what makes radical environmentalism appropriate fare for a book such as this one?

Of course, the fact that the FBI has labeled these activists a terrorist threat has something to do with it, but that reason is not the most interesting one, sociologically speaking. In his book *Stigma*, Goffman (1963) argued that acquiring and possessing a "spoiled identity" work in a variety of ways, but the way they operate in this case is fairly unusual. In the case of this radical social movement, the stigma that has been attached to the movement as a whole, with accusations of ecological terrorism and rampant misanthropy, has stigmatized individuals associated with the movement, even when there is no evidence that they are misanthropic or terrorists. (In fact, Earth First! has an explicit policy against harming people.) The original definition of "lowbagger" is someone who belongs to "a loosely-knit alternative community that shares resources when living/traveling," people who "are modern-day gypsies, bucking capitalism and living light on the land" (Mahan, 2005). More loosely interpreted, a lowbagger is someone who believes the condition of the Earth comes before corporate profits, someone who is willing to undermine—illegally, if necessary—industrial and housing development in environmentally fragile areas. How do a bunch of essentially harmless "lowbagger" pranksters come to be seen as so dangerous? More to the point, what about the way they are organized might lead to this outcome?

When you consider the goals and orientations of Earth First! and other organizations like it, you would be pretty hard-pressed to find a clear and convincing argument that they pose much threat to the country. Earth First!'s slogan reads, "No compromise in defense of Mother Earth." Their orientation of "biocentrism" suggests that all species are equally deserving of respect and that the elimination of other species is a tragedy that must be prevented. With mounting evidence of global climate change, and international treaties enacted to protect the environment and the planet both gaining widespread public acceptance, it seems as though the goals and orientations of Earth First! are actually fairly mainstream. What, then, makes Earth First! and other organizations like it different from organizations like Greenpeace or the Sierra Club? Why has one group become a terrorist threat while the others are seen as upstanding defenders of our collective interests (see Photo 6.1)?

One important difference has to do with institutional support for the goals of the organizations and their abilities to convince others that their approaches to those goals are reasonable, legitimate, and mainstream. As the authors of the selections in this section point out, Earth First! intentionally moved outside the usual mainstream political channels so they would not have to be beholden to the influences of a political system they saw and see as corrupt and deaf to their cries of injustice. Since Sierra Club raises funds through conventional channels and raises its concerns in conventional ways, their message comes across to the hypothetical mainstream as nonthreatening. Earth First! eschews those acceptable means in favor of slightly more dramatic methods like tree-sitting and "monkeywrenching," methods that deliberately reject the "proper" channels of airing grievances. It will probably come as no surprise to you, then, that the radical environmentalist movement is not organized in standard bureaucratic fashion, and its connections do not run deeply within normative political webs of influence. In standing outside the normative social structure, then, the radical environmentalist movement cannot enjoy the protection that norms and conformity afford. They are treated as terrorists, not because they pose a threat to the citizenry of the country, but rather because they don't have a lobby to protect them.

In a phrase, Earth First! has been deemed by the political mainstream to be an *illegitimate* environmentalist movement; its solution to the problem of the degradation of the natural world has been deemed *invalid*, its methods, off-limits. The social movement organization is treated as deviant and is seen, even by many mainstream environmentalists, as *contaminating* the environmentalist movement as a whole. Opponents of Earth First! have constructed the stigmatization process in two stages: (1) the tactics of the more extreme Earth First!

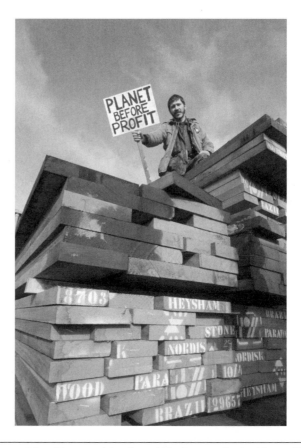

**Photo 6.1**    Protester on Pile of Imported Hardwood Timber. Earth First! is a militant social movement organization whose members are unwilling to compromise in protecting the environment. Its members believe that the ruthless quest for profits by capitalist economies has led to ecological degradation. Some of their efforts to halt damage to the earth are conventional, such as demonstrations and protests. But some of Earth First!'s methods to protect the environment have been illegal. Such methods include tearing down signs, throwing oneself under the wheels of earth-moving equipment, and even burning down luxury housing developments. Many mainstream supporters of the environmental movement regard Earth First! as a deviant organization.

SOURCE: Corbis.

members were identified with Earth First! as a whole; and (2) this radical image of Earth First! was identified with environmentalism as a whole. In this way, entirely reasonable movement activists are identified as radical "tree huggers," and their goal of preventing environmental degradation is ridiculed.

How, then, does Earth First! operate? How is it set up? How has that set-up contributed to the largely unsupported claims and stigmas that plague it? How do these organizational principles contribute to the spreading stigma that bleeds down from the organization, affecting people who, by most accounts, do not deserve the infamy? How has the evolution of the movement contributed to changes in the labels that are applied to its members, and how have they responded to those labels?

In this chapter, Rik Scarce and Douglas Lloyd Bevington each have interesting contributions to make to our understandings of how social movements work and how their structures, goals, orientations, and memberships contribute to the kinds of meanings those outside the movements are likely to assign to them and their members. As you read their articles, consider the relationship between the history of Earth First! and the many changing meanings or labels that have been assigned to it over the course of that history. This is a dynamic process. Do meanings go one way and only one way? Or do you see more give and take, jab and parry, move and countermove? Finally, consider the account of Earth First! founder, Mike Roselle. What does it tell us about deviance, stigma, keeping a non-normative activity a secret? What does it tell us about how one's identity can revolve around an activity mainstream society considers illicit and unacceptable? Does this account resonate with any activities you, the reader, have been involved with? What does it tell us about deviance in general?

# REFERENCES

Goffman, E. (1963). *Stigma: Notes on the management of spoiled identity.* Englewood Cliffs, NJ: Prentice Hall/Spectrum.

Mahan, J. (2005, February). *What is* lowbagger, *what is a lowbagger?* Retrieved from http://www.low bagger.org

# Earth First!

## Deviance Inside and Out

### *Rik Scarce*

One characteristic of social movements is their inherent deviance. True social movements—I'll explain what I mean by "true," below—consciously stand outside the norm, pointing to specific grievances that the activists involved in a given movement argue *must* be alleviated. In important ways, the history of the United States is a history of social movements—not solely of movements, of course, but it is a nation in which very little of great and lasting importance has occurred without the involvement of social move-ments. The United States was founded by move-ment activists who argued that citizens of the 13 colonies lived under the yoke of an uncaring and unjust monarch. The civil rights movement existed for more than a century before its grievances were adequately addressed in the 1960s, and female protestors advocating women's suffrage were jailed en masse when they protested in front of the White House nearly a century ago.

Equal rights for women and blacks are not the contentious issues they once were, thanks to the untold numbers of "deviants" who picketed, marched, gave speeches, and deliberately put them-selves up for arrest. Those grassroots activists viewed themselves as outsiders because their cause was so clearly at odds with dominant American norms—including the laws that encapsulated the objects of their grievances. Such grievances clearly identify a fundamental wrong perpetrated by society or some subgroup: a wrong worthy of direct confrontation by a group of people, at least in the minds of those people.

Here, I introduce another social movement, the radical environmental movement. I argue that its deviance exists on two levels: within the move-ment itself and between the movement and broader society. That is, even as the movement fights to end environmental destruction—its external struggle, if you will—activists who par-ticipate in the movement fight battles that escape the attention of most of us in society. At times, those internal conflicts are as important as those the movement wages against corporations and governments, and often the outcome of internal struggles shapes how the movement pursues its grievances against powerful social forces.

## What Makes a "True" Social Movement?

Phenomena like the women's rights and civil rights movements—and the radical environmental

movement—are characterized to varying degrees by several key dimensions. Each point in the list below contrasts "true" social movements with interest groups. The latter attract huge numbers of dues-paying members, and when people speak of one or another social movement, they often are actually speaking about interest groups. Doing so is a mistake, I argue, for true social movements are the real loci for much of the social change that seems to be constantly sweeping the United States, while interest groups are characterized not so much by a commitment to change society in fun-damental ways as by a drive to seek small, incre-mental changes. The distinction is especially notable along the following eight dimensions:

• As grassroots groups, true social movements identify their most important *resource* as the activists who join the groups. Such key resources are what any group or organization needs the most. In contrast to interest groups, whose key resource is money, which can be used to buy every-thing from labor to office space, grassroots groups rely most on the commitment of their members.

• *Leadership* positions, high-status roles in interest groups that are vested with a great deal of power and control, are often shared among activists in social movements. Instead of operating at the behest of strong leaders, grassroots groups work cooperatively through consensus-based decision making, ensuring that everyone has an equal voice.

• Similarly, activists share other duties as well. Because money is a comparatively unimportant resource, there may be no paid staff at all in a social movement, only volunteers. Thus, there is no *bureau-cracy* to speak of. Work and meetings often take place around kitchen tables or in members' living rooms, and tasks are divided according to expertise and availability—a notable contrast to the "corpo-rate" look of most interest groups in which roles are clearly defined and hierarchies are rigidly enforced.

• Social movements are located where the grievances are actually occurring, typically in people's back yards, while interest groups can be found near the seats of political power. *Location*, thus, is a fundamental point of difference between social movements and interest groups.

• Although interest groups seek to differentiate themselves as little as possible from the rest of society, social movements often create their own *culture*— including clothing, music, and their own vernacular. Activist culture creates a "we're all in it together" attitude that bonds members to one another and to the cause—so much so that the movement becomes a core part of activists' self-identity.

• An important component of that identity is the movement's *ideology*. Understood as a belief system that is acted upon, ideology operates much like a hypothesis does. Hypotheses identify variables and their relationships to one another; ideology supplies the movement's belief system, its grievances, the causes of those grievances, the appropriate means of addressing the grievances, and much more. Important as a clear ideology is to activist groups, interest group organizations typically avoid ideology because of their interest in being seen as "mainstream"—as part of everyday, dominant society.

• Mainstream interest groups participate in the political process in acceptable ways, particularly through participating in the compromise process. As such, they espouse incremental social change, and their *strategic vision*, their plans for the future, are muted or nonexistent. Among activist movement groups, strategy emerges from their ideology and typically points to dramatic, sweeping change at fundamental points in society.

• Finally, social movement *tactics* are confrontational. They involve legal protest behavior like speaking out at public meetings, carrying picket signs, and conducting street theater, but movements may also employ illegal behaviors like

civil disobedience (which is actually considered constitutionally protected free speech, though it involves illegal trespassing), property destruction, and—in extraordinary cases—physical confrontation. Interest groups are confrontational only in the narrow confines of the accepted decorum of legislatures, courtrooms, and regulatory agencies.

As is the case for many social movements and the interest groups who advocate for the same causes, this set of characteristics—in a sense, a running definition of social movements that distinguishes them from interest groups—applies to the radical environmental movement. That movement includes Earth First!, a group that stands in sharp contrast to better-known interest groups like the Sierra Club, Wilderness Society, Audubon Society, National Wildlife Federation, Environmental Defense Fund, and the like, which are interest groups, not true social movements. In the sections that follow, I discuss how the eight dimensions outlined above are manifested in Earth First!

## SHARED CONCERNS, FUNDAMENTAL DIFFERENCES

As is the case for the Sierra Club and many other mainstream environmental interest groups, Earth First! emphasizes "wilderness" issues. That is, chief among their grievances is the destruction of large expanses of undeveloped land. All of these groups argue that placing such tracts off-limits to road building, logging, mining, livestock grazing, and the like should be of paramount importance to government. But beyond a general shared concern for wilderness, Earth First! and the mainstream environmental organizations have little in common.

Above, I noted that mainstream environmental organizations are characterized by their close resemblance to dominant American society. Other than the issues they advocate, the Sierra Club and the other large environmental interest groups may as well be the National Rifle Association (NRA) or the American Association for Retired Persons (AARP), two of the largest and most respected interest groups in the nation. All such organizations seek to "look like America," to behave like the mythical average American would, to act in the "American tradition" without offending others while advocating for their causes.

As a social movement, Earth First! does not concern itself with those sorts of niceties. Driven by an "ecocentric" ideology that identifies ecological preservation as its sole ethical measuring stick, Earth First! activists have created a deviant, radical, loosely connected group that very nearly embodies the social movement ideal type outlined above (see Photo 6.2).

## MEMBERSHIP AND IDEOLOGY IN EARTH FIRST!

Even at the point of entry, Earth First! is a deviant group. To become an Earth First! member, one need only declare that one *is* an Earth First! member—say, by appearing at an Earth First! rally or by donning an Earth First! t-shirt. Silk-screened onto those shirts is the group's name over the likeness of a clenched fist, representative of rage and empowerment, with the group's motto below: No Compromise in Defense of Mother Earth! Of the hallowed names in U.S. environmentalism, none had uttered anything like it until Earth First! came along— though John Muir, founder of the Sierra Club, did when he said he might join the "beasts" should a

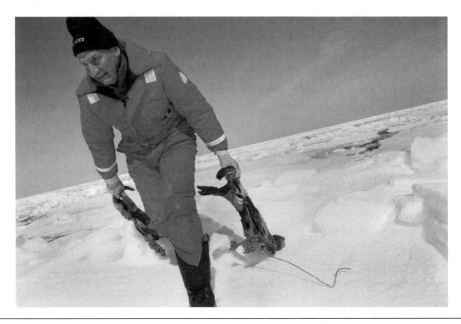

**Photo 6.2**   Baby Seal Hunt in Canada, 2001. Earth First!'s members believe that certain commercial activities that take place in the ocean—seal hunting in particular—should be stopped. The organization's members support forceful measures to prevent the slaughter of baby seals, even if some of these measures are illegal: blocking harbors, ramming sealing ships, and spraying organic dye on the backs of seals to prevent them from being turned into fur coats. "The days of being manipulated by moderates are over," proclaim some members.

SOURCE: Darren McCollester/Getty Images.

war erupt between them and humanity (Muir, 1916, p. 122).

That motto guides everything that Earth First! activists do. Perhaps most notably, it gives insight into Earth First! members' ideology. "Mother Earth" is the personification of the wilderness that is at the heart of radical environmentalists' efforts. She should be *defended*, the slogan goes, implying that She is under assault and that someone—or some group—needs to step forward to shield Her from those who would harm Her. As for "no compromise," implicit in those words are three notable points. First is a critique of the give-and-take that is at the core of interest group politics—some things should not, *must not* be negotiated away, "no compromise" implies. The second point is an extension of the first, and it points us toward the group's central grievance: that wilderness has, in fact, been compromised by mainstream environmental organizations' participation in the horse trading that characterizes U.S. politics. Third, understood in the motto is a pledge that Earth First! will do things differently, that it will not simply advocate for wilderness but that it will *fight* for it.

In each of these points we glimpse the role of ideology in creating Earth First!'s extreme stance—and, thus, its position as a deviant group. Through its no-compromise attitude, Earth First! violates norms that are at the core of the U.S. political system. It refuses to participate in that system, at least in the standard manner. Moreover, groups that are ostensibly "on the same side" as one another do not usually air their differences in public, yet Earth First! regularly critiques mainstream environmental interest groups.

Moreover, Earth First! ideology stands upon two conceptual "legs," ecocentrism and communal anarchy. Ecocentrism refers to Earth First!'s perspective on all human-environment relations. It is a philosophical outlook premised on the argument that ecology, not human interests, should be the guide for what humans do—*everything* that humans do (Devall, 1998; Devall & Sessions,

1985). As a group guided by its ideology, and given the location of ecocentrism at the core of that ideology, it is fair to say that the ecocentric outlook is responsible for virtually all of Earth First!'s deviant behaviors and attitudes.

Whether the issue is population growth, deforestation, agriculture, urban sprawl, genetic engineering, or nanotechnology, ecological well-being is the measuring stick for Earth First!'s stance. Earth First! cofounder Mike Roselle put it bluntly in response to assertions that the group's point of view, and some of its actions, amount to "terrorism." Turning the table on the logging industry that condemns all that Earth First! does, Roselle said, "These guys are terrorists. . . . And we think there's violence in cutting down a thousand-year-old tree to make lawn furniture, too" (cited in Scarce, 2006, p. 78). What humans may want—and perhaps even need—is irrelevant to Earth First! Or at least it has been historically; recently, however, the group's ecocentric ideology has been challenged by some within the group, as I discuss below.

Earth First!'s politics, also a key component of the group's ideology, is best described as communal anarchy. Communal anarchism emerged most forcefully in Western political thought in the mid-1800s, when an array of thinkers began to decry the social costs of capitalist economics. Today, Karl Marx is the best known of the critics of capitalism, but his perspective emerged out of a conflict with anarchist thinkers. The latter shared Marx's condemnation of capitalism's abuse of the working class and his call for revolution. But they rejected Marx's assertion that a strong, centralized state would be needed before workers could govern themselves.

Not only did Earth First! members look to anarchist thinkers for inspiration regarding their ideal sociopolitical future, they also found inspiration in Native American tribal cultures. Both communal anarchism and (many) Native American tribes embraced a thoroughgoing democracy that allowed all members of a community or a tribe to have a say in decision making. In practice, Earth First!

follows guidelines such as shared leadership, consensus-based decision making, and a rejection of bureaucracy—a far cry from top-down mainstream environmental interest groups, or, for that matter, most other forms of organization in American social life.

## MAKING IT EASY FOR THE MAINSTREAM

Ecocentrism is what Earth First! is about, not narrowly human concerns. However, it is, after all, a *social* movement. Earth First! may seek to preserve wild places and to defend the planet against a host of assaults, but its successes depend on its ability to effect social change—change outside the movement itself.

That observation was central to the movement's founders' view of Earth First!'s role in the broader environmental movement. Those founders had long been affiliated with mainstream environmental organizations, including Sierra Club and the Wilderness Society. They had, one said, "played the game, played by the rules. We were moderate, reasonable, professional. We had data, statistics, maps, graphs. And we got fucked" (cited in Scarce, 2006, p. 24). That bitter background led the earliest Earth First! members to see the new group's place strategically.

Earth First!, its founders hoped, would allow mainstream environmental organizations to be more successful because the radicals would be, well, *radical*. Earth First! would demand that every scrap of wilderness be preserved, that every endangered species be protected. One Earth First! co-founder said, "If Earth First! hadn't come along, somebody else would have come along with something like it. It was an idea whose time had come" (cited in Scarce, 2006, p. 59). The environment was in desperate shape, under assault from a host of powerful forces, and environmentalism needed an extreme wing, a true environmental movement.

The Earth First! founders figured that with Earth First! around, the "deviant" label—using the word pejoratively because that's the connotation that its users intended—would shift to it and away from the Sierra Club, the Wilderness Society, and the like. In turn, the theory went, those mainstream organizations would be more successful.

So, from its start, Earth First! was strategically deviant, created as it was to enable the mainstream to accomplish more, thanks to the Earth First! members' extremism. In 1989, one of Earth First!'s co-founders, Dave Foreman, argued, "Earth First! has made those groups more effective, and I think we have opened up more issues. We have been able to redefine the parameters of the debate" (cited in Scarce, 2006, p. 25). However, the movement's early strategic vision never worked to the extent Foreman and his compatriots envisioned.

The radicals *did* identify new issues, and they framed old ones differently. But the mainstream never followed through on its end of the bargain. It failed to find the courage to demand what Earth First! hoped to allow it to claim—more wilderness, the creation of wildlife corridors, the development of stronger endangered species, wetlands, anti-toxics laws. Earth First!'s deviance often proved toxic to the mainstream, fearful as the latter was of offending powerful decision makers by appearing to be taking advantage of Earth First!'s extremist positions.

## DEVIANTS AT WORK: THE STRUGGLE FOR HEADWATERS FOREST

One of Earth First!'s longest-running campaigns, the fight for Headwaters Forest, exemplifies the dangers—from Earth First!'s perspective—of collaborating with the mainstream. Headwaters was "discovered" in 1986 by a group of Earth First! members investigating Pacific Lumber Company property in northern California. Pacific Lumber, or "Palco," is the largest private owner of ancient redwood trees in the world. Redwoods are among the tallest and oldest trees in the world, reaching 250 feet tall and 2,000 years old. But the stately trees are prized for their lumber, commonly used to make patio decks and for other purposes where durable wood is needed. Redwood ecosystems had been decimated by industrial forestry of the sort practiced by Palco, and environmental advocates in Northern California had painted Palco as the poster child for irresponsible logging for years before Headwaters entered their consciousness.

Earth First! members protested Palco's plans to "liquidate" its redwoods—cut them all down to pay off debt, purely to make a profit for its parent company, Maxxam—in numerous ways. Among the first were lawsuits filed by the Sierra Club Legal Defense Fund (now "Earthjustice"), a litigation-oriented creation of the Club, and the Environmental Protection Information Center, a North Coast group that has long supported Earth First!-inspired legal tactics. Those lawsuits were successful for several years (Byrd, 1995, p. 1).

In time, however, legal roadblocks to Palco's destruction of Headwaters were all but removed. If the issue had been left to the Sierra Club, Headwaters would have been logged once the legal path to resisting Palco was cleared. But Earth First! had other ideas. It protested for the trees and against Palco's practices in a host of ways. Musicians penned songs about the evils the company perpetrated, and thousands marched through the heart of timber country in a show of popular support for redwood preservation (Bari, 1995, p. 6).

But some activists went a step further—a step over the legal line: Trespassing on Palco land, they disrupted logging by sitting in roads and refusing to move, giving themselves up for arrest in acts of "civil disobedience" (Ghent, 1995, pp. 1, 28). They even went beyond "road sits," conducting "tree sits," during which they occupied individual redwoods, and sometimes groups of them, for days and weeks at a time. One tree sitter, Julia Butterfly Hill, stayed in her tree for more than two years, supported by an on-the-ground crew that allowed her to maintain her perch all that time (Hill, 2001; see Photo 6.3).

The proximate, immediate goal of civil disobedience tactics, as Mahatma Gandhi and Martin Luther King honed them, was to create in non-activists a sense of moral outrage against a social movement's opponents. Secondary, broader goals, like nationhood for India or equality for blacks in the United States, would ideally follow from the public's new-found solidarity with activists, the activists argued. One Earth First! activist described the effect of civil disobedience this way: "I think when you can stand up and say why you did something, you make a tremendous sacrifice. You can speak directly to the public about why you did it" (cited in Scarce, 2006, p. 70). In a sense, then, the broader goal of civil disobedience is to strip deviant acts of their deviance, to humanize what seems to be an outrageous political position.

In the struggle for the redwoods, Earth First! pursued a similar line of reasoning. First, they hoped to attract the media's attention to the plight of ancient, "old growth" forests and the ancillary plants and animals—like the legally threatened marbled murrelet, a gull-like bird that nests in pristine redwood habitat—that depend upon mature trees, thereby creating moral indignation on the part of Americans and on behalf of ancient forests. In the process, Earth First! hoped to preserve those forests, fulfilling its ecocentric ideology.

Consider for a moment what Earth First! was attempting and how it was attempting it. In contrast to Gandhi and King, both of whom had a direct stake in their causes, and in contrast even with their respective British and white supporters, who had no stake in the respective fights but supported Indians' and blacks' struggles for justice and equality because they were humans who possessed "inalienable rights," the ecocentric Earth First! "tribe" advocated something like equality for *non-humans*. Never in Western history have others mounted the kind of tireless, selfless campaigns on behalf of "groups"—in this case, non-*Homo sapiens* species—that Earth First! and similar environmental advocates have attempted. Earth First!'s ecocentrism is a mark of extreme deviance unlike any other. Their acts are deviant not because they violate norms out of personal or even supra-personal,

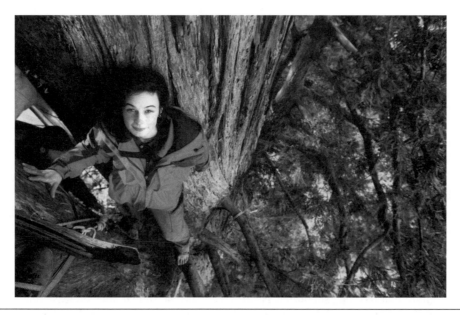

**Photo 6.3**    Julia Butterfly Hill Stands in a 200-Foot-Tall Old-Growth Redwood Tree in Humboldt County. Most trees used for commercial purposes, including paper products, are grown and harvested by wood companies; hence, there is no possibility of their depletion. In fact, more trees grow in the United States today than existed in 1900. However, the best and most expensive wood—that which contains timber most suited for construction—can be found in "old-growth" forests with trees that are hundreds of years old. Earth First! takes steps to protect these old-growth forests.

SOURCE: Gerard Burkhart/Getty Images.

human-focused concern. Rather, their deviance emerges out of the movement's activists' commitment to safeguarding that which is *not* human.

Within environmentalism—including both activist groups and interest groups—ecocentric ideology typically is marginalized. Think how foreign virtually every aspect of the Headwaters campaign, guided as it was by ecocentrism, must have seemed to mainstream environmental organizations. Marches, road sits, tree sits, and other forms of civil disobedience—none of those tactics was practiced by the mainstream as it lobbied, legislated, and litigated. Musical parody, common in Earth First!, was unknown to the mainstream because it did not seek to create its own culture. And rejecting compromise, as Earth First! steadfastly attempted, violated the central tenet of interest group politics.

After nearly 15 years, in 1999 a deal was finally struck for Headwaters—and, ironically but understandably, it was the mainstream's involvement that tipped the scales (Pickett, 1999, p. 5). Julia Butterfly's tree sit, having garnered the attention of the nation's media, appears to have been the thing that attracted the major environmental groups, led by the Sierra Club, to the fight. Once they got involved, politicians had the respectable "cover" they needed to bring about a deal for Headwaters. As one would expect, the mainstream didn't get everything the radicals would have liked. Rather, they brokered a compromise, one that allowed Palco to avoid some of the Endangered Species Act's requirements and that compensated it to the tune of nearly $500 million (Pickett, 1999, p. 5).

Headwaters was not the sort of victory Earth First! had in mind. Too little was saved, a few thousand acres, at too high a cost: not just monetary, but in effort, emotion, pain—peaceful protestors were repeatedly tortured by police, who swabbed pepper spray directly into their eyes (Littletree, 1997/1998, p. 5)—and even in lives. One popular activist was killed during the protests when a redwood that had just been cut fell on him ("Death is not," 1999, p. 32). In Headwaters, the movement found that the distance between its deviance and the mainstream's conservatism amounts to a gaping chasm. The Earth First! founders' dream of making life easier for the major environmental organizations proved, once and for all, to be just that: a dream.

Not everyone would agree with that assessment, however. After the Headwaters deal was announced, Sierra Club rebel David Orr wrote,

> Speaking for myself, I think the Sierra Club owes these visionary groups and the activists who run them a tremendous debt of gratitude for their pioneering and courageous efforts, sometimes facing life-threatening situations, doing work that some environmental leaders said was hopeless. Sometimes the Club wasn't there for them when they needed us, but they pressed on and made Headwaters Forest and "saving the redwoods" household words for an entire generation of young environmentalists. They plowed the political ground—for more than a decade—making it possible for the Sierra Club to play a key role in the political endgame. This is an example of cooperative campaigning, and we must look at it as a model for how—with improvements and refinements—the Club can move major campaigns in other areas in the future. (Orr, 1999)

Efforts like those that Orr advocates, presumably involving mainstream pressure at the centers of power to capitalize on movement activists' on-the-ground struggles at the point of environmental destruction, mirror the Earth First! founders' hopes of a radical-mainstream alliance. Such a vision has only rarely come to fruition. It is the case that Earth First! identified Headwaters as an environmental problem worth fighting for, but it took precious years for the mainstream to enter the fray. The major environmental advocacy organizations appear fearful of approaching the radicals' white-hot flame—a flame that continues to be fueled, in part, by anger at the mainstream's lack of effective action.

## SHIFTING TACTICS

The ways that Earth First! has gone about advocating its ecocentric perspective have, in many ways, remained the same over its 25 years. But they have also evolved in ways that many observers of the movement find disturbing. Initially, Earth First!'s tactics simply involved doing what the mainstream had never dared do. In the months following its founding in 1980, Earth First! placed a memorial plaque in a wilderness area, and shortly after that it symbolically "cracked" Glen Canyon Dam in Arizona by securing a 300-foot roll of plastic to the dam's face—from a distance, it really did look like a crack (McLeod, 1982). Earth First! sought to be the bad boys and girls of environmentalism, pushing buttons and violating cherished boundaries. For the mainstream, proper protest was presenting testimony to politicians. Earth First! had other ideas.

By 1985, Earth First! activists were sitting in trees to stop logging companies from destroying old growth—the era of civil disobedience on behalf of the planet had begun. The other tactic that came to define Earth First!, *monkeywrenching*, was inspired by Edward Abbey's novel *The Monkey Wrench Gang* but made its first appearance in 1970 when "The Fox," a Chicago-area activist, became the first *ecoteur*, dumping corporate CEOs' toxic waste in their own offices (Weissman, 2002).

In time, *ecotage* came to define Earth First! in many people's eyes, though nondestructive modes of protest were the group's primary tactic, and no form of monkeywrenching had a greater impact on the group's meaning than "tree spiking." Tree spiking involves hammering long nails, commonly called spikes, into trees. To ensure that the trees remain standing and that no logger or sawmill worker is injured cutting the spiked trees, activists inform the governmental agency (or private corporation) responsible for cutting trees in a given area that the trees have been spiked. Earth First! members characterized spiking as "inoculating" trees against cutting, but timber workers insisted it was nothing short of terrorism.

Ecotage, for Earth First!, was part of a broader strategy within any given campaign, typically a last resort when all other means had failed to preserve wilderness or otherwise halt environmental destruction. "The confrontation . . . creates the illumination," said Mike Roselle. "It brings these issues to light. . . . Obviously, signing a petition for a wilderness area isn't going to get it, it doesn't create the illumination. But shutting down a logging area does do it" (cited in Scarce, 2006, p. 73). Illuminating as ecotage may be, it has led to dozens of activists being jailed and has prompted intense investigation by the Federal Bureau of Investigation; it seems that when deviants confront the powerful, the powerful will use their position to confront right back (FBI annual report on domestic terrorism).

## DEVIANCE WITHIN THE MOVEMENT

Loud, shocking, and confrontational as Earth First! was to the outside world, it took less than a decade after its founding in 1980 for it to show signs of internal tension. The self-styled environmental deviants gained the ire of the mainstream even as they drew more deviants to the cause. Those new activists found a group that admitted anyone who accepted ecocentrism as the central tenet of their outlook on life, and they proceeded to change Earth First! in fundamental ways.

Ecocentrism alone was not enough to hold the group together. For example, some activists came to Earth First! through the animal rights movement. Those "animal liberators" tended to emphasize the importance of each individual animal's pain and suffering, prompting them to break into animal experimentation laboratories and make off with mice, cats, dogs, monkeys, and other animals (Scarce, 2006). In contrast, old-line Earth First! members focused on wilderness areas measured in thousands and millions of acres; the fate of individual animals on those lands was immaterial to them.

Animal liberators also brought with them a political critique that troubled some of the initial Earth First! adherents. Deviant as Earth First! was intended to be at the outset, its founders nevertheless insisted that they were acting in the spirit of traditional American values that could be traced back to the nation's founders. In the early years, they held the Round River Rendezvous, their annual gathering, on Independence Day, and they avoided a thoroughgoing critique of the U.S. government or the nation's capitalist economic system. America needed to be changed in many ways, but the capitalist state needn't be totally eliminated.

Newcomers, including the animal liberation activists and the political anarchists who flocked to Earth First! in the late 1980s, saw corporations and the federal government as beyond redemption. Those entities were the problem and could not possibly be part of the solution. Even something as simple as what activists ate around the campfire changed with the arrival of the animal liberators and the anarchists. The latter eschewed all animal products, from meat to leather shoes. They began grilling tofu, not hamburger, over Earth First! campfires. And in 1989, anarchists at the Round River Rendezvous burned an American flag (Scarce, 2006, p. 89).

Other fractures appeared within the movement as well. In Northern California, a union activist, musician, and forest advocate, Judi Bari, found herself confronting forest workers who condemned ecotage. They said they would have nothing to do with her efforts to create an Earth First!-loggers united front so long as Earth First! advocated tree spiking. Optimistic that she might actually succeed in creating an environmentalist-logger unified front, Bari renounced tree spiking in 1990. Her decision did not go over well. Many Earth First! members argued that Bari and her fellow North Coast activists had given away a key tactical tool when they pledged not to spike trees, arguing that North Coast Earth First! may not have compromised Mother Earth, but it had given away a key tactic used to defend Her. In response, Bari insisted that a greater tactical advantage could be won by securing the cooperation of loggers, without whom the trees could not be cut.

As a result of those differing points of view that emerged in the late 1980s and throughout the 1990s—the dietary and political perspectives advocated by animal liberators and anarchists, Bari's rejection of tree spiking, and other issues—Earth First!'s character began to change. In a sense, the deviants within the deviant movement won. Human-environment connections of the sort that Bari advocated became widely accepted in Earth First!, though debates continue regarding whether new initiatives—such as efforts to support the poor or Native Americans when their protests overlap with environmental issues—are within even the redefined ecocentric perspective that has emerged over the last decade. And Earth First!'s political rhetoric has changed as well, to the point that articles condemning capitalism appear in every issue of the group's newspaper, the *Earth First! Journal*.

A much deeper split than any that came before emerged in the mid-1990s, when the Earth Liberation Front (ELF) appeared on the scene. The ELF has sought to rewrite the radical environmental playbook by eliminating the strategy-tactics distinction and solely using destructive tactics. "Hard-core" anarchists driven by a political commitment to destroy capitalism, ELF activists act in defense of Mother Earth anywhere, anytime, not waiting until other avenues of protest have failed—or have even been attempted.

ELF rhetoric is different as well. Earth First! activists often have been outright victims of destructive forces themselves, as noted above; note, too, that Judi Bari and her activist-troubadour partner, Darryl Cherney, were nearly killed in a car bombing (Scarce, 2006). Thus, Earth First! activists have reason to portray themselves, like the environments they seek to protect, as victims. But the ELF has openly taken on the role of perpetrator. In some of its communiqués, it has come close to threatening the lives of those it opposes, and in practice has trashed their vehicles and homes, personalizing struggles in ways Earth First! never dreamt.

The ELF's rejection of Earth First!'s evolution of protest model (which asserted that any given campaign should develop roughly step-by-step from legal actions to civil disobedience to ecotage) has some activists within Earth First! insisting the ELF practices property destruction, not ecotage—one Earth First! activist commented, "Our motto is 'No Compromise in Defense of Mother Earth!' not 'Fuck Shit Up!'" (quoted in Baer, 1999, p. 3). But examples of that kind of internal deviance—rule-breaking within the movement—are nothing new, and one era's "deviant" is another's "taken for granted."

## Deviants' Debates

Whether it is what others eat around the campfire, what they think of the U.S. government, their willingness to compromise in small ways to win big battles, their efforts to admit human concerns into radical environmentalism's purview, or even who sits around the fire in the first place, activists within the movement have always struggled with one another. Dissent over deviance continues today as activists build upon the continued momentum against corporate globalization that began with the Seattle World Trade Organization protests in 1999. At protest after protest, labor activists have marched alongside human rights, women's rights, children's rights, and indigenous rights proponents—and activist environmentalists. Within the movement, however, some question whether it is possible to be ecocentric and uncompromising while building such bridges (Juliana, 1994, p. 9; Bell, 2003, p. 2).

And then there are those who struggle for a place for women and persons of color in the movement— deviants pointing out the irony that, while society at large is increasingly accepting of difference and diversity, the movement has not been so welcoming. Throughout its history, female activists in Earth First! have questioned men's willingness to make them full partners in the struggle. Those tensions have only risen in recent years as male activists have been outed for raping female tree sitters and otherwise resisting women's full participation in the movement—themselves deviant acts (Puck, 2004, pp. 30–33).

Like sexism, racism dogs Earth First! Environmentalism is seen by many as the purview of whites, but Earth First!'s ostensibly free and open community ought to be a welcoming place for nonwhite activists. However, most persons of color who experience the movement encounter a chilly climate, and the movement has a reputation, according to one environmental justice scholar I spoke to, for racism. In the eyes of some, some activists' misanthropy and support for extreme limits on immigration indicates a movement subtly promoting racism.

In many ways, groups like Earth First! are utopian. Whether they are viewed as lacking the mainstream's "realism" or gifted with a "vision of the future" that interest groups cannot seem to summon because of their deep connections with dominant society, true social movements consciously set themselves apart from society. They offer up an alternative vision both of what society is and what it might become. And in their deviance, they compel the vast majority of non-activists to acknowledge what matters most to us—and to consider whether those attitudes, values, symbols, behaviors, and institutions are truly those to which we aspire.

## REFERENCES

Baer, C. (1999, February 1). Thoughtful radicalism revisited: Because sometimes *#%ing shit up just isn't enough. *Earth First! Journal*, pp. 3, 29.

Bari, J. (1995, May 1). Headwaters forest still stands. *Earth First! Journal*, p. 6.

Bell, J. J. (2003, November 1). Hayduke, ecofeminism, and monkeywrenching: The fighting words of Earth First! *Earth First! Journal*, p. 2.

Byrd, M. C. (1995, March 21). Pacific lumber threatens headwaters. *Earth First! Journal*, pp. 1, 5.

Death is not the punishment for trespass. (1999, November 1). *Earth First! Journal*, p. 32.

Devall, B. (1998). *Simple in means, rich in ends.* Layton, UT: Gibbs M. Smith.

Devall, B., & Sessions, G. (1985). *Deep ecology.* Layton, UT: Gibbs M. Smith.

Ghent, R. (1995, September 23). Mass action for headwaters. *Earth First! Journal*, pp. 1, 28.

Hill, J. (2001). *The legacy of luna: The story of a tree, a woman and the struggle to save the redwoods.* San Francisco: HarperSanFrancisco.

Juliana, C. (1994, November 1). Say what? *Earth First! Journal*, pp. 2, 8–9.

Littletree, A. (1997/1998, Winter). Pepper spray and nonviolent protesters. *Redwood Nation Earth First!* pp. 5, 8.

McLeod, C. (Producer/Director). (1982). *The cracking of Glen Canyon Dam with Edward Abbey and Earth First!* [Short film]. LaHonda, CA: Earth Image Films.

Muir, J. (1916). *A thousand mile walk to the gulf.* Boston: Houghton Mifflin.

Orr, D. (1999). *David Orr thanks those who worked so hard on headwaters.* Retrieved from http://www.animated software.com/misc/stories/redwoods/do1999th.htm

Pickett, K. (1999, May 1). Headwaters deal. *Earth First! Journal*, p. 5.

Puck. (2004, September 1). Facing off the radical environmental lynch mob. *Earth First! Journal*, pp. 30–33.

Scarce, R. (2006). *Eco-warriors: Understanding the radical environmental movement.* Walnut Creek, CA: Left Coast Press.

Weissman, D. (2002, Spring). Farewell to the fox. *Chicago Wilderness.* Retrieved May 17, 2007, from http://www.chicagowildernessmag.org/issues/spring 2002/fox.html

# Strategic Experimentation and Stigmatization in Earth First!

## *Douglas Lloyd Bevington*

## EARTH FIRST! AND RADICAL
## SOCIAL MOVEMENTS

For the past 25 years, Earth First! has been the cornerstone of the radical wing of the environmental movement in the United States. Earth First! members have garnered substantial publicity for their daring actions in defense of wildlife and wild places. For example, Earth First! members have sat in the tops of ancient trees to prevent them from being cut and they have sabotaged bulldozers that were carving logging roads into wilderness areas. However, radical social movement groups such as Earth First! are often misunderstood and maligned. Discussions of radical groups usually focus on their most dramatic actions and their most controversial statements. But to focus only on these aspects risks overlooking the broader context of the group's activities. To appreciate this context, it is helpful to look at radical groups in terms of their strategy.

At the level of strategy, a radical group like Earth First! can be distinguished from mainstream organizations such as the Sierra Club or Wilderness Society by its overall approach to social change outside the bounds of conventional politics. Conventional politics consists of socially prescribed forms of political participation, such as lobbying a politician, endorsing a candidate, or making a campaign contribution. So why wouldn't a radical group rely on these familiar mechanisms? Radical activists are more likely to see the existing political institutions as slanted against them and unable to fairly or adequately address their issues.

In the case of Earth First!, its founders had worked for mainstream environmental organizations in the 1970s. They witnessed how those organizations were constrained by their commitment to conventional forms of political participation.

The mainstream organizations sought to appear reasonable and avoid controversies that might hurt their access to politicians. And as a result, they limited their demands to what was seen as politically feasible rather than what was actually needed to protect ecosystems and prevent wildlife from going extinct. Moreover, their main bargaining chip in negotiations with politicians was their willingness to endorse compromises that sacrificed some wild places for others. Earth First!'s founders were deeply troubled by the millions of acres of public lands that were being lost to logging and other development as a result. Howie Wolke, one of those cofounders, recounted,

> We played the game, we played by the rules. We were moderate, reasonable, professional. We had data, statistics, maps, graphs. And we got fucked. That's when I started thinking, "Something's missing, here. Something isn't working." That's what led to Earth First! more than anything else. (Scarce, 1990, p. 24)

Earth First! was created as a critique of and alternative to the approach of the mainstream environmental organizations. Earth First! members united under the slogan, "No compromise in defense of Mother Earth." Ultimately, the history of Earth First! is a story of activists searching outside conventional forms of political participation for a better way to protect the environment.

While the pathways for exerting influence through conventional politics are well-defined in our society, a group that steps outside those bounds enters uncharted territory. Radical groups must necessarily experiment to discover other routes. It is only when a radical group offers a free space for its activists to explore a broad range of approaches that they are likely to find more effective alternatives. But experimentation means trial and error. Not all paths are equally effective, and some experiments are likely to be controversial. This makes the radical groups quite vulnerable to stigmatization. It is tempting to focus primarily or solely on the most extreme and contentious actions and statements by those groups. But doing so may cause us to overlook other experiments within the group, as well as the overall impact of the experimentation. In keeping with the goals of this book, if we hope to better understand and appreciate radical social movement groups such as Earth First!, we must examine their most contentious aspects within the larger context of their strategic experimentation.

## EARTH FIRST! IN THE 1980s: CHARACTERISTICS AND STIGMAS

Earth First!'s emergence in the 1980s opened up a space of experimentation with new forms of environmental activism that were quite unlike those of the mainstream environmental organizations. During its first decade, Earth First! developed three defining characteristics in regard to its organizational structure, unifying philosophy, and tactics that distinguished it from the mainstream organizations. These characteristics allowed it to experiment more freely in developing alternative approaches to environmental protection.

However, these same characteristics left Earth First! members particularly susceptible to being stigmatized. Earth First! members were stigmatized in two primary ways: They were portrayed as misanthropes and as eco-terrorists. I will argue that both of these labels are misleading and that they are best understood in the context of the three defining characteristics of Earth First!

### Characteristic #1: No Formal Organization

One defining characteristic of Earth First! from its inception was its lack of formal organization.

The founders of Earth First! felt that the large mainstream environmental groups had become too bureaucratic and business-like, and that had reduced their effectiveness. Instead, they decided that Earth First! should have no formal organization, no official leaders, and no dues-paying members—just active participants. Anyone who shared Earth First!'s values and took part in its activities was considered an Earth First! member.

This approach had both advantages and disadvantages. On the one hand, it allowed for much greater freedom for Earth First! members to experiment with unconventional ideas and tactics without restrictions from leaders. On the other hand, this approach also meant that there was no formal system of accountability within Earth First!

The lack of accountability was most notably an issue around media coverage. In unstructured groups such as Earth First!, the media focus on the most attention-grabbing spokespeople within a group and treat them as leaders. In this case, Dave Foreman—one of Earth First!'s co-founders and most charismatic speakers—became the public face of Earth First! in the 1980s. Foreman emphasized Earth First!'s association with a contentious tactic known as monkeywrenching and promoted an interpretation of Earth First!'s philosophy of deep ecology that was antagonistic to social justice issues. However, he only represented one perspective within the diverse community of Earth First! Yet, all of the media attention on Foreman created the perception that his positions were indicative of Earth First! as a whole.

While outside observers tried to conjure up artificial leaders, in reality, Earth First! was only loosely organized through a network of autonomous local groups. Earth First! members throughout the country remained connected to each other through their publication, the *Earth First! Journal*. The journal offered activists a free space for the exchange of new ideas, no matter how controversial. This openness would leave Earth First! vulnerable to stigmatization, as we will see.

## Characteristic #2: Deep Ecology

Along with the *Earth First! Journal*, Earth First! members were connected by a shared philosophy known as deep ecology. A central premise of deep ecology that appealed to Earth First! members was the idea of *biocentrism*. Biocentrism is the belief that all species of life have intrinsic worth and an inherent right to exist, and the extinction of another species is a tragedy akin to genocide.

## Stigma #1: Misanthropy

Biocentrism is contrasted with anthropocentrism, the idea that other species matter only to the extent that they are useful as a resource for humans. Anthropocentrism is a premise of the dominant religious and philosophical systems in the modern world. It is not surprising, then, that Earth First! members' beliefs about the rights of other species might seem unusual or controversial to other members of society. What was more problematic was the way that Earth First! members' biocentrism was stigmatized as being misanthropic—the hatred of human beings.

This sort of stigmatization is a familiar pattern for radical social movements. Advocating strongly for an oppressed group is often reframed in negative terms as being hatred of the dominant group. For example, the ideas of radical African Americans in the late 1960s were labeled as "reverse racism" and radical feminists in the 1970s were depicted as "man-hating." This same pattern continued with Earth First! members' advocacy for the rights of other species being portrayed as misanthropic.

Despite the overall error of those depictions, one can always find some example to support the charge. In the case of Earth First!, critics pointed to a handful of controversial statements made by Earth First! members around the ecological impacts of human overpopulation. The most attention was focused on an article written by an Earth First! member using the pen name "Miss Ann Thropy." This name satirically embraced the misanthropy label placed on Earth First! members. And Miss Ann Thropy's article in the *Earth First! Journal* was deliberately provocative in this regard, raising the question of whether AIDS would have an environmental benefit in terms of reduced population (Thropy, 1987).

While Miss Ann Thropy's ideas are troubling, what was arguably more troubling was the way that critics used this article to broadly dismiss Earth First! as a whole as being misanthropic. Even in analyses of Earth First! written more than a decade after Miss Ann Thropy's article, it was still cited as the primary example to support the claim that Earth First! is misanthropic. But that focus is misleading. A review of *Earth First! Journal* after the Miss Ann Thropy piece finds only one other notable article in support of those ideas (Lee, 1995). Moreover, other Earth First! members published essays that were quite critical of Miss Ann Thropy. Miss Ann Thropy's article is more an indicator of the open space provided by the *Earth First! Journal* than of widespread misanthropy within Earth First! It is not surprising that some of the ideas that emerged in that space were contentious and provoked widespread disagreement. However, it was only through a process of open intellectual experimentation that more effective ideas could develop over time, as we will see later when we look at Earth First! in the 1990s.

## Characteristic #3: Direct Action

Just as Earth First! members experimented with new ideas, they also experimented with new tactics. Since Earth First! worked outside the political system, it did not rely on the usual lobbying tactics of the mainstream organizations. Rather than trying to appeal to politicians to protect nature, Earth First! members took action to directly stop environmentally destructive activities.

This direct action took two notable forms. One form was civil disobedience, in which Earth First! members used their own bodies to actively obstruct logging and other forms of environmentally destructive activity. However, the visibility of this type of action was initially overshadowed by a second type known as "monkeywrenching" or "ecotage" (ecological sabotage), which entailed stopping environmentally destructive activities by damaging the equipment involved in the activity. The goal of monkeywrenching actions, such as putting sand in a bulldozer's gas tank or pulling up the survey stakes used for road building, was to raise the costs of the project to a point where the companies involved would no longer find those activities profitable enough to pursue them.

Monkeywrenching became a quintessential part of Earth First!'s public image in the 1980s. But as sociologist Timothy Ingalsbee explained, it was a problematic identity:

> Monkeywrenching was a core identity construct that partially defined the movement's radical activism, and brought public and media attention to it far in excess of the movement's size and strength or the actual incidents of sabotage... few [Earth First!] activists and almost no organizers actually do any monkeywrenching. (Ingalsbee, 1995, pp. 151–152)

The media focused on monkeywrenching because it defied the conventional attitudes toward private property and had an element of danger. And that publicity swelled the ranks of Earth First!'s participants and supporters. It is not surprising, then, that Earth First! members such as Dave Foreman embraced this image as monkeywrenchers even if it was a comparatively small part of their activities. But at the same time, the emphasis of monkeywrenching gave a distorted view of Earth First! As public relations expert Herb Gunther summarized, "Early on the monkeywrenching gave them a boost because it got them attention that they would have never gotten otherwise. But then it started working against them" (Zakin, 1993, p. 307).

## Stigma #2: Eco-Terrorists

The monkeywrenching image worked against Earth First! when they were labeled "eco-terrorists" (a term invented by an anti-environmental think tank). The label was misleading. Earth First! had a clear nonviolence code that forbade hurting other people. Earth First!'s monkeywrenching was aimed at dismantling machines, not harming people. Nonetheless, as with the misanthropy label, there was a grain of fact that maintained the larger fiction. In their experimentation with different monkeywrenching techniques, Earth First! had rediscovered an old union tactic known as "tree spiking." Driving a spike into a tree did not injure the tree, but if the tree was cut and then sent to the mill, the spike could damage the saw blades at the mill. Earth First!'s method of tree spiking was to target areas of national forest that were scheduled to be cut and then to inform the Forest Service and the logging company that the area had been spiked. The assumption was that the risk of having to replace expensive sawmill blades would deter the company from cutting trees in the spiked area. The goal of tree spiking was to stop logging, not to damage mill equipment. And Earth First!'s guidelines on informing the authorities were intended to prevent any injuries to timber workers. Nonetheless, the potential risk of injury set tree spiking apart from other forms of monkeywrenching. And because of the danger, it received particular attention from the media. Critics of environmentalism tapped into this attention and then tried to broadly apply the eco-terrorist label to "any crime committed in the name of saving nature." As researchers Sheldon Rampton and John Stauber note, "This definition of 'eco-terrorism' is so broad that it even includes activities such as sit-ins and other forms of peaceful civil disobedience" (Rampton & Stauber, 2004, p. 186).

To many Earth First! members, the eco-terrorism label seemed particularly unfair given that while Earth First! members did not hurt people, they were often on the receiving end of violence from their opponents. But as with the misanthropy charge, there were some Earth First! members who satirically embraced this stigmatizing label. For example, a small group of Earth First! members in Arizona who monkeywrenched equipment for a ski resort that was expanding on national forest land issued a press release calling themselves the "Evan Mecham Eco Terrorist International Conspiracy" (EMETIC). The name was deliberately ironic. Evan Mecham was the anti-environmental Republican governor of Arizona at the time. It should also be noted that in later communiqués, the group changed the "T" from "terrorist" to "teasippers," stating, "We aren't really terrorists. We refuse to do anything that will physically injure anyone. We just needed a T word to make the acronym work" (Zakin, 1993, p. 426). But the humor was lost on the authorities. And the eco-terrorist label brought greater attention from the FBI.

In 1989, the four Earth First! members active in EMETIC and Dave Foreman were arrested for conspiring to cut down power lines in Arizona. The power line sabotage had been organized by an FBI infiltrator. Foreman was not directly involved in the action but was charged with allegedly providing funding for it. Foreman avoided jail in a 1991 plea bargain in which he agreed to stop advocating monkeywrenching. By then he had already publicly left Earth First! in frustration over different approaches that were developing within the group.

## THE LEGACY OF EARTH FIRST!: EXPERIMENTATION AFTER 1990

Many of the most notable accounts of Earth First! focus on its first decade, culminating with Foreman's arrest and departure (Lee, 1995; Manes, 1990; Scarce, 1990; Zakin, 1993). But Foreman's departure did not mark the end of Earth First! nor of the larger experiment in radical environmentalism. That experimentation continued within Earth

First! and also expanded out from Earth First! to include new organizations. From this ongoing experimentation, three distinct approaches to radical environmentalism emerged in the 1990s: Earth First! after Foreman, the Earth Liberation Front, and radical grassroots groups.

### Earth First! and the Headwaters Forest Campaign

Because Foreman was treated as the leader of Earth First! in the 1980s, his advocacy of monkeywrenching and more contentious interpretations of deep ecology had dominated the public image of Earth First! After his departure, other approaches to tactics and ideas that eschewed the stigmatizing labels of eco-terrorist and misanthrope became more visible in Earth First! One of the most prominent Earth First! organizers in the 1990s was Judi Bari, who actively resisted the association of biocentrism with misanthropy. She wrote an article titled "Why I Am Not a Misanthrope," and in her organizing work she emphasized the links between social justice and the protection of nature (Bari, 1994).

Bari worked on protecting the forests on timber corporations' properties in Northern California, including an area of gigantic 2,000-year-old redwood trees known as Headwaters Forest. The campaign to protect Headwaters Forest was one of Earth First!'s most noted accomplishments in the 1990s. It was also indicative of the continuing experimentation with tactics taking place within Earth First! Earth First! members in the Headwaters campaign renounced tree spiking and moved away from other forms of monkeywrenching as well. Instead, they focused on developing tactics in which they would put their bodies at risk in order to stop the logging. Perhaps the famous tactic of this type was "tree sitting." Tree sitting involved climbing up to the top of the tree that was about to be cut. The logging would then have to stop, for if the tree were cut down, the tree sitter would likely fall to her death. There were also other similar types of blockades, but the underlying premise was the same—Earth First! members put their own lives at risk to protect the forest.

This tactical experiment was effective on two levels. First, the actions stopped logging, at least temporarily. Second, these tactics attracted a lot of media attention because of the danger involved. Moreover, that media coverage was more sympathetic than news stories about tree spiking and emphasized the heroic quality of these actions. One of the most famous activists to come out of the Headwaters campaign was Julia "Butterfly" Hill. Hill was a young woman who had been a model and then got interested in protecting the redwoods. When she arrived in Northern California to work on this issue with no background in environmental activism, Earth First!'s participatory community offered her the training to learn how to safely do a tree sit. Up until then, tree sits had generally lasted anywhere from a couple of days to a couple of weeks. But Julia Butterfly wound up sitting in an old-growth redwood continuously for two years until the logging company agreed not to cut it. Her tree sit attracted international attention. Some opponents tried to label her as an "eco-terrorist" because she was trespassing on private property, but the label did not have much traction in this case. Indeed, even *Good Housekeeping* magazine nominated her as one of the most admired women of the year.

The Headwaters activists' emphasis on civil disobedience also allowed them to experiment with types of actions that allowed for broader participation by people who might not otherwise have been involved in Earth First! In 1996, as Headwaters was about to be logged, Earth First! organized a mass trespass onto the timber corporation's property near Headwaters. Over one thousand people participated in that action, making it the largest arrest for an environmental protest in U.S. history. The protesters came from all walks of life, and most had never been arrested before. The number of arrestees was so large that the police ran out of handcuffs and arrest forms well before the protest was done. The action brought national attention to the plight of the forest. And two weeks later, the government announced plans to purchase and protect the main grove of Headwaters Forest.

## Earth Liberation Front

As Earth First! moved away from monkey-wrenching in the 1990s, activists who favored property destruction tactics had to look outside Earth First! They found a unifying identity in the Earth Liberation Front (ELF). Arson became ELF's signature tactic, and its actions included burning a ski lodge, timber corporation facilities, and affluent houses under construction as well as setting fire to SUVs in car dealers' lots. (The fires were set when these places were uninhabited, in keeping with ELF's prohibition against hurting people.) Between 1997 and 2001, ELF caused over $40 million in damages (Rosebraugh, 2004, p. 257). However, these actions did not directly lead to the protection of any specific wilderness areas or endangered species. The use of arson also generated extensive media attention, but that coverage revived and intensified the eco-terrorist stigmatizing label. Moreover, the FBI drew on this eco-terrorist label to declare ELF to be the number one domestic terrorist threat in February, 2001, although ELF had never hurt any people (Rosebraugh, 2004, p. 213). The eco-terrorist label caused particular difficulties for ELF after September 11, 2001, with the subsequent "war on terror" leading to further stigmatization in the media and an intensified crackdown by the FBI. Overall, ELF was arguably a much less successful experiment in radical environmentalism than other approaches taking place during the same time period.

## Radical Grassroots Groups

While ELF received much attention, a third experiment in radical environmentalism that grew out of Earth First! has largely been overlooked, despite its significant accomplishments. This approach is embodied by the small, radical "grass-roots" environmental organizations that proliferated during the 1990s and played a central role in national forest and endangered species protection. Many of these groups were founded or staffed by people who had begun their environmental activism with Earth First! or drew inspiration from Earth First!'s radicalism. However, these groups used lawful tactics—particularly litigation—to stop logging and protect wildlife.

If these groups are considered only in terms of their tactics, they might appear to be a rejection of Earth First! But at the level of strategy, they were an outcome and extension of Earth First!'s quest to find an effective alternative to conventional politics. They had few resources and did not seek special access to politicians. Instead, they experimented with litigation to directly stop environmentally destructive projects. In this regard, their actions had a similar effect to the Earth First! tree sits. But because these grassroots groups were able to harness the authority of the courts to halt those projects, their litigation could have a larger and more lasting impact than direct action. At the same time, their approach was markedly different from the mainstream environmental organizations. While the mainstream organizations sometimes used litigation, they were reluctant to pursue lawsuits that might stir up controversy and upset their relations with politicians. However, because the grassroots groups did not depend on access to politicians to make change, these groups did not need to avoid controversy. And so, grassroots organizations were responsible for initiating much of the litigation to protect forests and wildlife in the 1990s and early 2000s.

For example, the Center for Biological Diversity was founded in 1989 by two Earth First! activists. Since that time, the Center has successfully protected more species of wildlife under the Endangered Species Act than any other group, including the largest mainstream organizations. In keeping with their biocentrism, the Center activists stood up for species that were shunned by the big environmental organizations either because the species were not particularly charismatic or because protection of those species would be politically controversial. As a result, by 2003, the Center was responsible for the protection of 281 species and 38 million acres of habitat for those species (McGivney, 2003).

Overall, in the period after 1990, there was a dramatic upsurge in the protection of endangered species and national forests. Radical grassroots environmental groups provided the primary impetus for this protection. And those groups grew out of the experimental space opened up by Earth First! to find more effective alternatives to mainstream environmentalism.

## CONCLUSION

Earth First! emerged out of the concern that the conventional political strategies of the mainstream environmental organizations could not adequately protect wildlife and wild places. But finding more effective alternative strategies was an experimental process because they lay outside of the socially prescribed forms of political participation. Earth First! created a free space where this sort of experimentation could take place without the restrictions found in more formal environmental organizations. The space opened up by Earth First! led to a proliferation of new ideas and tactics for protecting nature. They were unconventional and, at times, controversial. Certainly not all of the experiments were equally beneficial or effective. And some of the most extreme forms of this experimentation were particularly vulnerable to criticism and stigmatization. However, as we have seen, the main stigmatizing labels applied to Earth First! do not accurately reflect the overall character of that group. Moreover, that emphasis on the most contentious ideas and actions obscures the larger success of Earth First!'s experimentation.

Earth First!'s early use of monkeywrenching in the 1980s helped to give it the visibility to become a notable alternative to the mainstream organizations.

Then in the 1990s, Earth First! focused on civil disobedience tactics that allowed the group to broaden participation and win some notable victories, such as the Headwaters Forest campaign. At the same time, other activists coming out of Earth First! combined its radical strategy with legal tactics in a particularly potent combination. The grassroots groups they formed were central to many of the victories of the environmental movement in the 1990s and into the twenty-first century. In these ways, Earth First! succeeded in fostering effective radical alternatives to the limitations of mainstream environmentalism.

As the example of Earth First! illustrates, the same experimental qualities that make a radical group vulnerable to stigmatization can also allow it to discover innovative paths to social change. Focusing solely or primarily on the most stigmatized experiments may cause us to overlook the overall impact of the experimentation. It is thus only by examining radical social movement groups in the larger context of their strategic experimentation that we can hope to appreciate the role of these groups more fully.

REFERENCES

Bari, J. (1994). *Timber wars.* Monroe, ME: Common Courage Press.

Ingalsbee, T. (1995). *Earth First!: Consciousness in action in the unfolding of a new-social-movement.* Unpublished doctoral dissertation, Department of Sociology, University of Oregon, Eugene.

Lee, M. (1995). *Earth First!: Environmental apocalypse.* Syracuse, NY: Syracuse University Press.

Manes, C. (1990). *Green rage: Radical environmentalism and the unmaking of civilization.* Boston: Little, Brown & Company.

McGivney, A. (2003, February). Moses or menace? *Backpacker,* pp. 46+.

Rampton, S., & Stauber, J. (2004). *Banana republicans.* New York: Tarcher/Penguin.

Rosebraugh, C. (2004). *Burning rage of a dying planet: Speaking for the Earth Liberation Front.* New York: Lantern Books.

Scarce, R. (1990). *Eco-warriors: Understanding the radical environmental movement.* Chicago: Noble Press.

Thropy, A. (1987). Population and AIDS. *Earth First! Journal, 7*(4), 29.

Zakin, S. (1993). *Coyotes and town dogs: Earth First! and the environmental movement.* New York: Viking.

# I Am a Lowbagger

## Mike Roselle

I am a lowbagger. I have always been a lowbagger. I grew up with seven brothers and sisters and my father was usually away getting drunk, so we had to make do with what little we had. I was used to wearing hand-me-downs and eating meals of beans and greens. In Louisville, Kentucky's west end, this was pretty normal. Not only that, but few people aspired to live a different life. It was pretty much a given that people with more money were no happier, so there was little anger about the situation, only resignation. When I was 12 years old, my mother remarried and we moved to Los Angeles.

The suburbs of the San Gabriel Valley were very different from Kentucky. In LA, material possessions defined who you were. Your clothes, your car, even your lawn was a statement about who you were. Most of the neighbors thought we were trashy because we refused to play by these rules. Fortunately for me, the surfers and hippies were an antidote to this rigorous culture of materialism, and drugs and Levis were affordable even for the poor.

In Kentucky, I had always loved camping and hiking. Because my dad wasn't around when I was growing up, I belonged to the Boy Scouts and a few

Christian organizations for the sole purpose of going camping. In LA, it was a different story. The local Boy Scout Troop was run by a racist Christian and we only went camping once a year. I started going camping with my older brothers and their friends. My brother had a beat up '59 Ford Falcon station wagon and we would take it whenever we could to the San Gabriel Mountains or the Colorado River. We would take a lot of marijuana and LSD. I started reading underground newspapers and listening to underground radio stations. By Earth Day 1970, I was a radical environmentalist who admired Ralph Nader above all other living Americans. I was 16 years old, and the next year I left home to travel the country by hitch-hiking and working odd jobs. In 1975, I wound up in Jackson, Wyoming. I had come to hike in Yellowstone National Park and wound up staying there for seven years.

In my travels across the country, I'd visited many national parks and forests. I'd spend as much time in the woods as I could, including a yearly tradition of spending Christmas and New Year's as far away from civilization as was possible. I pretty much detested civilization and saw most people as slaves and hypocrites, unwilling to rebel against the grinding oppression of their daily lives. Out in the wilderness, you could wander naked with your girlfriend, high on LSD, and truly understand what it was like to be free. I met Cheryl in the Everglades in the spring of 1974. Her dad was a professor at MIT with a teaching assignment in Boulder, Colorado. She wanted to hike the length of the Continental Divide and meet up with her parents in Boulder. When we reached Jackson, it was so beautiful that we decided to stay. We were looking for an unobscured wilderness landscape, and Wyoming had it all. We both got jobs in restaurants and rented a small apartment north of town. Eventually Cheryl left and went back to school. Her parents did not approve of me, and I always thought that had something to do with her decision.

Wyoming in the seventies was the ideal place for a radical hippie: lots of tourists and rich white

kids, lots of low-paying work, and the best camping in the U.S.A. I took up cross-country skiing that year and it dawned on me that I could make more money selling pot to skiers than I could working at a restaurant. I also started meeting other people who I had more in common with, which was surprising, as I didn't think there was anyone out there that felt the way I did about wilderness. Bill and Howie were active environmentalists. Howie was radical, even rabid. He was a big fan of Edward Abbey's Monkey Wrench Gang, whose goal was to sabotage anti-environmentalist development, and would always fantasize about destroying logging and oil field equipment in the way that Abbey's characters did, but didn't actually do much because he worked for a national environmental organization and figured that he would be the first suspect. As it turned out, he was right.

On Sunday nights we would hang out after a day's skiing at the Stagecoach Bar in Wilson, Wyoming. On Sunday, the bar closed at 10 o' clock. We had had a few beers, and Bill and I were talking about cutting down the ugly billboards that littered the highways on every approach to town. The county had just outlawed them, but all the existing signs were exempted under a grandfather clause. The catch was that the existing signs could not be maintained beyond repainting. If the wind blew one over, it could not be replaced. But what if someone cut it down? Well, under the new law, that would be the same as the wind. We hopped in my VW van and went out and cut down a billboard. It was great fun, and the next day everyone was talking about it. Most everyone approved, except the owners of the Wagon Wheel Motel, who owned the sign. We kept our secret.

Over the next year, and always on a Sunday after 10 PM, we cut down every single billboard in Teton County and received praise from the local newspaper in their end-of-the-year edition. Our problem now was what to do on Sunday nights. That was soon remedied when Getty Oil announced their plans to develop an oilfield in the Gros Ventre

Mountains just east of the Tetons. Soon, fleets of oil exploration trucks were seen driving through town, setting up worker camps around town and starting seismic exploration of the area using dynamite and large thumper machines. Because of the jar-shaped geophones they placed in the ground to record the shock waves of the disturbances, they were usually referred to by the locals as "Juggies."

Most of the local people were horrified by this situation, and public outrage in our area was 90% against oil field development, yet the proposed field was on federally owned property so there was little the city could do about it. One Sunday night, in the Stagecoach Bar, four people declared war on the Juggies. In the ensuing months, mostly during Sunday evenings after 10 p.m., millions of dollars worth of exploration equipment was destroyed, and much more was defaced with graffiti declaring "Save the Gros Ventre!" The newspapers reported it as mindless vandalism, but even then the police were beginning to investigate Howie and me.

Not that it was very hard to investigate. I lived right across the street from the county courthouse, which housed the sheriff office, the police, courts, and the jail for this town of 5,000 people. It was from this house that I ran my marijuana business. We kept our mouths shut and things stayed cool. The problem was that because the press was describing our war against big oil as vandalism, we weren't getting any attention for our cause, which was to protect the Gros Ventre as a wilderness. We were causing all kinds of economic havoc, but we were voiceless. We decided to form an underground organization so we could send press releases to explain our actions. We named this group the Earth Liberation Front. We later would call it Earth First!

In a small town, it's hard to make a living dealing drugs. There are simply too many potential customers, the demand is high, supplies sometimes hard to get, and before long everyone in town knows who you are and is calling you or dropping by your house. The money is good, but the risks are extremely high. I usually tried to cultivate a clientele and sold only to friends. To create a cover, I usually worked at a job once in a while, so people wouldn't wonder how I supported myself. Since my first winter in Wyoming, when I was so broke I couldn't pay my rent, I had gone down to the town of Big Piney to work in the oil fields. I know this sounds hypocritical for environmentalists to work for the oil companies, but I saw no contradiction. We were simply saying back then that there are some places too special to drill for oil in, and the Gros Ventre was one of them. All the guys I worked with on the drilling rigs knew I was an environmentalist and didn't care. What they cared about was that I always had pot, and at least half of the wildcatters I met were potheads. I made more money selling them smoke than I did pulling pipe, but I actually enjoyed the work. Working on a drilling rig was like being on a ship at sea: You had a crew, a big piece of iron, and down in the hole, anything could happen. I loved the danger and the challenge of working high in the derrick.

In 1980, Getty was ready to drill in Little Granite Creek, the first of their planned oil fields for the region. I was working for Loffland Brothers Drilling at the time on the largest and newest drilling rig in the Northern Rockies. It was a plush assignment, only 45 minutes south of town, and I worked the midnight shift. Most nights I would drive to the rig from the Cowboy Bar and head to the pump house, smoke a joint, and go straight to sleep. We were running diamond drill bits on this hole and they would last for weeks, so most nights we didn't have to change the bit, so we just checked the gauges once in a while and watched the pipe turn to the right. It was the perfect job for a ski bum. One night, the drilling superintendent told me our next job was going to be up Little Granite Creek. I told him I didn't think the Feds were going to approve it. He said it was just a matter of paperwork.

Although it was well-known that I was an environmental activist, the ongoing war with the oil companies was still a secret known to only a few. I saw no reason to be paranoid. But with the drilling rig moving in at any day, the stakes were getting higher. The oil company had just surveyed and staked the road, getting it ready for grading and paving. I went up there with two friends and we pulled out all the survey stakes. When we got to the end of the road, we saw the survey crew sitting under a tree, eating lunch. We waved to them, and hiked the seven miles back down the trail. We got into my VW van and drove towards Dog Creek, where my landlord, Paul, was having his birthday party. Paul is an outfitter and a professional bear hunter. He has a hunting camp up Little Granite Creek and had joined the lawsuit against Getty Oil.

As we left the dirt road for the highway, we encountered the surveyors, who were now following us in their pickup truck. They were mad as hell. I just kept driving and had an orange survey ribbon tied around my head as a headband. I was wearing camouflage. We were busted. At the next intersection there was a payphone, so the surveyors stopped to call the police. Most of them were at Paul's birthday party in Dog Creek, and I showed up in my new headband. Everyone at the party knew where I had been. The next day I was approached by the police but refused to answer any questions and referred them to an attorney. The attorney assured me that no jury in the county would convict me. A week later, the governor of Wyoming, heeding the controversy, denied Getty a permit. This was the first time a state had ever stepped in to stop an oil well on federal land. The Gros Ventre Mountains are now within a federally protected wilderness area.

Meanwhile, Paul had been chosen to sit on a state grand jury investigating the local drug trade. Some high school kids were busted and turned in some older locals who were being grilled relentlessly by the new DA, a crusading Mormon. The investigation was getting close to home, and two of my colleagues were facing long prison sentences. Paul let on that he was suspicious of how I made my living. I gathered that my name had come up during the proceedings. Because I knew many influential people in town who would be concerned by my getting a subpoena and testifying in front of the grand jury, I decided to leave Jackson and go to Oregon. Some friends in the Siskiyou Mountain region had informed me that the Feds were planning a similar road into the Kalomiopsis Wilderness in order to log the old-growth forests. They wanted our help. I left town that spring and have only been back a few times to visit.

The Oregon campaign gained national notoriety for Earth First! We stopped the road that year by staging a series of nonviolent blockades over the spring that almost forced the contractor into bankruptcy. We recruited thousands of new activists across the country and built Earth First! into an influential national grass roots organization. In the meantime, we have been satirized on television sitcoms and stereotyped in television dramas. The longhaired, shaggy, dope-smoking environmental activist is now an American icon as much as the cowboy or gangster. People no longer see environmentalists simply as a class of elite, overeducated professionals and can now better grasp the diversity in our movement.

Of course, America is not the only place you will find such characters. Canada, Europe, and Australia all have them. In Australia they call them rat bags, in Britain, dirt bags. In America, we go by the name lowbagger. We are unashamed of our hippie roots and still believe that modern society is far too materialistic and lacks a proper reverence for nature. We are activists, but we try to practice what we preach. We are not anti-technology, but reject the view that new technology is needed to solve the world's problems, which we feel are mainly caused by human greed and indifference.

## Discussion Questions

1. Most studies of deviance focus on more informal patterns of organization (e.g., subcultures, social worlds, and the like). How is the study of a relatively more formalized organization like Earth First! similar to the study of less formal social worlds? How is it different? Is Earth First! really an organization?

2. Some aspects of Earth First!'s organizational structure have allowed it to become what it has become; others have interfered with its founders' ability to achieve their goals. If you could organize Earth First! from scratch, how would you do it differently? What problems might your changes create?

3. What's the sociological difference between an Earth First! member and an everyday environmentalist? Your answer should include a discussion of labeling and identity work.

4. Design a social movement organization to advance a cause near and dear to you. Design that organization on Earth First!'s model. Try to accomplish your organization's goals without being placed on the FBI's terrorist list. Can you do it? Why or why not? If you can, why couldn't Earth First!?

5. Design a course in Deviance and Social Control using the basic principles of Earth First! What will your students learn? Where will you hold class? Who will design the curriculum? Who will evaluate the students' progress? What evaluation instruments will you use? How will you ensure that your students learn anything?

# PART 7

# ENGAGING IN
# S&M SEXUAL PRACTICES

# S&M
## An Introduction

The first and most fundamental principle to keep in mind when considering deviance as a sociological phenomenon is "things are not always what they seem" (Berger, 1963). In other words, popular and widespread understanding of deviance may be spectacularly inaccurate. In very few other areas of deviance do we notice such a wide and yawning chasm between myth and reality as with S&M.

What is the public understanding of S&M? S&M, or sadism and masochism—or (in reverse) master and slave—is thought to be a sexual perversion, a psychological disorder; common wisdom has it that the sadist and the masochist are mentally ill. Most people believe that one partner (the sadist), the "active" partner, obtains sexual pleasure from inflicting pain on the passive or semi-unwilling partner (the masochist), who nonetheless obtains pleasure from receiving pain. In addition, it is assumed that the sadist often includes unwilling partners in his or her sexual practices, forcing them to submit to his or her twisted, perverted lust.

Another stereotype, among some radical feminists at any rate, is that S&M is a form of cruelty and hence, a model, paradigm, or slight exaggeration of conventional male-female relations, which contain a generous measure of coercion, domination, cruelty, and violence (Linden, Pagano, Russell, & Star, 1982, p. 78). Pornography, likewise, represents the essence of male domination and, whether in diluted or pure form, is based on sadism (Dworkin, 1981; Lederer, 1982).

A third stereotype is that S&M is an either-or proposition, that rough sex is either present in the sexual experience or absent, that there is no in-between territory; "abnormal" sex is a world apart from what we all regard as normal sexuality.

These views (which are not necessarily all held by the same ideological or intellectual circles) are mistaken, and for at least seven reasons.

First, pain is not the central or guiding principle of S&M. Indeed, it is not even essential to sadomasochistic activities (Baumeister, 1988, p. 37; Weinberg, 1995b, p. 291). In fact, it is the *illusion* of pain that is crucial; it is *symbolic* of dominance and control (Moser, 1988, p. 50). S&M is about dominance and submission, controlling and being controlled (Weinberg & Levi Kamel, 1995, p. 19). Pain is far from unknown in S&M, but the pain is secondary.

The second point is that the masochistic partner is far from passive. S&M is a *social* and *interactional* activity. The masochistic (or "bottom") partner emits cues to the sadistic (or "top") partner as to what he or she wants to do, and vice versa. Both partners "are actively involved in the development of the scenario" (Weinberg, 1995b, p. 294; Califia, 1994). Collaboration, not force, is the foundation of S&M. Sadists who force their partners to engage in activities against their will "are avoided and quickly find themselves without partners" (Weinberg & Levi Kamel, 1995, p. 19). Weinberg describes a scene in which a man was hoisted up onto a wall by a hook. At a certain point, the two women who were engaged in the action whispered into the man's ear to ask him whether he was uncomfortable. He nodded to assure them that he was okay (Weinberg, 1995b, p. 295).

The third point is an outgrowth of the second: It is *scripted* behavior—it is more or less planned in advance (Gebhard, 1969, p. 78). This does not mean that there are no departures from the script. Limits are negotiable, scripts may be tossed aside—but the partners involved map out the dynamics of the action before it takes place.

Another way of saying S&M is reciprocal and that it is scripted is that partners agree, in Goffman's (1963) terminology, on a particular S&M *frame*. S&M is theater, a world of make-believe, a shared fantasy that becomes a mutual creation. Frames inform participants "what is and is not proper, acceptable, and possible within their world. They define and categorize for their members situations, settings, scenes, identities, roles, and relationships" (Weinberg, 1995a, p. 134).

Just as frames can be constructed, they can also be violated. In the world of S&M, breaking frame is communicated in much the same way as in more conventional worlds. Brodsky (1995) describes a scene during an especially crowded weekend at the Mineshaft, an S&M bar, in which frame was broken. A man yelled out very loudly, "I said STOP THAT!" and struck another man. "The crowd was stunned, and in Goffman's terminology, the frame was obviously broken—no one knew what to do. All sound but the disco tapes ceased. People all around stopped what they were doing and stood frozen as if in a tableau." The assailant was removed from the scene, several people were distressed by what they had witnessed, left, several others moved in, "and the frame was reestablished within a few minutes" (p. 213).

Fourth, the two positions, sadist ("top") and masochist ("bottom"), are not fixed; there is a substantial amount of movement from one position to the other. In fact, far from being mutually exclusive or contradictory, being a "top" trains the participant to be a good "bottom," and vice versa. In one study, only 16% of the sample said that they were exclusively dominant or submissive; the remainder—the vast majority of the sample—was made up of "switchables" (Moser & Levitt, 1987).

Fifth, no evidence from any study based on a reasonable cross-section of S&M participants has demonstrated them to be any more mentally disordered than the population at large. Studies based on non-clinical samples have found that they are essentially normal (Moser & Levitt, 1987; Thompson, 1994, pp. 88–116; Weinberg, 1995b). The fourth edition of the American Psychiatric Association's *Diagnostic and Statistical Manual of Mental Disorders* (1994, pp. 529–530) is careful to distinguish between being sexually aroused by "real" as opposed to "simulated" beating, humiliation, and suffering. While men (and women) exist who are excited by real (and unscripted) pain and humiliation, for the most part, they are not devotees of S&M, and they are not part of the mainstream S&M subculture. If they were to attempt to participate in that subculture, chances are they would be avoided and stigmatized. There are, after all, proper rules of behavior, even in a deviant context, and a violation of rules constitutes deviance in any context (see Photo 7.1).

**Photo 7.1.**    Folsom Street Fair 2006 Poster. People who engage in power play get erotic satisfaction from giving and/or receiving pain. In most communities in the United States, S&M is extremely deviant, its practitioners keeping their activities a secret from nonparticipants. In contrast, in others, such as gay neighborhoods in San Francisco, though it is a minority practice, it is more likely to be tolerated.

SOURCE: Photo by Fredalert; design by Derivdesign.com.

Sixth, the extrapolation from S&M to ordinary male-female relations, as a few feminists have done (Linden et al., 1982), is misleading. (In many S&M circles, the man is typically the submissive partner and the female, the dominant one.) The question of whether or not violence, coercion, dominance and submission, and/or humiliation are characteristic or typical of male-female relations in this or any society is not related to how S&M is conducted. As we saw, S&M behavior is mutually arrived at, reciprocal, scripted, fantasy-oriented, theatrical, carefully choreographed, socially constructed, and subculturally framed.

And last, as Rebecca Plante's contribution below on sexual spanking demonstrates, rough sex, engaged in mutually by consenting partners, is a continuum, a matter of degree, not an either-or proposition. The degree of "roughness," constraint, control, pain—or its illusion—depends on the couple. Moreover, for most participants, some measure of S&M is, in a given experience, optional rather than compulsory. In other words, S&M is "extreme" only in its more extreme versions.

Not all participants in S&M are into the same activities. Partners who spank one another for sexual stimulation do not necessarily like to tie up one another; partners who are into

**Photo 7.2.**   S&M entails a wide continuum of activities, from married couples lightly spanking one another to practices involving the use of a variety of paraphernalia such as harnesses, gags, chains, whips, restraints, leather outfits, metal rings, and balls inserted into one or another orifice. Most of us would be shocked to find out that a friend or relative engaged in sex that involved what this woman is experiencing.

SOURCE: Copyright © MedicalToys.com.

leather are not necessarily into spanking. There is a great deal of variation in what partners engage in when they engage in rough sex. Many participants tolerate but do not participate in some of the more extreme S&M conduct, just as they recognize that not everyone who is interested in S&M partakes of some of their activities. Much deviant behavior is stereotyped by the majority, and most stereotypes "flatten" the people or their behavior into a misleadingly homogeneous consistency. S&M is far from consistent. Differences and distinctions within a particular unconventional scene and the role they play among their members are some of the more interesting aspects of deviance (see Photo 7.2).

In this section, Rebecca Plante discusses the process by which sexual spanking, a mild form of S&M, is justified by heterosexual males who try to make sense of their unusual sexual predilection. A very small minority of women find such behavior stimulating, and hence, the likelihood that a man who does will come into contact with such a woman is extremely small. Stigma adheres to the activity; hence, the activity must be hidden from non-participants and its stigma must be neutralized. The hold that conventional norms have even on participants of this unusual sexual practice is illustrated by the statement of one of Plante's interviewees who said, "I am not interested in a full S&M lifestyle, just in erotic spanking with members of the opposite sex." The implication is that if a clear and bright line can be drawn between S&M and spanking, then surely spanking is not so deviant after all! S&M and sexual spanking may not be pathological, but it *is* deviant in the normative sense. In a volume titled *Sexual Deviance*, Roy Baumeister and Jennifer Butler (1997) refer to S&M as "deviance without pathology." And in a volume on "sexual domination and submission," Gloria Brame and her colleagues refer to S&M as a "different loving" (Brame, Brame, & Jacobs, 1996). Deviant it is, and "different"—extreme S&M is so far off the charts for most Americans that it does not even appear in a survey of the public's sexual behavior or preferences (Michael, Gagnon, Laumann, & Kolata, 1994; Laumann, Gagnon, Michael, & Michaels, 1994)—but not pathological. It is kept secret to all but its participants; as Plante suggests, participants go to great lengths to engage in the practice, and it can be an occasion for rejecting a potential sexual partner.

Below, Marianne Apostolides defines some of the basic terms used among S&M aficionados, explains that their practice is "no longer a pathology," speculates about the origin of the S&M impulse, and establishes, as we explained, that it is one end point along the broad "sexual continuum." And "Jackie" contributes a first-hand account to illustrate the S&M experience for one participant.

# REFERENCES

American Psychiatric Association. (1994). *Diagnostic and statistical manual of mental disorders* (4th ed.). Washington, DC: Author.

Baumeister, R. F. (1988). Masochism as escape from self. *Journal of Sex Research, 25*(1), 25–59.

Baumeister, R. F., & Butler, J. L. (1997). Sexual masochism: Deviance without pathology. In D. R. Laws & W. O'Donohue (Eds.), *Sexual deviance: Theory, assessment, and treatment* (pp. 225–239). New York: Guilford Press.

Berger, P. (1963). *Invitation to sociology*. Garden City, NY: Doubleday Anchor.

Brame, G. G., Brame, W., & Jacobs, J. (1996). *Different loving: The world of sexual dominance and submission.* New York: Villard.

Brodsky, J. I. (1995). The mineshaft: A retrospective ethnography. In T. S. Weinberg (Ed.), *S&M: Studies in dominance and submission* (pp. 195–218). Buffalo, NY: Prometheus Books.

Califia, P. (1994). *Public sex: The culture of radical sex*. Pittsburgh, PA: Cleis Press.

Dworkin, A. (1981). *Pornography: Men possessing women.* New York: Perigee.

Gebhard, P. H. (1969). Fetishism and sadomasochism. In J. H. Masserman (Ed.), *Dynamics of deviant sexuality* (pp. 71–80). New York: Grune & Stratton.

Goffman, E. (1963). *Stigma: Notes on the management of spoiled identity.* Englewood Cliffs, NJ: Prentice Hall/Spectrum.

Laumann, E. O., Gagnon, J. H., Michael, R. T., & Michaels, S. (1994). *The social organization of sexuality: Sexual practices in the United States.* Chicago: University of Chicago Press.

Lederer, L. (Ed.). (1982). *Take back the night: Women on pornography.* New York: Bantam Books.

Linden, R. R., Pagano, D. R., Russell, D. E. H., & Star, S. L. (1982). *Against sado-masochism: A radical feminist analysis.* San Francisco: Frog in the Well Press.

Michael, R. T., Gagnon, J. H., Laumann, E. O., & Kolata, G. (1994). *Sex in America: A definitive survey.* Boston: Little, Brown.

Moser, C. (1988). Sadomasochism. *Journal of Social Work and Human Sexuality, 7*(1), 43–56.

Moser, C., & Levitt, E. E. (1987). An exploratory-descriptive study of a sadomasochistically-oriented sample. *Journal of Sex Research, 23,* 322–337.

Thompson, B. (1994). *Sadomasochism.* London & New York: Cassell.

Weinberg, T. S. (Ed.). (1995a). *S&M: Studies in dominance and submission.* Buffalo, NY: Prometheus Books.

Weinberg, T. S. (1995b). Sociological and social psychological issues in the study of sadomasochism. In T. S. Weinberg (Ed.), *S&M: Studies in dominance and submission* (pp. 289–303). Buffalo, NY: Prometheus Books.

Weinberg, T. S., & Levi Kamel, G. W. (1995). S&M: An introduction to the study of sadomasochism. In T. S. Weinberg (Ed.), *S&M: Studies in dominance and submission* (pp. 15–24). Buffalo, NY: Prometheus Books.

# The Pleasure of Pain

## *Marianne Apostolides*

*Bind my ankles with your white cotton rope so I cannot walk. Bind my wrists so I cannot push you away. Place me on the bed and wrap your rope tighter around my skin so it grips my flesh. Now I know that struggle is useless, that I must lie here and submit to your mouth and tongue and teeth, your hands and words and whims. I exist only as your object. Exposed.*

Of every 10 people who read these words, one or more has experimented with sadomasochism (S&M), which is most popular among educated, middle- and upper-middle-class men and women, according to psychologists and ethnographers who have studied the phenomenon. Charles Moser, Ph.D., M.D., of the Institute for Advanced Study of Human Sexuality in San Francisco, has researched S&M to learn the motivation behind it—to understand why in the world people would ask to be bound, whipped, and flogged. The reasons are as surprising as they are varied.

For James, the desire became apparent when he was a child playing war games—he always hoped to be captured. "I was frightened that I was sick," he says. But now, he adds, as a well-seasoned player on the scene, "I thank the leather gods I found this community."

At first the scene found him. When he was at a party in college, a professor chose him. She brought him home and tied him up, told him how bad he was for having these desires even as she fulfilled them. For the first time, he felt what he had only imagined, what he had read about in every S&M book he could find.

James, a father and manager, has a Type A personality—in control, hard working, intelligent, demanding. His intensity is evident on his face, in his posture, in his voice. But when he plays, his eyes drift and a peaceful energy flows through him

AUTHOR'S NOTE: Reprinted with permission from *Psychology Today Magazine* © copyright 1999 Sussex Publishers, Inc. Marianne Apostolides is author of *Inner Hunger: A Young Women's Struggle through Anorexia and Bulimia* (W.W. Norton, 1996).

as though he has injected heroin. With each addition of pain or restraint, he stiffens slightly, then falls into a deeper calm, a deeper peace, waiting to obey his mistress. "Some people have to be tied up to be free," he says.

As James's experience illustrates, sadomasochism involves a highly unbalanced power relationship established through role-playing, bondage, and/or the infliction of pain. The essential component is not the pain or bondage itself, but rather the knowledge that one person has complete control over the other, deciding what that person will hear, do, taste, touch, smell, and feel. We hear about men pretending to be little girls, women being bound in a leather corset, people screaming in pain with each strike of a flogger or drip of hot wax. We hear about it because it is happening in bedrooms and dungeons across the country.

For over a century, people who engaged in bondage, beatings, and humiliation for sexual pleasure were considered mentally ill. But in the 1980s, the American Psychiatric Association removed S&M as a category in its *Diagnostic and Statistical Manual of Mental Disorders*. This decision—like the decision to remove homosexuality as a category in 1973—was a big step toward the social acceptance of people whose sexual desires aren't traditional, or vanilla, as it's called in S&M circles.

What's new is that such desires are increasingly being considered normal, even healthy, as experts begin to recognize their potential psychological value. S&M, they are beginning to understand, offers a release of sexual and emotional energy that some people cannot get from traditional sex. "The satisfaction gained from S&M is something far more than sex," explains Roy Baumeister, Ph.D., a social psychologist at Case Western Reserve University. "It can be a total emotional release."

Although people report that they have better-than-usual sex immediately after a scene, the goal of S&M itself is not intercourse: "A good scene doesn't end in orgasm; it ends in catharsis."

## S&M: No Longer a Pathology

> If children at [an] early age witness sexual intercourse between adults . . . they inevitably regard the sexual act as a sort of ill-treatment or act of subjugation: they view it, that is, in a sadistic sense.
>
> —Sigmund Freud, 1905

Freud was one of the first to discuss S&M on a psychological level. During the 20 years he explored the topic, his theories crossed each other to create a maze of contradictions. But he maintained one constant: S&M was pathological.

People become sadistic, Freud said, as a way of regulating their desire to sexually dominate others. The desire to submit, on the other hand, he said, arises from guilt feelings over the desire to dominate. He also argued that the desire for S&M can arise on its own when a man wants to assume the passive female role, with bondage and beating signifying being "castrated or copulated with, or giving birth."

The view that S&M is pathological has been dismissed by the psychological community. Sexual sadism is a real problem, but it is a different phenomenon from S&M. Luc Granger, Ph.D., head of the department of psychology at the University of Montreal, created an intensive treatment program for sexual aggressors in La Macaza Prison in Quebec; he has also conducted research on the S&M community. "They are very separate populations," he says. While S&M is the regulated exchange of power among consensual participants, sexual sadism is the derivation of pleasure from either inflicting pain or completely controlling an unwilling person.

Lily Fine, a professional dominatrix who teaches S&M workshops across North America, explains, "I may hurt you, but I will not harm you: I will not hit you too hard, take you further than you want to go, or give you an infection."

Despite the research indicating that S&M does no real harm and is not associated with pathology,

Freud's successors in psychoanalysis continue to use mental illness overtones when discussing S&M. Sheldon Bach, Ph.D., clinical professor of psychology at New York University and supervising analyst at the New York Freudian Society, maintains that people are addicted to S&M. They feel compelled to be "anally abused or crawl on their knees and lick a boot or a penis or who knows what else. The problem," he continues, "is that they can't love. They are searching for love, and S&M is the only way they can try to find it because they are locked into sadomasochistic interactions they had with a parent."

## LINKING CHILDHOOD MEMORIES AND ADULT SEX

I can explore aspects of myself that I don't get a chance to explore otherwise. So even though I'm playing a role, I feel more connected with myself.

—Leanne Custer, M.S.W., AIDS counselor

Meredith Reynolds, Ph.D., the Sexuality Research Fellow of the Social Science Research Council, confirms that childhood experiences may shape a person's sexual outlook.

"Sexuality doesn't just arise at puberty," she says. "Like other parts of someone's personality, sexuality develops at birth and takes a developmental course through a person's life span."

In her work on sexual exploration among children, Reynolds has shown that while childhood experiences can indeed influence adult sexuality, the effects usually "wash out" as a person gains more sexual experience. But they can linger in some people, causing a connection between childhood memories and adult sexual play. In that case, Reynolds says, "the childhood experiences have affected something in the personality, and that in turn affects adult experiences."

Reynolds' theory helps us develop a greater understanding of the desire to be a whip-bearing mistress or a bootlicking slave. For example, if a child has been taught to feel shame about her body and desires, she may learn to disconnect herself from them. Even as she gets older and gains more experience with sex, her personality may retain some part of that need for separation. S&M play may act as a bridge: Lying naked on a bed bound to the bedposts with leather restraints, she is forced to be completely sexual. The restraint, the futility of struggle, the pain, the master's words telling her she is such a lovely slave—these cues enable her body to fully connect with her sexual self in a way that has been difficult during traditional sex.

Marina is a prime example. She knew from the time she was six years old that she was expected to succeed in school and sports. She learned to focus on achievement as a way to dismiss emotions and desires. "I learned very young that desires are dangerous," she says. She heard that message in the behavior of her parents: a depressive mother who let her emotions overtake her, and an obsessively health-conscious father who compulsively controlled his diet. When Marina began to have sexual desires, her instinct, cultivated by her upbringing, was to consider them too frightening, too dangerous. "So I became anorexic," she says. "And when you're anorexic, you don't feel desire; all you feel in your body is panic."

Marina didn't feel the desire for S&M until she was an adult and had outgrown her eating disorder. "One night, I asked my partner to put his hands around my neck and choke me. I was so surprised when those words came out of my mouth," she says. If she gave her partner total control over her body, she felt, she could allow herself to feel like a completely sexual being, with none of the hesitation and disconnection she sometimes felt during sex. "He wasn't into it, but now I'm with someone who is," Marina says. "S&M makes our vanilla sex better, too, because we trust each other more sexually, and we can communicate what we want."

## ESCAPING THE MODERN WESTERN EGO

Like alcohol abuse, binge eating, and meditation, sado masochism is a way people can forget themselves.

—Roy Baumeister, Ph.D., professor of psychology, Case Western Reserve University

It is human nature to try to maximize esteem and control: Those are two general principles governing the study of the self. Masochism runs contrary to both and was therefore an intriguing psychological puzzle for Baumeister, whose career has focused on the study of self and identity.

Through an analysis of S&M-related letters to the sex magazine *Variations,* Baumeister came to believe that "masochism is a set of techniques for helping people temporarily lose their normal identity." He reasoned that the modern Western ego is an incredibly elaborate structure, with our culture placing more demands on the individual self than any other culture in history. Such high demands increase the stress associated with living up to expectations and existing as the person you want to be. "That stress makes forgetting who you are an appealing escape," Baumeister says. That is the essence of "escape" theory, one of the main reasons people turn to S&M.

"Nothing matters except you, me, and the sound of my voice," Lily Fine tells the tied-up and exposed businessman who begged to be spanked before breakfast. She says it slowly, making her slave wait for every sound, forcing him to focus only on her, to float in anticipation of the sensations she will create inside him. Anxieties about mortgages and taxes, stresses about business partners and job deadlines are vanquished each time the flogger hits the flesh. The businessman is reduced to a physical creature existing only in the here and now, feeling the pain and pleasure.

"I'm interested in manipulating what's in the mind," Lily says. "The brain is the greatest erogenous zone."

In another S&M scene, Lily tells a woman to take off her clothes, then dresses her only with a blindfold. She commands the woman not to move. Lily then takes a tissue and begins moving it over the woman's body in different patterns and at varying speeds and angles. Sometimes she lets the edge of the tissue just barely brush the woman's stomach and breasts; sometimes she bunches the tissue and creates swirls on her back and all the way down. "The woman was quivering. She didn't know what I was doing to her, but she was liking it," Lily remembers with a smile.

Escape theory is further supported by an idea called "frame analysis," developed by the late Erving Goffman, Ph.D. According to Goffman, despite its popular conception as darkly wild and orgiastic, S&M play has complex rules, rituals, roles, and dynamics that create a "frame" around the experience.

"Frames suspend reality. They create expectations, norms and values that set this situation apart from other parts of life," confirms Thomas Weinberg, Ph.D., a sociologist at Buffalo State College in New York and the editor of *S&M: Studies in Dominance and Submission* (1995).

Once inside the frame, people are free to act and feel in ways they couldn't at other times.

## S&M: PART OF THE SEXUAL CONTINUUM

S&M has inspired the creation of many psychological theories in addition to the ones discussed here. Do we need so many? Perhaps not. According to Stephanie Saunders, Ph.D., associate director of the Kinsey Institute for Research in Sex, Gender, and Reproduction at Indiana University, "a lot of behaviors that are scrutinized because they are seen to be marginal are really a part of the continuum of sexuality and sexual behavior."

After all, the ingredients in good S&M play—communication, respect, and trust—are the same ingredients in good traditional sex. The outcome is the same, too—a feeling of connection to the body and the self.

Laura Antoniou, a writer whose work on S&M has been published by Masquerade Books in New York City, puts it another way: "When I was a child, I had nothing but S&M fantasies. I punished Barbie for being dirty. I did Bondage Barbie, dominance with GI Joe. S&M is simply what turns me on."

## Whip Smart: Beyond the Boundaries of Safe Play

While S&M can be a psychologically healthy activity—its motto is "safe, sane, and consensual"—sometimes things do get out of hand.

### Abuse

It is rare, but some "tops" get too involved in power and forget to monitor their treatment of the "bottom." "I call them 'Natural Born Tops,'" says dominatrix Lily Fine, "and I don't have time for them." Also, some bottoms want to be beaten because they have low self-esteem and think they deserve it. They are forlorn, absent, and unresponsive during and after a scene; in this case, S&M ceases to be play and becomes pathological.

### Boundaries

A small percentage of people inappropriately bring S&M power play into other facets of their life. "Most people in S&M circles are dominant or submissive in very specific situations, while in their everyday life they can play a whole range of roles," says psychology professor Luc Granger. But, he continues, if the only way a person can relate to someone else is through a kind of sadomasochistic game, then there is probably a deeper psychological problem.

### The Use of S&M as Therapy

People often confuse the fact that they feel good after S&M with the idea that S&M is therapy, says psychology professor Roy Baumeister. "But to prove that something is therapeutic, you have to prove that it has lasting beneficial effects on mental health . . . and it's hard to prove even that therapy is therapeutic." In mental health terms, S&M doesn't make you better and it doesn't make you worse.

## Excerpts From an S&M Glossary

Bondage and Discipline (B&D):   A subset of S&M not involving physical pain.

Bottom:   The submissive person in a scene; synonyms: submissive, sub, slave.

Dungeon:   A place designated for S&M play.

Dominatrix (pl. dominatrices):   A female top, usually a professional.

Fetish:   An object that is granted special powers, one of which is the ability to sexually gratify. It is often wrongly confused with S&M.

Lifestyle Dominant/Submissive:   A person involved in a relationship in which S&M is a defining dynamic.

Masochist:   A person who derives sexual pleasure from being abused by others. Sadist and masochist are sometimes used playfully in the S&M community, but are generally avoided because of psychiatric denotation.

Negotiating a Scene:   The process of loosely outlining what the players want to experience before they begin a scene.

Play:   Participation in a scene.

Sadist:   A person who derives sexual pleasure from inflicting pain on others.

Sadomasochism (S&M):   An activity involving the temporary creation of highly unbalanced power dynamics between two or more people for erotic or semi-erotic purposes.

Safe Word:   A prearranged word or phrase that may be used to end or renegotiate a scene. This is a clear signal meaning "Stop, this is too much for me."

Scene:   An episode of S&M activity; the S&M community.

Switch:   A person who enjoys being a top in some scenes and a bottom in others.

Top:   The dominant person in a scene; synonyms: dominant, dom, master/mistress.

Toy:   Any implement used to enhance S&M play.

Vanilla Sex:   Conventional heterosexual sex.

# Sexual Spanking

## *Rebecca F. Plante*

Traditionally, spanking, or its umbrella term, flagellation, has been administered as punishment. However, very possibly in every society, some individuals have found spanking sexually arousing and engage in it as an erotic practice. The *Kama Sutra,* the ancient Hindu sex manual, includes a section on "love blows," offering detailed instructions on how to administer the most arousing slaps and punches. Historically, a certain proportion of sexual workers, mainly prostitutes, have used flagellation as one way to excite their clients. Erotic spanking can be seen as a variety of bondage/domination and sadomasochism. The purpose of erotic spanking is to achieve the emotional and sexual gratification of either or both parties. It plays a part in fantasy scenes of punishment or misbehavior, which many participants find arousing.

Here, I highlight the activities of a group of heterosexual men who enjoy spanking consensual heterosexual women as an erotic, sexualized activity. I frame my investigation with several questions: How do people who engage in unconventional

sexual behavior understand and make sense of their stigmatized sexual interests? How do they mitigate the effects of stereotypical, and negative, sexual scripting? What is the larger social context for a type of sexual conduct that might appear, at first glance and for most audiences, to be the province of only a few, highly atypical, individuals?

Participants in this activity know about broader cultural narratives and social constructions of normal sexual expressions and are aware that their interests and activities are stigmatized and widely regarded as deviant. In this vein, they work to redefine deviance by means of several strategies and techniques for neutralizing stigma. They collect and share popular cultural references to sexualized spanking and suggest that most people are interested in spanking but simply aren't aware of it. Participants also know that conventional audiences would condemn them and what they do, and they have a repertoire of interactional devices with which to introduce, or avoid introducing, the subject to others.

EDITORS' NOTE: Adapted from "Sexual spanking, the self, and the construction of deviance," in *Journal of Homosexuality, 50*(3/4), copyright © 2005. Reprinted with permission of Haworth Press, Inc.

My participants differentiate themselves from sadomasochistic practitioners, defining themselves as interested solely in "the bottom" or the buttocks and in scenes specifically involving the erotic tableau of a man spanking a woman. Definitionally, spanking is one activity within a broader rubric of sexual bondage, domination, and sadomasochism. This encompasses a wide range of practices including, but not limited to, flagellation, humiliation, restraints, torture, and blindfolding. As a set of sexual practices and interests, sadomasochism (S&M) is ecumenical, with gay, lesbian, bisexual, heterosexual, pansexual, and transgendered practitioners. The fluidity of identities, roles, and fantasies opens S&M to participants with a broad range of sexual orientations, although minority practices and interests do coalesce within this broader umbrella, such as gay leather scenes, heterosexual infantilism, and so on.

Most prior research on the subject has emphasized the aberrant features of S&M participants, arguing that the activity plays a role in satisfying impulses derived from childhood pathologies. Sociological and ethnographic research is more recent and less abundant than psychoanalytic inquiries. Such research attempts to locate S&M and spanking within the framework of sexual scripts; it is guided by the question, "Why does anyone have the sexual interests he/she has, whether those interests are normative or nonnormative, mainstream or outside the mainstream, deviant or conventional?"

## The Context of Sexualized Spanking

Gagnon and Simon (1973, 2005) first advanced the idea of sexual scripts, those sociological blueprints that guide our erotic interests. Scripts specify the who, what, where, when, why, and how of sexualities and sexual practices. Scripts can be, from the broadest to the narrowest levels, cultural, subcultural, interpersonal, or intrapsychic. Intrapsychic scripts include the stories we tell ourselves, memories, and internal rehearsals. We assemble intrapsychic scripts based on cues from culture, subculture, and social interactions with others. Interpersonal scripts develop from interactions we have with others. Subcultural scripts include discourses, ideologies, and expectations at the small-group level, for example, based on ethnic or religious group membership. And the broadest, cultural scripts derive from discourses, ideologies, and expectations at the societal level.

Standard cultural scripts are nonmainstream and do not include sexual spanking. The standard heterosexual script eroticizes the basic sexual practices, such as kissing, breast fondling, genital stimulation, and penile-vaginal intercourse. How does someone come to adapt and transform this basic cultural script? How would an individual exposed to the larger or cultural definitions of appropriate sexual practices expand this script to include sexual spanking? More specifically, how does one adapt his or her sexual scripting to encompass a practice that is stigmatizing?

Stigma is an attribute that is discrediting to an individual's identity (Goffman, 1963). Persons interested in spanking have a *discrediting* stigma, one that has not yet been discovered, one that can be hidden from conventional others. According to Goffman, "Even where an individual has quite abnormal feelings and beliefs, he is likely to have quite normal concerns and employ quite normal strategies in attempting to conceal these abnormalities from others" (p. 131). Awareness of a stigmatizing condition requires impression management to determine to whom the attribute will be revealed, in order to maintain control over revelations of the discreditable attribute.

One coping mechanism that enables someone to continue engaging in nonmainstream sexual practices entails embracing the acceptability of said practices and rejecting the dominant norms that define such practices as unacceptable. With respect to sexual spanking, this often implies believing that everyone is actually interested in spanking, but most of us just aren't yet aware of it. Minority sexual subcultures often develop oppositional definitions that parody the practices of the sexual mainstream. A commonly-used description of those mainstream practices is "vanilla" sex, that is, sexual interests and practices that are bland, boring, and unexciting. Turning the mainstream into a negatively labeled category enables the sexual nonconformist to reject the standard cultural scripting, thus normalizing the self. This is a fairly straightforward form of stigma management.

Another strategy for interpreting the sexual self is to construct a story describing its attributes, tracing its history, and locating it within the nexus of cultural sexual scripting. Plummer (1995) looked at the sexual stories in circulation, arguing that they constitute patterned discourses that are constructed and given meaning within specific social contexts. In spite of the fact that these stories encompass the sexually different, they represent efforts to normalize unconventional actors, to place them into broader social contexts.

Simon (1996) noted the tendency to essentialize sexualities, locating them within the genes or as a product of innate tendencies. Thus, for example, increasingly, homosexuals will claim that they were born with a same-sex gender interest, that they are obeying an impulse that has been present all along, that it is an essential aspect of their sexual being. The culturally motivated interest in essentializing sexuality is linked to the social construction of what is acceptable—and unacceptable—practice. "Once the normal is constructed," Simon states, "its explanation organizes our understanding of all other variations by moving us to conceive of all other outcomes as violations or variations of the logic of the normal" (p. 14). By this logic, then, spanking is viewed as a violation of the normal, requiring an explanation of how and why such interest develops.

Looking at sexual spanking demands that we recognize the reality of stigma. "Vanilla" cultural scripts provide a foundation for identity development. Deviations from narrowly rendered norms force aficionados to recognize that mainstream members of the society may condemn and stigmatize them for their sexual practices and interests. To address such potential and actual stigma, persons with variant interests must develop coping strategies and design culturally and subculturally meaningful sexual stories. The spanking stories aficionados narrate address the management of stigma and provide a script that attempts to deflect stigma from the behavior they engage in.

## The Study

My fieldwork looks at participants in a loosely organized group of adults interested in consensual spanking. All participants were told of the research and gave consent to be included in my study. Because of the sensitivity of the topic, participants are described in such a way that they cannot be identified. Since this research included observation, it is appropriate to situate the author in the fieldwork. I obtained access to the group through a key informant, Jim, a longtime member of the scene. After we met at a professional conference and engaged in non-sexual conversations, Jim mentioned that he had long been interested in spanking. In making this admission, he sought to determine whether he could trust me. Jim was also curious whether I had an interest in being spanked. A year later, Jim confirmed that he had hoped that I was a "bottom" because men outnumber women, particularly younger ones, in the scene. Since my interests were strictly research related, the fieldwork was fraught with conflicts, dilemmas, and ambiguities so often experienced in qualitative research. I never misrepresented my sexual interests to gain access, and all my research was confined to observation.

Jim provided access to a complex and dynamic community of spanking aficionados. My fieldwork included spanking parties, discreetly held in small-town hotels on floors far from hotel traffic; formal interviews; casual conversations; and observations of private scenes between two people. Supplemental research included reading spanking stories, spanking newsletters, and spanking magazines. I examined participants' toy boxes, which included paddles, straps, hairbrushes, and whips. I expanded the scope of the research to include other aspects of the larger world of sadomasochism, including observations in sex clubs, scanning Web sites, interviews with persons who incorporate S&M into their sexual activities, and visits to commercial ventures such as Boston's Fetish Fair. The fieldwork took place in Boston, New Hampshire, metropolitan New York, New Jersey, and Atlanta between 1993 and 2000.

## SPANKING STORIES AND STRATEGIES OF NEUTRALIZATION

The narratives offered by the participants to explain or situate their interests in spanking are strikingly similar to narratives offered by others who adapt standard sexual scripts. Men who like to spank said that they had this interest for as long as they could remember. This is similar to gay men who are asked to explain the origin of their same-sex interests. Women who like to be spanked said that it took many years for them to realize that they were interested in being spanked, similar to most lesbians who report many heterosexually active years before realizing their same-sex orientation. The men tended to essentialize their interests, while the women tended to locate them in interpersonal scripting, describing the influence of partners who assisted the development of their sexual interests. With respect to spanking, both men and women explained their interest by asserting that everyone has hidden desires about spanking.

Researchers note that men tend to be more likely to develop an interest in S&M, and to develop it earlier, than women. Breslow, Evans, and Langley's (1985) sample of S&M practitioners surveyed 130 men and 52 women. Among the men, nine out of ten had acknowledged S&M interests by their early twenties, and by age 14, more than half had done so. Damond's (2002) study of 342 male S&M participants found that over nine in ten said that they had childhood or adolescent fantasies relating to S&M. To neutralize stigma, most developed an impression management strategy that entailed a variation on "I was born this way, this is hardwiring, I have no choice, so don't discriminate against me."

Some of these men offered stories of having been spanked as children and having made a connection at those early moments between sexual arousal and the punishment they received. This strategy seems designed to imply that the individual has not consciously orchestrated or chosen this sexual interest. Taylor and Ussher (2001) commented, "Such discourse usually involved some awareness of S&M as having a neuro-physiological component in which pain and arousal become inseparably paired" (p. 307). Others were never spanked as children but nonetheless asserted a long-standing interest in spanking. Even as a five-year-old—indeed, ever since Christina could remember, she explained to me—she wanted to be spanked. She thought she was weird and thought it best to keep the matter to herself for most of her life. Preston vividly recalled the first time he developed an interest in spanking. He was 12 years old and saw an ad depicting "a beautiful woman's bottom." He looked at it and thought, "That's ripe for spanking."

But the narratives differed slightly from person to person and encompassed a range of interests. Jim could not precisely pinpoint the development of his interest in spanking. His wife knew that he enjoyed spanking, but refused to participate and did not attend parties. Jim, Christina, and other participants described spanking relations that did not include intercourse or other stereotypically sexual activities. These relationships were forged with trust—female participants noted that trust was essential for a good scene—and comfort. The focus was on playing out fantasy scenes, with men providing erotic/sexual discipline. However, Christina and Belinda had confessed their interests to the men whom they later married. These husbands were able to integrate their sexual scripts of spanking and discipline with more "vanilla" sexual practices. Including spanking in these relationships enabled these and other women participants to feel much less alone, "less freakish," as Christina said.

Outside the contexts of relationships, it was difficult for participants to fully accept and understand themselves. Initially, Michael thought he was the only person in the world who was into this "bizarre perversion." Once he had been in the scene for four or five years and discovered publications on spanking, he felt he was not alone. Initially, he felt his affinity for spanking was "bizarre," a perspective that seemed to be borne out in the Midwestern state where he lived. Officials there had threatened to outlaw spanking publications, arguing that they depicted violence against women. Michael noted that it was especially important that he eventually found publications by "real" spanking aficionados because originally, the items he found "were done by people just looking to make a buck." They were less realistic and arousing than the later publications he found.

Several participants combed more general publications for mentions of spanking. Jim was extremely knowledgeable about popular culture references to spanking, seemingly non-sexualized, but to him, sexually charged. He situated his interest by arguing that everyone needs to try sexualized spanking, asserting that there is nothing "deviant" about his interests. About spanking aficionados, he said, "We wonder about ourselves and our 'perversion' endlessly."

Newer participants are especially prone to these musings. Andrew said, "You know, I can't believe that I'm here. I look around and wonder what the hell I'm doing here. I mean, I'm not like these other people. This isn't all I do or anything." He was trying to neutralize stigma to himself by

comparing himself to the other partygoers. He implied that the others have a single-minded focus on spanking but he is normal, that his interest in spanking is just a small piece of his identity. He also told me that he finds me "stereotypically attractive," attempting to neutralize the perceived stigma of spanking by validating his attraction.

Another stigma neutralization technique followed this path: an attempt to broaden spanking parties beyond the ostensible reason for gathering. Several male partygoers noted that the parties they attended seemed "especially sterile." Michael said, "Especially among the men, there's this tendency to talk about sports, politics—anything but spanking." In dancing around or avoiding the subject that had drawn the group together, participants could diminish its seeming importance and, like Andrew, present the impression that they have interests and identities beyond spanking.

Another stigma neutralization strategy was common among spanking aficionados. Many men took care to mention that those interested in spanking were different from those interested in S&M more generally. There is a spectrum of activities included in S&M, including play with whips, bondage devices, clothing such as leather and latex, and role playing. Much of the specific lingo has been reluctantly borrowed from S&M, according to participants. Spanking and other forms of flagellation are sometimes included in spanking activities, thus the apparent need for participants to differentiate themselves from S&M practitioners. But participants generally defined S&M as "truly kinky" and "where the real weirdos go." In this strategy, members of one group denigrate another fringe group in order to mitigate the stigmatizing effects on them: "We are more normal than they are; they are the true deviants."

## The Party and Subcultural Rules

At the party I observed, something occurred that constituted a defining moment in an attempt to normalize the activity and differentiate spanking from S&M. The party included about 50 people, perhaps 15 women and 35 men, almost all white and middle to upper middle class. Some had traveled from the West Coast and Midwest to this East Coast event. It was a social event where people of like minds could meet. For many of the participants, communication had only been through correspondence; this rendezvous was their first face-to-face meeting. Others brought regular spanking dates. Scenes only entailed spanking and fantasies; penile-vaginal and oral intercourse were limited to marital and dating partners. One married couple described their spanking scenes as separate from but also integral to intercourse.

Party organizers had leeway with respect to how much planning to do. Men tended to simply arrange the time, place, and basic snacks, while women tended to make more elaborate preparations, including decorating and organizing public spankings and demonstrations. Occasionally, partygoers provided their own public demonstrations, playing out a scene in the main gathering space while attendees watched avidly.

The organizer of this particular party planned a "Bid-a-Swat" auction. The women at the party would bid on men with the number of swats they wished to receive. The men were expected to display forearms, biceps, and hand spans. The auction hostess demonstrated her hand span for comparison so that bidding women could assess the spanking potential of the men. Finally, each man was told to say, in his sternest possible voice, "Young lady, get over my knee now!" The most stereotypically attractive men, the men with the largest hand spans, and the two men who were known to be good spankers were bid on the most.

A group of six women monopolized the bidding. Many of the women made comments about one particular woman, Annalisa, because of her bidding behavior. She had won a cute young man with a high bid of 600 swats, after already having won a large-handed man with a bid of 400 swats. When two other women grouped their bid to get a total of 500 swats from Michael, who was known as a good spanker, someone with just the right touch, sternness, and trustworthiness, they asked Annalisa whether she was splitting her 600-swat bid with anyone.

"No," she responded emphatically, and seemed offended at the suggestion that she would share her swats with anyone. Behind Annalisa's back, the other women were moved to judge her behavior. One said, "There's no way she can do all that! She's going to need a pillow on the plane back!" The other women who had been bidding whispered to each other, "Wow, she's crazy," and looked at her disdainfully.

These women attributed her apparent desire to receive over a thousand swats from several men to masochism, the desire to receive pain. The women at the party did not link spanking with masochism, pain, or S&M. Belinda told me, "It's more about knowing that someone cares about me to discipline me, to keep me in line when I act like a brat." The women's desire to be spanked was seen as an emotionally laden activity within a caring context—not as the desire for pain or humiliation. One man captured the group's shared distinction between S&M and spanking in the following words: "It's tough for male first-timers to get to spank anyone because there is a shortage of women, and they like to go with men they know they can trust. It's also difficult to know a woman's limits because there she is, crying out, 'No, no, stop,' and your natural inclination is to heed her cries." This hints at a presumed difference between sadism and spanking, with participants believing that men who spank do so for the emotional fulfillment of women, not to hurt them. This rationale is supported in numerous spanking short stories and fantasies, and in Belinda's words about someone caring enough to "provide discipline."

Other male and female participants described their interests in similar terms, though men were more likely to readily acknowledge a sexual element. Male participants admitted that there is an erotic charge in having "a squirming, bare-bottomed woman over your knee," as Cooper explained. Thus, the apparent "Goldilocks" rule was revealed: There is a just-right amount of spanking to administer or receive, or a just-right amount of discipline to desire, and a just-right amount of eroticism to derive. Bidding for too many swats is constructed in this context as beyond the pale: no longer just about having been a brat, but more about pain and masochism.

Other apparently unspoken rules were revealed at this party when one woman dared to offer to spank men. Since this party was billed and constructed as a gathering of women who like to be spanked and men who like to do the spanking, most of the women were offended by this act of switching. Only four men ended up bidding on the woman's services. She looked uncomfortable throughout the auction. She refused to say, "Young man, get over my knee, now!" Finally, she offered to let all the men come to her room so she could line them up and spank them all.

Some of the partygoers were in awe of this woman's offer, but most seemed disdainful of the fact that she was switching, knowing that she would spank men and be spanked herself. "She doesn't even know what she is," one woman said. The woman who switched does have her limits, however. Melanie asked whether she would spank women too, and her very cold response was, "No." Although in this particular setting she was clearly seen as deviant, she remained resolutely heterosexual, in accordance with broader sexual scripts about sexual orientation.

However, in line with the subcultural scripting in this particular community, all of the behavior described above was transgressive. A woman wanting too many swats, from more than one man, all of whom were strangers to her—this was outside the unspoken rules. A woman offering to spank men at an event that had been constructed with specific roles and rules—that is, only men spank women—was also deviant in this community. Before the party, a male participant had said, "Women who want to spank are borderline with being tops in the S&M scene. Most [heterosexual] men in the spanking scene would be loathe to admit an interest in being spanked—as opposed to men in the S&M scene," in which men tend to be bottoms, or the masochistic partner. The harshest judgment was reserved for transgressive women, instead of the men who offered their bottoms or the multiple swats, most likely because women's participation in the constructed and overt order of things was crucial. With women outnumbered almost three to one, men were eager to become accepted in the scene, trusted by women, and thus, desired as a spanking partner. Women were the gatekeepers for men being able to participate in "what they came for," according to Brett. The men had come to spank willing women, not to be spanked.

## DISCUSSION

The participants in this study delighted in discussing public and popular references to spanking as a way of emphasizing the normality of their interests. Particularly pleasing were the references to stories that participants thought suggested the sexualized component of the activity, even if one needed to split hairs to find the sexual symbolism. For example, several participants recounted the spanking activities in the household of all-American singer and entertainer Pat Boone. One said, "There was far too much spanking going on for it to lack any sexual charge for him." In *Starving for Attention*, the autobiography of Boone's daughter, the sexual edge is conveyed in the following words:

> I knew disobedience would result in swift, sure punishment. . . . I was strangely thankful for the uncommon spanking I did receive because it created a kind of penitential release for me—a victory over the nagging, inner torment of guilt. There would be a time of praying, crying, and hugging after the punishment and this seemed to give me a new lease on life. (Boone O'Neill, 1982, p. 37)

This was precisely the kind of anecdote my informants enjoyed most because they interpreted it to mean that Cherry actually enjoyed this form of punishment, an interpretation most readers would not draw.

In a similar vein, participants recounted numerous references to sexualized spanking as validation of the normalcy of their activity. For instance, a song by Madonna, popular in the early 1990s, referred to spanking in a casual and favorable manner. In the early 1990s, the *Arsenio Hall Show*, a popular talk show, twice featured guests who extolled the virtues of a good spanking. Actor Robert Pastorelli of *Murphy Brown*, a popular early 1990s sitcom depicting a stubborn, clever female television journalist, commented that the Candice Bergen character, Murphy Brown, could use a good spanking. Participants pointed out that FM talk show host and "shock jock" Howard Stern mentioned spanking quite a bit in his autobiography, *Private Parts*, and that actors Ryan O'Neal and Farrah Fawcett had made veiled references to her being spanked during their long-term relationship. Stern had tried to convince NBC executives to broadcast him spanking a woman on Jay Leno's late night television variety show, but censors refused to allow it.

What is the significance of these and other widely circulated references to an activity that may have a clear sexual meaning to some but only punitive meaning to others? For spanking aficionados, these references are like unpolished gems, indicative of the larger context of their special sexual interests. They believe that these anecdotes reveal a cultural fascination with corporeal punishment in all forms, and they offer these anecdotes as proof that they are neither alone nor deviant in their interests. The efforts within the spanking community to delineate themselves from and disavow S&M practices are offered as proof, again, that they are not deviant, at least not as deviant as others.

Is it really true that S&M, an exotic and unusual pleasure, is part of all of us? If so, does it reveal itself in timid and unrecognized ways, such as spanking? How do spanking aficionados understand and explain themselves?

One intention of the many spanking publications, videos, toys, and Internet statements is to draw a distinction between S&M and spanking. At the same time, the differences between and among spanking, flagellation, and S&M are obscured by the casual use of all three terms. But participants insist on drawing a bright line between S&M and spanking. "I am not interested in a full S&M lifestyle," said one, "just in erotic spankings and discipline with members of the opposite sex."

What does this foray into one sexual subculture suggest about sexual scripts, the neutralization of stigma, impression management, and the development of the sexual self?

First, we might conclude that the social norms are pervasive, even in a sexually radical subculture. This subculture's participants compared themselves to each other, made microlevel distinctions about the just-right or "Goldilocks" amount of spanking, and offered justifications for their interests. They made within-group judgments, redefinitions, and made use of stigma neutralization techniques. This echoes the discourses that surround us in the cultural scripting of what is regarded as normal and deviant.

These observations suggest that sexualities are enormously complex. The sexual self is clearly fluid, variable, and is simultaneously individually and culturally contextualized. Sexual scripts are blueprints, yes, but they can clearly be adapted and revised for the user. Sexual spanking should be viewed as one of many sexual adaptations individuals make, based on interactions and changes to intrapsychic and interpersonal scripts. An expanded view of sexualities, seen as the potent interaction between cultures and individuals instead of a series of simple rights and wrongs, can only benefit all who seek to find sexual paths of comfort, pleasure, and pain.

To understand participation in sexual spanking, we need to ask large questions about sexual participation. Why does anyone do what they do sexually? Why is the society as concerned as it is about what is sexually normal and abnormal, normative and deviant? We need to learn a great deal more than we know about nonmainstream sexual activities and the role they play in their participants' lives.

## REFERENCES

Boone O'Neill, C. (1982). *Starving for attention.* New York: Continuum.

Breslow, N., Evans, L., & Langley, J. (1985). On the prevalence and roles of females in the sadomasochistic subculture: Report on an empirical study. *Archives of Sexual Behavior, 14,* 303–314.

Damond, W. D. (2002). *Patterns of power: A test of two approaches to understanding sadomasochistic sexual behavior in heterosexual men.* Unpublished manuscript, University of Chicago.

Gagnon, J., & Simon, W. (1973). *Sexual conduct: The social sources of human sexuality.* Chicago: Aldine.

Gagnon, J., & Simon, W. (2005). *Sexual conduct: The social sources of human sexuality* (2nd ed.). New Brunswick, NJ: Aldine Transaction.

Goffman, E. (1963). *Stigma: Notes on the management of spoiled identity.* Englewood Cliffs, NJ: Prentice Hall/Spectrum.

Plummer, K. (1995). *Telling sexual stories: Power, change, and social worlds.* London & New York: Routledge.

Simon, W. (1996). *Postmodernist sexualities.* London & New York: Routledge.

Taylor, G. W., & Ussher, J. M. (2001). Making sense of S&M: A discourse analytic account. *Sexualities, 4,* 93–314.

# The S&M Experience

## *Jackie*

I am a 21-year-old bisexual female who, in the BDSM [bondage-discipline-sadism-masochism] community, is known as a "switch." I was raised Catholic in an interesting sort of family life. My mother is a diagnosed antisocial psychopath. My father raised his siblings because his mother was the town drunk while his dad abused both him and his siblings; he, in turn, grew up to be a rage-aholic, a verbal and physical child abuser. I lived off and on with my "grandmother"—one of my half-sister's grandparents—who has been more of a parent than anyone else. I began studying psychology in an attempt to work with children so I would be able to remove them from the sorts of abusive situations I had to endure as a child.

I have always thought women were attractive. I remember watching beautiful women when I was younger. My mother was a beautiful woman. My mother was a very sexual woman, and there was a constant stream of men in the house. She used them to get things, not for sex—that was part of her disorder. Because of this, I grew up seeing men and women in much the same light. I don't think I fully admitted this to myself until I was in college. I have always done a lot of nudes in my paintings, females preferably because I like their lines better. When I visited my high school art teacher—also a close friend—because I was having a crisis over the stress of admitting I was gay, she informed me she had known that since she met me. Even my guy friends in high school knew. Recently, I asked John how he knew about me. He said the whole time he had known me I had looked at men and women with the same interest and desire, whereas usually, people choose one or the other. Specifically, he said, most men look at women and drool, whereas he looked at other attractive men and wished he looked more like them. John said I looked at attractive women *and* men with a drooling look.

At one point, I tried telling my grandmother. I could never tell my mother—she was a gay-basher—or my father, whom I don't feel close to. My grandmother said it was a phase. At some point or another, every woman had fantasies about other women. She "knew me," she said. I'd meet some knight in shining armor and get married; I'd live in a nice house surrounded by a picket fence. Besides, she'd say, even if I were a lesbian—it wasn't possible to like both sexes, she believed—I could never marry another women. And I couldn't live in sin—I was a Catholic, after all. And so I'd have to live my life alone.

I've had relationships primarily with men, but a few with women. Men are easier to come by. There is more of a selection of males to choose from, and I am picky with the people I date. It's harder finding same-sex partners, although it's easier living so close to a big city than in a less urban area. I'm not openly gay. My first gay relationship was with Emily, my best friend in high school. I was at her house, fooling around with a guy friend. I was young and most definitely stupid. I remember feeling uncomfortable with this guy. I really wasn't into fooling around with this guy, but he was and he kept going. Finally I called Emily over and she began kissing me on the neck and breasts and I felt exhilarated. We drove our friend home and she and I talked. Apparently, we have been attracted to each other since we had met but we were just afraid to act on our desires. Within the week, we were dating and were constantly with one another. My family knew that she was my best friend, so they didn't suspect anything. Her mom knew about us but she also knew how much we cared for each other as friends, so she never minded my staying over, although we never had sex when we stayed over. There are some things I just considered too uncomfortable.

I've always believed in monogamy no matter who my partner was. I always hated the stigma

that bisexuals are "easy," into having sex with as many people as possible simply because they like both sexes. Even now, most of my friends don't know I am bisexual. Definitely not my roommates or my mother. My roommates are a little more tolerant than my mother, but when you're living in a house full of girls, they start getting uncomfortable. One of my housemates in particular, Jennifer, whom I love dearly—in a strictly platonic way, mind you—had a run-in because one of her past roommates was bi and told her not to worry because she wasn't attracted to her. Instead of feeling less anxious, she got insulted. It's like me saying, I am not going to grope you in your sleep so you can rest easy and not live in terror.

During my freshman year of college, I worked in an office in a work-study program. I didn't think anything of being bisexual until one day my supervisor began talking about a guy in the department she thought was gay. I couldn't believe it when I heard her refer to this kind, intelligent man as a "fag"; then she began making jokes about the fact that he was a homosexual. I wanted to crawl into my skin or a deep hole and never come out. I knew if anyone at my job found out I would be harassed or, even worse, I'd lose my job. Sometimes the nicest people make a complete change of face when they find out someone is gay. There is a lot of stigma associated with being bisexual. Most people think we are lascivious, can't make up our minds, sick, perverse—you name it, we are pretty much labeled it.

I think about who will be reading this account. I hardly share any of this with outsiders. If anyone were to find out how I lead my sexual life, I could lose all credibility as a therapist simply because of the stigma of how perverse I am. The things I do would shock anyone, I guess. For as long as I can remember, seeing men and women tied up, spanked, smacked, or interacting in violent or sexually aggressive ways has always been a turn-on [for me]. No one else I knew seemed to have these feelings. Having had the background I did, I couldn't tell if it was my own form of self-abuse, mental illness, or seeking the familiar. My childhood was very abusive. I thought it may be possible that I seek humiliation, abuse, and power in relationships because I was trying to act out familiar patterns. That didn't really make sense, though, since in sex, I played the dominant or dominatrix role. I have always had some form of a power dynamic in my relationships, even with partners who weren't into being kinky. The first woman I dated, I told her that I had a surprise. I came home and blindfolded her and I tied her up and tickled and tease her as I watched her writhe until I was satisfied that her release and satisfaction were completely dependent on my will. In the beginning, I didn't really consider it kinky; I saw it mainly as experimentation.

Most of the time my actions got really negative responses. I can remember one guy I dated in high school. When I pulled his hair and tried to bite his neck, he kinda freaked out. From then on in that relationship, I never tried anything out of order again. I did remain the "top" partner, though, the person who causes the sensation. That was doing what I wanted—getting my way, staying in control, and enjoying every minute of it. I wanted to take the dominant role in pleasing a partner. At the time, I didn't realize there was a community and a literature about all this that explained that what I was doing could please both me and my partner. Women were a lot more welcoming with my tendencies than men. Men never seemed to understand what I was up to, or they would see my dominance as challenging their masculinity. The women I dated liked being tied up, blindfolded, bitten, degraded, smacked, and used sexually. I guess this is one reason why I always like to dominate women. I don't think another woman could ever dominate me. I just don't have that mind-frame. I enjoy watching them too much.

You could look at this and say that I am trying to assume a power role because I was badly abused in childhood. Being dominant in my sexual relationships is safer because I call the shots. But the fact is, I never really saw myself as a victim. In school, when I was living with my parents, I thought these behaviors—shaking, hitting, punching, throwing across the room, leaving bruises—happened to everyone. When I was living with my mom, I hadn't known anything different. My sense of what should happen in a family was kind of skewed. I've thought a lot about it, though. Maybe my whole reason for seeing this as interesting and arousing is that it uses sex as manipulation as my mom did. It's a possibility; she was my earliest role model. No one can be born liking this, right? When I was younger, I still viewed this as sick and twisted.

Every time I was abused at home, I swore I would never hurt anyone like that. So I went through extreme bouts of cognitive dissonance. I was thinking along one track while trying to do the exact opposite. For me, sexual activity was fun, but without certain elements, I never really got fulfilled. There came a time when I knew I wanted to try something different. I wanted to be in the other role. I wanted to be subservient. I craved it. I tried prompting boyfriends at the time by bringing up non-scary items, such as scarves. I could tell there was something wrong with me. I still wasn't fulfilled because those boyfriends were terrible at doing what I wanted them to do, but I was also terrible at trying to explain how to do it in a way that wouldn't send them running. So I continued to remain dominant.

Don't get me wrong: Bad things can happen both during sex and during a relationship. There is a population of people who believe that bondage and discipline is all about force—real abuse, real rape. I had a relationship with a guy. For a while, things were pretty good. I was usually dominant, but occasionally, things switched the other way. He became verbally and emotionally abusive, taking out his anger at his exes on me. He eerily reminded me of my father. We were very volatile, providing catalysts for one another. We went through phases when we would cut things off and end up sleeping with one another, over and over again. I thought maybe we could be just friends, but I realized I was being naïve and foolish. One night, I went to his place thinking that he was going to help me find parts for my car. When he wanted to have sex, I told him no. I tried to pull away from him but couldn't because he was stronger. He tied me up from hand to foot. Before, we had played with handcuffs and ropes, but I just never thought he would use them without my consent. I felt very violated that night. I walked home, shaking. I couldn't sleep. I sat on the fire escape outside my bedroom, smoked two packs of cigarettes, and watched the sun rise. I thought that if I kept doing these bad things I would end up with more people who would take advantage of me. My next relationship was with a very conventional guy. I guess there's a Catch-22 situation here: When I engaged in bondage and discipline, bad things happened; when I didn't, bad things happened.

The conventional guy, we talked about marriage and kids, but he hated anything even remotely kinky, even the non-scary things. He saw bondage and discipline as abusive to women. He accused me of being a nymphomaniac—apparently all I wanted was sex. I became extremely depressed and began taking antidepressants. I realize now that I wasn't satisfied with the sex I engaged in, so I tried to make up with it in quantity. He ended the relationship, and I got upset because he was perfect for leading the life my family wanted me to lead: the husband, the family, a two-car garage, a good income—and most definitely no collars or handcuffs. I felt guilty about the failure of the relationship. I had screwed up what would have been perfect if I could just be normal. This was everything I was supposed to want by conventional standards. I won't ever have a normal life, I thought.

I started visiting specialty adult stores. I accumulated a little collection of the toys I enjoyed. This is part of me, I realized. When I fight who I am, I end up miserable. It didn't take me long to get over this guy.

Through a friend, I met Jason, the guy I've had my most recent relationship with. I completely brushed him off, and he thought I was a total bitch. We met again three months later. We decided to change our stances toward one another. At first, we talked as friends online. He told me things about myself no one had ever bothered to notice. He was supportive when we were talking about sex. He felt the same things. He had problems with sex earlier because he didn't want to see himself as abusive. He took the teacher role, showing me books and answering my questions. He wasn't sickened by me, and he gave me an opportunity to fulfill my need for being submissive. He became my friend, lover, and above all, master. He explained what being submissive entails. The dominant partner has to earn the trust and respect from the submissive to play the role. He told me that whatever may go on in the bedroom—degradation, humiliation— they happen because the submissive partner wishes to fulfill the role that involves those activities. He would treat me in this way because he respects the dynamic between us. In turn, I would allow him to treat me like that because I would have the control to say who treats me as such and when. He also set up what's called a "safe word" for me. Sometimes things can become so intense that the words you might speak in a typical dialogue during a scene won't stop the action. You need a safe word that you would never say during a scene that would be a signal to stop the action so that the participants can try to fix anything that may be going wrong. S&M is all about communication. My safe word is "blue." I think I picked it because I think primarily in colors and it reminds me of feeling scared. It seemed right.

We have a library of books that explain techniques of the bondage and dominance "lifestyle." Occasionally, when I'm reading one of them, one of my roommates will walk in and see my book, and so I explain it away as a book for research on deviance or aesthetics or some other such thing. As for my toys, they are usually kept in a duffle bag or in drawers in my closet. One aspect of the bondage and discipline lifestyle is covering up evidence of how we live, including bruises and bite marks, or simply putting away the toys so that no one will ever find out about it and accuse us of abuse. We have many friends in the bondage and discipline community because it tends to be very tightly knit. We choose to keep it private among ourselves.

Some people in this community find romance in pieces of glass—that is, bloodletting, cutting the skin to achieve sexual arousal. I enjoy many different things. Sometimes the simple act of being tied or having something placed around my neck will send me into a frenzy of arousal, wanting to do anything to please, to earn pleasure. Sometimes I surprise Jason by setting up a scene for him when he comes home from work. One such scene involved 12 lit candles lining each side of the corridor to the bedroom door and red rose petals scattered on the floor. Inside the bedroom, I trailed petals up to the bed with candles lighting the windowsill. A rope trailed zig-zag through the petals under the door and onto the bed, connected to the collar I was wearing. It was then my turn to wait, having mentally prepared myself for him to come home, when he would decide what happened next. One night, paddling or flogging; the next night, maybe hot wax, anal intercourse, or bondage and teasing.

There is a sensation called "floating" a lot of submissives describe. It's when you get so far into your personal head-space that sensation floods you and everything feels like soft pillows. After we have a vigorous scene, my master usually gathers me into his arms or holds me and we talk about everything we felt and went through in our minds, things that happened—and maybe didn't happen—during the session. This is the most fulfilling and loving relationship I have been in. In the morning, we're like every other couple. We get up and shower, brush our teeth, dress and the like, and go about our normal lives; for him, it is his work, for me, to school and therapy sessions—where we await the next time we see each other.

When we get together, we're distinctly not like other couples.

It excites me to think I will be able to spend the rest of my life with someone who fills me with such joy—emotionally, intellectually, and physically. Someone who pushes me to be the best I can, someone who makes me dinner when I am stressed or gives me a back rub or surprises me by putting up Christmas lights or bringing my favorite candies for a devious blindfolded study break. Someone who won't judge me. To me that doesn't seem deviant. It's really all in the way you look at it.

I have a job I enjoy tremendously, trying to make the lives of children better. I am in my last year of college. I won't talk about private members' clubs for bondage and discipline participants in my deviance course because all eyes would turn to me in accusation. If people in my everyday life knew about my sex life, they would accuse me of being sick, being just like a child molester, accuse me of doing things with my clients with the same ignorant thought processes that lead people to think you can "catch" homosexuality. I won't discuss anything that happened the night before, when I subjected myself to any number of abuses and perversities. I will put on the mask of a confident, conventional, heterosexual woman. I will hope that I remembered to put all my toys away, that I haven't left a trail that may lead to being scrutinized, judged, evaluated, stigmatized. And I will love being comfortable, finally, with who I am.

Everyone wants to feel accepted. I spent most of my life either not admitting things to myself or thinking I was a bad person because I felt a certain way. Now that I feel accepted in one area of my life, I have a much easier time separating the two halves of my life and not worrying about one affecting the other as much. Now that I have confidence in my sexual self, I am much more confident in my social self. Jason says it is funny that my family never liked any of the guys I dated in the past who were supposed to be so acceptable. Now that my family knows Jason—the one person who shouldn't be acceptable—they've fallen in love with him. Jason says, "Being comfortable allows other people to be comfortable with you." I don't consider myself "normal" in the way that the "American dream" is normal, but I am the way I want to be.

## Discussion Questions

1. How do the popular and the "insider" or sociological views of S&M differ? Discuss some implications of this fact.

2. Discuss the relevance of Erving Goffman's concept "frame" or "framing" in the world of S&M.

3. How do participants in S&M explain their interest in their unconventional sexual activities?

4. Place the forms of extreme deviance discussed in this book along a continuum or spectrum of "extremeness." On what basis would you construct this continuum? Can such a continuum be constructed?

# INDEX